EXPERIMENTAL BUSINESS RESEARCH

EXPERIMENTAL BUSINESS RESEARCH

Edited by

Rami Zwick

Hong Kong University of Science and Technology

and

Amnon Rapoport

University of Arizona, USA

KLUWER ACADEMIC PUBLISHERS
Boston / Dordrecht / London

Distributors for North, Central and South America:
Kluwer Academic Publishers
101 Philip Drive
Assinippi Park
Norwell, Massachusetts 02061 USA
Telephone (781) 871-6600
Fax (781) 871-6528
E-Mail < kluwer@wkap.com >

Distributors for all other countries:
Kluwer Academic Publishers Group
Distribution Centre
Post Office Box 322
3300 AH Dordrecht, THE NETHERLANDS
Telephone 31 78 6392 392
Fax 31 78 6546 474
E-Mail < orderdept@wkap.nl >

 Electronic Services < http://www.wkap.nl >

Library of Congress Cataloging-in-Publication Data

A C.I.P. Catalogue record for this book is available from the Library of Congress.

Contents

PART II AUCTIONS

PART III LEARNING AND CONSTRUCTION

PART IV BARGAINING AND CONTRACTS

Preface

This volume includes papers that were presented at the First Asian Conference on Experimental Business Research held at the Hong Kong University of Science and Technology (HKUST) on December 7–10, 1999. The conference was organized by the Center for Experimental Business Research (cEBR) at HKUST and was chaired by Amnon Rapoport. The organizing committee members were Paul Brewer, Soo Hong Chew, and Rami Zwick. The papers presented at the conference and a few others that were solicited especially for this volume contain original research on individual and interactive decision behavior in various branches of business research including, but not limited to, economics, marketing, management, finance, and accounting.

The impetus for the conference, reflected in the mission of cEBR, is to promote the use of experimental methods in business research, expand experimental methodology through research and teaching, and apply this methodology to solve practical problems faced by firms, corporations, and governmental agencies. Three agendas have been proposed to accomplish this mission: research, education, and networking and outreach programs. The conference organized by cEBR and the resulting volume contribute in various degrees to all three agendas by presenting original research ideas in the field of business to a wide audience, fostering stronger ties among researchers, and enhancing communication between researchers and industry representatives.

Richard Feynman, one of the leading theoretical physicists of the twentieth century, wrote: "The principle of science, the definition, almost, is the following: The test of all knowledge is experiment. Experiment is the sole judge of scientific 'truth'." In today's postmodern approach this might seem to be an old-fashioned view. Nevertheless, we accept it as self-evident, and proceed on what might be considered a naïve faith in the contribution of experiments to science. We make a few introductory comments below about the place and role of experimentation in the social sciences. More comprehensive discussions of this issue can be found in Kagel and Roth (1995) and the various references in the present volume.

Experimental methods have played a critical role in the natural sciences. From the beginning of the 20th century, in an attempt to achieve scientific legitimacy, social scientists have believed that progress could be achieved by embracing the experimental methodology advocated by the natural sciences while abandoning the subjective, introspective methodology that was so common earlier. Ignoring the debate whether it is appropriate to base the social sciences on the foundations erected by the natural sciences, experimental methodology is now as common in the social sciences as in the natural sciences.

Progress in adopting the experimental methodology has been uneven. Several social science disciplines, most notably psychology, have embraced the experimental methodology enthusiastically. Experiments presently constitute a central part of theory development and testing in these disciplines. Mastering the experimental methodology, including experimental design, data analysis, and reporting represent a major effort in educating graduates and postgraduate students in these fields. Other social science disciplines, most notably economics, have been more reluctant to adopt the experimental methodology. The different attitudes toward experimentation within the various disciplines of social science reflect the scientists' evaluation of the status of their field vis-à-vis the nature of the inquiry. If the scientific inquest relates to how people should behave under well specified conditions, including goals and beliefs of self and others, then no experimental evidence can provide any deep insight, except for the observation that people follow or do not follow the normative prescription. On the other hand, if the goal of the scientific inquiry is to understand the underlining reasons why people do, or do not, follow normative principles and to uncover systematic and replicable patterns of behavior, then experimental evidence is essential. Fields of social science that perceive their main domain to be normative and prescriptive have been slower to adopt the experimental methodology. Only when these fields have come to recognize that no meaningful prescription is possible without understanding the human cognitive system that experimental methodology has assumed it rightful status.

Academic business professors often seem to exhibit schizophrenic symptoms in the practice of their discipline. Perhaps these symptoms may better be described as multiple personality disorders because the schism in schizophrenia is a split with reality. The person in active schizophrenia has lost touch with reality, whereas the schism in the business disciplines is exactly the awareness that reality does exist and by the nature of the inquiry must be relevant. The various business disciplines are invariably described as scientific, professional, applied, and concrete. We provide professional education that contains management principles and offers basic tools for practicing them. We teach theory, develop abstract principles, and at the same time advocate concrete practices that businesses can emulate. We espouse ideas that originated in a wide gamut of fields from the natural sciences to spirituality, and teach from books that are labeled "The art and practice of . . ." and "The art and science of . . ." We quote from both hard-core scientists, and feel equally justified borrowing from motivational speakers and management gurus. We teach concepts that have achieved religious-like status such as reengineering, total quality, and CRM, and at the same time teach game theory and equilibrium concepts. No wonder that some business professors struggle daily to assert their identity.

We believe that the experimental methodology can provide partial relief to these split personality syndromes. Experiments can provide the link as well as the justification for the scientific inquiry in the business discipline. To support this argument, let us first briefly describe the main ingredients commonly found in business experiments. The first is the environment, which specifies the initial endowments, preferences, goals, and costs that motivate the decision-makers. Second, an experiment also uses an institution, which defines the language (messages) of market communication (e.g., bids, offers, prices, rejections, acceptances), the rules governing the exchange of information, and the rules under which messages become binding contracts. These institutions are typically implemented by instructions that are commonly computer-controlled. Finally, there is the observed behavior of the participants as a function of the environment and institution that constitute the experimental variables (Smith, 1994).

Each of the three components of the business experimental setting constructs and at the same time confirms the link between reality and the stylistic experimental environment. The direct relevancy of the findings is judged vis-à-vis the assumptions about the environment and the institutions. This is not to say that experiments that investigate an environment or study an institution that does not exist outside the realm of the experiment are not relevant or important. On the contrary, such findings can often point out possibilities that have not been taken advantage of. The question is not whether or not such an environment or an institution already exists, but rather whether it can exist. If the answer is positive, the informational value of the study can often exceed that of a study that explores an existing setting.

Using this framework, several prominent reasons for conducting business experiments have been forwarded. First, several of the important roles of experimentation involve its relation to theory. Experiments may provide evidence in support of a theory, refute a theory, hint to the mathematical structure of a theory, and serve as evidence presented by researchers to the scientific community when two or more theories are competing to explain the same phenomenon. This is accomplished by comparing the behavioral regularities to the theory's predictions. Examples can be found in the auction and portfolio selection literature. Second, business experiments have been conducted to explore the causes of a theory's failure. This exploration is essential to any research program concerned with modifying a theory. Examples are to be found in the bargaining literature, accounting literature, and literature on the provision of public goods. Third, although experiments often take their importance from their relation to theory, they often have a life of their own, independent of theory. Because well-formulated theories in most sciences tend to be preceded by systematically collected observations, business experiments can and have been used in order to establish empirical regularities as a basis for the construction of new theories. These empirical regularities may vary considerably from one population of agents to another, depending on a variety of independent variables including culture, socio-economic status, previous experience, expertise of the agents, and gender. Fourth, experiments can be used to compare environments, using the same institution, or compare institutions, while holding the environment constant. Fifth, perhaps less known is the use of experiments as a testing ground for institutional design. For example, Smith (1994) mentions early experiments that studied the one-price sealed bid auction for Treasury securities in the USA, which subsequently helped motivating the USA Treasury in the early 1970's to offer some long-term bond issues. Experiments can and have also been used to evaluate policy proposals. Examples can be found in the area of voting systems, where different voting systems are evaluated experimentally in terms of the proportion of misrepresentation of the voter's preferences (so called "sophisticated voting"). In the past decade, both private industry and governmental agencies in the USA have funded studies of the incentives for off-floor trading in continuous double auction markets, alternative institutions for auctioning emissions permits, and market mechanisms for allocating airport slots. Six, experiments have been used as demonstrations to communicate with the non-academic world, in a way that theorems about equilibrium behavior, for example, can not do. As new markets are designed, experiments will have a natural role to play as scale model tests of their operating characteristics, and even as demonstrations to skeptical patrons and potential users. Finally, there is now ample evidence that learning through experimentation is a very effective way of acquiring new concepts and procedures and gaining insights into business processes. Consequently, gaming and experimentation are now common in MBA and executive education worldwide.

At the same time, there is an extensive and long tradition of using experiments to guide business decisions in various industrial functions in the private and public sectors, most notably in marketing, independent of the academic inquiry. For example, testing a range of creative executions and media scheduling in different test markets often precedes introduction of a large-scale advertising campaign, and a new product introduction and corresponding pricing decisions are made with the help of laboratory and field experiments. These experiments that are performed for purely utilitarian purposes are nevertheless not devoid of theory. The researcher presumes understanding of the underlining forces that would make, for example, an advertising campaign attractive and persuasive, or a desirable product often direct the researcher to narrow down the set of theoretically infinite versions to a manageable number of levels to be manipulated experimentally.

The interplay between testing and experimentation is not unique to the business discipline. Although the physics of flying is relatively well understood, no pilot would feel safe to fly an airplane that has not been extensively tested in wind tunnel. Similarly, firms can maximize their learning by testing several different approaches in small-scale experiments. By evaluating radical ideas through an interactive process of prototyping, testing, and refinement, companies can successfully manage the risk of future endeavors. Experiments in this sense are the scouting units of the company, pointing dead ends and suggesting alternative and attractive (profitable) new paths to pursue. Business experiments can range in scope from small lab studies with few participants to a large field study that is virtually the "real thing" except limited in scope along geographical, demographic or other relevant variables. Generalizability and control are, of course, the variables the researchers trade off when determining the scope of their study.

Several previous conferences and edited books such as "Games and Human Behavior" edited by Budescu, Erev, and Zwick (1999), or the proceedings of the conference on the behavioral foundations of economic theory held in 1985 in Chicago (Hogarth & Reder, 1986) have explored the different perspectives of economic and psychology on human decisions in individual and interactive contexts. One of the main issues for comparison was the differences and similarities between economics and psychology with regard to the use of experiments. This issue seems to be well understood, and numerous articles have been written on this subject (for a recent review see Hertwig & Ortmann, 2001). We find it interesting that echos of this dichotomy can be heard within the various branches of the academic business disciplines, where the more psychological oriented disciples of marketing, organizational behavior, and to a lesser extent accounting adopted the experimental methodology quite early and mimicked, for the most part, the experimental psychology tradition. On the other hand, economics and to some extent finance, have developed the experimental methodology along independent lines. Similar to the benefits derived from integrating economic and psychological approaches to experimentation, we believe that it is important to open a line of communication among experimentalists within the various academic branches of business administration. The present volume is step in this direction.

This volume includes 16 chapters coauthored by 37 contributors. The authors come from many of the disciplines that correspond to the different departments in a modern business school. In particular, the chapters represent different experimental approaches in accounting, economic, marketing, and management. The book is organized in four sections: six chapters on coordination and dynamic decision-making, four chapters on auction, three chapters on learning and constructions, and three chapters on bargaining and contracts. They are all unified not by their themes but by the experimental methodology.

This volume should be viewed as work in progress rather than a state of the art summary, or a guide for future research. The conference and the resulting book were designed to provide a place for intellectual exchange of ideas between experimentalists within the various business disciplines. We hope that the exposure we provide for the experimental method in business will inspire the reader to pursue the method and take it to new heights.

ACKNOWLEDGEMENTS

We owe thanks to many for the successful completion of this volume. Most importantly, we express our gratitude to the contributors who attended the conference, participated in insightful discussions, and later served as reviewers for the chapters in this volume. The conference was supported financially by a grant from the Hong Kong University Grant Commission to cEBR that provided seed money under the Areas of Excellence initiative (Project No. AOE97/98.BM03), and by an RGC Postgraduate Students Conference/Seminar Grant (Project No. PSCG98/99.BM01) to Wang Jing and Rami Zwick. Additional financial support was given by HKUST. Special thanks are due to Professor Yuk Shee Chan who, at the time of the conference, served as the Dean of the HKUST Business School and is currently the acting Vice-President for Academic Affairs at HKUST. We wish to thank Maya Rosenblatt, the conference secretary, without her help the conference would have been a total chaos, and Benjamin Hak-Fung Chiao, the heart and soul of cEBR, for the splendid and dedicated work in preparing and formatting all the chapters for publication. We also thank Kluwer for supporting this project.

Rami Zwick and Amnon Rapoport
July 2001

REFERENCES

Budescu, D., Erev, I., and Zwick, R. (Eds.), (1999) *Games and Human Behavior: Essays in Honor of Amnon Rapoport*. Mahwah, NJ, USA: Lawrence Erlbaum Associates.

Hertwig, R. and Ortman, A. (2001). Experimental Practices in Economics: A Methodological Challenge for Psychologists?: *Behavioral and Brain Sciences*, 24(4).

Hogarth, R. M. and Reder, M. W. (1986). Editors' comments: Perspectives from economics and psychology. *The Journal of Business*, 59, 185–207.

Kagel, J. and Roth A. E. (Eds.) (1995). *Handbook of Experimental Economics*. Princeton: Princeton University Press.

Smith, V. (1994). Economics in the Laboratory. *Journal of Economic Perspectives*, 8(1), 113–131.

Part I

COORDINATION & DYNAMIC DECISION MAKING

Chapter 1 (Germany)

AN EXPERIMENTAL STUDY OF SAVING AND INVESTING IN A COMPLEX STOCHASTIC ENVIRONMENT

D80 G31
D14

Vital Anderhub
Humboldt-University of Berlin

Werner Güth
Humboldt-University of Berlin

Florian Knust
Humboldt-University of Berlin

1.   INTRODUCTION

Optimal intertemporal decision making in a stochastic environment requires considerable analytical skills. Boundedly rational decision makers typically fail in achieving the best outcome. Thus, experimental studies of intertemporal decision making (see the selective survey[1] of Anderhub and Güth, 1999) may offer stylized facts which can guide our intuition about how boundedly rational decision makers generate choices.

The study at hand continues previous experimental research (Anderhub, Güth, Müller, and Strobel, forthcoming, Anderhub, 1998, Anderhub, Müller, and Schmidt, forthcoming, Brandstätter and Güth, forthcoming) based on variations of the same basic experimental design. The idea is that "life" expectation is not a constant but has to be updated during "life". Experimentally this has been captured by three (differently coloured) dice representing three markedly different "life" expectations. By taking out first one and then another die "life" expectation changes. An intuitive interpretation of such changes is the effect of a serious medical examination. While learning about such effects participants have to decide how much of their resources to spend in each period. Thus the task combines the difficulties of Bayesian updating with those of dynamic programming (studies with stationary stochastic processes are Hey and Dardanoni, 1988, and Köhler, 1996).

According to the basic experimental setup a "life" consists of at least 3 and at most 6 periods $t = 1, 2, \ldots, T$ with $3 \leq T \leq 6$. At the beginning, an initial endowment of 11.92 ECU (Experimental Currency Unit) is available. Denote by x_t the expenditures in period t and by S_t the remaining capital in period t, i.e., $S_1 = 11.92$. Since $S_{t+1} = S_t - x_t$, a participant decides between spending more in period t or keeping more for the future. Although Anderhub et al. (forthcoming) have also studied another intertemporal utility function, we restrict attention to the version where

$$U = x_1 \cdot \ldots \cdot x_T = \prod_{t \leq T} x_t.$$

If $T < 6$ and $S_{T+1} > 0$, the amount kept for the future is lost. Conversely, $x_t = 0$ implies the worst result. This illustrates the conflict when saving for an uncertain future.

In the experiment, the final period T is stochastically determined by three differently colored dice (green, yellow, and red) representing three different termination probabilities ($\frac{1}{6}$ for green, $\frac{1}{3}$ for yellow, and $\frac{1}{2}$ for red) to be applied after the 3rd period. After the choice of x_1, one die is taken out, and after choosing x_2 the second one is taken out. Thus, only from the 3rd period on a participant encounters a constant termination probability which is then applied repeatedly to determine whether "life" extends over $T = 3, 4, 5,$ or 6 periods.

To allow for learning a participant did not "live" once but experienced 12 successive "lives". A minor experimental control concerned the possible sequences of "initial chance moves", namely, the taking out of dice. A participant experienced all 6 sequences in a random order (1st cycle) and then again the 6 sequences in another random order (2nd cycle).[2] In other words: The 1st cycle comprises the first 6 "lives" and the 2nd cycle the last 6 "lives" where exactly one of the first 6 "lives" and one of the second 6 "lives" relies on the same sequence of firstly and secondly taken out die. Instead of requiring that participants are paid according to their average success U (in the 12 successive "lives") or according to a randomly chosen "life", participants can choose the payoff mode before starting to play. If one, for instance, considers the choice of the random mode as a signal of risk loving, participants would signal their attitude toward risk. In this sense the choice of the payoff mode offers some form of self-screening. In the present study we allow for even more self screening.

Whereas Anderhub (1998) has reduced stochastic uncertainty (the dice represented certain "life" expectations, namely $T = 6$ for green, $T = 5$ for yellow, and $T = 4$ for red), in our experiment participants could add another uncertainty concerning their future expectations. Specifically, after choosing x_1 and before excluding the first die, a participant could invest any amount y with $0 \leq y \leq S_1 - x_1 = 11.92 - x_1$ into a risky "asset" yielding $\frac{4}{3}y$ with probability $\frac{2}{3}$ and $\frac{2}{3}y$ with probability $\frac{1}{3}$ in period 2, i.e.

$$S_2 = 11.92 - x_1 + \frac{y}{3} \text{ with probability } \frac{2}{3}.$$

and

$$S_2 = 11.92 - x_1 - \frac{y}{3} \text{ with probability } \frac{1}{3}.$$

The possibility to invest into such a risky asset with the positive expected dividend of $\frac{y}{9}$ has been restricted to just one period. We were afraid of over-burdening participants with too many investment decisions and also wanted to limit the maximal possible payoff U of the participants. A large investment level y signals a readiness for taking chances although, due to the uncertainty of T, the situation is already very risky (a combination of investment risk with an uncertain horizon is also explored by Rapoport and Jones, 1970, and Rapoport et al., 1977). Clearly, the new experimental scenario offers now two possibilities for self-selection: The old discrete one of A-types (average payoff) and R-types (random payoff) and the new continuous investment level y with $0 \leq y \leq S_1 - x_1$ indicating how willing a participant is to invest into a risky but profitable asset.

Compared to other studies in experimental economics (for a survey see Camerer, 1995) of risky investments, our experimental scenario has the advantage that the risk resulting from investing is not the only one. It is rather embedded in a highly stochastic environment where self-imposed investment uncertainty combines with exogenously imposed uncertainty, here whether T will be 3, 4, 5, or 6. Will the unavoidable uncertainty of T induce risk averse behavior? Or does an uncertain "life" expectation render self-imposed risks like the random payoff mode or positive risky investments y as more accept-able? In other word: We want to learn whether exogenously given risks crowd in or out voluntary risk taking.

As in Anderhub et al. (forthcoming) and Anderhub (1998), we have derived the optimal trajectories for a risk neutral decision maker whose expected payoff is $U = 80.54\,\text{ECU}$ (see Figure 1). After the initial choices $x_1 = 2.19$ and $y = 9.73$, chance determines whether the investment $y = 9.73$ is yielding $\frac{4}{3}y$ (with probability $\frac{2}{3}$) or $\frac{2}{3}y$ (with probability $\frac{1}{3}$). This is followed by the chance move determining whether the green ($\neg green$), the yellow ($\neg yellow$), or the red ($\neg red$) die is taken out. After x_2 is chosen, the second die is taken out. Finally, after x_t for $t \geq 3$, it is randomly determined whether $T = 3, 4, 5,$ or 6. The optimal choices for the respective chance events are listed inside the boxes whereas the residual funds S_t inducing those choices are indicated above the boxes. Our experimental software automatically implemented the choice $x_6 = S_6$.

2. EXPERIMENTAL DESIGN

Our design corresponds to the one of Anderhub et al. (forthcoming) except for the necessary changes in the instructions as well as in the software required by the additional second decision in period $t = 1$ when a participant chooses y with $0 \leq y \leq S_1 - x_1$. In the instructions (see appendix for English translation) the novel sections are indicated in italics. Participants could use a calculator.

Fifty participants were invited by leaflets to register for an experiment which would last at most two hours. Actually, the time needed for the twelve

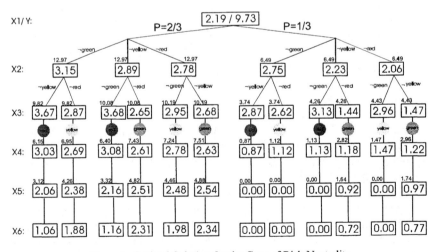

Figure 1. Optimal Solution for the Case of Risk Neutrality

successive "lives" ranged from 13 to 103 minutes (without the time for reading and understanding the instructions in the beginning). In addition to the payoff relevant choices x_t and y, we also asked for plans regarding future expenditure levels. Previous results have shown that most participants try to answer such questions quickly rather than carefully. Dropping such questions might, however, have influenced behavior and thus the possibility to compare our results to previous ones. Each participant finally answered the 16PA-personality questionnaire (Brandstätter, 1988) which can be used to account for individual differences in intertemporal decision making (Brandstätter and Güth, forthcoming).

Participants were mainly students of economics and business administration of Humboldt University of Berlin. Although the maximal payoff expectation U is much larger due to the possibility of engaging once into a risky but profitable asset, the average earning does not reflect this. The maximal payoff expectation $U = 80.54$ ECU (1 ECU $= 0.50$ DM) exceeds the one of $U = 35.16$ ECU (1 ECU $= 1$ DM) in the Anderhub et al. (forthcoming)-experiment, but the average earning of 39.72 ECU (49% efficiency) is much smaller than the average payoff 27.62 ECU (79% efficiency) in the experiment of Anderhub et al.

To illustrate how sensitive the payoff expectation is to changes in the new decision variable y we have derived for all possible decisions y the optimal intertemporal allocation behavior $x_t^*(y)$ for $t = 1, 2, \ldots, 6$ and all possible chance events for the case of risk neutrality.[3] For any given y one computes the optimal consumption as in Figure 1 for $y^* = 9.73$. Let $U(y)$ denote the payoff expectation resulting from these optimal trajectories for a given investment y. Figure 2 graphically illustrates how $U(y)$ depends on the investment level y. To the right hand side of the optimal investment level $y^* = 9.73$ the decline of $U(y)$ is much steeper.[4] In general, wrong choices y can drastically reduce the payoff expectation $U(y)$.

One cannot expect that participants are aware of how $U(y)$ depends on y. But they may understand the risk of too large investments, e.g., in the sense of $y \geq 11$, and that underinvestments, e.g., in the sense of $y < 5$, are less dangerous. A general attitude to under- and even more to overinvest could explain why participants have earned less than in the previous experiment.

3. EXPERIMENTAL RESULTS

In this study we are mainly interested in the investment decision y. The choice of y will inform us about the (different) willingness to increase stochastic complexity by inducing a stochastic consumption fund S_2 and how such (different) attitudes are interrelated with intertemporal allocation patterns. On average, more than half of $S_1 - x_1$ is invested in the risky prospect (see Figure 3 which displays the average y and available funds $S_1 - x_1$ for the 12

U(y)

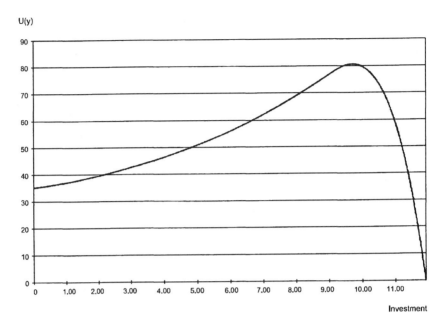

Figure 2. Expected Value $U(y)$ Depending on Investment y

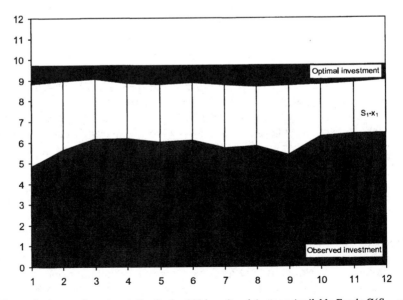

Figure 3. Average Investment $Øy$, Optimal Value y^* and Average Available Funds $Ø(S_1 - x_1)$

successive "lives"). The fact that the sum of average observed investment (the lower dark area) and $S_1 - x_1$ (the light area) leave an upper dark area reveals a constant tendency to overspend in period 1 (on average the observed x_1 is with 3.07 much larger than its benchmark level of 2.19, cf. Figures 1 and 6). Of course, larger investments y imply on average a larger variance of actual earnings (see scatter plot in Figure 4). The linear regression line $U_i(y_i) = \alpha + \beta y_i = 21.55 + 3.14 y_i$ included in Figure 4 explains $R^2 = .06$ of the variance in individual earning per round. Both the coefficients α and β are significantly different from zero at the one percent level. We also estimated the quadratic specification $V_i(y_i) = \alpha + \beta y_i + \gamma y_i^2$ which, however, did not increase R^2 significantly.

Of the altogether $50 \cdot 12 = 600$ plays, 224 (37.33%) rely on full investment $y = 11.92 - x_1$. How the average absolute and relative investment share $\varnothing y$ and $\varnothing y / (11.92 - x_1)$, respectively, depends on the payoff type (R for random and A for average) as well as on experience (1st versus 2nd cycle) is described by Table 1. A-types slightly increase their investment and R-types slightly decrease it with experience, both absolutely and relatively. Note, that only five participants chose the random payoff procedure.[5]

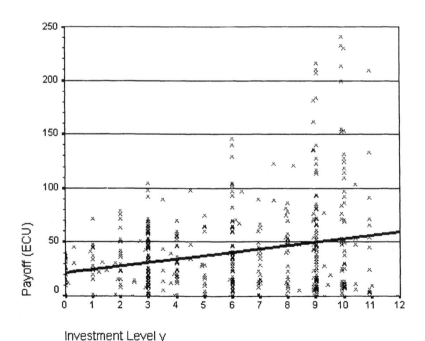

Figure 4. Investment y and the Resulting Monetary Gains U

Table 1. Average Investment (Øy) and Average Investment Share (Ø(y/(11.92 − x₁))) Depending on Payoff Mode and Experience

	payoff type					
	A (N = 45)		R (N = 5)		*both* (N = 50)	
	1st cycle	2nd cycle	1st cycle	2nd cycle	1st cycle	2nd cycle
Øy	5.86	6.11	5.50	5.05	5.83	6.00
Ø(y/(11.92 − x₁))	.66	.69	.59	.55	.65	.68

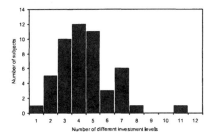 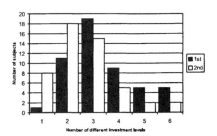

Figure 5. Number of Different Investment Levels (all 12 Rounds Left – Separated by Cycles Right)

Figure 5 illustrates how often participants have chosen different y-levels. None of the 50 participants has chosen 12 different investment level y, and only one participant has always relied on the same y-choice, namely $y = 3.00$ ECU.

During the second cycle the average number of different y-levels 2.62 is smaller than the corresponding level 3.42 for the first cycle. The number of investment levels stabilizes at using 1 to 3 different levels. y-choices are often prominent numbers: 3.00, 4.00, 6.00, 9.00, 9.92, or 10.00 are chosen 104, 28, 86, 80, 26, and 39 (in total 363 of 600) times. The more frequent numbers can be divided by 3 (3.00, 6.00, and 9.00), i.e. they yield also prominent returns from investment.

Figure 6 shows that lucky investments (411 of 600 plays) led to higher average consumption choices $\emptyset x_t$ in periods $t = 2$ to 6 than unlucky ones (189 of 600 plays) where the common starting condition is $\emptyset x_1 = 3.07$ and $\emptyset y = 5.91$. Even in the last and most unlikely period $t = 6$ one usually consumes much more after a lucky investment than after an unlucky one (the frequency of $x_6 = 0$ is 8.1% (11/136) for the left branch of Figure 6 and 16.8% (9/57) for the right one.[6] The mean of x_1 is much higher than for the benchmark solu-

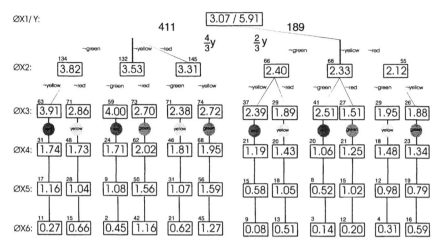

Figure 6. Average Observations

tion. Even though the optimal x_1-decision $x_1 = 2.19$ is lower than for $y = 0$ ($x_1 = 2.49$, see Anderhub et al., forthcoming), the observed average value $\emptyset x_1 = 3.07$ is significantly (Mann-Whitney-U test, $p = 0.019$) higher than for the compulsory $y = 0$-game where $\emptyset x_1 = 2.64$. One could justify this by wishful thinking, i.e. that investors are more certain of being lucky than captured by its probability of 2/3.

Like in other experimental studies of risk-taking (e.g. Levin, Snyder and Chapman, 1988), a gender effect has been observed: For the altogether 38 male and 12 female participants the mean investments are significantly higher for male ($\emptyset y = 6.53$) than for female ($\emptyset y = 4.00$) participants (Mann-Whitney-U test, $p = 0.003$).

Directional learning (e.g., as applied by Selten and Buchta, 1999) predicts that success of an action strengthens the tendency for this particular action. Applied to investment behavior, lucky investments should lead to larger or equal investments later. On the other hand, it has been argued (Kahneman and Tversky, 1979) that losses lead to more risk taking since one wants to recapture what has been lost (on financial markets this can explain the frequent phenomenon of "overriding losses", e.g., Weber and Camerer, 1992). In Table 2 we distinguish the three possibilities, namely, an increase of the investment level ($y_l > y_{l-1}$), equal ($y_l = y_{l-1}$), or lower ($y_l < y_{l-1}$) investments for the two possible chance events. The share 78.36% of cases with ($y_l \geq y_{l-1}$) after bad luck exceeds slightly the corresponding share 74.41% for previous good luck. For the more narrow concept of strict adaptation (in the sense of $y_l \neq y_{l-1}$) the results are with 32.16% for bad and 27.44%

Table 2. Directional Learning

	unlucky in $l-1$	lucky in $l-1$	Total
$y_{l-1} > y_l$	37	97	134
$y_{l-1} = y_l$	79	178	257
$y_{l-1} < y_l$	55	104	159
Total	171	379	550

Table 3. Reacting to an Uncertain Future

	Cases	%		Cases	%		Cases	%
$T \geq 4$	402	100.0	$T \geq 5$	278	100.0	$T = 6$	193	100.0
$x_3 > x_4$	293	72.9	$x_3 > x_4\,x_5$	146	52.5	$x_3 > x_4 > x_5 > x_6$	78	40.4
$x_3 \geq x_4$	370	92.0	$x_3 \geq x_4 \geq x_5$	226	81.3	$x_3 \geq x_4 \geq x_5 \geq x_6$	143	74.1
$T \geq 5$	278	100.0	$T = 6$	193	100.0			
$x_4 > x_5$	199	71.6	$x_4 > x_5 > x_6$	108	70.6			
$x_4 \geq x_5$	251	90.3	$x_4 \geq x_5 \geq x_6$	158	81.9			
$T = 6$	193	100.0						
$x_5 > x_6$	147	76.1						
$x_5 \geq x_6$	171	88.6						

for good luck not very encouraging. It seems that both directional learning and recapturing losses are poor predictors when the stochastic nature of success is obvious.

Since from $t = 3$ on a later period $t + 1$ is less likely, even boundedly rational intertemporal allocation behavior should satisfy the requirement $x_t > x_{t+1}$ for $t = 3, 4$, and 5. For the 402 plays with $T \geq 4$ we can, in general, only check the requirement $x_3 > x_4$ which is satisfied in 293 (72.9%) cases. Of the remaining plays with $T \geq 4$ the equality $x_3 = x_4$ is observed in 77 cases whereas 32 plays rely on $x_3 < x_4$. When $T \geq 5$ or even $T = 6$ one can check quite similarly the more demanding criteria $x_3 > x_4 > x_5$ and $x_3 > x_4 > x_5 > x_6$, respectively. According to Table 3 many participants set often the same value even when the future is uncertain, i.e., $x_t = x_{t+1}$ (for $3 \leq t \leq 5$). For $T = 6$, for instance, only 40.4% of the 193 plays[7] are characterized by $x_3 > x_4 > x_5 > x_6$ whereas 74.1% satisfy the weaker requirement $x_3 \geq x_4 \geq x_5 \geq x_6$ (for similar results see Anderhub et al., forthcoming).

4. SELF-SELECTION AND INTERTEMPORAL ALLOCATION BEHAVIOR

As in Table 1 for R(andom) and A(verage) types, we are interested whether participants with low (below median) or high (above median) average investment levels or with low (below median) or large (above median) variance of individual investments differ in their intertemporal consumption pattern. To answer such questions we introduce some individual measures:

$$c = \frac{x_1 + x_2 + x_3}{11.92 \pm y/3}:$$ Share of totally available funds $11.92 \pm y/3$ spent in the certain periods 1, 2, and 3

$$S_6:$$ Amount left for consumption x_6 in period 6

$$v = \sum_{l=1}^{11} |y_l - y_{l+1}|:$$ Volatility of investment levels over time

We distinguish rounds with high or low investment and whether investment was profitable or not. The optimal value c^* can be computed with the help of Figure 1 as the expected value c for all equally probable 6 sequences of taking out two of three dice. Compared to the benchmark level for lucky $c^* = 0.54$ and $c^* = 0.80$ for unlucky investment, the observed average c-shares (see Table 4) are less sensitive to success. The critical level separating low and high investors is the median of the individual average (over the 12 "lives") y-levels. But the c-values for good luck are significantly larger than those for bad luck (Mann-Whitney-U test: low investment $p = .088$; high investment $p = .011$; all investment $p = .004$). In our view, this qualitatively contrary effect, when compared to c^*, is mainly due to the much smaller observed investment amounts which imply a lower volatility of S_2 than the benchmark solution. The average difference ΔS_6 of S_6 between good and bad luck is naturally larger for high $(y > \bar{y})$ than for low $(y < \underline{y})$ investments. Compared to the difference

Table 4. Measures of Low and High Investors

	$y < \bar{y}$ (low investment)		$y > \bar{y}$ (high investment)	
	unlucky	lucky	unlucky	lucky
$c = \dfrac{x_1 + x_2 + x_3}{11.92 \pm y/3}$	.73	.76	.71	.73
S_6 (if $t = 5$)	0.56	0.68	0.28	1.12

Table 5. Number of Different Types of Participants Based on Median Splits (Independence would Imply the Frequencies in Brackets)

		Mean Investment		Σ
		low ($y > \bar{y} = 5.91$)	high ($y > \bar{y} = 5.91$)	
$v = \sum_{l=1}^{11} \lvert y_l - y_{l+1} \rvert$	Low (<13.78)	16 (14)	14 (16)	30
	high (>13.78)	8 (10)	12 (10)	20
Σ		24	26	50

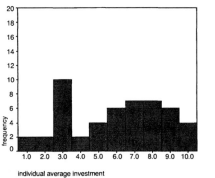 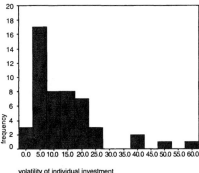

Figure 7. Histogram of Individual Average Investment (Left) and Volatility of Investment (Right)

$\Delta S_6^* = 1.54$ for $y^* = 9.73$ implied by optimality, even for "high investors" the observed distance $\Delta S_6 = .84$ is small.

Let us compare the individual average investment level with the individual volatility v for each participant.[8] The larger average volatility v for high ($v = 14,79$) than for low ($v = 12.69$) investors had to be expected. The v-distributions of high and low investors, however, do not differ significantly (Mann-Whitney-U test, $p = .225$). The distribution of individual average investment levels $\bar{y}$ is double peaked with a spike at $\bar{y} \sim 3$ and another more dispersed peak for $\bar{y} \sim 7$ and 8 (see Figure 7 – left). Figure 7 (right) displays the distribution of v, i.e., the volatility of individual investments over time which is essentially single-peaked. Independence of low or high volatility and low or high investment level would yield the frequencies in brackets of Table 5 which differ from the observed ones by two in all four cases. There seems to be no clear-cut deviation from independence.

Table 6. Percentage of $x_t > x_{t+1}$ $(t \geq 3)$

$\sum\limits_{t=1}^{11} \lvert y_t - y_{t+1} \rvert$	Mean Investment		Σ
	low $(y < \bar{y} = 5.91)$	high $(y > \bar{y} = 5.91)$	
low (<13.78)	.76	.67	.72
high (>13.78)	.75	.67	.71
Σ	.76	.67	.72

Table 6 reveals for all 12 ("lives") $\cdot$ 50 (participants) = 600 plays how the %-confirmation of the basic rationality requirement $x_t > x_{t+1}$ for $t \geq 3$ depends on (low or high) volatility, respectively investment. Comparing the distribution of $x_t > x_{t+1}$-percentages for low $(y < \bar{y})$ with the one for high investors $(y > \bar{y})$, shows that the higher rationality of low investors is not significant (Mann-Whitney-U test, $p = .258$). High but unlucky investors apparently became less careful after experiencing a major loss.

5. CONCLUSIONS

The "savings game" confronts participants with highly stochastic future prospects. Some uncertainty (concerning the termination probability to be applied after period $t = 3$) is gradually resolved (by taking out dice) and some remains, namely whether "life" ends in period $T = 3, 4, 5,$ or 6. In our experiment participants can voluntarily add another risk by investing more or less of the available funds $11.92 - x_1$ into a profitable but risky prospect. Such an experiment allows the study of investment behavior when investment risk is just one of many uncertainties. Other experimental (economics, see otherwise Rapoport and Jones, 1970, and Rapoport et al., 1977) studies of decision making under uncertainty (see Camerer, 1995, for a survey) usually focus on situations where the investment risk is the only experimentally controlled risk.

By repeating the modified savings game we could investigate how stable investment attitudes are. Since most y-levels, namely 58.5%, were interior in the sense of $0 < y < 11.92 - x_1$, most participants were neither extremely risk averse nor risk neutral or risk loving. Furthermore, the rather large individual average volatility $v = 13.78$ indicates that risk attitudes were rather unstable or path dependent. Normative decision theory offers nothing to account for this phenomenon (income effects are negligible in our context). In our view, people are not either risk loving or risk averse but rather capable of both. One needs more data to determine when which risk attitude applies.

The individual investment choices provide another (continuous) variable for self-selection in addition to the distinction of the A- or R-payment mode. Only 5 of our 50 participants chose the R-mode who, on average, invested less in absolute and relative terms (see Table 1). Since the R-mode causes already one additional uncertainty, namely, whether a successful or unsuccessful "life" will determine the monetary win, the R-choice seems to crowd out risky investments.[9]

Our detailed analysis of "low and high investors" did not reveal any striking differences in their intertemporal allocation behavior as, for instance, measured by the c, S_6, and v-parameters. What matters more is whether one has been lucky in investing or not where this is, of course, more important for large investments. We conclude from our findings that individual risk attitudes matter more for self-imposed risks (here voluntarily choosing $y > 0$) than for the ways of coping with exogenously imposed risks (here the uncertainty of T). As suggested by the theory of mental accounting (see, for instance, Thaler, 1985), we seem to account for different types of risks by different considerations: A very bold, respectively cautious investor may be very cautious, respectively careless when health risks are concerned.

ACKNOWLEDGEMENT

The financial support of the Deutsche Forschungsgemeinschaft (SFB 373, C5) and the TMR-project "Savings and Pensions" by the European Commission is gratefully acknowledged. We thank Simon Gächter and Amnon Rapoport for their helpful advice how to improve the paper.

NOTES

1. The authors review only studies in experimental economics and thus neglect related research in mathematical psychology, e.g., Rapoport (1995), Rapoport and Jones (1970), Rapoport et al. (1977) and in economic psychology (Wärneryd, 1999).
2. Anderhub et al. (forthcoming) did not find any evidence indicating that participants detected this regularity.
3. Note that risk neutrality implies that the optimal investment level y^* is the maximal one, i.e. $y^* = S_1 - x_1$.
4. If y approaches $S_1 = 11.92$ this means that x_1 converges to 0 so that $U(y) \rightarrow 0$.
5. Without the investment opportunity 16 of the 50 participants have chosen the R-payoff mode. Thus one can argue that the more relevant voluntary risk (positive y) crowds out the seemingly less relevant voluntary risk (the R-payoff mode).
6. The frequency of reaching a certain box, i.e. of the respective chance moves, is always indicated above the respective box.
7. These plays occur, of course, in all three columns of Table 3 since they meet all requirements of Table 3.

8. The average volatility is 13.78 (the benchmark solution prescribes, of course, $v^* = 0$).
9. In view of the small number of R-types the difference can not be tested for significance.

REFERENCES

Anderhub, V. (1998). "Savings Decisions when Uncertainty is Reduced." SFB Discussion Paper, Humboldt University of Berlin.

Anderhub, V., W. Güth, W. Müller, and M. Strobel (forthcoming). "On Saving, Updating and Dynamic Programming – An Experimental Analysis." *Experimental Economics*.

Anderhub, V., R. Müller, and C. Schmidt (forthcoming). "Design and Evaluation of an Economic Experiment via the Internet." *Journal of Economic Behavior and Organisation*.

Anderhub, V., and W. Güth (1999). "On Intertemporal Allocation Behavior – A Selective Survey of Saving Experiments." *ifo-Studien* 3, 303–33.

Brandstätter, H. (1988). "Sechzehn Persönlichkeits-Adjektivskalen (16 PA) als Forschungsinstrument anstelle des 16PF." *Zeitschrift für experimentelle und angewandte Psychologie* 35, 370–91.

Brandstätter, H., and W. Güth (forthcoming). "A Psychological Approach to Individual Differences in Intertemporal Consumption Patterns." *Journal of Economic Psychology*.

Camerer, C. (1995). "Individual Decision Making." In *The Handbook of Experimental Economics*, edited by J. H. Kagel and A. E. Roth, 587–703. Princeton: Princeton University Press.

Hey, J., and V. Dardanoni (1998). "Optimal Consumption under Uncertainty: An Experimental Investigation." *The Economic Journal* 98, 105–16.

Kahneman, D., and A. Tversky (1979). "An Analysis of Decision under Risk." *Econometrica* 47, 263–91.

Köhler, J. (1996). "Making Saving Easy: An Experimental Analysis of Savings Decisions." Mimeo., Department of Economics and Related Studies, University of York.

Levin, I. P., M. A. Snyder, and D. Chapman (1988). "The Interaction of Experimental and Situational Factors and Gender in a Simulated Risky Decision Making Task." *The Journal of Psychology* 122, 173–81.

Rapoport, A. (1975). "Research Paradigms for Studying Decision Behavior." In *Utility, Probability, and Human Decision Making*, edited by D. Wendt and C. A. J. Vlek. Dordrecht, Holland: D. Reidel.

Rapoport, A., and L. V. Jones (1970). "Gambling Behavior in Two-Outcome Multistage Betting Games." *Journal of Mathematical Psychology* 7, 163–87.

Rapoport, A. et al. (1977). "How One Gambles if One Must: Effects of Differing Return Rates on Multistage Betting Decisions." *Journal of Mathematical Psychology* 15, 169–98.

Selten, R., and J. Buchta (1999). "Experimental Sealed Bid First Price Auction with Directly Observed Bid Functions." In *Games and Human Behavior: Essays in the Honor of Amnon Rapoport*, edited by D. Budescu, I. Erev, and R. Zwick. Mahwah, NJ: Lawrence Erlbaum Associates.

Thaler, R. (1985). "Mental Accounting and Consumer Choice." *Marketing Science* 4, 199–214.

Müller, W. (1999). "Strategies, Heuristics and the Relevance of Risk Aversion in a Dynamic Decision Problem." SFB Discussion Paper 61, Humboldt University of Berlin.

Wärneryd, K.-E. (1999). *The Psychology of Saving – A Study on Economic Psychology*. Cheltenham: Edward Elgar Publishing.

Weber, M., and C. Camerer (1992). "Recent Developments in Modelling Preferences: Uncertainty and Ambiguity." *Journal of Risk and Uncertainty* 5, 325–70.

APPENDIX: INSTRUCTIONS

Your task in every round is to distribute an amount of money over several periods. The better you do this, the higher is your payoff. Altogether you will play 12 rounds. In the beginning of the experiment you can choose whether we should draw lots to select one round for which you are paid. Otherwise, you will receive the mean of your payoffs in all rounds. In any case you get your payoff in cash according to you own decisions.

The general task in each round is to distribute a certain amount of money over several periods. Your payoff for one round is calculated by the product of the amounts allocated to the single periods. *In addition, you can invest any amount of the remaining money in the first period in a profitable but risky prospect which increases your disposable amount in period 2 when you are lucky and reduces it when you are unlucky.*

The difficulty is that there is no certainty about the number of periods over which you have to distribute your money. The game can last for three, four, five, or six periods. Every round will last at least three periods. Whether you reach the fourth, fifth, or sixth period will be determined by throwing a die. There are altogether three different dice with the colors red, yellow, and green. The following table shows in which cases you reach a next period.

The number of periods in a single round can not be higher than six. In the beginning of a round you will not know which die is used. You will receive this information after you have made some decisions. The play proceeds as follows:

COLOUR OF DIE	NO FURTHER PERIOD IF DIE SHOWS	NEW PERIOD IF DIE SHOWS
RED	1, 2, 3	4, 5, 6
YELLOW	1, 2	3, 4, 5, 6
GREEN	1	2, 3, 4, 5, 6

1st period)   You will get a total amount of money S which you can spend in the coming periods. Altogether you can only spend this amount. You can choose an amount x_1 that you want to spend in the first period. Consider carefully how much you want to spend and how much you want to save for the following periods. *In addition, you have (only) in the first period the opportunity to invest some of the residual amount $S - x_1$. You can choose any amount y with $0 \leq y \leq S - x_1$. Now a die is thrown. If the die shows 1, 2, 3, or 4 the amount invested will increase by 1/3. If the die shows 5 or 6 the amount invested will decrease by 1/3. Accordingly, your disposable amount for the second period will be higher or lower.* After your decision, one of the three dice is excluded. One of the two remaining dice will determine whether you reach the fourth, fifth, and sixth period.

2nd period)   You choose an amount x_2 which you want to spend in the second period. You can not spend more than you have left of the total amount after the first period. After your decision, another die is excluded. Now you know which die will be thrown to determine whether the fourth, fifth, and sixth period is reached.

3rd period)   You choose an amount x_3 which you want to spend in the third period. After this decision, the computer will throw the remaining die in order to decide whether you reach the fourth period. If you do not reach the fourth period, the round ends here. The amount which is not spent until now is lost.

4ᵗʰ period) If you have reached the fourth period, you choose an amount x_4. For reaching the fifth period, the die will be thrown again.

5ᵗʰ period) If you have reached the fifth period, you choose an amount x_5. For reaching the sixth period, the die will be thrown again.

6ᵗʰ period) If you reach the sixth period, all remaining money is spent automatically.

Your payoff is calculated as the product of all amounts you spent in the periods you have reached. If you experienced, for instance, exactly four periods, your payoff is determined as $G = x_1 \cdot x_2 \cdot x_3 \cdot x_4$. When you have reached, for instance, all six periods, your payoff is determined as $G = x_1 \cdot x_2 \cdot x_3 \cdot x_4 \cdot x_5 \cdot x_6$ where x_6 is the amount you have left after the fifth period. Please, notice: If you spend in one period an amount of 0, your payoff is 0 since one of the factors determining G is 0. This can happen, for instance, if you spend all the money in the fourth period and reach the fifth period. Then you spend 0 in the fifth and perhaps also in the sixth period and receive the payoff of 0. You have to decide between the risk of spending all your money early or wasting your money if the game ends earlier than expected.

Chapter 2

DYNAMIC DECISION MAKING IN MARKETING CHANNELS
AN EXPERIMENTAL STUDY OF CYCLE TIME, SHARED INFORMATION AND CUSTOMER DEMAND PATTERNS

Sunil Gupta

M 3 1

Principal, Thinktodo, LLC and
Senior Consultant, David Shepard Associates

Joel H. Steckel
New York University

Anirvan Banerji
Economic Cycle Research Institute

1. INTRODUCTION

In traditional channels, orders flow upstream and shipments move downstream (as, for example in Figure 1).

Based on the locally available information (the flows of incoming orders from downstream members and shipments from upstream members), each channel member attempts to simultaneously minimize inventory-on-hand and stockouts. These dual tasks are rendered especially complex because of: *i*) ordering and shipping delays between channel members; *ii*) uncertainties regarding customer demand and the external environment; and *iii*) the dependence of each channel member's performance on the quality of other channel members' decision making (e.g., poor decision making by the wholesaler can adversely impact the in-stock position of a retailer, even if the retailer is

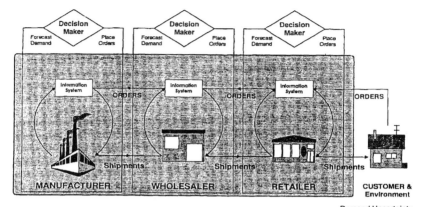

Figure 1. A Traditional Distribution Channel

perfectly prescient about incoming orders from customers). The resulting set of dynamic and interdependent decisions have often been found to result in large inefficiencies for the channel as a whole. For example, Hammond (1992) reports that, on an annual basis, the 100 billion dollar apparel industry incurs a penalty of as much as 25 billion dollars for being out of stock at some times, and having to offer markdowns because of excess inventory at others. Similar alternating periods of stockouts and surpluses have plagued many industries (e.g., personal computer memory chips, textiles, shoe leather) throughout a wide span of time (Burke 1988; Fisher, Hammond, Obermeyer and Raman 1994; Mack 1956).

Impatient with the inefficiencies so typical of many traditional channels, several companies have invested (e.g., Buzzell and Ortmeyer, 1994, mention Wal-Mart, P&G, GE's Appliance Division and Baxter), or are considering investing large sums of money to re-engineer their distribution processes (Coopers & Lybrand 1992, National Retail Federation and Andersen Consulting 1992). The hope is that greater decision making efficiency will result in substantial economies. Recently, Kurt Salmon and Associates (1993) estimated that re-engineered processes and more efficient decision making could save the grocery industry as much as thirty billion dollars in inventory costs.

Academic research on decision-making in such dynamic and interde-pendent task environments is rare. Whereas the marketing channels literature provides many studies regarding the nature of relationships between channel members (see, e.g., Dwyer, Schurr and Oh 1987, and Frazier, Spekman and

O'Neal 1988), and the impact of a channel members' strategy on the strategic behavior of other channel members (see, e.g., McGuire and Staelin 1983 and Moorthy 1988), studies of day-to-day operating decisions, the resulting need for coordinated actions, and the impact of various channel flows on efficiency are absent. In the decision making literature, save Sterman (1989a and b) and Glazer, Steckel and Winer (1992), most studies either deal with static situations, or fail to account for interdependence among multiple decision makers (Brehmer 1992). With the current and anticipated growth of technology based systems which speed up the flows of information and goods among channel members (e.g., Quick Response, Efficient Consumer Response, or even just Electronic Data Interchange) we believe it is crucial to begin the systematic study of managerial decision making under a wide variety of channel and external conditions.

Using a simulated channel experiment (based on the well known "Beer Game", see Senge 1990, Sterman 1989a) our objectives in this paper are to address the following specific issues:

   i) To what extent do structural changes which speed up the order and delivery cycles (by reducing the order processing, manufacturing, storing and shipping lags) impact decision-making efficiency and the mental model employed by each channel member?
   ii) To what extent does timely sharing of information between channel members (by transmitting the retailer's Point-of Sale (POS) information to all other channel members) impact decision making efficiency and the mental model employed by each channel member?
   iii) What is the impact of the nature and extent of uncertainty in customer demand (as represented by the shape and volatility of incoming customer demand) on the results obtained in (*i*) and (*ii*) above?

We found that reducing the cycle time through shorter lags, predictably, reduces the inventory and stockout costs. But, the effect of POS information availability was contingent on the nature of the customer demand being served by the channel. Whereas POS availability led to the expected improvements in the simplest demand environment, efficiency was not helped and was even impaired for some channel members under more realistic (and less predictable) patterns of customer demand! Further, by examining the decision maker's (DM's) mental model under a variety of experimental conditions we surmise that in addition to paying insufficient attention to the supply line (as posited by Sterman 1989a), the quality of decision making suffers due to: the *complexity* of the decision; *inadequate coordination* among DMs; and *overreaction* to small or irrelevant changes in demand.

2.   BACKGROUND

Our study builds on Sterman's (1989a) experiment of interdependent decision-making in a dynamic, but traditional distribution system. In his experiment, Sterman found that a single one-time change in customer demand resulted in long-term inefficiencies within a distribution channel. Specifically, orders and inventory were characterized by large fluctuations (*oscillations*), increasing amplitude and variance the further away the DM was from the end consumer (*amplification*), and later peaks in order rates as one moved further up the channel (*phase lag*).

Two classes of possible causes emerge for these results. First, the channel design itself may be inefficient (e.g., too many levels, long delays between and/or within levels, poor transfer of information between levels, etc.) rendering decision making much too complex. Several authors (e.g., Martin 1993, Stalk and Hout 1990) have suggested that efforts be concentrated on *speeding up the intra- and inter-channel flows and simplifying the system*. Several companies have benefited from following this approach (see, Buzzell and Ortmeyer 1994, and Davidow and Malone 1992). Second, the sub-optimality could result from the limitations and biases so often observed in judgment and decision-making (e.g., ignoring interdependence, biased forecasting, inadequate updating of the DM's mental model of the task at hand, etc.). In particular Sterman (1989a, p. 334) concluded from his experiment that:

> To understand the source of the oscillations it is necessary to consider how the subjects dealt with long time lags between placing and receiving orders – the supply line. The results show that **most subjects failed to account adequately for the supply line** (emphasis added). . . . Thus it appears that subjects failed to allow for sufficient (product) in the pipeline to achieve their desired inventory level.

In agreement with Sterman's conclusion, Senge (1990) and Kleinmuntz (1990) suggest that efforts should also be focused on improving the *quality* of the decision-making activity. Kleinmuntz, in particular, suggests that the biases and inefficiencies noted in Sterman's paper should be more closely examined under a variety of circumstances where the DM is better and more easily informed about customer demand and the state of the pipeline. Senge suggests that a systematic analysis of the cognitive biases in DMs' mental models provides a promising direction for improving the quality of dynamic decisions made in the context of an interdependent system.

Clearly, both approaches (re-engineering and improved understanding of the decision environment) have merit. In fact, Kurt Salmon and Associates' (1993) report for the Food Marketing Institute emphasizes that companies who want to make significant improvement will have to do both. A systematic research effort aimed at understanding the efficacy of re-engineering the traditional channel under various environmental scenarios, the critical role of judgmental decision making (Kleinmuntz 1990, Towill 1992), and the interaction between these factors should therefore prove fruitful.

The complexities characteristic of an interdependent multi-level system render the calculation of optimal behavior virtually impossible for the individual channel member (Sterman 1989a). Thus, we assume that DMs resort to simplifying heuristics (Cyert and March 1963; Simon 1982). The mental model of each DM is therefore represented with the anchoring and adjustment heuristic (Tversky and Kahneman 1974) adopted by Sterman (1989a), and routinely used to model industry level sales and inventory data in the production smoothing literature (see e.g., Bechter and Stanley 1992, and Blinder and Maccini 1990). Specifically, each DM's calculus for any given period is represented thus:

DESIRED ORDER	= **Expected Incoming Orders**	+ **Adjustment for Desired Inventory Level**	+ **Adjustment for Desired Supply Line**	(1)
Where each term is based on	• DM's forecast of future incoming orders	• Desired safety stock • Current inventory/ backlog	• Total delay in receiving shipments against orders • Average sales per period expected • Pending shipments	

Note that (1) implies that past decisions and outcomes will influence current and future decisions (dynamics), and the required adjustments depend crucially upon others' performance (interdependence). We shall use (1) to model the subjects' mental model and gain insights about the reasons for variations in channel and individual performance.

2.1. The Value of Re-Engineering, or, Shortening Order and Delivery Lags

Longer lead times should make the channel less efficient for several reasons. First, because orders placed and shipments sent a long time ago might still be in the pipeline, the DM must make appropriate adjustments for pipeline delays (the third term in (1), the DM's calculus). Past research shows that paying attention to complex relationships among events and decisions in the past is difficult (Hambrick 1982; Sterman 1989a and b). Second, longer delays in feedback impede learning (Hogarth 1987), compounding the first problem. In a single-DM task Brehmer (1992) found that even minimal delays effectively prevented the DM from making any significant adjustments at all. Finally, longer lead time makes the forecasting task (the first term in (1)) less accurate because predictions must be made for a period farther out into the future. Greater demand uncertainty calls for an increase in the desired inventory (the second term in (1)) and results in higher costs (Fisher et al. 1994).

We examine two conditions: one with two period ordering and shipping delays between each successive stage in the channel, and a shorter single period delay.

2.2. The Value of Shared POS Information

Each channel member incurs carrying and stockout costs based on the ability to fill orders received from the channel member immediately downstream (e.g., the distributor is most immediately concerned about filling the orders received from the wholesaler). Consequently, accurate knowledge of *final* customer demand is of obvious importance to the retailer. But, it is important to recognize that *ultimately* the entire channel is also attempting to fill this *same* customer demand. So, if the only information about customer demand transferred to upstream members is in the form of orders from downstream members, the attendant distortion could mislead the upstream members in their inventory and ordering decisions for two important reasons. First, there is an obvious problem due to the delays created by ordering lead times. Second, the upstream member is forced to guess how much of the change from the downstream member's "normal" order level is due to future expectations of customer demand, and how much of the change reflects adjustments to the downstream member's safety stock (the first and second terms of (1) are completely confounded). Because it is natural to expect the incoming orders to be noisy themselves, mismatching of downstream orders with upstream expectations can cause the variance of orders to increase as one moves upstream (the amplification phenomenon) (Lee, Padmanabhan and Whang 1997). Providing customer demand information to each channel member, however, could mitigate this consequence by allowing channel members to "coordinate" their decisions without explicit communications. Thus, shared POS information can be expected to reduce the uncertainty faced by each DM and increase efficiency (Towill 1992).

A potential drawback of providing the extra information is that it could overload the DM's cognitive abilities (Kleinmuntz 1990), resulting in poor performance. As Glazer, Steckel and Winer (1992) have shown, salient information can have a distracting, deleterious effect on managerial performance, *even if the DMs know how to use it!* This happens because managerial attention is drawn away from other relevant (but less salient) pieces of information. The extent to which the benefits from implicit "coordination" and reduced uncertainty will be countered by cognitive overload and distraction deserves careful examination. We examine two conditions: one where the customer demand is known to the retailer only, and another where the POS information is made immediately available to every channel member.

2.3. Patterns of Customer Demand

Clearly, meeting customer demand efficiently is easiest when it is stable or constant. The more meaningful issue is how well DMs adjust to changes? In Sterman's study, a single change in (what was before and what is after a constant level of) customer demand in period 5 continued to cause order and inventory fluctuations until period 36! But, for most subjects, a one-time only change in demand is very unusual (the priors on encountering such a pattern would be extremely small). In fact, Sterman (1989a, p. 336) himself wondered whether "subjects' behavior (would) differ if customer demand followed a more realistic pattern."

How well can we expect DMs to perform when customer demand changes according to a more realistic and expected pattern? To a population of business school students, an S-shaped curve is probably much more realistic and expected. But, while a more familiar pattern should be expected to help improve performance, Wagenaar and Timmers (1979) found that subjects display a "non-linear extrapolation" bias, systematically under-forecasting an (exponentially) increasing process. For S-shaped demand, this should lead to shortfalls and stockouts during the growth phase. The precise manner in which such a consistent tendency towards more frequent stockouts can be expected to impact stability and amplification upstream deserves careful examination.

Finally, while it is clear that overall efficiency will decrease as random volatility in customer demand increases, the impact of such a pattern on upstream variance and amplification deserves further study. Consequently, we investigate the effects of the channel modifications (shorter delays, shared information) under three separate demand environments: a Step-up demand function similar to Sterman's, an errorless S-shaped pattern, and an S-shaped pattern with added error. See Figure 2.

The "Beer Game" developed and used over the years at MIT (Forrester 1958, Sterman 1992, 1989a) for teaching and research is a natural choice for simulating decision making in an interdependent channel under a wide range of conditions. We describe it next.

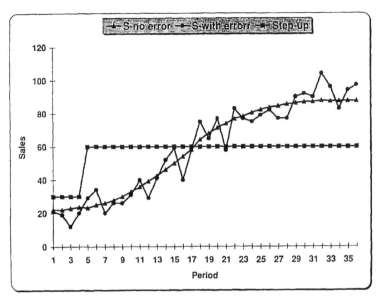

Figure 2. Customer Demand Patterns

2.4. The "Beer Game"

In the basic "Beer Game" setup, depicted in Figure 3, the retailer receives customers' orders and places orders with the wholesaler.[1] In turn, the wholesaler places orders with the distributor, and the distributor with the factory. At each stage, there is a two period delay in order transmission. Upon receipt of orders, each DM ships as much as current inventory allows, and backlogs the rest for future delivery (with the exceptions that unfilled orders at retail are lost forever and the factory is always able to ship the ordered amount after the two period delay). It takes two additional periods for the shipments to reach the next downstream entity. Thus, it takes *at least* four periods for a retailer to receive shipments against a particular order. However, if the wholesaler does not have sufficient inventory, the delay can be much longer (an out-of-stock wholesaler would have to wait additional periods for shipments to arrive from the distributor, who also may be out of stock!). Finally, each DM has access only to local information (own past orders, current and past incoming orders, inventory and incoming shipments). So, neither the wholesaler nor the distributor observes actual customer demand at the retail level. Nor is anyone aware of the current inventory and order position of other channel partners.

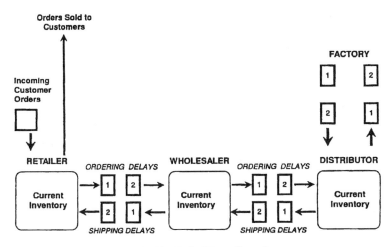

Figure 3. The Typical Beer Game Setup

Players of the "Beer Game" are instructed to minimize their costs during the game. Costs are composed of two elements, inventory holding costs and stockout costs (cost for each unfilled order) with stockout cost per unit being twice holding cost per unit. Costs are assessed at each level of the channel. The game consists of a series of decisions. It begins with each channel member having an initial inventory. The first step in each decision period involves the receipt of incoming inventory that is added to the current stock. Of course, this inventory was ordered at least four periods ago (more in the case of upstream stockouts). At the beginning of the game, the pipeline is well stocked in the sense that each player is told that they have ordered a specified number of units over the last four periods. This is done to ensure that no order backlogs will exist until at least the first orders placed by the players are received. The next step involves the filling of orders to the extent possible. The amount of inventory it takes to fill an order is the sum of incoming orders and any backlog (unfilled orders from previous periods) carried from the prior period. These must be satisfied whenever encountered by the wholesaler and distributor. The final step in each period, *and the only step that involves a decision*, is the placement of orders for the next period.

In the typical application of the "Beer Game", end-customer demand follows a simple Step-up function. It begins at a constant level, stays there for four periods, and then doubles in period five. It remains at this level for the remainder of the game. The game lasts 36 periods. For additional detail the reader is referred to Senge (1990), and Sterman (1992, 1989a).

3.   EXPERIMENTAL PROCEDURES

3.1. Experimental Design

The experimental design is a 2 (order and shipping LAGs of 1 or 2 periods) X 2 (POS information is available to all channel members–*y*, or only to the retailer–*n*) X 3 (customer DEMAND patterns; Step-up–SU, S-shaped without error–SN, and S-shaped with error–SE) full factorial. In all, usable data were collected for 100 channels. Individual cell sizes are shown below (due to scheduling conflicts and a few computer errors, the cell sizes are unequal).

Lag	1	1	1	1	1	1	2	2	2	2	2	2
POS	N	N	N	Y	Y	Y	N	N	N	Y	Y	Y
Demand	SU	SN	SE	SU	SN	SE	SU	SN	SE	SU	SN	SE
Number	9	7	8	10	5	9	11	5	9	13	6	8

The simulation was run using personal computers connected through a Novell network. Among other things, the computerized version provided the subjects with historical data and information about incoming shipments (by pressing specific function keys), helped the subjects with the basic accounting arithmetic, and afforded greater control over intra-channel communications than is usually possible in the standard board game implementation of the simulation. Note that the history and information screens also provided additional feedback to the DMs, as recommended by Kleinmuntz (1990).

Computerization also considerably eased the task of operationalizing the treatments. For the *POS* = *y* condition, where every channel member can see the retail level demand, simply pressing the F5 key brought up a screen showing those sales up to the current period. Those in the *POS* = *n* condition simply did not have access to the F5 key. Shipping and ordering delays were changed by transmitting the orders (shipments) to the upstream(downstream) member two periods (LAG = 2) or one period (LAG = 1) after its initiation. Finally, the input consumer demand patterns were readily changed by choosing one of three historical patterns (see Figure 2) available to the program.

3.2. Procedures

Two days before their assigned simulation, participants (day and evening students in an MBA program) were given a basic description of the game and provided reading material to familiarize themselves with the computerized setup. Upon arrival on the scheduled date, channel roles were assigned and additional role-specific information provided. All orders and shipments flowed *within* a 3-person channel. Each participant sat at a separate computer terminal. Several channels were run simultaneously. The retailers were all seated in one bank, then the distributors in another, and finally the wholesalers. Participants were unaware of who their other channel partners were. There was no interaction *across* channels.

The simulation began with an eight-period trial phase. Each trial period lasted two minutes, with additional stoppages for answering questions. After the trial phase, participants began what they believed was the actual 48 period simulation (we stopped in period 36 to minimize end-game effects). Costs incurred during this 36 period phase (stockout costs: $1 per case, holding costs: $0.50 per case) were used to determine each participant's final payoff. To make their decisions, participants had 90 seconds during the first six periods, and 70 seconds subsequently. Extensive pre-testing had shown these lengths to provide a reasonable balance between rushing the decisions and having too much time. A timer displayed the elapsed time on screen, and the input box flashed during the last 15 seconds in the event that no decision had been entered. The pipeline was initialized with inventory-on-hand of 50,000 cases and incoming shipments of 30,000 cases. These initial values ensured that channel members had neither too much nor too little inventory on hand during the initial periods.

Each period, the computer screen displayed the incoming and on-hand amounts for orders and shipments, and provided the subjects an opportunity to examine historical data. The cumulative stockout, inventory holding and total costs incurred by each member were also displayed. After the end of the simulation, participants' payments were determined according to the total costs incurred by their entire channel. So, their motivation was to make the best decisions for the entire channel, not just for themselves. Possible payoffs ranged from five to twenty-five dollars. The average was fifteen.

4.   ANALYSIS AND RESULTS

4.1. The Impact of LAG on Costs

Figure 4 shows the total costs (stockout plus inventory carrying) for each channel member and the entire channel, for each LAG within each Demand condition. Table 1 indicates whether the LAG effect is significant or not. For example, for the S with Error condition the cost difference due to LAG for the retailer (1.320–0.969) is significantly different from zero at the .10 level. However, for the distributor, the analogous difference (3.111–3.529) is not significant (see Figure 4 and Table 1).

The benefits of reducing the ordering and shipping delays are clear for the Step-up and S-no error demand patterns. Once error is introduced, however, the benefits are not as clear, especially for the distributor. The

a) **Set-Up Demand**

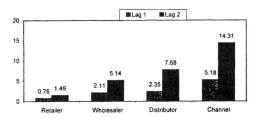

b) **S-Shaped Demand without Error**

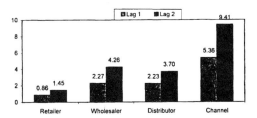

c) **S-Shaped Demand with Error**

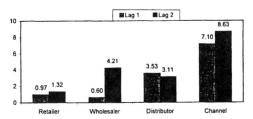

Figure 4. Costs by LAG and Demand Conditions

Table 1. Are Costs Significantly Different Between LAG Conditions?

	Retailer	Wholesaler	Distributor	Channel
Step-Up	Yes	Yes	Yes	Yes
S, no Error	Yes	Yes	Yes	Yes
S, with Error	Yes	Yes	No	No

Table 2. Are Cost Differences between Channel Member Pairs Significantly Different from Zero?

	LAG = 1		LAG = 2	
	Wholesaler-Retailer	Distributor-Wholesaler	Wholesaler-Retailer	Distributor-Wholesaler
Step-Up	Yes	Yes	Yes	Yes
S, No Error	Yes	No	Yes	Yes
S, with Error	Yes	Yes	Yes	Yes

channel still does show improved performance, but because the distributor actually does worse (though not significantly) for the shorter lag, the improvement is not significant. The important conclusion is that faster cycle times do help, but the magnitude of improvement is moderated by the underlying demand pattern. The differences are clearest for the simpler demand patterns (Step-up and S-no error).

Next, consider the propagation of inefficiency as we go up the channel (amplification). Amplification would require significant positive differences in total costs between pairs of upstream-downstream channels members. Table 2 shows whether the differences are significant (one-sided test, p-value < .10) or not.

For Step-up, as in Sterman, the effects of amplification on cost are clear in both LAG conditions. However, this result does not hold up for either one of the S-shaped patterns. The relatively high costs of the wholesaler actually cause the difference to be *negative* for the distributor-wholesaler pair! Why does this happen? We believe that one explanation may lie in the relative complexity of the task faced by the DM. The wholesaler faces irregularities in retailer orders (composed of the actual changes in customer orders and the retailer's added noise), and variations in lead times for distributor shipments. Neither of the other DMs must contend with both (the retailer sees the actual demand, and the distributor is guaranteed shipment in 2 or 4 periods). The complexity faced by the wholesaler is magnified in the S-shaped conditions because these patterns may be more difficult to "learn". Finally, the penalty incurred by the wholesaler in these conditions is smaller for the easier LAG = 1 condition.

Together, these results imply that the propagation of inefficiency due to the quality of decisions made by channel members is not inevitable. This phenomenon may well be contingent on the complexity of the customer demand pattern (which is generally not under managerial control), and also on the predictability of downstream and upstream channel members' actions (which may well be responsive to managerial actions).

4.2. Impact of POS Information Availability on Costs

Figure 5 shows the total costs (stockout plus inventory carrying) for each channel member and the entire channel, for each POS condition within each Demand condition. Table 3 indicates whether the POS effect is significant or not.

The benefits of providing POS information are clearest for the Step-up demand function. *It is the only demand pattern for which there is any improvement in total channel costs!* By contrast, the two S-shaped demand patterns actually result in *worse* performance with POS information. Examining the

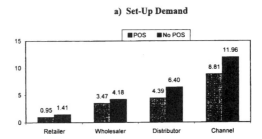

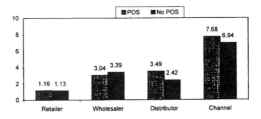

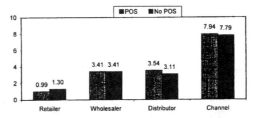

Figure 5. Costs by POS and Demand Conditions

Table 3. Are Costs Significantly Different between POS Conditions?

	Retailer	Wholesaler	Distributor	Channel
Step-Up	Yes	No	No	Yes
S, No Error	No	No	Yes	No
S, with Error	Yes	No	No	No

Table 4. Are Cost Differences between Channel Member Pairs Significantly Different from Zero?

	POS = n		*POS = y*	
	Wholesaler- Retailer	Distributor- Wholesaler	Wholesaler- Retailer	Distributor- Wholesaler
Step-Up	Yes	Yes	Yes	Yes
S, no Error	Yes	Yes	Yes	Yes
S, with Error	Yes	No	Yes	No

means in Figure 5, it is clear that whereas the retailer and the wholesaler do not benefit greatly, the distributor actually does *worse* with the POS information available. A possible explanation is that the salience of the POS information is distracting the distributor from other information, such as wholesaler orders, that is more relevant to her task (Glazer, Steckel and Winer 1992). By reacting independently to customer demand, performance actually worsens! This problem is not as serious for the wholesaler, perhaps, because greater proximity to the final customer makes the salient POS information more relevant too (we shall return to the issue of independent versus coordinated actions later). Indeed, the information is that which directly impacts the decisions of the agent immediately downstream from the wholesaler. Thus, paying more attention to customer demand, rather than the orders coming in from the retailer, should prove less harmful to the wholesaler than to the more distant distributor. Empirically, too, we do not see the wholesaler's costs increase with availability of POS information.

Regarding amplification, we find additional evidence supporting the earlier conjecture regarding the wholesaler's difficult position in complex conditions. For S-shaped demand patterns the wholesaler's costs are greater than the distributor's in the most complex environment ($POS = n$) (3.41 to 3.11; see Figure 5, and Table 4 for significance results). However, when the dependence of the wholesaler on the vagaries of retailer's orders is reduced, (in the "simpler" $POS = y$ condition), the distributor-wholesaler cost difference returns to the expected positive sign.

The pattern of costs examined thus far shows that the basic results reported by Sterman do in fact persist for the Step-up pattern even when the cycle time is shortened, and channel members have shared POS information. However, the result pattern does not fully survive under S-shaped customer demand patterns. Perhaps most surprisingly, we find that the availability of POS information can sometimes even *impair* the distributors and consequently the entire channel's performance. Among the reasons for the observed results, we find some evidence in support of the hypothesis that the wholesaler, most vulnerable to decision biases of other members, performs most poorly under the most complex conditions (S-shaped demand with error, 2 period lags, and no POS information). Further, we find indications that, overly influenced by the POS information, the distributor may be making inappropriate independent adjustments detrimental to her own and the entire channel's performance.

4.3. Subjects' Mental Model and Attention to the Pipeline

As quoted earlier, Sterman found that an important reason for the observed inefficiencies lay in the participants' tendency to pay insufficient attention to the pipeline. To reach this conclusion Sterman operationalized the basic mental model form (1), as follows:

$$DO_t = F_t + \alpha_1(I^* - I_t) + \alpha_{SL}\left(\lambda F_t - \sum_{i=1}^{\lambda} O_{t-1}\right) \tag{2}$$

where DO_t is the desired order at time t; F_t is the forecast of downstream member's incoming order for period t (a function perhaps of the historical ordering pattern of the downstream customer); I_t is the inventory on hand in period t; I^* is the desired inventory level; λ is the length of the supply line; α_1 is an inventory adjustment parameter; and α_{SL} is the supply line adjustment parameter. The actual order placed in any given period is $O_t = Max(0, DO_t)$.

Following Kleinmuntz (1990), however, we make a slight change in the formulation by making the current period's desired order a function of the previous period alone, as follows:

$$DO_t = L_{t-1} + \alpha_1(I^* - I_t) + \alpha_{SL}(L_{t-1} - O_{t-1}) \tag{3}$$

where the forecast, F_t, is set equal to L_{t-1}, the order received from the downstream customer in the previous period, and only last period's outgoing orders, O_{t-1} are accounted for in the supply line. We choose this formulation because: *i*) it considerably simplifies the estimation process; *ii*) as Kleinmuntz has shown, in many instances this form and Sterman's more complete form result in very similar ordering patterns; *iii*) given Sterman's results, we already know that participants do not pay attention to far-in-time events and dropping them from the estimation equation is unlikely to cause any meaningful biases; and *iv*) results in the production smoothing literature (see, e.g., Blinder 1986 and Bechter and Stanley 1992) show that more sophisticated models add little.

Equation (3) can be estimated by nonlinear regression. However, for the S-shaped patterns an important caveat applies. For these patterns it is likely that as end-customer demand increases, channel members would desire to maintain larger safety stocks, I*. Strictly speaking, then, I* is time variant. Specifying the estimation equation as such would render the econometrics extremely difficult and unreliable. Thus, we estimate it as a single value. Such an estimated value will likely represent an average value of the parameter over the 36 periods. Therefore, magnitude comparisons across experimental conditions are still meaningful.

Overall, the mental model fit the subjects' orders quite well. The following table summarizes the average ratio of explained to total variance for each role under each LAG condition (these values do not vary appreciably for the three separate demand conditions, nor does POS have a significant effect on this pattern):

	Retailer	Wholesaler	Distributor
LAG = 1	0.91	0.77	0.68
LAG = 2	0.86	0.78	0.61

In his analysis, Sterman relied on the size of the supply line coefficient α_{SL} to judge how much attention the subjects were paying to the supply line. Our average estimates for α_{SL} for both LAG conditions for each channel role under each demand condition are summarized in the (a) part of Table 5.

Note first that, as in Sterman's study, our subjects are unable to fully account for the supply line and the estimates of α_{SL} are close to zero. Nonetheless, the estimates for LAG = 1 condition tend to be larger than for LAG = 2 (and sometimes significantly so). Further, even though they are small, distributors do consistently have the largest supply line coefficients. Together these results suggest that while participants do underweight the supply line, they tend to correct for this somewhat when the supply line itself gets less complex. Clearly, accounting for the supply line is easier when delays are shorter (LAG = 1). Also, recall that the distributor's supply line is perfectly predictable. By contrast, the total time taken to receive shipments can and did vary greatly for retailers and wholesalers. Consequently, their supply line is much less predictable and therefore less emphasized in decision-making.

Table 5. The Effects of Lag Time Reduction on Subjects' Mental Model

a) Average Supply Line Coefficients (α_{SL})

	LAG = 2			LAG = 1		
	Retailer	Wholesaler	Distributor	Retailer	Wholesaler	Distributor
Step-Up	0.00[a]	0.00	0.00[a]	0.07	0.03	0.19
S-no Error	0.00	0.01	0.08	0.00	0.05	0.17
S, with Error	0.01	0.00	0.06[a]	0.02	0.03	0.15

b) Average Desired Inventory Level, I*

	LAG = 2			LAG = 1		
	Retailer	Wholesaler	Distributor	Retailer	Wholesaler	Distributor
Step-Up	12.98[a]	137.59	301.59[a]	3.58	114.71	124.32
S-no Error	74.39	123.72	133.84	5.10	44.85	97.03
S-with Error	26.04	100.64	141.16[a]	8.41	102.26	180.83

[a] difference in parameter values between the two *LAG* conditions is significant at the 0.1 level.

Further insights into the subjects' ability to adjust for delays and lags in the supply line can be gleaned by examining the impact of LAG and channel role on the estimated desired inventory levels, I* (see Table 5, part b).

First, note that in general the desired inventory levels are smaller (even though not always significantly so) for LAG = 1. Thus, participants do make reasonable adjustments to their desired inventory levels. Second, it is interesting to note the consistent increase in desired inventory levels as we travel upstream. Clearly, each DM is making separate and, therefore, redundant adjustments to deal with demand uncertainties. As Lee et. al. (1997) have shown, such uncoordinated behavior is sufficient to cause large inefficiencies that get amplified up the channel.

In summary, while we find basic support for Sterman's earlier results, closer examination also suggests that inadequate attention to the supply line may not be an inherent bias but may result due to the *complexity* of fully accounting for the supply line. When the task is made simpler, the supply line coefficients do increase and participants show the ability to react appropriately to changes in supply line length by adjusting the desired inventory levels. Finally, due perhaps to the lack of explicit communication among channel members, we find that the desired inventory levels increase redundantly up the supply chain. Consequently, re-engineering the supply chain and better coordination should together prove most useful for improving channel efficiency.

4.4. Impact of POS on Decision Making

It is intriguing to find that channel members' costs are higher for S-shaped patterns when every channel member has access to POS information. The ability to implicitly coordinate through this shared information was expected to help improve efficiency. However, the pattern of results examined so far seems to show that the distracting effect of such salient information, and independent redundant adjustments may have ended up hurting more. We examine the nature of decision making under the two POS conditions further to gain some insights into these results.

First, consider the impact of POS information on the order size. Table 6 (part a) shows the average order sizes for each channel role for each demand pattern and the associated significance comparisons.

Note that for the Step-up pattern, order sizes are smaller under $POS = y$. Recall that for the typical channel, orders increase too much following the one time change in demand. When the customer demand pattern can be seen, participants make adjustments in the appropriate direction. On the other hand, the average order size *increases* for the S-shaped pattern. Directionally, this too is reasonable because without being able to see the actual demand, the tendency is to underestimate the growth in customer demand (Wagenaar and Timmers 1979). However, part (b) of Table 6 shows that this increase in order

Table 6. The Effects of POS Information on Subjects' Mental Model

a) **Average Order Sizes** (in units of thousands)

	Retailer		Wholesaler		Distributor	
	$POS = n$	$POS = y$	$POS = n$	$POS = y$	$POS = n$	$POS = y$
Step-Up	50	47	56	48[b]	65	54[b]
S-no Error	47	55[b]	46	56[b]	48	62[b]
S, with Error	51	56	52	60[b]	56	68[b]

b) **Average Variance of Effective Inventory** (in units of thousands)

	Retailer		Wholesaler		Distributor	
	$POS = n$	$POS = y$	$POS = n$	$POS = y$	$POS = n$	$POS = y$
Step-Up	10	3[b]	41	79[b]	78	199[b]
S-no Error	3	11	21	18	49	16[b]
S, with Error	7	3	34	27[b]	56	30[b]

[b] difference in parameter values between the two POS conditions is significant at the 0.1 level.

size for the S-shaped patterns is accompanied by greater volatility in channel members' effective inventory (current inventory minus order backlog), especially for the distributor. By contrast, being able to see the actual demand for the Step-up pattern helps reduce the variance considerably. These results suggest that when the underlying phenomenon is less clear (S-Shaped demand), subjects may well be *overreacting* to far away changes (evidenced by the high levels of variance in effective inventory). Future research should examine this possibility more closely.

5.   DISCUSSION

5.1. Summary

In this paper we have examined decision making in a dynamic and inter-dependent task environment. While such environments typify the operations of many distribution channels, decision oriented research is generally lacking. Building upon Sterman's pioneering work we examined the "Beer Game" under a wider range of circumstances. Specifically, we examined how channel efficiency and individual decision-making are affected by changes in the time it takes to transmit orders and shipments (LAG), the availability of POS information, and the pattern of changes in customer DEMAND.

Regarding channel costs and efficiency we find that reducing the cycle time (LAG) results in the greatest positive benefits across all experimental conditions, though the extent of improvement is somewhat mitigated by the pattern of change in customer demand. Surprisingly, we find that making POS information available is unambiguously beneficial in only the simplest scenarios. As the pattern of pattern of change in customer demand becomes more complicated, performance deteriorates. Overall, we find that the basic results reported by Sterman are replicated only for the Step-up demand pattern.

Regarding the manner in which decisions are made and insights into the causes for observed inefficiencies, once again, we find support for Sterman's basic assertion that participants fail to pay sufficient attention to the supply line. But the more complete examination afforded by our experiment also leads to new and refined insights. First, from observing the adjustments made to desired inventory levels as LAG increases, we find that a subject's mental model is affected by the length of the pipeline, and in a directionally appropriate manner. Rather than finding a systematic bias towards disregarding the supply line we find greater support in favor of a *complexity* argument. As LAG decreases and the supply line gets more predictable (as for the distributor), complexity decreases and the weights participants give to supply line considerations increase.

In addition to the supply line bias and complexity, our analysis uncovered two other sources of inefficient decision-making. First, with the availability of POS information, increasing fluctuations in effective inventory and larger distributor costs imply the possibility of *overreaction* by these DMs to less relevant information. Indeed, in studying how people use "useless" information. Bastardi and Shafir (1998) show that people will place positive weight on information that has no objective value whatsoever to making the decision if that information might be presumed not to always be available. Clearly POS information is relevant. Nevertheless, the overweighting of it is apparently a source of the inefficiencies in our study.

Finally, we found that changes in customer demand caused channel members to make separate adjustments to their desired inventory levels. As Lee et al. (1997) have analytically demonstrated, such lack of *coordination* among channel members can lead to gross inefficiencies of the kind observed in our experiment. Further, contrary to expectations, merely providing shared POS information across the channel does not induce sufficient implicit coordination.

In sum, our results imply that the future research needs to closely examine the individual and joint effects of speeding up the cycle time, improving the communication and coordination among channel members, and reductions in the cognitive complexity of the task through appropriate decision support for individual DMs. Some suggestions for such a research agenda are discussed next.

5.2. Future Research

Future research on operational decision-making in distribution channels needs to proceed in at least two related directions. First, there is a need to study how ordering and shipping decisions are actually being made in corporations, and the kinds of problems and inefficiencies that are commonly encountered. The other possibility is to expand and enrich the experimental agenda (based, perhaps, on the kinds of observations suggested above). Enriching the "Beer Game" by increasing its external validity, and further exploring the shortcomings of dynamic, interdependent decision making in a controlled laboratory setting is likely to prove beneficial. Our suggestions are in the latter vein.

5.2.1. Overreaction

Our results showed that due to the tendency to overreact, providing more information might not always be beneficial. In our case, more information was operationalized as the availability of POS information. However, more information can also result from more frequent availability of the same data. For example, providing daily rather than weekly POS information is technically feasible. However, if the underlying phenomenon changes at a slower pace, it is possible that DMs might overreact to the noise in day-to-day information and efficiency might actually suffer. In a series of studies, Wagenaar and Timmers (1978a, 1978b) found that for exponential growth tasks, subjects were better at long-range extrapolation with fewer data points (e.g., weekly rather than daily POS data).

To explore this possibility, we conducted a separate "Beer Game" experiment in which half the subjects received 36 periods of "monthly" data, and the other half received 36 periods of "bi-monthly" data (following an S-with Error pattern). For the second group, each of the first 18 months of data was the sum of two of the "monthly" sales numbers seen by the first group. Thus, the sum of all 36 periods of demand for the first group, was exactly equal to sum of the first 18 periods of the second groups' demand. *The 36-period average forecasting errors for the first group were significantly **higher** than the 18 average forecasting errors for the second group*, in agreement with our conjecture. Faster may not always be better!

Similar over-reaction problems have also been noted in JIT systems under volatile customer demand conditions (Karmarkar 1989, Zipkin 1991). Together with our results, and casual experimental observations, we believe that the *match* between the time it takes for the system to respond to a DM (related to the lag time), the frequency with which information is made available, and the pace with which customer demand is itself changing deserves to be examined in greater detail. We expect, for example, that shorter lead times and more frequent decision opportunities will be most helpful if underlying customer demand is changing rapidly. However, if the period-to-period change in retail sales is more the result of random variation rather than a basic change in customer needs, shorter lead times and/or more frequent observations should affect channel efficiency adversely. Careful examination of such hypotheses may suggest that the processes developed to deal with one type of demand environment might be predictably inefficient in others.

5.2.2. Complexity

Our results document the gross inefficiencies in decision-making created due to the complexity of dynamic interdependent task environments. Future research should now examine how human DMs can learn to operate more efficiently, and how they can be aided in making their decisions.

Prior research has shown that incentives are not likely to be very effective (Arkes 1991).

The vast literature on multiple cue probabilistic learning (MCPL) shows that feedback plays a critical role in learning (Balzer et al. 1992, 1989, Castellan 1974, Hogarth 1987). In the basic "Beer Game" setup, the only feedback provided to each DM is through incoming orders from the channel member below, and incoming shipments from the channel member above. This type of information is akin to *outcome* feedback (Balzer et al. 1989, Gupta 1994, Sengupta and Abdel-Hamid 1993). The DM can see what happened, but how and why are unclear. MCPL research shows that outcome feedback alone rarely helps the DM learn in an uncertain environment. Brehmer (1992), and Sengupta and Abdel-Hamid (1993) have found support for this in single-person dynamic decision-making tasks. The practice of selective hypothesis testing, described by Sanbomatsu et al. (1998), structures the search for and interpretation of evidence in a way that confirms any prior mental model the DM may have had (Snyder and Whyte 1981). Recent research using real managers as subjects has shown that such a *confirmation bias* may actually be more prevalent in group contexts than individual ones. Shulz-Hardt et al. (2000) found that groups of DMs preference for information that supports (rather than contradicts) a preferred view (i.e. mental model) in a hypothetical case about a chemical company in a developing country was often intensified when the DM was placed in a group.

The alternative to outcome feedback is to provide cognitive feedback (Balzer et al. 1989). Cognitive feedback includes information about relations in the task environment, the DM's mental model, and relations between the DM's mental model and the task environment. In the context of the "Beer Game" this would include, for example: information about current and past inventory/backlogs at *other* levels in the channel, information about the length of time it actually was taking for orders to be filled, and information about the particular manner in which the DM was using the three elements in the mental model (e.g., displaying the supply line coefficients). Such feedback will in Arkes' (1991) words "cue a debiasing behavior." In particular, DMs will likely realize that they were paying inadequate attention to the supply line.

The drawback of providing all of this information is that it could overload the DM's cognitive abilities (Kleinmuntz 1990). Consequently, it is important to investigate what types of cognitive feedback are more effective than others, and how best to present the information. Gupta (1994) and Kleinmuntz and Thomas (1987), among others, have found that providing a *decision aid* that allows the DM to process the available information more readily can prove helpful. Future research on how such aids can be used in the distribution channel context should prove especially beneficial.

5.2.3. Coordination

Our results, and Lee et al.'s analysis, clearly show that even after speeding up the cycle the need for coordinated decision making remains. Our results also show that merely providing common retail demand information does not significantly improve the results. The role of more explicit coordination needs examination.

From the perspective of upstream channel members, there is a need to account for uncertainty in primary customer demand, and the secondary uncertainty created through the decisions made by downstream members (e.g., are changes in orders from downstream members due to poor decision making, due to a changed policy, or due to other strategic considerations?). Downstream members must deal with uncertainty in incoming orders and the supply reliability of upstream members. Management of these uncertainties through better intra-channel coordination is a hallmark of the partnership arrangements (e.g., Quick Response Systems, Efficient Consumer Response, etc.) emerging in several industries. But, because greater coordination is expensive and requires sharing sensitive information, it is important to understand exactly what aspects must be coordinated and what the resulting benefits are. For example, our results show that compared to improving the lag times, sharing POS information with upstream suppliers is much less effective. However, there is a need to examine whether even greater sharing of information, and perhaps even joint decision making, might result in significant improvements (e.g., by reducing the uncertainty surrounding the strategic intentions of other channel members). Further, research on the contractual aspects of how the benefits of coordinated decision making might be shared among the channel members and how far up the channel such coordination may prove beneficial also need to be examined. The "Beer Game", with variations in the payoff functions, the number of channel members, and opportunities for controlled communications among channel members provides a systematic opportunity for examining these issues.

With the great changes currently underway in relations between vendors and their channel customers, it is incumbent upon the research community to begin a concerted effort to understand how the new relations can be managed most efficiently. One approach for such research is a systematic laboratory exploration of the issues identified here.

ACKNOWLEDGEMENT

This research was supported, in part, by a grant from the Marketing Science Institute. The authors would also like to thank the Research Funds of the Michigan Business School and the Stern School. Professor Noel Capon's assistance in data collection is appreciated.

NOTE

1. Figure 3 presents a shortened version of the "Beer Game". The original setup contains one more middleman. We eliminated this intermediary in order to economize on subjects (each channel would require three instead of four, or an extra 100 subjects) for our experiment.

REFERENCES

Arkes, Hal R. (1991). "Costs and Benefits of Judgment Errors: Implications for Debiasing." *Psychological Bulletin* 110, 486–98.

Balzer, William K., Michael E. Doherty, and Raymond O'Connor Jr. (1989). "Effects of Cognitive Feedback on Performance." *Psychological Bulletin* 106, 410–33.

Balzer, William K., Lorne M. Sulsky, Leslie B. Hammer, and Kenneth M. Sumner (1992). "Task Information, Cognitive Information, or Functional Validity Information: Which Components of Cognitive Feedback Affect Performance?" *Organizational Behavior and Human Decision Processes* 53, 35–54.

Bastardi, Anthony, and Eldar Shafir (1998). "On the Pursuit and Misuse of Useless Information." *Journal of Personality and Social Psychology* 75, 19–32.

Bechter, Dan M., and Stephen Stanley (1992). "Evidence of Improved Inventory Control, Federal Reserve Bank of Richmond." *Economic Review* 78, 3–12.

Blinder, Alan S. (1986). "Can the Production Smoothing Model of Inventory Behavior be Saved?" *Quarterly Journal of Economics* 101, 431–53.

Blinder, Alan S., and Louis J. Maccini (1990). "The Resurgence of Inventory Research: What Have We Learned?" Working Paper No. 3408, National Bureau of Economic Research.

Brehmer, Berndt (1992). "Dynamic Decision Making: Human Control of Complex Systems." *Acta Psychologica* 81, 211–41.

Burke, Steven (1988). "Chip Manufacturers Find a Pot of Gold in DRAM." *PC Week*, 31 May, 107.

Buzzell, Robert D., and Gwen Ortmeyer. "Channel Partnerships: A New Approach to Streamlining Distribution." Report No. 94-104, Marketing Science Institute, Cambridge, MA.

Castellan, N. John Jr. (1974). "The Effect of Different Types of Feedback in Multiple-Cue Probability Learning." *Organizational Behavior and Human Performance* 11, 44–64.

Coopers & Lybrand (1992). *Competing for the American Consumer: Partnering for Quick Response*. NY: Coopers & Lybrand.

Davidow, William H., and Michael S. Malone (1992). *The Virtual Corporation: Restructuring and Revitalizing the Corporation for the 21st Century*. NY: Harper Business.

Dwyer, F. Robert, Paul Schurr, and Sejo Oh (1987). "Developing Buyer-Seller Relationships." *Journal of Marketing Research* 51, 11–27.

Fisher, Marshall L., Janice H. Hammond, Walter R. Obermeyer, and Ananth Raman (1994). "Making Supply Meet Demand in an Uncertain World." *Harvard Business Review* 72, 83–93.

Forrester, Jay W. (1958). "Industrial Dynamics: A Major Breakthrough for Decision Makers." *Harvard Business Review* 36, 37–66.

Frazier, Gary L., Robert E. Spekman, and Charles R. O'Neal (1988). "Just-in-Time Exchange Relationships in Industrial Markets." *Journal of Marketing* 52, 52–67.

Glazer, Rashi, Joel H. Steckel, and Russell S. Winer (1992). "Locally Rational Decision Making: The Distracting Effect of Information on Managerial Performance." *Management Science* 38, 212–26.

Gupta, Sunil (1994). "Managerial Judgment and Forecast Combination: An Experimental Study." *Marketing Letters* 5, 5–17.

Hambrick, Donald C. (1982). "Environmental Scanning and Organizational Strategy." *Strategic Management Journal* 3, 159–74.

Hammond, Janice H. (1992). "Coordination as the Basis for Quick Response: A Case for 'Virtual' Integration in Supply Networks." Working Paper 92-007, Graduate School of Business Administration, Harvard University.

Hogarth, Robin M. (1987). *Judgment and Choice*. 2nd ed. NY: Wiley.

Karmarkar, Uday (1989). "Getting Control of Just-in-Time." *Harvard Business Review* 67, 122–31.

Kleinmuntz, Don N. (1990). "Information Processing and the Misperception of Feedback in Dynamic Decision Making." Presented at the 1990 International System Dynamics Conference, Boston, College of Commerce and Business Administration, University of Illinois at Urbana-Champaign.

Kleinmuntz, Don N., and James B. Thomas (1987). "The Value of Action and Inference in Dynamic Decision Making." *Organizational Behavior and Human Decision Processes* 39, 341–64.

Kurt Salmon Associates (1993). "Efficient Consumer Response: Enhancing Consumer Value in the Grocery Industry." Food Marketing Institute, Washington D.C.

Lee, Hau, Paddy Padmanabhan, and Seungjin Whang (1997). "Information Distortion in a Supply Chain: The Bullwhip Effect." *Management Science* 43, 546–58.

Mack, Ruth P. (1956). "Consumption and Business Fluctuations: A Case Study of the Shoe, Leather, Hide Sequence." National Bureau of Economic Research, NY.

Martin, Andre J. (1993). *Distribution Resource Planning: The Gateway to True Quick Response and Continuous Replenishment*. Rev. ed. Essex Junction, VT: Oliver Wight.

McGuire, T., and R. Staelin (1983). "An Industry Equilibrium Analysis of Downstream Vertical Integration." *Marketing Science* 2, 161–92.

Moorthy, K. Sridhar (1988). "Strategic Decentralization in Channels." *Marketing Science* 7, 335–55.

National Retail Federation and Andersen Consulting (1992). "Strategic Vendor Partnership Survey Results." Andersen Consulting, 92–2016.

Sanbonmatsu, David M., Steven S. Posavac, Frank R. Kardes, and Susan P. Mantel (1998). "Selective Hypothesis Testing." *Psychonomic Bulletin and Review* 5, 197–220.

Senge, Peter (1990). *The Fifth Discipline: The Art and Practice of The Learning Organization*. NY: Doubleday Currency.

Sengupta, Kishore, and Tarek K. Abdel-Hamid (1993). "Alternative Conceptions of Feedback in Dynamic Decision Environments: An Experimental Investigation." *Management Science* 39, 411–28.

Schulz-Hardt, Stefan, Dieter Frey, Carsten Luthgens, and Serge Moscovici (2000). "Biased Information Search in Group Decision Making." *Journal of Personality and Social Psychology* 78, 655–69.

Snyder, M., and P. White (1981). "Testing Hypotheses about Other People's Strategies of Verification and Falsification." *Personality and Social Psychology Bulletin* 7, 39–43.

Stalk, George, and Thomas Hout (1990). *Competing Against Time*. NY: Free Press.

Sterman, John D. (1992). "Teaching Takes Off: Flight Simulators for Management Education." *OR/MS Today* 19, 40–4.

Sterman, John D. (1989a). "Modeling Managerial Behavior: Misperceptions of Feedback in a Dynamic Decision-Making Environment." *Management Science* 35, 321–39.

Sterman, John D. (1989b). "Misperceptions of Feedback in Dynamic Decision Making." *Organizational Behavior and Human Decision Processes* 43, 301–35.

Towill, Denis R. (1992). "Supply Chain Dynamics." *International Journal of Computer Integrated Manufacturing* 40, 197–208.

Tversky, Amos, and Daniel Kahneman (1974). "Judgment under Uncertainty: Heuristics and Biases." *Science* 185, 1124–31.

Wagenaar, W. A., and H. Timmers (1978a). "Extrapolation of Exponential Time Series is not Enhanced by Having More Data Points." *Perception and Psychophysics* 24, 182–4.

Wagenaar, W. A., and H. Timmers (1978b). "Intuitive Prediction of Growth." In *Environmental Assessment of Socioeconomic Systems*, edited by D. F. Burkhardt and W. H. Ittelson. NY: Plenum Press.

Wagenaar, W. A., and H. Timmers (1979). "The Pond and Duckweed Problem: Three Experiments on the Misperception of Exponential Growth." *Acta Psychologica* 43, 239–51.

Zipkin, Paul H. (1991). "Does Manufacturing Need a JIT Revolution." *Harvard Business Review* 69, 40–50.

Chapter 3 (U5|

COOPERATION IN SINGLE PLAY, TWO-PERSON EXTENSIVE FORM GAMES BETWEEN ANONYMOUSLY MATCHED PLAYERS

Kevin McCabe
George Mason University

C7|

D64

Mary Rigdon
George Mason University

Vernon Smith
George Mason University

1. INTRODUCTION: BACKGROUND AND MOTIVATION

Experimentalists have long observed that many subjects in two-person extensive form games choose cooperative strategies even when they will be played only once matched with another person whose identity will never be revealed to them.[1] This phenomenon has been observed most prominently, and replicated many times, in the large literature on ultimatum (and dictator) games, beginning with Güth, Schmittberger and Schwartz (1982). In the ultimatum game two anonymously paired subjects split k units of money. Player 1 proposes a split of x for Player 2 and k-x for Player 1. If Player 2 accepts, the money is split as proposed; if rejected, each gets zero. The modal outcome

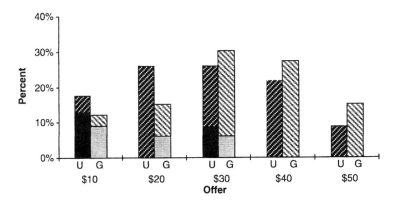

U Offers Accepted   ■ U Offers Rejected   G Offers Accepted   G Offers Rejected

Figure 1. Comparison of Undergraduates (U) and Graduates (G) in $100 Ultimatum Game. Contest/Exchange Treatment

in these experiments is for Player 1 to offer half of the pie represented by k units of money; the mean offer is about $0.47k$. Players 2 rarely reject offers as high as $x = 0.4k$ and regularly reject offers of $0.1k$, $0.2k$ and even $0.3k$, where $k = \$10.^2$ These results are little changed when the stakes are greatly increased to $k = \$100$ (Hoffman, McCabe and Smith, 1996). Yet game theory predicts that Player 1 will offer the minimum unit of account, say $1, when k consists of 10 one-dollar bills, and Player 2 will accept. Although offers are significantly lower when the game is formulated as a trade between a buyer and seller, and/or the Player 1 position is "earned" by outscoring others (who become Players 2) on a general knowledge pretest (Hoffman, McCabe, Shachat and Smith, 1994; hereafter, HMSS), it is still the case that Players 1 tend to offer an average of 25–30 percent of k.

Figure 1 depicts a bar chart showing the frequency distribution of ultimatum game first-mover offers, and the frequency of rejection of these offers for both undergraduate and graduate students. The stakes are $k = \$100$, available in the form of 10 ten dollar bills, and the treatment condition combines the contest (the Player 1 position is earned in the pretest) and exchange (buyer/seller format) protocols. The advanced (3rd and 4th year) graduate student subjects were attending a workshop in experimental economics. These subjects are very "sophisticated" relative to the average undergraduate student in that they have all studied economic theory including game theory. The undergraduate results, also shown in Figure 1, are those reported in Hoffman, McCabe and Smith (1996), when $k = \$100$. Note that the graduate students make somewhat more generous offers than do the undergraduates.

In dictator games (Player 2 cannot reject the offer of Player 1), Players 1 offer (give) much less to their counterpart: 20% give nothing, but 80% transfer from 1 to 5 dollars (Forsythe et al., 1994). These results, however, are drastically altered when conducted "double blind" so that it is transparent to Players 1 that no one can possibly know their decisions: some two-thirds give nothing; 84% give 0 or 1 dollar (HMSS). Burnham (1998) and Eckel and Grossman (1996) have replicated the HMSS experiments and report very similar results that do not differ statistically. Systematic variations on these HMSS procedures, however, yield systematically different results, showing clearly how sensitive cooperation is to the fine structure of its context. (Bolton and Zwick, 1998; Hoffman, McCabe and Smith, 1996).

In this paper we present results from several extensive form alternating play games that exhibit comparably high frequencies of play that deviate from the predictions of noncooperative game theory. The games and results we present have been chosen to test various hypotheses as to why we tend to observe "too much" cooperation relative to the predictions of the game theoretic self-interested player model.

2. COOPERATIVE VERSUS SUBGAME PERFECT (NONCOOPERATIVE) PLAY: THREE GAMES

Consider the two-person game in Figure 2. The subgame perfect (SP) equilibrium of this game is for Player 1 to move right at node 1, yielding $10 for Player 1 (the upper payoff), and $10 for Player 2 (the lower payoff). This is because if Player 1 moves down, Player 2, in his/her immediate self-interest, will move down (defect) yielding zero for Player 1 and $40 for Player 2. If each player is self-interested in the sense of always choosing *dominant* outcomes; if each player assumes the other is self-interested; and if players analyze the game using backward induction, then Player 1 will see that Player 2 will not choose the cooperative outcome, right at node 2, and, logically, Player 1 will choose SP. We call this game the "Invest $10 Trust Game." (This is because it represents a reduced form of a two-stage investment game involving trust studied by Berg, Dickhaut and McCabe, 1995.) In Figure 2 think of a move down as representing an investment of $10 by Player 1; the $10 is tripled to $30, and Player 2 can either divide the $30 equally or take it all. This description, however, is not part of the instructional protocol, which simply presents the tree in Figure 2 as an abstract decision task. The game in Figure 2 is played in sessions consisting of 12 undergraduate subjects. Subjects are carefully screened to yield individuals who have not previously been to the laboratory to participate in bargaining experiments. Each subject is paid $5 upon arriving on time for the experiment, and is immediately escorted to a computer terminal in a large room containing 40 terminals. Each terminal is in a separate stall, and the 12 subjects are dispersed so that no subject can see the terminal screen of another. The subjects are randomly assigned to one of six pairs, and randomly assigned to the role of Player 1 or Player 2. Each reads the instruc-

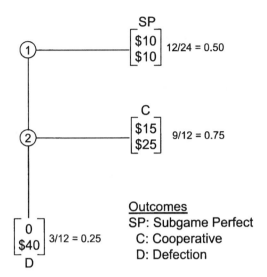

Figure 2. Invest $10 Trust Game

tions for the experiment in which words like "game," "player," etc. are not used. Rather, reference is made to Decision Maker 1 or 2 (DM1 or DM2), who move sequentially until they reach a payoff box. No subject knows the personal identity of his/her paired counterpart, although they can easily infer that they are paired with another "like" person (undergraduate) and may thus have a non-conscious group identity. After the experiment is completed, each person is called out of the room one at a time, paid the amount earned in cash, and dismissed. Each subject participates in one and only one such experiment.

The results for 48 subjects (24 pairs) are displayed adjacent to the payoff brackets of Figure 2. Half of the 24 Players 1 choose the SP outcome, but half choose to move "down." Of the 12 Players 1 who pass to Players 2, 9 (75%) Players 2 choose the cooperative outcome, while 3 (25%) Players 2 choose the defection outcome.

Figure 3 displays a payoff variation on the game in Figure 2, the "Invest $5 Trust Game." Note that the outcome frequencies are statistically quite similar to these in Figure 1: the 50% and 55.6% frequencies of SP choice in Figures 2 and 3 respectfully do not differ significantly; similarly for the 75% and 66.7% C outcomes.

A variation on the trust game in Figure 3 is to expand it into the three-stage trust/punishment game shown in Figure 4. Now if Player 1 chooses "down," Player 2 can respond by moving right for the cooperative outcome or he/she can defect by choosing "down." But Player 1, controlling the final outcome, can either accept the defection (AD) which is in her or his dominant

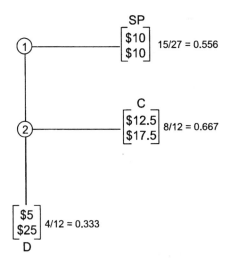

Figure 3. Invest $5 Trust Game

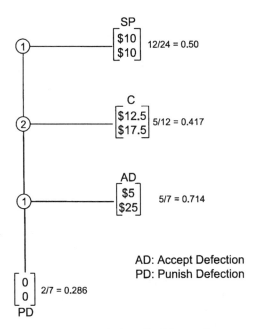

AD: Accept Defection
PD: Punish Defection

Figure 4. Invest $5 Trust/Punishment Game

payoff interest, or, at a personal opportunity cost ($5), move "down," choosing an action clearly intended to punish (PD) player 2 for defecting on player 1's initial offer to cooperate. Note that the game theoretic outcome is unambiguously the SP outcome, obtained by backward induction assuming "rational" (choose dominant payoffs) players. This is because, as the game protocol is played, Player 1 cannot credibly threaten the punishment outcome as a trigger strategy to induce Player 2 to cooperate in her self-interest.

The outcome frequencies are shown adjacent to each payoff alternative in Figure 4. Two observations are noteworthy: (1) Players 1 choose half right and half down, much as in Figures 2 and 3; (2) two of the seven defecting Players 2 are punished by their counterparts. The use of costly punishment strategies in single play games presages the potential for cooperation to persist when subjects engage in repeat play with distinct counterparts.

In section 4 we will return to a more systematic comparison of a trust game with and without punishment in protocols in which play is repeated but with distinct subjects paired on each game trial.

3.   WHY SO MUCH COOPERATION?

In the above game roughly half the Players 1 fail to play the SP equilibrium, and far too many Players 2 forego the choice of their dominant strategy, and respond cooperatively. What accounts for these "other-regarding" (HMSS, Hoffman, McCabe and Smith, 1996) forms of behavior? We discuss and provide evidence on three alternative answers (hypotheses):

(1) Naïve subjects
(2) Other-regarding preferences
(3) Reciprocity and Mindreading

3.1. Naïve Subjects

A common objection to the results reported above using undergraduate subjects is that their lack of sophistication, training and/or experience cause the results to be suspect, special to that population and condition, and not generalizable to "real world" decision problems. This objection is also sometimes made as a corollary of the low monetary stakes normally used in such experiments. In this case the stakes, up to $40 per subject pair, for an experiment requiring less than 30 minutes total time from arrival to completion, is substantially above what the typical participant can otherwise earn. Such objections are difficult to test empirically, since any subpopulation is special, and one can always defend the theory against the test outcome on the grounds that what failed was the particular auxiliary hypothesis used to implement the test – in this case that the subjects chosen constituted an acceptable test population, or that the payoffs were adequate. This is the Duhem-Quine problem according to which all tests of any theory require auxiliary hypotheses, and falsifying outcomes can be dismissed by the argument that it is the auxiliary hypothesis not the theory that is to be rejected. Thus, suppose an outcome is said to be due to inadequate stakes. You increase the stakes by a factor of ten, and get the same results, as in the ultimatum games discussed in the introduction. Since whatever are the stakes one can imagine still larger stakes, it can always be argued that they were inadequate. Hence, the theory is not falsifiable.

Whatever one might feel about the merit of these methodological arguments, it is always of worth to determine the effect of varying subject populations (or stakes) as a vehicle for examining robustness. Accordingly in section 4 below we report comparisons between undergraduate and other subject populations in games like those in Figures 2 and 3.

The effect of experience on cooperation is reported for trust games with and without punishment in section 6.

3.2. Other-Regarding Preferences

Ever since Harsanyi (1967) introduced the concept of player types, identified in terms of their utility functions, game theorists have used variations on assumed player utilities to explain variations in behavior. Thus, Rabin (1993) has sought to articulate a utilitarian basis for explaining ultimatum game results, in which player types want to be "fair," want to be treated "fairly," and incur personal costs to punish "unfair" behavior. Bolton and Ockenfels (2000) model some simple games with players whose utility is increasing in own and relative payoff, called ERC (equity, reciprocity and competition). Fehr and Schmidt (1999) also develop a model which has a player's utility depend not only on her own payoff, but also on the difference between her payoff and the other players' payoff. Many of the choices below can be rationalized, expost with such preferences. Cox (1999) has also proposed a preference explanation of cooperation in the investment trust game. In the games of Figures 2–4 Players 1 may choose "down" because they value an increased payoff for their counterpart. In section 5 we introduce two trust games – one with and one without punishment that allow subjects to choose an altruistic option, among others; that is, Player 1 can opt out at small cost, giving Player 2 a large payoff, relative to the SP equilibrium. We also summarize the results from several games that cannot be explained by ERC or Fehr-Schmidt's model.

3.3. Reciprocity and "Mindreading"

An alternative hypothesis, explaining why we observe cooperation under its least likely conditions, is that people perceive a game, such as the one in

Figure 1, as a reciprocal exchange. Reciprocity, like the use of natural (spoken) language is a human universal (Brown, 1991, pp. 107–8, passim; Gouldner, 1960). Friends and associates, without conscious calculation, exchange favors, goods and services across time without the use of money, any formal reckoning of accounts, or a cosigned memorandum of agreement. Such day-to-day social practices, we suppose, are a manifestation of the autonomic social brain. Apparently, in Figure 2, half the Players 1 do not think, "I am paired anonymously with someone in this room who cannot know my identity, and therefore if I play 'down,' I will get $0." Similarly, three-quarters of the Players 2 do not think, "By passing to me my counterpart has chosen stupidly; surreptitiously I can take the whole $40." To quote David Hume (1739; 1886, p. 235) "The rules of morality . . . are not conclusions of our reason." "Norms" that constitute the rules of morality emerge from social and coevolutionary experience, and, we hypothesize, can be so powerful that the behavior survives in purely anonymous interactions. While such norms can be rationalized by interdependent preferences in some games, this approach is inadequate in accounting for the full range of behavioral data. Reciprocity proposes that context matters in strategic interaction because people form expectations about each other's intentions using mental modules adapted to processing contextual information.

Positive reciprocity as a model of exchange based on trust requires two conditions: there must be gains from the exchange, shared by each person, and each party must incur or risk a strictly positive opportunity cost.[3] Thus, in Figure 2 for Player 1 to play "down" is to give up the certain payoff of $10, signaling to Player 2 the intention of achieving C, increasing 2's return by 150% and 1's return by 50%. Player 2 reciprocates by choosing C, completing the exchange at a personal opportunity cost of $15 (= $25 − $40) relative to the defection outcome. If Player 2 defects, then Player 1 realizes an opportunity cost of $10 relative to SP. Consequently, both players incur significant opportunity costs in reaching C.

Negative reciprocity, illustrated in Figure 4, requires two conditions: an offer to cooperate through reciprocity fails due to opportunistic behavior by the second party, and the first party incurs a personal cost to punish this behavior. Thus, in Figure 4, two of the seven defecting Players 2, are punished by counterpart Players 1 who incur an opportunity cost of $5.

4.   COMPARING LESS WITH MORE SOPHISTICATED SUBJECT TYPES

In our introductory discussion of ultimatum and dictator games, we presented the results from ultimatum game experiments using 33 pairs of advanced graduate students with training in game theory. Most of these same subjects also participated in the game shown in Figure 2. Consequently, the protocols normally used for recruiting subjects, as in the results reported in Figure 2, were not followed for this sample. In addition to their greater maturity, education level, and training in economics the graduate students also differed from typical undergraduate subjects in that they had been recruited from dispersed educational communities throughout the United States and Europe. Against their greater knowledge of theory we note, however, that in each group, the reported experiments were conducted on the second day, of a seven day workshop, by which time each group had already become a community, interacting in experiments, classroom discussion, and in social events. Consequently, although individuals interacted anonymously in the bargaining games they might have a strong group identity capable of tempering their theoretical training.[4]

It is against this background that we compare in Figure 5 the results for the graduate students (G) with those for the undergraduates (U) repeated from Figure 2. There is no statistically significant behavioral difference between the outcomes of the two subject samples.[5]

A similar comparison using a game with the same two-stage reciprocity characteristics (shared potential gains from exchange, with each player incurring an opportunity cost to achieve the C outcome), but different payoffs, is reported by Coricelli, McCabe and Smith (2000). They compare undergraduates with participants in an experimental economics workshop for visiting economics faculty. In addition to recording all moves in the game, they also report the time each player took to choose a move. The results are as follows: under-

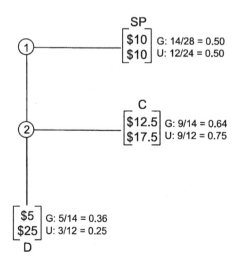

Figure 5. Invest $10 Trust Game Comparing Undergraduates and Graduates

graduates take less time to decide, and make more money than faculty, because the undergraduates are more likely to offer cooperation, and defections are much less frequent.

The above results, together with those of the Ultimatum games discussed in section I, lead to an important conjecture: although individuals in all these groups interact anonymously, they "mindread" each other in their respective groups very well. Both the undergraduates and graduates in the Player 1 position in Figure 5 expect high reciprocity from their counterpart Player 2, offer to cooperate, and the Players 2 predominately tend to fulfill those expectations of players 1 by reciprocating. Similarly, the economics faculty subjects (Players 1) expect high defection rates, most choose the SP, and the few who attempt cooperation encounter high defection rates by their counterpart Players 2.

This observation implies that if we prescreen Player 2 subjects on some characteristic that Players 1 cannot detect, and that makes the former more likely to defect, then we should observe the normal propensity to choose "down" by Players 1, but an increased defection rate by Players 2. Gunnthorsdottir, McCabe and Smith (1999) use the Machiavellian scale, administered to some eighteen hundred freshman, to prescreen subjects, using the highest scores on the Mach test to identify people we predicted were more likely to defect in the Player 2 position. Low and average scoring Mach subjects are screened to participate in both player roles. The results were dramatic in that the high Mach scoring subjects defected at twice the rate of the low and average scoring subjects in the Player 2 position.

5.   IS COOPERATION THE RESULT OF OTHER-REGARDING PREFERENCES? ALTRUISM AND RELATIVE PAYOFF EXPLANATIONS

In this and the next section we summarize some published results, and provide some new unpublished results from the games shown in Figure 6. Note that SP is in the right branch of the tree, ($8, $8), C in the left branch, ($10, $10), and that in Game 1 Player 1 can defect on 2's offer to cooperate by forcing Player 2 to choose between accept defection (AD) or punish defection (PD). Hence, Game 1 is strategically similar to the one in Figure 4 except that we also have an outside option, ($7, $14) at the top of the tree for altruistic (A) Players 1.

A variation on the game, also shown in Figure 6, is Game 2, formed from Game 1 by interchanging the C and AD payoffs in Game 1. Now the game becomes a pure trust game like the one shown in Figure 2: Player 1 can defect (D) and collect $12 without any prospect of punishment by Player 2.

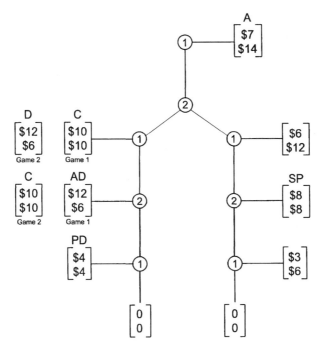

Figure 6. Two Multistage Games. Game 1: Trust/Punishment. Game 2: Trust

For both of these games, if we regard SP, strategically, as the "sure thing" benchmark (Player 1 can earn at least $8 whichever branch of the tree played by Player 2), then if Player 1 is an altruist, he can incur an opportunity cost of only one-eighth of SP and increase Player 2's return by six-eighths, or a multiple of six times the opportunity cost to Player 1. McCabe, Rassenti and Smith (1996) report data on 30 single plays of Game 1 and 26 single plays of Game 2 in Figure 6. Not one of these 56 observations support outcome A. This is consistent with the data from ultimatum, dictator, and other games summarized by Bolton and Ockenfels (2000), but it is contrary to the results reported by Cox (1999).

Because of the poor predictive performance of both selfish and altruistic preferences in many games, Bolton and Ockenfels (2000) proposed their ERC preference function for two-person games in which utility or preference is increasing in own payoff, y_i, but also depends on relative reward $\sigma_i = y_i/(y_1 + y_2)$, $i = 1, 2$; i.e., $v_i = v_i(y_i, \sigma_i)$, where v_i is nondecreasing in y_i, but decreasing in deviations of σ_i from the equity level, $\frac{1}{2}$. Fehr and Schmidt (1999) also propose a model based on inequity aversion (self-centered inequity aversion or SCIA). With two players, the SCIA utility function is $U(x_i, x_j) = x_i -$

$\alpha_i \max\{x_j - x_i, 0\} - \beta_i \max\{x_i - x_j, 0\}$ where α_i measures how much Player i dislikes inequitable outcomes which favor Player j and β_i measures how much Player i dislikes inequitable outcomes which favor himself (with $\beta_i \le \alpha_i$). These are parameter-rich utility specifications, consistent with much of the data in prisoner's dilemma, ultimatum, dictator and competitive market games. These approaches would appear, however, to be inconsistent with the following observations in which decision behavior is altered by instructional treatments (common information), while payoffs, and therefore putative utilities, are not changed. We say "appear" because of the traditional view that utility is an ultimate given, stable across alternative contexts to which it is applied. If we identify utility with emotions of pleasure and discomfort, however, then the instructional state may affect behavior through intermediate manipulations of feelings. It is in this sense that we have never ruled out a possible role for utility as an intermediate explanatory variable based on how the brain might work. But utility explanations such as ERC or SCIA are pleasure explanations. It is pleasure that requires explaining, not the choices pleasure produces, since these follow by construction.

5.1. Dictator Games

Comparing dictator offers under a double blind protocol (no one, including the experimenter, can know the dictator's decision) with standard single blind anonymity condition (the experimenter, but not the recipient, knows the identity of the dictator) offers in the former condition yields a mean = $1.19, while in the latter we have a mean = $2.75. These differences are significant. (See HMSS, Table 2, 3, and Figures 4(a) and 4(c)). Since payoffs are the same in the single blind and double blind treatments, ERC and SCIA utilities are the same, and cannot account for the results.

5.2. Ultimatum Games

The mean ultimatum offer in the random property right treatment ($3.71) is significantly less than in the earned property right exchange treatment ($4.38) (HMSS, Tables 2, 3, Figures 3(a) and 3(d)). Payoffs and utilities are the same in the two treatments, and neither ERC or SCIA utilities can account for the results.

5.3. Trust Games: "Partners" versus "Opponents"

Burnham, McCabe and Smith (2000) study the trust Game 2 in Figure 6 using only two instructional treatments: (1) in treatment P, the individuals in each matched pair are referred to as "partners"; (2) in treatment O, they are referred to as "opponents."

In repeat single play, both trust (the frequency of offers to cooperate) and trustworthiness (the frequency with which such offers are accepted) are significantly greater in the P than in the O treatment. Again, payoffs and utilities are the same in the P and O treatments, and ERC and SCIA utilities cannot account for the treatment differences. It is of interest to note that cooperation declines over time in these pure trust games under both the P and O condition. This contrasts sharply with the results reported below for the trust/punishment game (section 4).

5.4. Extensive versus Normal (Strategic) Form

As in standard game theory, if preferences are as specified in ERC or SCIA, there should be no difference in the propensities to cooperate whether a game is played in extensive or its "equivalent" normal form. In Rapoport (1997) and in McCabe, Smith and LePore (2000) several different games are studied in which it is shown that choice behavior differs significantly between the two forms of the same game. The latter compares the two forms using Game 2 in Figure 6. In the single play protocols 46.2% of the pairs play the left branch in extensive form, while 29% play the left branch in the normal form. Conditional on left branch play, 50% cooperate in the extensive form, only 14% in the normal form. Similarly, under repeat play with same pairs, left play and cooperation are more frequent in the extensive form. This is one more problematic experimental treatment for the models proposed by Bolton and Ockenfels (2000) and Fehr and Schmidt (1999).[6]

6. DOES COOPERATION DEGENERATE WITH REPEAT SINGLE PLAY?

Repeat single play is a matching procedure in which play is repeated, but always between distinct paired subjects. Thus, each subject plays every other subject exactly once, and this protocol is common information among all subjects. Consequently, subjects acquire experience, and can modify their behavior in the light of such experience, but it is not possible (consciously) to build a reputation across repetitions with any other subject. The Roth et al. (1991) ultimatum games report data using this protocol (see note 1 above) in which the rejection rates are much higher than in single play.

In this section we examine data from a previously published source based on Game 1 (See McCabe, Rassenti and Smith, 1996) and new data which are for repeat single with each subject in the same role in all plays of Game 1.

6.1. Results from Trust/Punishment Game 1

We provide first the results for Game 1 when the subjects alternate between the role of Player 1 and Player 2: in each of three sessions, 16 subjects each play every other subject exactly once, alternating roles for a total of 15 periods ($N = 24$). Figure 7 provides a bar graph summarizing outcome frequencies in each of the three five-period blocks: 1 to 5, 6 to 10, and 11–15. Left branch play fluctuates between 55 and 61 percent, but does not change to any important degree across the 15 periods of play. Similarly, cooperation (conditional upon left branch play) does not deteriorate and in fact rises slightly across the three five-trial blocks from 63 to 68 percent. Defection declines slightly across the three five-trial blocks, while punishment persists at substantial rates in every five-trial block, averaging above half the defections.

In the new data on Game 1 subjects retain their original randomly assigned roles as Player 1 or 2: in each of three sessions, 20 subjects each play every other subject exactly once in their fixed roles. This yields 10 observations per session with $N = 30$. Figure 8 charts the outcome frequencies for the first and second five-period block. Left branch play increases from 64.6% to 72.3% from the first to the second five-period block. Cooperation increases from 67.4% to 75.7%, with over half the defections punished in each trial block.

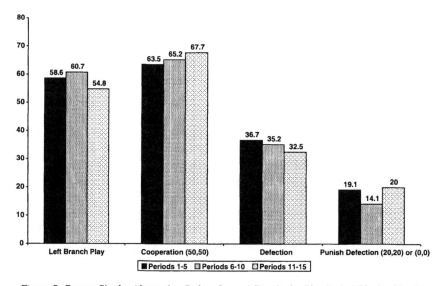

Figure 7. Repeat Single, Alternating Roles, Game 1 Results by Five Period Blocks, N = 24

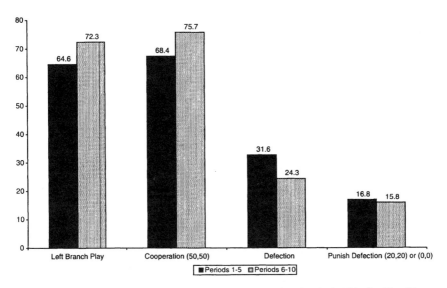

Figure 8. Repeat Single, Same Roles, Game 1 Results by Five Period Blocks, N = 30

6.2. Logit Analysis of Game 1

The logit regression of $p(t)/[1 - p(t)]$, where $p(t)$ is the proportion of left game (trust) play, is shown in Table 1(a). The independent variables are $t = 1$, $2, \ldots, 10$ (the play round), and an indicator variable for role (0 if alternating roles; 1 if same roles). Trust is significantly increased by the same-role treatment, but the increase in trust over time is not significant.

Table 1(b) shows the logit regression results when p(t) is the proportion of plays that are cooperative on round t, conditional on left branch play. The slight decline in cooperation over successive rounds is not significant, and there is no significant difference between the dichotomous treatments, same vs. alternative rules.

These results confirm that there is no significant tendency, under r epeat single play conditions, for the proportion of trusting play by Players 1, or the use of reciprocal trustworthy responses by Players 2, to unravel across time. The mechanism of sustained cooperation by strangers who interact repeatedly is assured by the persistence with which defectors are punished. In Figure 6 defectors in Game 1 intend to increase their payoff from $10 to $12. In fact they consistently earn less than the $10 they give up. This stems the tide of defection, and with defection held to low levels, Players 2 on average earn more by playing the left side of the tree than the SP return on the right.

Table 1.

(a) Logit Estimates of the Odds, $p(t)/[1 - p(t)]$, that Player 1 Will Trust, $p(t)$ = Frequency of Left Branch Play Game 1

Dependent Variable	Coefficient	Standard Error	t – ratio	Significance Probability
Constant	−0.572	0.382	−1.50	0.153
Period t	0.014	0.036	1.01	0.327
Same versus Alternating Roles	0.511	0.207	2.47	0.024

(b) Logit Estimates of the Odds, $P(t)/[1 - P(t)]$, that Player 2 Will Cooperate, $P(t)$ = Frequency of Cooperation by Player 2

Dependent Variable	Coefficient	Standard Error	t – ratio	Significance Probability
Constant	2.80	6.07	0.461	0.651
Period t	−0.875	0.572	−1.53	0.144
Same versus Alternating Roles	2.96	3.29	0.90	0.379

6.3. Why Do So Many Players 2 Punish Defection?

Given the high rate at which defection is punished it follows that defection does not pay. Since defection does not pay it follows that defection should decline, cooperation increase, and trust should produce an increase in earnings over time. This is what we observe. The antecedents are rational responses to the condition that defection is punished at a high rate. But it is *not* rational to punish defection. Rationally, individual Players 2 should accept defection, avoid the cost of punishment, and free ride on others who might punish defection. Hence, reciprocity as a cooperative mechanism for increasing the gains from exchange depends crucially on the irrational propensity to punish cheaters, as in the above data (Also see the cheater detection experiments of Cosmides, 1985).

7. CONCLUSION

Given the ample experimental evidence which suggests that many subjects choose cooperative strategies, in this paper we ask "Why so much cooperation?". There are currently two main approaches to answering this question:

preference models and reciprocity explanations. Preference models, such as ERC and SCIA, vary player utilities to explain variations in behavior. Reciprocity models, on the other hand, emphasize the role of intentions in achieving cooperative outcomes in personal exchange. We present evidence from a wide variety of games for which utility explanations cannot account, but are indeed predicted by trust and reciprocity. Furthermore, we describe data in repeated-play trust/punishment games demonstrating that cooperation does not degenerate with repeat single play, regardless of whether subjects maintain the same role. This tendency for cooperation rates to remain high is due to the amount of punishment inflicted on the defectors, i.e., negative reciprocity.

NOTES

1. In some Coase bargaining experiments, subjects bargain face-to-face over the division of $14, one of them having been randomly assigned an outside option of $12. This person should never agree to a division giving her less than $12. However, one hundred percent of the subjects split the $14 evenly, $7 each. This is clearly a violation of individual rationality (See Hoffman and Spitzer, 1982, 1985).
2. For a summary of results from these and other alternating offer games see Kagel and Roth (1995, pp. 253–348). Roth et al. (1991) report much higher rejection rates and rejection levels than those summarized in the text. In the text we report the results of single play games, while the Roth et al. (1991) study examines ultimatum game behavior in 10 round play sequences in which each play is with a distinct pairing of subjects. Under these conditions rejections of $0.4k$ are common and even rejection of offers of half the pie are observed. These observations are consistent with the well-documented tendency of people to punish cheaters in social exchange contexts (Cosmides, 1985). The tendency to punish defectors on offers to cooperate also emerges in some of the games we study below.
3. Deck (2000) reports data on a two-person game similar to the trust game in Figure 2 with gains from exchange that are imputed entirely to the first mover at the cooperative outcome. He observes little cooperation, suggesting that second movers are prone to defect if they do not share positively in the gains.
4. For this reason we would not interpret the results of Figure 1 as implying that the somewhat greater generosity of the graduate students was *due* to their greater sophistication. Rather, we would say that their greater knowledge of game theory was insufficient to overcome the treatment difference in socialization between the graduate and undergraduate subjects.
5. The results (G) in Figure 5 were for the final of two plays by the graduate students, each pair composed of the same people, and playing the same role (player 1 or 2). Game theory predicts the SP equilibrium for each of the two plays. In the first play the conditional outcome frequencies were 25% for ($10, $10), 75% for ($15, $25), 25% for (0, $40). As we expected, the Players 1 more strongly cooperated in the first play as a means of building reputation.
6. For more recent experimental data which are also problematic for ERC and SCIA, but explained well by intentions based models, see McCabe, Rigdon, and Smith (2000).

REFERENCES

Berg, Joyce, John Dickhaut, and Kevin McCabe (1995). "Trust, Reciprocity and Social History." *Games and Economic Behavior* 10, 122–42.
Bolton, Gary, and Axel Ockenfels (2000). "ERC: A Theory of Equity, Reciprocity, and Competition." *American Economic Review* 90, 166–93.
Bolton, Gary, and Rami Zwick (1998). "Anonymity versus Punishment in Ultimatum Bargaining." *Games and Economic Behavior* 10, 95–121.
Brown, Donald E. (1991). *Human Universals*. NY: McGraw-Hill.
Burnham, Terence (1998). "Engineering Altruism: An Experimental Investigation of Anonymity Gift Giving." Manuscript, Kennedy School of Government, Harvard University, Cambridge, MA.
Burnham, Terence, Kevin McCabe, and Vernon Smith (2000). "Friend-or-Foe Intentionality Priming in an Extensive Form Trust Game." *Journal of Economic Behavior and Organization* 1244, 1–17.
Coricelli, Georgio, Kevin McCabe, and Vernon Smith (2000). "Theory-of-Mind Mechanism in Personal Exchange." Proceedings 13th Annual Toyota Conference on Affective Minds.
Cosmides, Leda (1985). "The Logic of Social Exchange: Has Natural Selection Shaped How Human Reason?" *Cognition* 31, 187–276.
Cox, James C. (1999). "Trust Reciprocity and Other-Regarding Preferences of Individuals and Groups." Department of Economics and Economic Science Laboratory, University of Arizona.
Deck, Cary (2000). "A Test of Game Theoretic and Behavioral Models of Play in Exchange and Insurance Environments." Economic Science Laboratory, University of Arizona.
Eckel, Catherine, and Philip Grossman (1996). "Altruism in Anonymous Dictator Games." *Games and Economic Behavior* 16, 181–91.
Fehr, Ernst, and Klaus M. Schmidt (1999). "A Theory of Fairness, Competition, and Cooperation." *Quarterly Journal of Economics* 114, 817–68.
Forsythe, Robert, Joel Horwitz, N. E. Savin, and Martin Sefton (1994). "Fairness in Simple Bargaining Experiments." *Games and Economic Behavior* 6, 347–69.
Gouldner, Alvin W. (1960). "The Norm of Reciprocity." *American Sociological Review* 25, 161–78.
Gunnthorsdottir, Anna, Kevin McCabe, and Vernon Smith (1999). "Using the Machiavellianism Instrument to Predict Trustworthiness in a Bargaining Game."
Güth, W., R. Schmittberger, and V. Schwartz (1982). "An Experimental Analysis of Ultimatum Bargaining." *Journal of Economic Behavior and Organization* 3, 367–88.
Harsanyi, John (1967). "Games with Incomplete Information Played by "Bayesian" Players (Part I)." *Management Science* 14, 159–82.
Hoffman, Elizabeth, Kevin McCabe, Keith Shachat, and Vernon Smith (1994). "Preferences, Property Rights and Anonymity in Bargaining Games." *Games and Economic Behavior* 7, 346–80.
Hoffman, Elizabeth, Kevin McCabe, and Vernon Smith (1996). "Social Distance of Other-Regarding Behavior in Dictator Games." *American Economic Review* 86, 653–60.
Hoffman, Elizabeth, and Matthew Spitzer (1982). "The Coase Theorem: Some Experimental Tests." *Journal of Law and Economics* 25, 73–98.
Hoffman, Elizabeth (1985). "Entitlements, Rights and Fairness." *Journal of Legal Studies* 14, 259–97.
Hume, David (1886). *A Treatise of Human Nature*. Vol. 2, edited by T. H. Green and T. H. Grose, 235. London: Longmans, Green.
Kagel, John, and Alvin Roth (1995). *The Handbook of Experimental Economics*. Princeton: Princeton University Press.

McCabe, Kevin, Stephen Rassenti, and Vernon Smith (1996). "Game Theory and Reciprocity in Some Extensive Form Experimental Games." *Proceedings of the National Academy of Sciences* 93, 13421–8.

McCabe, Kevin, Mary Rigdon, and Vernon Smith (2000). "Positive Reciprocity and Intentions in Trust Games." Working Paper, University of Arizona.

McCabe, Kevin, Vernon Smith, and Michael LePore (2000). "Intentionality Detection and "Mindreading": Why Does Game Form Matter." *Proceedings of the National Academy of Sciences* 97, 4404–9.

Rabin, Matthew (1993). "Incorporating Fairness into Game Theory and Economics." *American Economic Review* 83, 1281–302.

Rapoport, Amnon (1997). "Order of Play in Strategically Equivalent Games in Extensive Form." *International Journal of Game Theory* 26, 113–36.

Roth, Alvin E., Vesna Prasnikar, Masahiro Okuno-Fujiwara, and Shmuel Zamir (1991). "Bargaining and Market Behavior in Jerusalem, Ljubljana, Pittsburgh and Tokyo." *American Economic Review* 81, 1068–95.

Chapter 4

COORDINATION IN THE AGGREGATE
WITHOUT COMMON KNOWLEDGE OR
OUTCOME INFORMATION

Amnon Rapoport
University of Arizona

Darryl A. Seale
University of Nevada Las Vegas

James E. Parco
University of Arizona

1.   INTRODUCTION

In his book *"Micromotives and Macrobehavior"* Schelling set the stage for a systematic analysis that explores the relation "between the behavior characteristics of the *individuals* who comprise some social aggregate, and the characteristics of the *aggregate*" (1978, p.13). This analysis is both challenging and difficult because the entire aggregate outcome is evaluated, not merely how each individual does within the constraints of her own environment. Aggregate behavior necessarily involves some sort of coordination. In reflecting on how ant colonies work, Schelling noted (see also Gordon, 1999) that "why the system works as it does, and as efficiently as it does, is a dynamic problem of social and genetic evolution" (1978, p. 21).

Theoretical analysis is in general not sufficient to account for the tacit coordination of decentralized decisions in large aggregates. Rather, coordination

EXPERIMENTAL BUSINESS RESEARCH. Copyright © 2002. Kluwer Academic Publishers. Boston. All rights reserved.

in interactive decision situations that can appropriately be modeled as non-cooperative games with multiple equilibria is typically achieved by the players invoking some coordination principle. This may take the form of a convention, social norm, or focal point (Cooper, DeJong, Forsythe, & Ross, 1990; Mehta, Starmer, & Sugden, 1994a, 1994b; Schelling, 1960, 1978). Rapoport, Seale, and Winter (henceforth RSW, 1997) extended the experimental investigation of tacit coordination in large groups (aggregates) to a class of iterated noncooperative n-person market entry games with a relatively large number (n = 20) of asymmetric players. This class of games allows for no conventions and elicits no social norms. Nevertheless, RSW reported a remarkable degree of tacit coordination, successfully accounted for by the Nash equilibrium solution, when the market entry game was iterated for a large number of periods.

RSW induced asymmetry between the players by charging differential entry fees. Entry fee was private knowledge but the distribution of entry fees was common knowledge. In particular, each player knew the exact number of players who were charged the same entry fee. In addition, at the end of each period each player was independently informed of a summary statistic, namely, the total number of entrants into the market as well as her own payoff. Information about the decisions and payoffs of others was withheld. The first source of information renders the distribution of entry fees common knowledge. Without this common knowledge the Nash equilibria for the stage game cannot be constructed. The second source of information provides trial-to-trial outcome feedback without which no adaptive learning is typically assumed to take place over time. Both sources of information are present in almost all experiments on interactive decision making that attempt to establish if and when the Nash equilibrium can be justified as a steady state of some adaptive learning process (e.g., Cachon & Camerer, 1996; Ochs, 1990; Rapoport, Seale, Erev, & Sundali, 1998; van Huyck, Battalio, & Beil, 1990, 1991; van Huyck, Gillette, & Battalio, 1992).

The purpose of the present study is to assess the importance and differential impact of these two independent sources of information in the iterated market entry game. It reports the results of two experiments that replicate the experiment of RSW but depart from it in two important ways. Experiment 1 replicates the RSW experiment with one major exception, namely, it eliminates all information about the entry fees of the other players. Although outcome feedback is provided at the end of each period, as in the original RSW study, this information cannot possibly be used to infer the parameters of the distribution of entry fees or, indeed, even to deduce that the players are asymmetric. Experiment 2 replicates the RSW experiment with another major exception, namely, it provides no outcome information at the end of each period. Presumably, without some sort of outcome information no learning is possible in the iterated game.

The present study transcends the conventional setting in experimental economics with its common knowledge assumptions. In Experiment 1 it does so by precluding any prior information on the distribution of types – subsets of players with different entry fees – in the population. We do not claim that the Bayesian Nash equilibrium could not apply in this setting. Clearly, one could model this setup as one with common knowledge about how the distribution of types was originated: The n players know that the distribution of entry fees in Experiment 1 was chosen by the experimenter, they may share the same model of how this was accomplished, etc. One can construct a game theoretical model of the market entry game without *explicitly* requiring that the n players have common knowledge. Although this is certainly possible, we argue below that it is not very plausible, and that the coordination we observe in Experiment 1 is achieved by some process of adaptation for which common knowledge of the type distribution is not required.

Experiment 2 departs from the conventional way of conducting iterated games (but see Weber, 2000) by precluding any information about the outcome at the end of each period. Nevertheless, we report small but systematic changes in behavior across iterations of the market entry game in Experiment 2, which – we argue below – could only be due to introspection gained with experience in playing the game. Comparison of the results of both experiments with the findings reported by RSW shows that the Nash equilibrium organizes the group frequency of entry as well as it did in the original RSW study.

The rest of the paper is organized as follows. Section 2 describes the market entry game and its multiple equilibria. Section 3 reports the results of Experiment 1, and Section 4 reports the results of Experiment 2. The implications of the findings are discussed in Section 5.

2. THE MARKET ENTRY GAME AND ITS EQUILIBRIA

2.1. The MEFC Game

The market entry game with fixed capacity (MEFC) is a noncooperative n-person game with binary decisions played by a group N of n players for T periods. The stage game has the following features. At the beginning of stage t ($t = 1, 2, \ldots, T$), a (possibly different) positive integer c ($1 \leq c \leq n$) is publicly announced. In both experiments c is interpreted as the "capacity of the market." Then, each player i ($i \in N$) is privately informed of her entry fee for the period (h_i), if she decides to enter the market. The entry fee h_i is fixed across iterations of the stage game. The values of T and the exact number of players who share the same entry fee are assumed to be common knowledge. Once the value of c is publicly announced, each player i decides on each period privately and anonymously whether to enter the market ($d_i = 1$) or stay out of it ($d_i = 0$). Communication during the experiment is prohibited. Individual payoffs for each period, denoted by $H_i(\mathbf{d})$, are determined from

$$H_i(\mathbf{d}) = \begin{array}{ll} v, & \text{if } d_i = 0 \\ k + r(c - m) - h_i, & \text{if } d_i = 1 \end{array} \tag{1}$$

where v, k, and r are real-valued, commonly known constants that remain fixed across all the T iterations of the stage game, $\mathbf{d} = (d_1, d_2, \ldots, d_n)$ is the vector of the n (binary) decisions for the period, and m is the actual number of entrants ($0 \leq m \leq n$).

The parameter v represents the riskless payoff for staying out of the market; it can be positive or negative. The parameter r can be interpreted as the volatility of the market; the larger is r the more volatile the market. Finally, the parameter k is simply the intercept of the linear function that determines the payoff of each entrant. At the end of period t, each player is informed of the actual number of entrants (m) and her payoff for the period. Once the player is informed of the value of m, she can compute $H_i(\mathbf{d})$ directly from (1). Information about the individual decisions of the other players and their payoffs for the period is not disclosed.

Asymmetry between the players is induced by charging differential entry fees. In both the RSW and the present studies, we fixed n = 20 and randomly sampled values of c without replacement from the set of ten odd integers C = {1, 3, 5, 7, 9, 11, 13, 15, 17, 19}. We also assigned to every four players the same entry fee. We shall refer to players with the same entry fee h_j as "type j" players. With n = 20, there are five types and four players of each type who are symmetric within but not between types.

2.2. The Equilibria

In the present study, v = 1, k = 1, and r = 2. As these are the same parameter values used by RSW, they allow for a direct comparison of the two studies. Table 1 lists all the pure-strategy equilibria for two selected values of c, namely, c = 9 and c = 15. The full set of pure-strategy equilibria for all ten values of c is presented in the RSW paper. The equilibrium number of entrants of type j is denoted by $m_j^*(c)$, an equilibrium is denoted by the vector ($m_1^*(c)$, $m_2^*(c)$, $m_3^*(c)$, $m_4^*(c)$, $m_5^*(c)$), and the total number of entrants across the five types is denoted by $m^*(c)$. For example, the first equilibrium listed in Table 1 for c = 9 is (4, 3, 0, 0, 0) with an associated $m^*(c = 9)$ value of 7 entrants, the second is (4, 2, 1, 0, 0) with an associated $m^*(c = 9)$ value of 7 entrants, and so on. The group payoffs, denoted by G, appear on the right-hand column.

The equilibrium solutions are Pareto deficient: the n players could collectively gain a considerably higher payoff by decreasing their frequency of entry. For example, consider the equilibrium (4, 2, 3, 4, 0) for the case c = 15. The total group payoff associated with this equilibrium is 39 (see Table 1). If, instead, only four players of type 1 and two players of type 2 were to enter, the total group payoff would have increased by a factor of three to 120.

RSW classified the equilibria as *monotonic* if $m_j^*(c) \geq m_{j+1}^*(c)$ (j = 1, 2, 3, 4), and as *compact* if they are monotonic and , in addition, there is at most one $m_j^*(c)$ that differs from either 0 or 4. Compactness means that for at least 4 of the 5 types, all the players of the same type behave in the same way. For example, consider the case c = 9. The equilibrium (4, 1, 1, 1, 0) is monotonic but not compact, the equilibrium (4, 3, 0, 0, 0) is compact, and the equilibrium (4, 0, 1, 2, 0) is non-monotonic.

The equilibrium solutions imply several testable predictions that differ from one another in their level of specificity (or refutability). The most specific prediction is that the profile of observed decisions of the five types of players, $(m_1(c), m_2(c), m_3(c), m_4(c), m_5(c))$ will correspond to one of the equilibria. Although there are multiple pure-strategy equilibria for each value of c (Table 1), this prediction has a lot of bite because the set of equilibria is a subset of a considerably larger set of all profiles. For example, there are 11 pure-strategy equilibria for c = 9 (Table 1) of which 4 are monotonic, whereas there are $5^5 = 3125$ possible profiles $(m_1, m_2, m_3, m_4, m_5)$ in which m_j can take on any value in the set {0, 1, 2, 3, 4}.

Basic economic reasoning would lead one to expect monotonic equilibria. For each of the values of c, one would expect the number of entrants with a higher entry fee to be no larger than the number of entrants with a lower entry fee. There are at most four monotonic equilibria for each of the ten values of c presented in the present study. Monotonicity implies several predictions about type behavior, some of which are listed below:

If c ≥ 9, all players of type 1 should enter.
If c ≤ 7, no player of types 3, 4, or 5 should enter.
If c ≥ 17, all players of types 2 and 3 should enter.
If c ≤ 15, no player of type 5 should enter.

Compactness further reduces the number of pure-strategy equilibria. It is, therefore, easier to refute compactness than monotonicity. There are at most two compact equilibria for each of the ten values of c in the present study. Compactness also implies several testable predictions that concern different player types:

If c ≥ 5, all players of type 1 should enter.
If c ≥ 11, all players of type 2 should enter.

Table 1. Pure Strategy Equilibria for Two of the Ten Values of
c in the MEFC Game

c	m*(c)	m₁(c)	m₂(c)	m₃(c)	m₄(c)	m₅(c)	G
9	7	4	3	0	0	0	38#*
9	7	4	2	1	0	0	37#
9	7	4	1	2	0	0	36
9	7	4	2	0	1	0	36
9	7	4	0	3	0	0	35
9	7	4	1	1	1	0	35#
9	7	4	0	2	1	0	34
9	7	4	1	0	2	0	34
9	7	4	0	1	2	0	33
9	7	4	0	0	3	0	32
9	8	4	4	0	0	0	24#*
15	12	4	4	4	0	0	68#*
15	13	4	4	4	1	0	44#*
15	13	4	4	3	2	0	43#
15	13	4	3	4	2	0	42
15	13	4	4	2	3	0	42
15	13	4	3	3	3	0	41#
15	13	4	4	1	4	0	41
15	13	4	2	4	3	0	40
15	13	4	3	2	4	0	40
15	13	4	2	3	4	0	39
!5	13	4	1	4	4	0	38

\# Monotonic equilibrium.
* Compact equilibrium.

If $c \geq 15$, all players of type 3 should enter.
If $c \leq 13$, players of type 4 should never enter.
Players of type 5 should never enter.

Yet another test of the equilibrium solution concerns the total number of
entrants across types. Table 1 shows that if $c = 9$, then $m^*(9) = 8$ or 9, and if
$c = 15$, then $m^*(15) = 12$ or 13. The full set of equilibria for the ten values of
c shows that $m^*(c)$ assumes a single value for six of the ten values of c used
in the present study, and two values for the remaining four values of c. Tests
of these predictions will be reported below.

Denote by p_j the probability of type j player entering the market, and
by $\mathbf{p} = (p_1, p_2, p_3, p_4, p_5)$ a vector of completely mixed strategy equilibria in
which each type j player enters with probability $p_j > 0$. RSW proved that there
exist no such symmetric completely mixed equilibria because no more than

two types can mix. There do exist symmetric and partly mixed equilibria. For example, if c = 11, there exists an equilibrium in which all players of types 1 and 2 enter, all players of types 4 and 5 stay out, and each of the players of type 3 enters with probability $p_3 = 1/6$. Because on later examination of individual data we find no evidence for mixing, we shall only focus on tests of the pure-strategy equilibria.

3. EXPERIMENT 1

3.1. Method

3.1.1. Subjects

Two groups of subjects, each consisting of 20 players, participated in the experiment. Group 1 ("sophisticated") included graduate and post-graduate students of economics from different countries, who in the summer of 1999 participated in a workshop on experimental economics organized by the Economic Science Laboratory at the University of Arizona. All the members of this group had prior knowledge of the basic concepts of game theory and considerable interest in experimental economics. Indeed, they were selected to take part in the workshop on the basis of their interest. Payoff in the experiment, which was contingent on performance, was used to defray the subjects' travel costs to the workshop. In addition, the subjects of Group 1 were told that their decisions would be discussed later in a post-experimental lecture. Therefore, the subjects took much care in making their decisions. It would be difficult to have a group of more sophisticated and better motivated subjects. Group 2 ("naïve") included University of Arizona students, mostly undergraduates, who volunteered to take part in a decision making experiment for monetary reward contingent on performance.

3.1.2. Procedure

The experiment was conducted at the University of Arizona. Group 1 participated in the Economic Science Laboratory, which consists of 40 networked desktop computers in individual cubicles. Group 2 participated in the Enterprise Room, which is comprised of 24 networked stations separated into two groups with individual stations spaced apart from each other. Upon arrival, the subjects were seated randomly at one of the computer workstations. Communication between the subjects during the experiment was prohibited. Hard copies of the instructions (see Appendix) were made available during the experiment.

At the beginning of the experiment, each subject received an endowment of 34 "francs" (a fictitious currency later converted into US dollars). The subjects were told that their cumulative earnings (which could be positive or negative) would be added to the endowment at the end of the session.

Each period (trial) consisted of two parts. In the first part, a value of c was sampled from the set C and displayed on all the twenty computer screens. The payoff function had the form (Equation 1):

$$\text{Your payoff} = \begin{array}{ll} 1, & \text{if ``stay out''} \\ 1 + 2(c - m) - h_j, & \text{if ``enter''} \end{array}$$

The subjects were divided into five types with four members each. Type j's entry fee was set at $h_j = j$ ($j = 1, 2, 3, 4, 5$). There was no indication in the instructions that the subjects differed from one another in their entry fees. Two examples were included in the instructions to illustrate the computation of the payoff for the trial. One included an entry fee of $h_j = 1$, and the other of $h_j = 6$ – an entry fee that, in fact, was not assigned to any of the subjects.

To eliminate the burden of computation and provide information about all the possible payoffs, the computer displayed on each period a table listing all the 21 possible payoffs – one for each value of m – associated with the player type and market capacity value presented on that period. Five different types of tables, one for each player type, were displayed to reflect the difference in entry fees. Each subject only saw the table relevant to his type.

In the second part of the experiment, each subject was asked to use the computer mouse in order to choose either "enter" or "stay out" via a graphical computer interface. Each trial was self-paced. Once all the twenty decisions were entered, each subject was informed of the number of entrants m, the subject's payoff for the period $H_i(\mathbf{d})$, and her cumulative payoff. The computer then advanced all the subjects to the next trial, unless it was the last one.

Ten values of c were presented to the subjects. In each block of ten trials, these values were sampled randomly and without replacement from the set C. The subjects of Group 1 were considerably more deliberate in making their decisions and completed only 90 trials (9 blocks) in a session that lasted more than two hours. Group 2 subjects completed 100 trials (10 blocks) in about half the time. Thus, each subject was presented with the same value of c either 9 (Group 1) or 10 (Group 2) times during the entire session but in a different order within each block. On the average, ten periods separated the successive presentations of the same value of c.

At the end of the session, the cumulative payoffs were converted into US dollars at the rate 10 francs = $3.00 for Group 1 and 10 francs = $1.50 for Group 2. Group 2 subjects also received a $5.00 show-up fee. The mean payoff was $51.02 for Group 1 and $27.48 for Group 2. Payoffs differed considerably between and within player types.

3.2. Results

To allow comparison between Experiment 1 and the RSW study, the present section has been organized in a similar way. We first test several hypotheses derived from the equilibrium solution on the group level, disregarding differences between types. We then examine more closely the effects of differential entry fees (types) and subsequently shift the focus of the investigation to individual behavior. Finally, we test a simple reinforcement-based learning model proposed by RSW to account for the emergence of coordination on the aggregate level.

3.2.1. Aggregate Behavior across Types

Table 2 presents the frequency of entry decisions by market capacity value and block of trials for each of the two groups separately. The ten values of c are presented in each panel in an ascending order and not in their order of presentation that, due to the random sampling, differed from block to block. Column 12 of each panel presents the total number of entry decisions across blocks, whereas the next two columns display the mean and standard deviations of number of entries. The next to the last row of each panel displays the number of entries summed across all ten values of c for each block separately. The bottom row presents for each block separately the product-moment correlation between the ten frequencies of entry in the block and the ten values of c.

Table 2 exhibits remarkable coordination on the group level. The ten frequencies of entry in each block increase in the value of c; we observe few departures from monotonicity that decrease both in number and magnitude across blocks. For example, the frequencies of entry in block 9 of Group 1 increase monotonically in c with only a single inversion. The correlation between the frequencies of entry and values of c in block 9 is 0.99. The frequencies of entry in block 10 of Group 2 increase monotonically in c with no inversions. The corresponding correlation in this case is equal to 1.00.

The hypothesis of equality of frequencies of entry in the two groups was tested statistically. For each value of c separately, we used a t-test to compare the two means of frequency of entry of the two groups. None of the ten t-tests rejected the null hypothesis of equality of the two means ($p > 0.3$). Inspection of the means (column 13) of the two groups verifies that they are, indeed, very close to each other.

Table 2. Total Number of Observed Entry Frequencies by Market Capacity Value, Block, and Group (Experiment 1, Present Study)

Group 1

c	Block										Total	Mean	SD	m*(c)
	1	2	3	4	5	6	7	8	9	10				
1	0	1	1	1	1	1	2	0	0	—	7	0.78	0.7	0
3	5	4	3	3	2	2	2	2	2	—	25	2.78	1.1	2
5	7	3	4	4	4	3	4	6	4	—	39	4.33	1.3	4
7	4	6	6	6	6	5	5	5	6	—	49	5.44	0.7	5 (6)
9	10	10	6	5	7	7	8	6	7	—	66	7.33	1.7	7 (8)
11	5	8	8	10	7	10	8	8	9	—	73	8.11	1.5	9
13	14	11	11	11	12	12	11	11	11	—	104	11.56	1.0	11
15	12	14	8	17	10	15	15	15	10	—	116	12.89	3.0	12 (13)
17	13	17	11	18	14	13	13	16	14	—	129	14.33	2.2	14 (15)
19	19	13	16	17	16	17	16	16	16	—	146	16.22	1.6	16
Total	89	87	74	92	79	85	84	85	79	—	754	83.78		80 (84)
Corr.	0.89	0.94	0.94	0.96	0.98	0.98	0.98	0.97	0.99	—				

Group 2

c	Block										Total	Mean	SD	m*(c)
	1	2	3	4	5	6	7	8	9	10				
1	0	0	1	1	0	0	0	0	0	0	2	0.2	0.4	0
3	2	2	2	2	2	1	3	2	2	1	19	1.9	0.6	2
5	7	4	4	5	3	3	3	6	5	4	44	4.4	1.4	4
7	3	5	6	5	7	6	7	7	6	5	57	5.7	1.3	5 (6)
9	18	6	7	8	8	7	6	7	6	7	81	8.1	3.5	7 (8)
11	8	9	9	10	10	8	9	9	9	10	91	9.1	0.7	9
13	14	10	11	9	12	11	12	11	12	11	113	11.3	1.4	11
15	13	13	12	16	11	13	14	11	12	12	127	12.7	1.5	12 (13)
17	14	14	13	16	15	15	15	14	14	14	144	14.4	0.8	14 (15)
19	17	18	15	16	16	16	16	16	16	16	162	16.2	0.8	16
Total	96	81	80	88	84	80	85	83	83	80	840	84.0		80 (84)
Corr.	0.82	0.99	1.00	0.97	0.98	1.00	0.99	0.98	0.99	1.00				

In yet another test of the equality of the two groups that focuses on individual differences, we counted for each subject separately the total number of entries across market capacity values and blocks. This statistic could take on any value between 0 to 90 in Group 1 and between 0 to 100 in Group 2. In actuality, the individual total number of entries in Group 1 ranged between 9 to 85 and in Group 2 between 3 to 80. A comparison of the mean individual total number of entries *per block* failed to reject the null hypothesis of equality of individual number of entries between the two different groups ($p > 0.5$). Therefore, subsequent analyses combine the frequencies of entry across the two groups.

The equilibrium total number of entries within block ranges between 80 and 84 (see the right-hand column in the two panels of Table 2). Inspection of the bottom row in each panel shows that the total number of entry decisions in each block first fluctuated and then after about five blocks converged to a frequency between 82 and 83. The correlations at the bottom rows of both panels display a similar pattern of convergence to unity. In both groups, the coordination in block 1 is not at all impressive; there are substantial departures from monotonicity, and the correlations between the entry frequencies and the values of c are below 0.90. Coordination improves rapidly with experience, particularly in Group 2. Comparison of the two panels suggests that the naïve subjects of Group 2 coordinated their actions at a slightly faster rate than the more sophisticated members of Group 1.

The equilibrium total number of entries, $m^*(c)$, are displayed in the right-hand column of Table 2. The null hypothesis that the mean number of entries is equal to $m^*(c)$ could not be rejected by a t-test in all twenty cases (2 groups times 10 values of c). Not only did the frequencies of entry converge after about five blocks, but they converged in each case to the (Pareto deficient) equilibrium solution.

Table 3 presents the frequencies of entry of the two groups in the RSW study. All the statistical tests that we conducted (not reported here) for comparing the aggregate results between the two studies failed to reject the null hypothesis of equality in frequencies of entry. Comparison of the total number of entries and the correlations in the bottom two rows of Tables 2 and 3 shows similar speed of convergence to equilibrium in both studies. We conclude that prior information about the distribution of entry fees – indeed, about the exact number of players of each type – had no significant effect on group coordination. The systematic block effects in both the total number of entries and the correlations between observed number of entries and market capacity values suggest that convergence to equilibrium was reached through some sort of adaptive learning that does not incorporate any common knowledge of the distribution of types. Before examining this process, we turn next to investigate the effects of the differential entry fees on the subjects' entry decisions.

Table 3. Total Number of Observed Entry Frequencies by Market Capacity Value, Block, and Group (RSW Study)

Group 1

c	Block										Total	Mean	SD	m*(c)
	1	2	3	4	5	6	7	8	9	10				
1	2	0	0	0	0	1	0	0	0	0	3	0.3	0.7	0
3	0	1	2	2	3	4	2	1	2	2	19	1.9	1.1	2
5	7	6	2	3	5	3	3	4	5	4	42	4.2	1.6	4
7	1	9	3	7	6	7	7	5	4	5	54	5.4	2.3	5 (6)
9	9	3	11	9	8	7	8	8	7	7	77	7.7	2.1	7 (8)
11	9	7	16	9	11	8	10	9	10	9	98	9.8	2.4	9
13	11	10	10	8	13	11	11	10	12	12	108	10.8	1.4	11
15	7	16	15	10	13	12	13	13	15	12	126	12.6	2.6	12 (13)
17	12	15	12	11	15	15	15	15	14	16	140	14.0	1.7	14 (15)
19	13	18	14	14	16	16	17	17	17	16	158	15.8	1.6	16
Total	71	85	85	73	90	84	86	82	86	83	825	82.5		80 (84)
Corr.	0.86	0.90	0.86	0.95	0.99	0.98	0.99	0.99	0.99	1.00				

Group 2

c	Block										Total	Mean	SD	m*(c)
	1	2	3	4	5	6	7	8	9	10				
1	5	1	1	0	1	0	1	0	0	0	9	0.9	1.5	0
3	2	4	1	4	2	1	2	3	2	1	22	2.2	1.1	2
5	3	4	4	5	4	6	2	3	3	4	38	3.8	1.1	4
7	6	7	5	6	8	7	7	9	6	5	66	6.6	1.3	5 (6)
9	14	8	11	7	6	9	5	6	8	8	82	8.2	2.7	7 (8)
11	9	12	8	10	8	11	9	8	10	8	93	9.3	1.4	9
13	12	11	13	11	12	9	13	10	12	10	113	11.3	1.3	11
15	14	15	11	14	13	14	12	15	11	15	134	13.4	1.6	12 (13)
17	16	14	15	17	13	15	15	13	14	15	147	14.7	1.3	14 (15)
19	15	17	18	16	16	17	17	15	16	17	164	16.4	1.0	16
Total	96	93	87	90	83	89	83	82	82	83	868	86.8		80 (84)
Corr.	0.88	0.98	0.96	0.98	0.97	0.97	0.94	0.98	0.98	0.99				

3.2.2. Effects of Player Type

As each value of c was iterated 9 times in Group 1, the number of decisions for each value of c across the four members of each type was $4 \times 9 =$
36. The corresponding number of decisions in Group 2 was $4 \times 10 = 40$ for
a total of 76 decisions by each type across the two groups. The upper left-
hand panel of Table 4 presents the percentage of entry decisions for each value
of c by player type. For example, when c = 5 was presented, players of type
1 in Group 1 entered the market a total of 22 (out of 36) times, whereas players

Table 4. Percentage of Entry Decisions across Blocks by Market Capacity Value, Player Type,
and Study

	Experiment 1, Present Study Player Type						RSW Study Player Type					
c	1	2	3	4	5	**Mean**	1	2	3	4	5	**Mean**
1	1.3	6.6	1.3	2.6	0	**2.37**	0	2.5	8.7	1.2	2.5	**3.00**
3	32.9	21.1	2.6	1.3	0	**11.58**	6.3	33.8	5.0	1.2	5.0	**10.25**
5	56.6	38.2	10.5	2.6	1.3	**21.84**	20.0	52.5	15.0	10.0	2.5	**20.00**
7	68.4	50.0	18.4	1.3	1.3	**27.89**	31.2	60.0	28.8	13.7	16.2	**30.00**
9	72.4	63.2	28.9	7.9	7.9	**38.68**	37.5	72.5	40.0	20.0	28.7	**39.75**
11	85.5	64.5	43.4	11.8	10.5	**43.16**	50.0	85.0	50.0	26.3	27.5	**47.75**
13	88.2	80.3	52.6	43.4	21.1	**57.11**	65.0	81.2	61.3	31.2	37.5	**55.25**
15	93.4	75.0	67.1	48.7	35.5	**63.95**	82.5	80.0	67.5	52.5	42.5	**65.00**
17	81.6	92.1	86.8	63.2	35.5	**71.84**	85.0	92.5	86.3	53.7	41.3	**71.75**
19	88.2	85.5	89.5	78.9	63.2	**81.05**	85.0	97.5	88.7	80.0	51.3	**80.50**
Mean	**68.2**	**57.6**	**40.1**	**26.2**	**17.6**	**41.95**	**46.3**	**65.8**	**45.1**	**29.0**	**25.5**	**42.33**

	Experiment 2, Present Study Player Type						Simulation Results for Exp. 1 Player Type					
c	1	2	3	4	5	**Mean**	1	2	3	4	5	**Mean**
1	1.8	1.8	3.6	0	12.5	**3.93**	6.2	1.0	0.7	0.3	0.2	**1.7**
3	37.5	3.6	12.5	5.4	12.5	**14.29**	33.8	1.6	0	0	0	**7.1**
5	60.7	17.9	19.6	14.3	32.1	**28.93**	73.0	12.5	2.1	1.3	1.2	**18.0**
7	69.6	28.6	19.6	10.7	30.4	**31.79**	88.8	48.2	5.4	2.5	2.2	**29.4**
9	69.6	58.9	21.4	23.2	37.5	**42.14**	95.0	85.0	12.4	3.82	2.8	**39.8**
11	67.9	64.3	26.9	25.0	44.6	**45.71**	95.8	93.8	37.4	4.2	1.6	**46.6**
13	66.1	80.4	42.9	46.4	42.9	**55.71**	99.1	96.4	83.4	13.3	6.3	**59.7**
15	69.6	71.4	60.7	58.9	50.0	**62.14**	99.5	98.6	93.6	30.7	10.9	**66.7**
17	82.1	75.0	78.6	75.0	58.9	**73.90**	99.6	99.3	98.0	76.1	22.4	**79.1**
19	91.1	83.9	83.9	75.0	66.1	**80.00**	99.2	99.2	98.7	94.9	65.5	**91.5**
Mean	**61.6**	**48.6**	**37.0**	**33.4**	**38.9**	**43.86**	**79.0**	**63.6**	**43.2**	**22.7**	**11.3**	**44.0**

of type 1 in Group 2 entered the market a total of 21 (out of 40) times. Therefore, the percentage of entry by type 1 players across the two groups in this
case was $43/76 = 56.6$. The upper right-hand panel in Table 4 presents the corresponding percentages of entry decisions computed across the two groups in
the RSW study.

Inspection of the two upper panels in Table 4 shows that, for each of the
five types, the percentages of entry decisions increase in the value of c. There
are a few exceptions for high values of c presented to type 1 and 2 players,
but they are mostly minor. The bottom row of the upper left-hand panel shows
that, as might be expected, the mean percentage of entry in Experiment 1
sharply decreases across types from 68.2 for type 1 to 17.6 for type 5. In correspondence with monotonicity of the equilibria and basic economic reasoning, the lower the entry fee the higher the rate of entry. This is not the case
for the RSW study, in which the type 2 players were shown to enter the market
significantly more often than the type 1 players (see RSW for details). A comparison of the two upper panels shows that, quite unexpectedly, elimination of
the common knowledge of the distribution of types actually *improved* the coordination between types.

The hypotheses derived above from the monotonicity of the equilibria
are statements of the type "100% of all players of type x will enter," or
"0% of all players of type x will not enter." Clearly, all of these extreme
hypotheses are rejected by the results presented in Table 4. Stronger support
for them is reported if we relax the criteria for hypothesis testing by substituting 85% for 100% and 15% for 0% in these statements. The hypothesis that if $c \geq 9$, then all players of type 1 will enter is supported for $c \geq 11$
but not $c = 9$. The hypothesis that if $c \geq 17$, then all players of types 2 and 3
will enter is clearly supported. The hypothesis that if $c \leq 7$, then no player
of types 3, 4, or 5 will enter is supported for all cases except $c = 7$ for
type 3. The fourth hypothesis that if $c \leq 15$, then players of type 5 will
never enter is supported for $1 \leq c \leq 11$ but not $13 \leq c \leq 15$. We observe percentages of entry for type 5 players as high as 21.1 for $c = 13$ and 35.5 for
$c = 15$. Overall, support for the monotonicity of the equilibria within types
is moderate.

3.2.3. Cutoff Decision Rules

The findings reported above indicate remarkable coordination on the
group and slightly worse coordination on the type level. The latter finding is
mostly due to the tendency of low entry players not to enter as often as predicted and high entry fee players to enter too often. Table 2 shows fluctuations
in the frequencies of entry that decline with experience. However, even after
the frequencies stabilize in the second part of the session, the group results

tell us nothing about individual behavior. RSW reported switches in individual decisions between successive presentations of the same value of c, which decreased across blocks but did not disappear completely. This led them to hypothesize that individual players use cutoff decision rules of the kind

"enter if and only if $c \geq c_i^*(t)$"

where $c_i^*(t)$ is some positive real valued number that may vary across players. Moreover, RSW hypothesized that the value of the individual cutoff value changes across trials but that the magnitude of the change decreases with experience. This implies convergence to individual decision rules with *fixed* cutoff: $c_i^*(t) \rightarrow c_i^*$ as $t \rightarrow \infty$. A uniform distribution of the cutoff values c_i^* across the n players constitutes a sufficient condition for equilibrium behavior by the aggregate. If, in addition, these cutoff values increase with entry fee, the frequency of entry decisions will decrease as the entry fee increases.

To test the RSW hypothesis, we examined the (binary) decisions of each subject by block. We classified a subject as using a cutoff decision rule in a given block of ten trials, if, corresponding to the ascending values of c, her *ten decisions* could be arranged as a sequence of k No decisions followed by a sequence of 10 − k Yes decisions (k = 0, 1, . . . , 10). For example, if the subject entered on all ten values of c, then k = 0; if she never entered, then k = 10; and if she only entered on c = 1, 3, 5, and 7, then k = 4.

The top row of Table 5 presents the percentages of the (inferred) cutoff decision rules in Experiment 1. Each entry in blocks 1 through 9 is based on 40 cases; the entry in block 10 is based only on the 20 decisions of the members of Group 2. Table 5 shows a steady increase in the percentage of cutoff decision rules from 25 in block 1 to 90 in block 10. These results strongly support the RSW hypothesis. For comparison purposes, the second row of Table 5 displays the percentages of (inferred) cutoff decision rules for the 40 subjects in the RSW study. We used a t-test, one for each block, to test the null hypothesis of equality of percentage of cutoff decision rules between

Table 5. Percentage of Cutoff Decision Rules across Player Types by Block and Study

	Block									
	1	2	3	4	5	6	7	8	9	10
Experiment 1	25.0	50.0	62.5	60.0	62.5	80.0	65.0	77.5	75.0	90.0
RSW Study	32.5	47.5	42.5	52.5	62.5	60.0	75.0	75.0	82.5	85.0
Simulation	36.8	65.8	74.7	81.1	89.3	93.2	95.7	97.0	98.2	98.5
Experiment 2	35.0	47.5	42.5	37.5	50.0	50.0	47.5	–	–	–

Experiment 1 and the RSW study. None of the ten t-tests rejected the equality hypothesis.

If a subject displayed a cutoff decision rule by staying on all market capacity values smaller than c' and entering on all values equal to or larger than c', we estimated his cutoff value for this block to be equal to c'. Of the 40 subjects in Experiment 1, 30 (75%) used a cutoff decision rule on the last block of trials (block 9 for Group 1 and block 10 for Group 2). The frequencies of the inferred cutoff values c' for these 30 cases are listed below:

c'	1	3	5	7	9	11	13	15	17	19	20
Frequency	0	3	4	0	3	3	3	1	2	6	5

Five subjects who never entered on the last block were assigned a cutoff values of $c' = 20$. We cannot reject the hypothesis that the estimated values of c' on the last block are distributed uniformly on the interval [3, 20] $(\chi^2(4) = 7.33, p > 0.1.)$

3.2.4. Adaptive Learning

To account for the emergence of coordination in their study, RSW proposed a parsimonious model of adaptive learning. Briefly, the model assumes that initially the players' decisions are determined by cutoff decision rules with cutoff values that may differ across players. Different cutoff values possibly reflect differences between players in risk attitude that are not necessarily related to player type. The model further assumes that the individual cutoff values $c_i^*(t)$ vary from trial t to trial t + 1 depending on player i's decision and payoff on trial t. The effect of the two parameters that govern the change in the cutoff values is assumed to diminish with experience. Because the model makes no use of the prior common knowledge of the distribution of types, it is testable with the data of Experiment 1. Thus, Experiment 1 provides an *independent* set of data for testing the RSW model.

Formally, the RSW model assumes that initially, at the beginning of trial 1 before the value of c is chosen and presented, each player determines his decision by using a cutoff decision rule of the kind

"enter if and only if $c \geq c_i^*(t = 1)$."

We make no attempt to estimate the initial cutoff values from the data. Rather, as in RSW, we assume that they are drawn randomly from a uniform distribution defined over the real interval $[1, n]$. In particular, $c_i^*(t = 1)$ does not depend on player type.

In revising the cutoff values, the model treats differently players who either entered or stayed out on trial t. Player i of type j who *stayed out* on trial t is assumed to compare his payoff (v) to the payoff that he would have received if entering $(k + r(c - m) - h_j)$. His cutoff value is revised as follows:

$$c_i^*(t+1) = \begin{matrix} c_i^*(t) - w^+(t)[(k + r(c - m) - h_j) - v], \text{ if } k + r(c - m) - h_j > v \\ c_i^*(t), \qquad\qquad\qquad\qquad\qquad \text{otherwise.} \end{matrix} \qquad (2)$$

The parameter $w^+(t)$ is a decision weight reflecting the effect of the opportunity loss due to staying out on trial t. Similarly to RSW, we assume the same decision weight for all the n players in order to achieve parsimony.

Player i of type j who *entered* the market on trial t is assumed to compare his payoff to the payoff he would have received if staying out. His cutoff value is revised as follows:

$$c_i^*(t+1) = \begin{matrix} c_i^*(t) + w^-(t)[v - (k + r(c - m) - h_j)], \text{ if } v \geq (k + r(c - m) - h_j) \\ c_i^*(t), \qquad\qquad\qquad\qquad\qquad \text{otherwise.} \end{matrix} \qquad (3)$$

The parameter $w^-(t)$ has the same opportunity loss interpretation as $w^+(t)$. The two decision weights are assumed to be discounted in time:

$$w^+(t+1) = (1 - d)w^+(t)$$

and

$$w^-(t+1) = (1 - d)w^-(t),$$

where d $(0 \leq d < 1)$ is a discount parameter. To compare our results with RSW, we assume the same discount rate for both decision weights.

We also follow RSW by allowing for deviations from the cutoff decision rule. This is accomplished by assuming that player i follows the cutoff decision rule with probability $1 - e_i(t)$, but makes the opposite decision than that prescribed by the rule with ("error") probability $e_i(t)$, where

$$e_i(t) = q_i(t)\exp[-|c - c_i^*(t)|].$$

Thus, the probability of deviating from the cutoff decision rule increases as the absolute difference between the market capacity value and the cutoff value decreases. In the present study, we assume that $q_i(t)$ does not change across trials: $q_i(t) = q_i$ for all t.

To recapitulate, the RSW learning model includes four parameters: the two decision weights $w^+(t)$ and $w^-(t)$, which are discounted with time, the common discount factor d, and the individual "error" parameter q_i. The former three parameters assume the same values for all the n players, whereas the latter parameter varies across players. In testing the model, we search for the best fitting values of the former three parameters, but assume that the values of q_i are randomly sampled from a uniform distribution defined on the real interval [0, 1].

Parameter values were estimated by simulating the model with 100 groups each including n = 20 artificial players. The simulated players were subjected to the same sequence of c values as the real subjects in Groups 1 and 2. Thus, the 100 simulations for each of the two experimental groups only differed from one another in the seed numbers that determined the initial cutoff values $c_i^*(t = 1)$ and the individual error parameters q_i. Table 6 presents the three best fitting parameter values for each group separately and the associated sum of squared deviations (SSD) between the observed and simulated frequencies of entry. The best fitting parameter values were found through an extensive search of a 3-dimensional grid. With a coarse grid, one cannot search all possible values of the parameters. It is possible, therefore, that the search terminated with an inferior saddle point. However, if this were the case, any superior set of parameter values would only improve the goodness of fit of the model. Table 6 shows that the estimated parameter values for the two groups are very similar to each other, reflecting the similarity between the two groups that we reported earlier. We observe a smaller SSD value for Group 2 than Group 1, again reflecting the better coordination achieved by the naïve subjects.

Table 7 presents the simulated mean frequencies of entry using the same format as Tables 2 and 3. The simulated results are reported separately for each group. Similarly to Table 2, we do not notice any significant differences between the simulated entry frequencies of the two groups. Comparison of Tables 2 and 7 shows that the model captures the major trends in the data. There seem to be only two differences between the observed and simulated entry frequencies. First, the simulated entry frequencies for c = 19 and to a lesser degree for c = 17 are higher than the corresponding frequencies of the real subjects. For c = 19, the model yields higher frequencies of entry than those observed

Table 6. Best Fitting Parameter Values for the Simulations of the Learning Model for Experiment 1

Group	$w^+ (t = 1)$	$w^- (t = 1)$	d	SSD
1	0.96	0.82	0.036	46,296
2	0.97	0.61	0.028	41,594

Table 7. Mean Number of Simulated Entry Frequencies by Market Capacity Value, Block, and Group (Experiment 1, Present Study)

Group 1

c	Block										Total	Mean	SD	m*(c)
	1	2	3	4	5	6	7	8	9	10				
1	1.1	0.3	0.3	0.3	0.3	0.1	0.1	0.2	0.1	—	2.7	0.3	0.3	0
3	0.2	0.8	0.9	1.3	1.4	1.4	1.7	2.0	1.9	—	11.6	1.3	0.6	2
5	3.4	2.9	2.5	2.9	4.0	4.1	4.1	4.0	4.0	—	31.8	3.5	0.6	4
7	5.4	5.0	5.8	4.8	6.5	6.3	5.9	6.1	6.2	—	52.0	5.8	0.6	5 (6)
9	9.0	6.5	7.9	8.0	7.9	7.9	7.9	8.0	8.0	—	71.0	7.9	0.6	7 (8)
11	6.7	10.4	9.1	9.2	10.1	9.2	9.4	9.1	8.9	—	81.9	9.1	1.0	9
13	14.5	10.6	11.9	11.3	11.9	11.5	11.8	11.8	11.9	—	107.2	11.9	1.1	11
15	15.7	13.5	12.9	14.1	13.6	12.7	12.5	12.4	12.4	—	119.6	13.3	1.1	12 (13)
17	15.4	17.6	15.6	16.2	15.5	15.4	15.1	15.3	15.1	—	141.2	15.6	0.8	14 (15)
19	18.3	18.3	18.9	18.4	18.5	18.3	18.1	18.0	17.6	—	164.4	18.3	0.3	16
Total	89.6	85.9	85.8	86.5	89.5	87.0	86.5	86.7	86.2	—	783.6	87.1		80 (84)
Corr.	0.96	0.99	0.99	0.99	1.00	1.00	1.00	1.00	1.00	—				

Group 2

c	Block										Total	Mean	SD	m*(c)
	1	2	3	4	5	6	7	8	9	10				
1	1.0	0.4	0.5	0.3	0.4	0.2	0.3	0.3	0.2	0.1	3.5	0.4	0.3	0
3	0.2	0.9	1.3	1.4	1.6	1.6	1.8	2.0	2.3	2.3	15.4	1.5	0.7	2
5	3.4	2.8	2.4	3.2	4.5	4.2	4.0	4.0	4.1	4.0	36.6	3.7	0.7	4
7	5.9	5.4	5.9	5.0	6.6	6.3	6.0	6.1	6.3	6.2	59.8	6.0	0.5	5 (6)
9	9.5	6.7	8.1	8.3	7.8	8.0	7.9	8.0	8.0	7.9	80.1	8.0	0.7	7 (8)
11	7.1	10.7	9.2	9.2	10.3	9.5	9.8	9.2	9.0	9.0	93.0	9.3	1.0	9
13	14.5	10.9	12.5	11.4	11.9	11.6	11.7	11.8	11.8	11.8	119.8	12.0	1.0	11
15	15.9	13.6	13.3	14.1	13.8	12.8	12.6	12.6	12.5	12.3	133.6	13.4	1.1	12 (13)
17	16.8	17.4	16.2	16.4	15.8	15.7	15.2	15.3	15.2	15.2	159.2	15.9	0.8	14 (15)
19	18.3	18.5	18.9	18.3	18.6	18.3	18.2	18.1	18.0	18.0	183.2	18.3	0.3	16
Total	92.6	87.3	88.2	87.6	91.2	88.1	87.5	87.4	87.2	86.9	884.2	88.4		80 (84)
Corr.	0.97	0.99	0.99	0.99	1.00	1.00	1.00	1.00	1.00	1.00				

in Groups 1 and 2 and the ones predicted by the equilibrium solution. Second, the simulated players seem to achieve coordination faster than the real subjects. The latter difference, however, is mostly an artifact due to averaging across 100 groups of simulated players. Inspection of individual groups of simulated players shows the same degree of departure from monotonicity in the earlier blocks and, consequently, a slower convergence of the correlations to unity than that suggested by the bottom row in the two panels of Table 7.

The lower right-hand panel in Table 4 shows the mean percentages of the simulated entry decisions by type. Comparison of the two panels in Table 4 – the upper left-hand panel for the real subjects in Experiment 1 and the lower right-hand panel for the simulation – shows that the model accounts for the basic patterns of the observed results. For each type, the mean percentages of the simulated entry decisions increase in c, and for each c they decrease with the entry fee. We observe the same tendency of the simulated players to enter more frequently than the real subjects when c assumes its highest values of 17 and 19.

The third row of Table 5 shows the mean percentages of cutoff decision rules for the simulated players. Comparison of rows 1 and 3 shows a similar pattern of percentages of cutoff decision rules that, with minor exceptions, increase steadily across blocks. However, the rate of increase is faster in the simulated results. Whereas only 25% of the real subjects used cutoff decision rules in block 1, the corresponding percentage for the simulated players is 36.8, and whereas 90% of the real players used cutoff decision rules in block 10, the corresponding percentage for the simulated player is 98.5.

Figure 1 exhibits the mean cutoff values for the simulated subjects. We present the results for Group 2 only; the results for Group 1 are similar and, therefore, omitted. Each point on each of the five lines is the mean cutoff value of 20 simulated subjects of a give type. Because the initial cutoff values were chosen from the uniform distribution defined on the real interval [1, 20], the mean cutoff values for each of the five player types start at 10. Figure 1 shows that the five means diverge quickly, and then each converges slowly to a different value. The numbers presented right to the table are the mean cutoff values at the last trial. Asymptotically, the model predicts that type 5 players will enter on c = 19 about 50% of the time. This is the major reason for the relatively high frequency of entry of the simulated players on c = 19.

3.3. Discussion

As mentioned earlier, it is possible to construct game theoretical models of the market entry game without requiring the players to be provided with common knowledge of the distribution of types, construct the equilibria, and

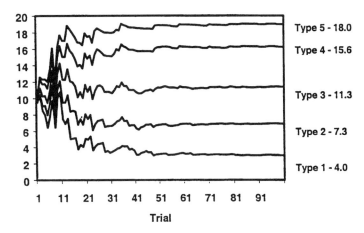

Figure 1. Mean Cutoff Values for Simulated Subjects by Player Type and Trial

then compare them to the observed entry frequencies. We contend that such models are not very plausible. First, it is difficult to justify the assumption that twenty independent players could come up with the same model of how the experimenter chose the distribution of entry fees or learned it during the course of the game. Second, the instructions provided a potentially misleading clue. As mentioned earlier, of the two examples presented in the instructions, one included an entry fee ($h_j = 6$) that was not assigned in the experiment. Third and perhaps more importantly, an informal interrogation of many of the subjects in Group 1 indicated that they had no accurate knowledge of the distribution of types after completing the session. Some the subjects believed that the same entry fee was assigned to all of them. Others suspected the presence of differential entry fees but specified the distribution incorrectly. Most subjects believed that at most two different entry fees were assigned.

Rather, our results suggest that convergence to equilibrium is achieved by some process of adaptive learning that ignores prior information about the distribution of types. The reinforcement-based learning model proposed by RSW does a reasonably good job in accounting for the data on the group level and to a lesser extent on the type level. It also accounts for the increase in the frequency of individual cutoff decision rules across time. Our results show several systematic discrepancies between observed and predicted results. In particular, the simulated players learned faster and entered more frequently on the two highest values of c than the real subjects. We could tinker with the model and improve its descriptive power by placing an upper limit on the value that $c_i^*(t)$ could take (say, restricting the value of $c_i^*(t)$ to a range between 1 and n). Another alternative would be to increase the real interval from which the values of $q_i(t)$ are randomly drawn and at the same time discount them over time. The data indicate a higher frequency of "erratic" behavior in the first part of the experiment. Yet, a third possibility is to introduce different discount factors for the two decision weights, or even go further and introduce decision weights that depend on c value, player type, or both.

However, we prefer neither to add new parameters nor modify the assumptions of the original learning model. While the purpose of modeling in experimental economics is to choose one model from a set of competing models that best captures the underlying cognitive processes of the individual players, one often chooses a model that best fits a particular set of data. The justification for this procedure is that the model providing the best fit is the one that mostly approximates the underlying cognitive process. However, as shown for example by Myong (2000) in the case of model comparison in cognitive psychology, this justification is unwarranted "for a highly complex model can provide a good fit without necessarily bearing any interpretable relationship with the underlying process "(Myong, 2000, p. 190). We believe that the right tradeoff between *accuracy* and *simplicity* of the model (see, e.g., Busemeyer & Wang, 2000; Cutting, 2000; and other articles in special issue of the *Journal of Mathematical Psychology* Vol. 44 on model selection) is best achieved by competitively testing the model against alternative models. Until other models are proposed to account for the coordination in several market entry studies (Seale & Rapoport, 2000; Rapoport et al., 1998; the present study), maintaining parsimony of the model is judged to more than offset the potential improvement in goodness of fit.

4.   EXPERIMENT 2

4.1. Method

4.1.1. Subjects

Two groups of twenty subjects each, mostly undergraduate students at the University of Arizona, participated in Experiment 2. All the subjects volunteered to take part in a single session, two-hour decision making experiment for monetary payoff contingent on performance. None of the subjects had participated in previous market entry games.

4.1.2. Procedure

All sessions took place at the Enterprise Room. The procedure was identical to Experiment 1 with four exceptions. First, the instructions provided complete information about the distribution of types. They informed the subjects that there were five types of players differing from one another in their entry fee, and that the entry fee of type j players was equal to j. Second, and in sharp contrast to Experiment 1, absolutely no information about the number of entrants and individual payoff was provided at the end of the period. The only difference between the trials was in the values of c that were randomly chosen from the set C without replacement (exactly as in Experiment 1). Third, because no learning was assumed to take place without outcome information, each session included seven rather than ten blocks of trials. Fourth, the individual endowment was set at 50 rather than 34 francs.

The individual payoffs for the session were determined as in Experiment 1 by converting the cumulative payoffs in "francs" into US dollars. The exchange rate was 6 francs = $1.00. The mean payoff per subject, including a $5.00 show-up fee, was $25.41 for Group 1 and $25.01 for Group 2.

4.2. Results

4.2.1. Aggregate Behavior across Types

The observed frequencies of entry are shown in Table 8. The entry frequencies are presented for each group separately using the same format as in Table 2. The most notable finding is the very high degree of coordination obtained with no outcome information. The mean frequencies across blocks in Group 1 increase monotonically in the value of c. There is only one inversion of monotonicity for $c = 9$. The mean frequencies for Group 2 show no such inversion. Despite the fact that no information was provided about the trial outcome, there is evidence for learning with entry frequencies approaching equilibrium. Thus, the frequencies of entry for $c = 3$ in Group 1 decrease across blocks form 3 to 2, and the frequencies of entry for $c = 9$ decrease from 14 to 9. The respective equilibrium numbers of entries are 2 and 7 (8). These patterns of change are seen to improve coordination: the correlations between frequencies of entry and c values in Group 1 increase steadily from 0.91 in block 1 to 0.97 in block 7. We observe no trend in the correlations across blocks in Experiment 2. A very high degree of coordination ($r = 0.98$) was already achieved in block 1.

We find no significant differences in the frequencies of entry between the two groups. Across blocks and c values, the percentages of entry in Groups 1 and 2 are 43.5 and 44.2, respectively. Comparison of the mean frequencies of entry by c value rejected the null hypothesis in only one of ten cases: when $c = 9$, the mean for Group 1 (10.3) was significantly higher than the corresponding mean for Group 2 (6.6). Although the players in Group 1 entered more frequently in block 1 than the players in Group 2, the frequencies in both

Table 8. Total Number of Observed Entry Frequencies by Market Capacity Value, Block, and Group (Experiment 2, Present Study)

Group 1

				Block							
c	1	2	3	4	5	6	7	Total	Mean	SD	m*(c)
1	2	1	0	0	0	0	0	3	0.4	0.8	**0**
3	3	3	3	2	2	1	2	16	2.3	0.8	**2**
5	9	5	4	5	5	7	4	39	5.6	1.8	**4**
7	7	8	6	4	8	6	7	46	6.6	1.4	**5 (6)**
9	14	11	13	9	7	9	9	72	10.3	2.5	**7 (8)**
11	9	8	7	8	10	8	10	60	8.6	1.1	**9**
13	14	11	13	9	10	11	10	78	11.1	1.8	**11**
15	17	14	13	15	12	11	13	95	13.6	2.0	**12 (13)**
17	16	15	13	13	14	14	16	101	14.4	1.3	**14 (15)**
19	16	16	17	14	17	15	14	109	15.6	1.3	**16**
Total	107	92	89	79	85	82	85	619	88.43		**80 (84)**
Corr.	0.91	0.96	0.93	0.95	0.98	0.96	0.97				

Group 2

				Block							
c	1	2	3	4	5	6	7	Total	Mean	SD	m*(c)
1	1	1	1	2	1	1	1	8	1.1	0.4	**0**
3	3	2	2	5	4	5	3	24	3.4	1.3	**2**
5	4	5	7	6	7	7	6	42	6.0	1.2	**4**
7	5	7	6	5	7	6	7	43	6.1	0.9	**5 (6)**
9	8	6	5	5	7	8	7	46	6.6	1.3	**7 (8)**
11	11	9	8	13	11	9	7	68	9.7	2.1	**9**
13	12	14	10	11	10	10	11	78	11.1	1.5	**11**
15	15	13	9	14	10	9	9	79	11.3	2.6	**12 (13)**
17	17	17	14	15	15	14	14	106	15.1	1.4	**14 (15)**
19	15	17	18	16	16	18	15	115	16.4	1.3	**16**
Total	91	91	80	92	88	87	80	609	87.00		**80 (84)**
Corr.	0.98	0.98	0.94	0.94	0.96	0.94	0.96				

groups are seen to converge to the equilibrium. The mean frequency of entry in the last two blocks of trials was 83.5 for each of the two groups.

4.2.2. Effects of Player Type

The percentages of entry decisions by player type are presented in the lower left-hand panel of Table 4. Because the two groups did not differ from each other in the frequencies of entry, the results are averaged across groups. There is a strong evidence for the effect of entry fees on entry frequencies; the mean frequencies across the ten c values decrease from 61.6 for type 1 to 33.4 for type 4. The only exception is due to the type 5 players who, on the average, entered slightly more often than the type 4 players. Inspection of the individual data shows that this exception is mostly due to a single type 5 subject in Group 2, who used a "reverse" cutoff decision rule entering on *low* values of c ($c = 1, \ldots, 9$) and staying out on *high* values of c ($c = 11, \ldots, 19$). If $h_j = 5$, entering on $c = 1$ and $c = 3$ is clearly irrational, as the player is guaranteed to lose money even if he is the sole entrant. This subject is the only one who exhibited this pattern and the only one of his group who ended the session with negative payoff. If he misunderstood the game, he received no feedback that might have led him to correct his behavior. Once he was removed from the analysis, the anomaly reported above disappeared. These results indicate that information about the distribution of types serves as a strong coordination cue when trial-to-trial payoff outcome is not disclosed.

4.2.3. Cutoff Decision Rules

The bottom row of Table 5 presents the percentages of cutoff decision rules computed across the two groups in Experiment 2. The percentage in block 1 (35) is not significantly different from the one reported by RSW (32.5). Table 5 shows that the percentage of cutoff decision rules increases with experience in playing the game but not as rapidly as in the RSW study.

4.2.4. Analysis of Switches in Decision

Additional evidence for learning without trial-to-trial feedback comes from the analysis of switches in decisions between adjacent blocks. For each subject separately, we counted the number of times that she switched her decision for the same value of c from block b to $b + 1$ ($b = 1, 2, \ldots, 6$). If a subject did not change any of her decisions between adjacent blocks, the number of switches for the block is 0. If she switched every decision, this number is 10. Therefore, across the six transitions between adjacent blocks, the minimum and maximum numbers of switches per subject are 0 and 60, respectively. In actuality, the observed number of switches per subject in Group 1 varied from 0 to 19 with a mean of 10.5, and in Group 2 from 0 to 21 with a mean of 10.75. Here, too, we find no differences between the two groups in the mean individual frequency of switching ($t < 1$, $p > 0.8$). On the average, the subjects in Experiment 2 switched their decisions between

Table 9. Observed Frequencies of Switches between Adjacent
Blocks by Market Capacity Value and Block (Experiment 2,
Present Study)

c	Block						
	2	3	4	5	6	7	Total
1	3	1	1	1	0	0	6
3	3	4	6	1	2	3	19
5	9	5	10	3	2	6	35
7	11	5	7	8	5	4	40
9	13	9	10	6	9	7	54
11	13	20	10	10	8	12	73
13	15	12	13	8	9	6	63
15	7	7	9	11	6	8	48
17	7	11	11	5	7	6	47
19	10	4	5	7	6	8	40
Total	91	78	82	60	54	60	425

adjacent blocks 17.8% of the time. These results are comparable to those reported by RSW.

Table 9 presents the observed frequencies of switches across groups. The frequencies are displayed in terms of the value of c and block. The total frequencies on the right-hand column exhibit the same pattern of results reported by RSW: the frequencies first increase and then decrease as the value of c increases. The most notable finding is the gradual decrease in the total number of switches across blocks from 90 in the transition from block 1 to 2 to 60 in the transition between blocks 6 and 7. Table 5 suggests that the decrease in the frequency of switches is mainly due to an increase in the number of subjects who, with more experience, moved to adopt cutoff decision rules.[1]

5. CONCLUSION

Coordination of entry decisions in the iterated MEFC game with asymmetric players and varying market capacity values can be achieved either without common knowledge of the distribution of types or without trial-to-trial information about number of entrants and individual payoff. Comparison of the results of each of the two experiments with the earlier findings reported by RSW shows that removing either of these two sources of information does not affect coordination on the aggregate level and possibly improves it on the type level. The Nash equilibrium solution accounts for the results of both experiments. The underlying mental processes that lead players to coordinate their actions seem to differ from Experiment 1 to 2. Coordination without common knowledge is achieved by some sort of learning with players steadily increasing their use of cutoff decision rules that more or less sort themselves into types. RSW reported similar results when they compared the individual decision profiles in the first and last block of trials. In Experiment 2 it is the differential entry fees that serve as focal points for coordination. We observe steady changes in frequency of entry and switches across trials that we attribute to deeper introspection and better understanding of the game gained with experience.

Experiments on interactive decision making that are driven by the Nash equilibrium solution try to ensure that the assumptions underlying the solution are fully implemented. The findings of Experiment 1 suggest that providing the subjects with common knowledge of the game may not be necessary if the game is iterated for sufficiently many periods. The findings of Experiment 2 seem to indicate that in the absence of an opportunity to learn, players will use whatever cues they have to coordinate their actions. These latter findings agree with the results reported by Rapoport and Fuller (1998) on 3-person coordination games and Cooper et al. (1990) on 2-person coordination games in which information about the order of play was used as a coordination device. Additional experiments on group behavior in a variety of settings that systematically delete sources of information about the game are needed in order to ascertain the generality and importance of these findings.

ACKNOWLEDGEMENT

This research has been supported by a grant from the Hong Kong Research Grants Council (Project No. CA98/99.BM01, Rami Zwick P. I.). We wish to thank Maya Rosenblatt for her help in data collection and E. Haruvi for his constructive comments.

NOTE

1. The results of Experiment 2 show systematic changes in behavior over time without trial-to-trial reinforcement. Similar results were reported by Weber (2000) in his study of the iterated competitive guessing game. These results point to a major flaw of reinforcement-based learning models that do not allow for changes in behavior over time without trial-to-trial reinforcement. One could argue that when significant improvement in goodness of fit with a reinforcement-based model is observed, some of the change is, in fact, due to introspection. Although this argument could be tested by estimating one or more reinforcement-based models with the data reported in Experiment 2, we do not pursue this line of inquiry in the present paper.

REFERENCES

Busemeyer, J. R., and Y.-M. Wang (2000). "Model Comparisons and Model Selections Based on Generalization Criterion Models." *Journal of Mathematical Psychology* 44, 171–89.

Cachon, G. P., and C. F. Camerer (1996). "Loss Avoidance and Forward Induction in Experimental Coordination Games." *Quarterly Journal of Economics* 111, 165–94.

Cooper, R. D., D. DeJong, R. Forsythe, and T. Ross (1990). "Selection Criteria in Coordination Games: Some Experimental Results." *American Economic Review* 80, 218–33.

Cutting, J. E. (2000). "Accuracy, Scope, and Flexibility of Models." *Journal of Mathematical Psychology* 44, 3–19.

Gordon, D. (1999). *Ants at Work*. NY: Free Press.

Mehta, J., C. Starmer, and R. Sugden (1994a). "Focal Points in Pure Coordination Games: An Experimental Investigation." *Theory and Decision* 36, 163–85.

Mehta, J., C. Starmer, and R. Sugden (1994b). "The Nature of Salience: An Experimental Investigation of Pure Coordination Games." *American Economic Review* 84, 658–73.

Myong, I. J. (2000). "The Importance of Complexity in Model Selection." *Journal of Mathematical Psychology* 44, 190–204.

Ochs, J. (1990). "The Coordination Problem in Decentralized Markets: An Experimental Study." *Quarterly Journal of Economics* 105, 545–59.

Rapoport, A., and M. A. Fuller (1998). "Coordination in Noncooperative Three-Person Games under Different Information Structures." *Group Decision and Negotiation* 7, 363–82.

Rapoport, A., D. A. Seale, I. Erev, and J. A. Sundali (1998). "Coordination Success in Market Entry Games: Tests of Equilibrium and Adaptive Learning Models." *Management Science* 44, 119–41.

Rapoport, A., D. A. Seale, and E. Winter (1997). "Coordination and Learning Behavior in Large Groups with Asymmetric Players." MKTG 97.098, Department of Marketing, Hong Kong University of Science & Technology.

Schelling, T. (1960). *The Strategy of Conflict*. Cambridge: Harvard University Press.

Schelling, T. (1978). *Micromotives and Macrobehavior*. NY: W. W. Norton.

Seale, D. A., and A. Rapoport (2000). "Elicitation of Strategy Profiles in Large Group Coordination Games." *Experimental Economics* 3, 153–79.

van Huyck, J., R. Battalio, and R. Beil (1990). "Tacit Coordination Games, Strategic Uncertainty, and Coordination Failure." *American Economic Review* 80, 234–48.

van Huyck, J., R. Battalio, and R. Beil (1991). "Strategic Uncertainty, Equilibrium Selection, and Coordination Failure in Average Opinion Games." *Quarterly Journal of Economics* 106, 885–910.

van Huyck, J., A. Gillette, and R. Battalio (1992). "Credible Assignments in Coordination Games." *Games and Economic Behavior* 4, 606–26.

Weber, R. A. (2000). "'Learning' with No Feedback in a Competitive Guessing Game." Working Paper, Social and Decision Sciences, Carnegie Mellon University.

Market Entry Experiment

SUBJECT'S INSTRUCTIONS

WELCOME

This experiment has been designed to study economic decisions. The instructions are simple. If you follow them carefully and make good decisions, you may earn a considerable amount of money. The money you earn will be paid to you, in cash, at the end of the session.

Description of the Task

This experiment is concerned with the decisions firms make whether or not to enter a newly established market for some product. The capacity of the market is public knowledge. Excluding entry fees, which may vary from one firm to another, the market capacity is simply the number of firms that can enter the market without losing money.

You are one of 20 subjects (firms) in this experiment. Communication between the subjects is strictly forbidden. Before making your market entry decision the computer will advise you of the capacity of the market in the present period. We denote the market capacity by the letter c. The market capacity value c will vary from period to period. It will always be an integer between 1 and 20.

Once you are informed of the value of c (market capacity) for the period, the computer will ask you to make one of the two decisions:

Stay out of the market

Enter the market

If you *stay out* of the market, you will earn 1 "franc" (a fictitious currency to be converted later to US dollars) for the period regardless of the decisions of the other subjects.

If you *enter* the market, your earnings will depend on the total number of entrants for this period (which we denote by E), and on your cost of entering the market (which we denote by T).

The present experiment is designed to simulate two basic features of market entry situations in real life. The first feature is that if a firm enters the market its payoff increases if it has fewer competitors. The second feature is that, in general, firms that consider entering a new market differ from one another in their entry costs. In general, the entry cost is private knowledge — only the firm knows its own entry cost.

Your payoff (in francs) for a given period will be calculated from the following equation, which is intended to incorporate the two features mentioned above:

$$\text{Your payoff} = \begin{array}{ll} 1, & \textbf{if you stay out of the market} \\ 1 + 2(c - E) - T, & \textbf{if you enter the market} \end{array}$$

In this equation, c denotes the market capacity for the period. As mentioned earlier, the value of c for the period will be made known to all twenty members of the group. E denotes the total number of entrants for this period. You will be informed of the value of E after all twenty group members make their decision to either enter the market or stay out. Finally, T denotes your entry cost. Entry costs are private knowledge. They may differ from one group member to another. The computer will advise you of your entry cost at the beginning of the experiment, but not the entry costs of the other group members. Each player's entry cost will remain fixed throughout the experiment.

To recapitulate, the computer will inform you of the market capacity for the period and your private entry cost (T). If you decide to stay out of the market, you will earn 1 franc with certainty. If you decide to enter the market, your payoff will be determined from the following equation:

$$1 + 2(c - E) - T$$

Example

To illustrate the equation determining your payoff, suppose that the market capacity for the period is $c = 7$ (this is common knowledge). Suppose that your entry cost is $T = 6$.

If you stay out of the market, you will earn 1 franc for the period, regardless of the decisions of the other group members.

If you enter the market, your payoff for the period may take any of the values in the table below (depending on the number of entrants, E):

Number of Entrants (E)	Payoff	Number of Entrants (E)	Payoff
1	7	11	−13
2	5	12	−15
3	3	13	−17
4	1	14	−19
5	−1	15	−21
6	−3	16	−23
7	−5	17	−25
8	−7	18	−27
9	−9	19	−29
10	−11	20	−31

If, in the same example, T = 2 (rather than T = 6), then your payoff for the period may take any of the values in the table below (depending on the number of entrants in this period):

Number of Entrants (E)	Payoff	Number of Entrants (E)	Payoff
1	11	11	−9
2	9	12	−11
3	7	13	−13
4	5	14	−15
5	3	15	−17
6	1	16	−19
7	−1	17	−21
8	−3	18	−22
9	−5	19	−25
10	−7	20	−27

The payoffs reported in the table above were computed from the formula:

$$1 + 2(c - E) - T,$$

where c = 7 and T = 2.

As you can see, if you enter the market you may either win or lose, depending on your entry cost and the decisions of the other group members. Please note that you are not required to calculate your potential payoffs on each trial. The computer will provide you with a table, similar to the one above, that reflects your (private) entry cost.

You will play a total of 100 trials. All of the trials have the same structure; they only differ from one another in the value of the market capacity c.

To begin the experiment, you have been given an initial endowment of 34 francs. Regardless of his or her entry fee, everyone begins the experiment with the same endowment. Consider an endowment as capital or income that an existing firm has already earned. Your subsequent earnings (positive or negative) will be accumulated over all the trials and added or subtracted from this endowment. The money you earn will be paid to you, in cash, at the end of the experiment at the exchange rate: 6 francs = $1.00.

After the final trial is concluded, please remain in your seat. When experimenter calls your station number, please come to the front of the room to receive your payment. You may then leave the laboratory.

Once you complete reading the instructions, please look up so that the experimenter will know that you are ready. The experiment will start in a couple of minutes.

Thank you for your participation.

Chapter 5

BEHAVIORAL ACCOUNTING EXPERIMENTS IN MARKET AND GAME SETTINGS

M4||

William S. Waller
University of Arizona and
Hong Kong University of Science and Technology

> *Critics are our friends; they remind us of our flaws.*
> Benjamin Franklin

Behavioral accounting research concerns the implications of empirically valid assumptions about human behavior for economic decision-making in relation to accounting systems. Past experiments in the area typically used non-interactive settings. This paper discusses the prospects for re-setting the setting of behavioral accounting experiments to include interactive processes. As background, the first section explains the unique role of behavioral accounting research, relative to other areas of accounting research. The second and third sections discuss the prospects for behavioral accounting experiments in market and game settings, respectively. The last section provides concluding remarks.

1. RE-SETTING THE SETTING

The purpose of accounting is to improve economic decision-making. This *decision premise* is at the foundation of accounting research. Decision-makers with scarce resources seek a satisfactory, if not maximum, return when choosing from among alternatives. Accounting systems can add value by providing signals that, directly or indirectly, inform the decision-making process. Consider examples from the four main substantive areas of accounting, i.e., cost/management accounting, financial accounting, auditing, and tax. In organizational settings, cost accountants estimate the effects on net income of make-or-buy decisions, product design decisions, and product mix decisions. Management accountants generate performance measures that influence the effort decisions of both supervisors and employees under their control. In capital market settings, corporate accountants make financial disclosures that inform predictions of cash flow for investment and credit decisions. External auditors enhance the credibility of financial disclosures by evaluating them against generally accepted reporting criteria. In tax settings, government auditors affect taxpayers' decisions about legal compliance when filing their returns. The research question of every accounting study stems from the decision premise.

1.1. Diversity in Accounting Research

Despite sharing the decision premise, accounting studies are diverse in methodology. Figure 1 classifies accounting research on three dimensions. One dimension concerns a study's assumptions about human behavior. Some accounting studies assume an extreme form of rational self-interest. Individuals thoroughly understand all aspects of their decision problem, including the effect of each alternative on their welfare. When uncertain about critical variables, e.g., state of the world or actions taken by others in the setting, individuals make precise probability assessments and always choose the alternative that maximizes their expected payoff or wealth. In contrast, other studies assume a more limited form of rationality, an expanded form of self-interest, or both. Individuals face cognitive constraints, and cope by using simplified decision procedures that usually produce satisfactory results, but sometimes cause systematic errors. In addition to wealth, individuals place value on personal or social factors, e.g., fairness, which sometimes leads to behavior that sacrifices material gain.

Another dimension concerns the method of analysis. Some accounting studies rely strictly on mathematical modeling. Given assumptions about the decision problem and economic setting, in addition to assumptions about human behavior, modelers derive the logical implications. For example, management accounting research contains many studies that derive the optimal employment contract between an owner and a manager, taking into account available information (Baiman 1982, 1990). Besides mathematical modeling, there are two prominent methods of empirical data analysis. One empirical method uses archival data relating to individuals' decisions in field settings. For example, financial accounting research contains innumerable studies examining the association between accounting disclosures and investors' decisions to buy and sell stocks (Beaver 1998). The other empirical method uses experimental data that capture subject responses in laboratory or similar settings. For example, auditing research contains many experimental studies that examine auditors' judgments and decisions when performing specific audit tasks (Ashton & Ashton 1995).

The third dimension is the setting, or level of aggregation. Some accounting studies focus on questions about individual behavior in non-interactive settings. How does a manager decide whether to investigate the cause of a production cost variance? How does an auditor update his or her belief about possible misstatements in financial disclosures when processing audit evidence? Other studies focus on questions about the strategic interaction of two or more individuals with conflicting interests and differing information. When allocating resources in a decentralized firm, how can central management provide incentives for division managers to reveal their private information about capital projects? When deciding whether to conduct an audit examination, how does a tax auditor take into account the taxpayer's reported income and deductions? Still other studies focus on questions about market outcomes that result from the combined decisions of many individuals. Does between-firm variation in accounting systems moderate stock price reactions to financial disclosures?

Extant accounting research is not evenly distributed among the cells of Figure 1. Instead, there are concentrations in three cells, which are labeled B for *behavioral*, A for *archival*, and M for *mathematical modeling*. Curiously, one may distinguish studies in these cells largely on the basis of theories and methods imported from other disciplines. Since the late 1970s, studies in cell M have employed the economic theory of games to examine strategic behavior in abstract settings. A standard assumption of game theory is that all players are rational, i.e., they maximize expected utility. Further, all players know that all players are rational, all players know that all players know that all players are rational, *ad infinitum*. Common knowledge of rationality is an important assumption in deriving an equilibrium solution of games, and has become a defining feature of mathematical analyses in accounting research. Since the late 1960s, studies in cell A have employed theories of capital markets, and econometric methods, from finance. Consistent with such theories, many archival studies in accounting assume that capital market outcomes are rational, or efficient, in that prices fully and accurately reflect all available information that is relevant to predicting future returns. Since the mid-1970s, studies in cell B have employed theories and methods from psychology, especially the branch pertaining to individual judgment and decision-making. A common assumption of psychology is that unaided human memory is subject to information processing limitations. Many behavioral

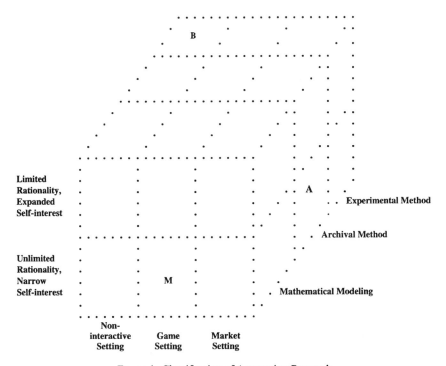

Figure 1. Classification of Accounting Research

studies in accounting make a similar assumption, and search for systematic errors in the judgments and decisions of accountants and users of accounting information.

In principle, there are gains from diversity in methodology. Triangulation, or viewing the same phenomena from multiple perspectives, can enrich knowledge and understanding. Because studies in the three cells share the decision premise, there is considerable overlap in their research questions. In the search for answers, studies from each cell can make a contribution. Mathematical analyses are strong as to internal consistency among theoretical variables, but are problematic as to external validity. Empirical testing of model-based predictions using archival or experimental data can address this problem. In empirical testing, archival data typically do not provide pure operational measures of theoretical variables. Instead, these data also reflect the effects of extraneous variables, which are difficult to eliminate entirely through sample selection or statistical procedures. Experimentation permits tighter control by systematically manipulating theoretical variables, while holding

constant extraneous variables. Such control rules out many alternative explanations of observed patterns. However, experiments are subject to both internal and external validity problems. To enhance internal validity, experimenters
benefit from basing their designs on applicable mathematical models. To
enhance external validity, experimenters benefit from looking for similar
patterns in archival data.

1.2. Response to Criticism

In actuality, the gains from diversity go largely unrealized. There is lack
of synergy, or even constructive criticism, among researchers representing the
three cells. But, there is no lack of criticism. Empirically minded critics accuse
mathematical modelers of making unrealistic assumptions, working on "toy"
problems, and emphasizing technique over substance. Theoretically minded
critics accuse archival researchers of conducting "dustbowl" empiricism in
search of statistical significance, without formal structures for developing
hypotheses and interpreting the results. When critics consider experimentation at all, they accuse experimenters of creating artificial settings, using
unrepresentative subjects, and generating irrelevant evidence. How should
researchers who represent one cell react to criticism from those representing
other cells? One response is to reiterate the relative strengths of their methodology. After all, each method of analysis unavoidably trades off strengths
and weaknesses. When critics accuse experimenters of poor external validity,
a standard response is that experiments enhance control. Uncertain external
validity is the cost of achieving internal validity. Although reasonable, this
response is not entirely satisfying. Old critics and their progeny continue to
repeat, *ad nauseam*, the same concerns about the unacceptably low external
validity of accounting experiments.

A more progressive response is to consider whether the methodology
under scrutiny, with careful modification, can directly address the criticism.
Does the critic's essential point involve a condition or process that might upset
the conclusions of prior studies using the methodology? If so, can new studies
revise or extend the methodology to include the condition or process, and test
the robustness of the prior conclusions? To illustrate, at a recent accounting
conference attended by researchers from all three cells, a behavioral accounting researcher presented an experimental study on individual decision-making
in relation to financial accounting disclosures. A person in the audience, as if
reading from a yellowed script, repeated an old criticism of such studies: "Who
cares about individual behavior? The market is all that matters." The presen-
ter's response, and ensuing discussion, emphasized methodological differences
and the trade-off between internal and external validity.

An alternative response begins by dissecting the criticism to reveal its essence. Expressed logically, the argument of the conference critic consists of three premises and a conclusion:

Premise 1.   Market outcomes are the only legitimate focus for financial accounting research.
Premise 2.   Market outcomes cannot be predicted on the basis of individual behavior in non-interactive settings.
Premise 3.   Your study examines individual behavior in a non-interactive setting.
Conclusion.   Your study is irrelevant to financial accounting research.

The critic's argument is weak, because premise 1 cannot be assessed objectively as true or false. By analogy, suppose that medical researchers asserted: "Who cares about individual patients? The population at large is the only legitimate focus for medical research." The treatments applied by individual physicians, e.g., surgery, drugs, acupuncture, herbs, leeching, or neglect, and the effects on individual patients, are irrelevant. Only population statistics, e.g., mortality and morbidity rates, need to be taken into account. This view is unlikely to have much support inside or outside the medical community. Like medical research, a goal of accounting research is to improve practice. Prescriptions should be based on an understanding of underlying causal mechanisms, and not just past successes in predicting aggregate outcomes.

Unfortunately, refuting the critic's argument does not save the experimenter. Consider a revised statement of the argument:

Premise 1.   Either market outcomes or individual behavior in market settings are legitimate foci for financial accounting research.
Premise 2.   Neither market outcomes nor individual behavior in market settings can be predicted on the basis of individual behavior in non-interactive settings.
Premise 3.   Your study examines individual behavior in a non-interactive setting.
Conclusion.   Your study is irrelevant to financial accounting research.

The revised argument may be correct, depending on the empirical validity of premise 2. Two testable propositions are implicit in this premise. First, individual behavior in market settings may differ from individual behavior in non-interactive settings. An individual may change his decision-making process in a market setting, because he knows that other participants would exploit serious errors. Second, even without change in individual decision-making, the aggregation process may produce outcomes that differ from the average response of non-interacting individuals. In a sequential process, one individual's behavior may alter the next individual's choice problem. After transforming criticism into testable propositions, researchers can design and conduct studies that modify the existing methodology to focus on the critic's essential point. Behavioral accounting researchers can address criticism about external validity, in part, by conducting new experiments that compare individual behavior in interactive vs. non-interactive settings.

The progressive modification of an existing methodology has benefits that go beyond appeasing old critics. Changing the setting of accounting experiments to include interactive processes re-directs attention to new questions that experiments with non-interactive settings could never examine. How does one reconcile the behavioral assumption of limited rationality at the individual level with efficient outcomes at the market level? It is wrong to presume, without direct evidence, that the behavioral assumption of limited rationality is invalid or that market efficiency is illusory. Instead, the question can and should be addressed by new experiments that examine individual behavior in market settings. How does individual decision-making change when the setting involves strategic interaction with another participant? It is wrong to presume, without direct evidence, that individuals are oblivious to strategic considerations or that they intuit the equilibrium solutions of game theorists. Instead, the question can and should be addressed by new experiments that examine individual behavior in game settings. Responding to criticism by systematically modifying extant methodology can open a new and invigorating agenda for future research. In this way, critics are our friends.

As Figure 1 suggests, past behavioral accounting research typically has three features. These studies emphasize empirically valid assumptions about human behavior, employ experimental data analysis, and focus on individual behavior in non-interactive settings. Moving forward, only the first feature is essential to the area. A study is *behavioral*, because its assumptions about human behavior and their empirical validity take priority. Behavioral accounting researchers ask the basic question: "What are the implications of empirically valid behavioral assumptions for economic decision-making in relation to accounting systems?" In the search for answers, behavioral accounting researchers are not constrained to the use of experiments with non-interactive settings. On the contrary, the viability of the area may depend on greater diversification in its methods and settings. Behavioral accounting researchers need to break out of their corner cell in Figure 1, with the ultimate goal of occupying and developing *all* cells in the upper half of the figure. As part of this effort, the remainder of the paper discusses the prospects for re-setting the setting of behavioral accounting experiments to include interactive processes. The discussion first focuses on market settings, and then game settings.

2.   MARKET SETTINGS

2.1. Psychological Experiments and Experimental Economics

Discussions about the external validity of behavioral accounting experiments often mirror the larger debate between economics and psychology (Waller 1995). Psychology and economics both focus on individual decision-making, but from fundamentally different perspectives (Lopes 1994). Psychologists view individuals as cognitive information processing systems that translate environmental stimuli, joined with prior knowledge, into behavioral responses. This processing involves simplified procedures, or heuristics, that cope with a limited capacity for encoding, retrieving, and manipulating information (Simon 1986). Although generally effective, heuristics may cause biased responses, relative to probability and utility theory (Tversky & Kahneman 1986). Numerous psychological experiments have demonstrated such biases in non-interactive settings (Connolly et al. 2000). In contrast, economists build theories of aggregate outcomes, e.g., equilibrium prices and quantities in competitive markets, based on the assumption that individuals maximize profit or utility (Milgrom & Roberts 1992). The difference in perspectives has led to considerable discussion about the behavioral foundations of microeconomics and whether biases observed in non-interactive settings persist in markets (Hogarth & Reder 1986).

A contentious view of the debate sees a contest between psychology and economics about the empirical validity of rational-choice theory. A more integrative view discerns limitations on both sides, and looks for ways in which economics might alleviate the limitations of psychology, and *vice versa* (Smith 1991). Drawing from experimental economics, Smith (1991) stated two conclusions from hundreds of laboratory market studies: economic theory generally provides a correct first approximation of equilibrium outcomes, but is weak in describing the processes of convergence and economizing on decision cost. Economic theory derives its aggregate predictions based on methodological individualism (Blaug 1992). Efficient equilibrium outcomes logically follow from *assumedly* rational choice at the individual level, along with other conditions. This derivation is open as to the *actual* causal mechanisms that produce aggregate outcomes and, *a fortiori*, does not require a process involving rational choice by actual individuals (Nelson & Winter 1982). Although achieving predictive success, economic theory offers limited insight into causal mechanisms. Although validly describing cognitive processes and constraints, psychological experiments suffer from the use of non-interactive settings that isolate the individual from market forces. From an integrative view, a key question is:

> Why is it that human subjects in the laboratory frequently violate the canons of rational choice when tested as isolated individuals, but in the social context of exchange institutions serve up decisions that are consistent (as though by magic) with predictive models based on individual rationality (Smith 1991, p. 894)?

As partial answer to this question, experimental economics emphasizes the role of trading institutions, incentives, and information for learning.

A major contribution of experimental economics has been extensive empirical evidence regarding the effects of trading institutions on the nature and rate of market convergence. For example, double auctions in which each subject may offer or accept either bids or asks induce rapid convergence, whereas posted-price institutions in which sellers make take-it-or-leave-it offers induce slower convergence. Perhaps the most striking demonstrations of institutional effects have been market simulations with zero-intelligence traders programmed to generate *random* bids and asks, subject to only a budget constraint and an endogenous choice set (Gode & Sunder 1993). Using double auctions, these simulations achieved almost 100% efficiency, despite the absence of arbitrage, bankruptcy, incentives, learning, or even use of heuristics. Efficient market outcomes emerge as a result of the institution and environment, not from the rational choice of individuals. Institutional effects are a primary difference between non-interactive and market settings.

Although not necessary for market efficiency, incentives and learning can strongly influence the convergence process. Standard procedures in experimental economics include subject payments under performance-based incentives and repeated trading periods with feedback to allow for learning. Regarding incentives, in contrast with the mixed evidence in psychology (Hogarth & Reder 1986), the preponderance of evidence in experimental economics indicates that incentives matter in markets, by reducing inconsistencies between actual and rational choice (Smith & Walker 1993). The effects of incentives in markets may be enhanced by the presence of multiple, self-interested participants who affect each other's payoff through the institution. At a minimum, incentives reduce noise when more cognitive effort can improve performance. Regarding learning, the typical pattern of convergence in laboratory markets is for efficiency to be relatively low in the first trading period, increase significantly in the next few periods, and increase more gradually in subsequent periods. While this pattern presumably reflects subjects' revisions in bids and asks in light of performance feedback, experimental economics contains few systematic attempts to describe individual learning as it relates to market convergence. This omission may suggest an opportunity for psychology to inform economics about adaptation by cognitive information processing systems. As with incentives, however, generalization from non-interactive to market settings is problematic. The primary difference is that learning is an interactive, social phenomenon in markets where each subject's performance feedback and observations of market activity depend on the actions of others through the institution.

Several studies in experimental economics have examined whether biases observed in non-interactive settings persist in markets. Psychological experiments have shown that subjects apply the representativeness heuristic when making probability judgments, which causes biases such as ignoring base rates (Kahneman & Tversky 1972). Camerer (1987) ran laboratory markets in which subjects traded assets that paid a state-dependent dividend. Asset demand depended on subjects' posterior probabilities, given sample information, and parameters were specified such that representativeness vs. Bayesian revision implied different prices. Observed prices tended toward Bayesian predictions, with only a small bias attributable to representativeness (see also Duh & Sunder 1986). In contrast, Ganguly et al. (1994) reported that prices in their asset markets were persistently closer to representativeness vs. Bayesian predictions, especially in markets where representativeness implied higher prices. Few subjects made unbiased, pre-trading probability judgments, and these subjects were not sufficiently active to drive prices to Bayesian predictions.

Preference reversal is another frequent finding in psychology (Slovic & Lichtenstein 1983). In such experiments, subjects perform two tasks: (1) choose between lottery A with a high probability of a moderate payoff and lottery B with a lower probability of a higher payoff, and (2) value A and B on a monetary scale. Many subjects choose A but place a higher value on B. Cox & Grether (1996) examined preference reversals by manipulating the response mode (choice vs. valuation), monetary incentives (strong vs. moderate vs. none), and setting (non-interactive vs. market). There were task repetitions to allow for learning. Observed rates of preference reversal were high in the first repetition, but much lower by the last repetition, especially in markets. As subjects in markets repeated the task, they incorporated past prices into their offers.

In summary, experimental economics contributes evidence from hundreds of laboratory market studies (not focused on individual biases) that generally confirms the equilibrium predictions of economic theory. This evidence provides indirect support for the orthodox assumption of unlimited rationality, and apparently contradicts the findings of many psychological experiments that used non-interactive settings. A much smaller group of studies focused on individual biases in markets yields more equivocal evidence. Some studies found that individual biases were reduced, if not eliminated, in market settings. Other studies found that individual biases had persistent effects on market offers and prices. Before drawing general conclusions, there is need for more research on the mechanisms that drive markets, including psychological processes, and on the conditions under which these mechanisms induce or fail to induce rational decisions.

2.2. Behavioral Accounting Experiments in Market Settings

Despite their focus on psychological issues, behavioral accounting researchers recognize the relevance of economic institutions, incentives, and information for learning over multiple periods (Libby 1989). Until recently, however, they have not incorporated the *combination* of these market features into their experiments. This step clearly is feasible, by applying the standard procedures of experimental economics for running laboratory markets. Reliance on such procedures allows researchers to examine information processing and decision-making at both individual and market levels, and address basic issues regarding the effects of individual behavior on market outcomes and effects of markets on individual behavior (Berg et al. 1995). The contribution of *behavioral* accounting applications of experimental economics is to examine the implications of limited rationality, and expanded self-interest, for economic decision-making and accounting systems in market settings.[1] An agenda for behavioral accounting experiments in market settings consists of two stages. The first stage, which already is underway, addresses an external validity question. Do biases observed in experiments using non-interactive settings occur at equilibrium in laboratory markets? The rest of this section reviews three studies representing the first stage. The second stage concerns a more ambitious question. In light of empirically valid behavioral assumptions, how do accounting systems add value to economic decision-making in laboratory markets? When future research develops the second stage, its main focus is likely to be the market convergence process (e.g., trader learning given accounting feedback), rather than equilibrium *per se*.

2.2.1. Sunk Cost and Pricing Decisions

Formal training in accounting emphasizes that sunk costs are irrelevant to current decisions. Nevertheless, accountants routinely report profit feedback that compares sales revenue with the historical cost of sales. A possible consequence of such feedback is *loss aversion* (Tversky & Kahneman 1991). Firm decision-makers may be unwilling to accept transactions that result in a paper loss, even when economic profit (i.e., price minus opportunity cost) is positive. A rational explanation of loss aversion involves lack of goal congruence between the firm and decision-maker *qua* employee. The decision-maker's direct personal cost due to the paper loss may exceed his indirect benefit due to increasing the firm's economic profit. For one-person firms, however, this explanation is not available. Loss aversion for a seller with the goal of maximizing economic profit is an error. Experiments using non-interactive settings, in psychology (Arkes & Blumer 1985) and accounting (Vera-Munoz 1998), have demonstrated many variations of over-weighting sunk cost, and under-weighting opportunity cost.

Kachelmeier (1996) examined loss aversion in laboratory asset markets using double auctions. In each market, subjects were five sellers and five buyers of a security. There were 12 trading periods, and the equilibrium price range was 500 to 600 francs, the experimental currency. Prior to trading, each seller received one unit of the security, with an assigned historical cost and a redemption value. The historical cost was normatively irrelevant for trading decisions, whereas the redemption value was the seller's opportunity cost. Any trade with a price exceeding the redemption value increased the seller's economic profit, even if the price was below historical cost. Each buyer received a redemption value if and only if he bought a unit from a seller. A between-market manipulation was the cost of sale in the seller's profit feedback report. In the redemption value (RV) markets, the report compared the seller's price and redemption value. In the historical cost (HC) markets, the report compared the seller's price and historical cost. In all markets, the computation of the seller's reward depended on cash flow, and not on the cosmetic reporting of profit feedback. The buyer's profit feedback was simply his redemption value minus purchase price.

Kachelmeier (1996) tested four hypotheses pertaining to the cosmetic reporting variable. H1 predicted that sellers' asks would be higher in the HC vs. RV markets, because of loss aversion. H2 predicted that buyers' bids also would be higher in the HC vs. RV markets. That is, market interaction would transform a bias in sellers' asks into a bias in buyers' bids. H3 predicted that negotiated prices would be higher in the HC vs. RV markets. Importantly, higher asks and bids do not necessarily imply higher prices. Prices are the result of trades at the margin, regardless of prior asks and bids. Also, double auctions permit either sellers or buyers to close the bid-ask spread. Prices could be the same in the HC vs. RV markets, despite systematic differences in offers, if there were compensating differences in the frequency of trades initiated by sellers vs. buyers. H4 predicted that efficiency would be lower in the HC vs. RV markets.

Regarding H1 and H2, Kachelmeier (1996) computed the median ask and bid in each market, to reduce the effects of unusually high or low offers, and compared the means of the medians for the HC and RV markets. The results showed that both asks and bids were persistently higher in the HC vs. RV markets. The mean ask (bid) for the last two periods was 623 (497) francs in the HC markets, vs. 606 (409) francs in the RV markets. Each t-test for a treatment effect was significant at $p = .05$. Regarding H3 and H4, the results showed no significant difference in either prices or efficiency for the HC vs.

RV markets. Cosmetic reporting affected the subjects' offers, but not aggregate market outcomes. An explanation is that the between-market difference in offers was offset by a difference in the frequency of trades initiated by buyers vs. sellers. In the RV markets, the vast majority of trades occurred when a buyer accepted a seller's ask. In the HC markets, this frequency was much lower.

Kachelmeier (1996) is a good example of how behavioral accounting researchers can adapt the procedures of experimental economics to examine implications of limited rationality in laboratory markets. Reliance on these procedures permitted clear expectations about market outcomes in the absence of a cognitive bias. The experimental setting included market features (e.g., trading institution, incentives, and information for learning) with the potential to discipline and eliminate systematic error. The between-market variable of cosmetic reporting provided the necessary contrast for determining whether the use of historical cost in profit feedback induced loss aversion. The results were interesting and informative. Despite market forces, sellers were subject to loss aversion when placing asks. Further, through market interaction, the sellers' bias induced a corresponding bias in buyers' bids. Finally, prices and efficiency were not sensitive to the cosmetic reporting variable, as the aggregation process negated a significant effect of individual bias on market outcomes. None of these results could have been validly observed in a non-interactive setting.

2.2.2. Absorption vs. Variable Costing and Pricing Decisions

Two functions of accounting in organizational settings are to facilitate economic decisions and, as part of control systems, to align employee behavior with organizational goals. A basic issue is the relative effectiveness of alternative accounting systems in performing these functions. As to decision facilitation, there is much interest in how alternative costing systems affect product pricing (Kaplan & Atkinson 1998). Surveys indicate that many firms set initial prices equal to unit cost plus target profit (Dorward 1987). For example, Govindarajan & Anthony (1983) asked representatives from large industrial firms to specify: "the method that comes closest to the one you usually use in arriving at the normal selling price for your typical product." About 80% specified variations of absorption cost-based pricing, and the rest specified variations of variable cost-based pricing. Under absorption costing, unit cost includes a share of fixed cost as well as variable cost. Under variable costing, unit cost includes only variable cost.

Orthodox economists are critical of cost-based pricing procedures (Oxenfeldt & Baxter 1961). For example, absorption costing includes fixed cost, which is normatively irrelevant to pricing in the short run. In contrast, behavioral economists see cost-based pricing as a reasonable procedure when firm decision-makers have limited knowledge about demand and opportunity cost (Cyert & March 1963). As long as initial prices are subject to revision, given the reactions of customers and competitors, cost-based pricing may be *procedurally* rational (i.e., economizing on decision cost), although not *substantively* rational (i.e., optimal without regard to decision cost). Despite having no role in orthodox models that predict equilibrium prices based on substantive rationality, costing systems may play a key role in the market process of price formation. In this regard, an important issue is whether alternative costing systems, e.g., absorption vs. variable costing, cause pricing biases in the convergence process. Many accounting experiments using non-interactive settings have examined whether absorption vs. variable costing affects sellers' pricing decisions (Ashton 1976; Swieringa et al. 1979; Hilton et al. 1988). A frequent finding is the tendency of higher prices under absorption costing, apparently because of the higher unit cost basis.

Waller et al. (1999) examined the effects of absorption vs. variable costing on pricing decisions in laboratory markets with a posted-price institution. In each market, absorption or variable costing was randomly assigned to ten sellers. Sellers competed by making offers to sell units at a price equal to the reported unit cost (i.e., absorption or variable cost per unit) plus a profit markup. Although their costing systems differed, all sellers faced the same increasing marginal cost function with an unavoidable fixed cost and a variable cost that depended on unit sales. Sellers realized a profit or loss from trades with buyers, observed other sellers' trades, and revised their price offers, for each of 48 periods (i.e., six sets of eight periods). Buyers were automated using a computer program that executed downward sloping demand functions. A bankruptcy occurred when a seller's capital balance (i.e., initial endowment plus cumulative profit or loss) was negative. Predictions of optimal prices and quantities at competitive equilibrium were derived independently of the costing systems. Product demand was manipulated within and between markets. The within-market manipulation involved a random shift for each set of periods. This permitted repeated observations of seller learning (i.e., price revisions) from the starting point of ignorance about demand. The between-market manipulation involved the threat of bankruptcy. Only five (ten) optimizing sellers could break even on average in the markets with relatively low (high) demand. This permitted observation of whether seller learning accelerated when the threat of bankruptcy was higher.

Waller et al. (1999) tested four hypotheses. H1 predicted that the sellers' price errors (i.e., absolute difference between price offer and optimal price) would approach zero over the eight periods of each set. Confirming this hypothesis was necessary to establish a general correspondence between this study's market setting and that of other laboratory market studies in experimental economics. H2 predicted that a bias in price offers due to absorption vs. variable costing would not persist over the eight periods of each set, because of market interaction. H3 predicted that price revisions would depend on feedback regarding profit and price variances. Under this hypothesis, seller learning is a linear function of a prior period's profit variance (i.e., difference between actual and target profit) and price variance (i.e., difference between price offer and average market price), consistent with the adaptive model underlying the behavioral theory of the firm (Cyert & March 1963). H4 predicted that a greater threat of bankruptcy would increase the rate of price revision in the early periods of a set.

Comparable to many laboratory market studies, sellers' price offers converged toward optimum in each set of periods (H1). Overall, the median price error decreased by more than 80%, from period 1 to 8 of a set. Absorption vs. variable costing caused a significant bias in price offers *only* in the first period of the first set, when sellers had not yet observed actual trades and were ignorant about demand (H2). The effects of demand conditions, as revealed through trading, quickly overwhelmed this bias, and costing systems had no long run effect on profitability or survival. Price revisions were highly associated with profit variances and especially price variances (H3). The threat of bankruptcy accelerated seller learning, in that relative price revision in the first and second periods was larger in the markets with low vs. high demand (H4), although this effect reversed in the next few periods.

Waller et al.'s (1999) results resembled those of prior accounting experiments using non-interactive settings only in the initial period. Given feedback from market interaction, the bias did not persist, as sellers revised their price offers toward optimum without regard to absorption vs. variable cost signals. Further, the bias did not re-emerge in the first period of subsequent sets, when sellers again were ignorant about demand. Market convergence did not require individual rationality. Instead, a simple learning process was effective in moving sellers' biased decisions toward optimum. Seller learning from feedback is a market mechanism that helps to reconcile the view of many economists that markets induce optimal decisions at equilibrium and the view of many psychologists that individual decisions are subject to bias. Besides addressing the external validity of past experiments, these results are relevant to accounting instruction. Cost accounting textbooks give detailed examples of how alternative costing systems affect pricing decisions. The examples normally involve a mechanical markup rule, without regard to price revisions caused by market interaction. Consequently, such examples overstate the decision relevance of alternative costing systems.

The finding of no-difference for alternative costing systems may be unsettling for accountants, especially when surveys indicate variation in practice. One possibility is that costing systems, instead of performing a decision-facilitation function, help to control employee behavior in decentralized firms. Accounting serves as a behavioral constraint. Specifically, sales agents often have a degree of discretion in negotiating prices with customers. When rewarded on the basis of revenue, agents may make deals that increase short run revenue, but impair long run profit. For durable products, expected firm profit may be higher if units are held in inventory for sale in future periods, rather than being sold currently under weak demand conditions. Use of absorption costing, along with a policy that prohibits pricing below cost, constrains the behavior of agents with a short run horizon. For non-durable products that must be sold currently, use of variable costing allows agents to make deals that increase contribution margin, ignoring fixed cost. Waller (2000) is investigating this possibility.

2.2.3. Budgets and Framing Effects

Incentive pay contracts for employees have many forms (Prendergast 1999). A linear contract pays an amount that is proportional to an employee's measured performance:

$$w = a + bx,$$

where w is pay and x is measured performance. The contract's motivational effect depends on the employee's marginal utility for b vs. the personal cost of effort, e, that is required to achieve increases in x. A budget-based contract consists of two functions:

$$w = g(x), \quad \text{if } x < t,$$
$$= h(x), \quad \text{if } x \geq t,$$

where t is a budget or target for measured performance. Under certain conditions, a budget-based contract can achieve the same motivational effect with improved risk sharing, relative to a linear contract (Demski & Feltham 1978). In the simplest budget-based contract, pay is either of two amounts:

$$w = w_l, \qquad\qquad \text{if } x < t,$$
$$= w_h = w_l + d, \quad \text{if } x \geq t,$$

where $d > 0$. The design and execution of budget-based contracts often involve the firm's accounting system.

There are different ways to frame incentive pay in a budget-based contract. A *bonus* frame specifies base pay as w_l, and the employee earns a bonus of d, if $x \geq t$. A *penalty* frame specifies base pay as w_h, and the employee incurs a penalty of $-d$, if $x < t$. Although the frame has no economic significance, incentive contracts in practice frequently adopt the bonus frame (Baker et al. 1988). A cognitive explanation is that employees view a bonus as a gain, and a penalty as a loss. Because a loss looms larger than a gain of equal magnitude (Kahneman & Tversky 1979), employees prefer contracts with a bonus frame. In an accounting experiment using a non-interactive setting, Luft (1994) reported evidence that supports a bonus preference. Suppose that w_m is a moderate amount (i.e., $w_l < w_m < w_h$), and that subjects choose between w_m and an incentive contract that pays w_h, if $x \geq t$, and w_l otherwise. Manipulating the contract frame on a between-group basis, Luft (1994) reported results indicating that the indifference point of w_m was higher under the bonus vs. penalty frame, controlling for w_h and w_l.

Orchard (2000) examined whether a bonus preference persists at equilibrium in a laboratory labor market. The study employed a three-step approach. The first step was to replicate Luft's (1994) finding of a bonus preference, but in a modified non-interactive setting. Subjects were employees who made two decisions: (1) between w_m and an incentive contract that paid w_h, if $x \geq t$, and w_l otherwise, and (2) between low and high effort, given the first decision. For each effort level, subjects knew their personal cost and $P(x \geq t \mid e)$. By varying $t(t = 1, \ldots, 13)$, while holding constant w_l and w_h, Orchard (2000) identified each subject's "switchover" point, i.e., the budget at which his contract choice changed from fixed pay to incentive pay. As in Luft (1994), one group faced a bonus frame, while another group faced a penalty frame. The switchover point for the bonus group (median of $t = 8$) was higher than that for the penalty group (median of $t = 7$). Statistically, the group difference was weaker than Luft's (1994) result, and did not emerge until subjects had gone through several task repetitions. Even so, the results support a bonus preference in another non-interactive setting.

The second step was to determine whether a consistent bonus preference, with a magnitude equal to that observed in the non-interactive setting, would have a significant impact on aggregate market outcomes. In each market, subjects were four employers who competed by offering incentive contracts to 16 automated employees. Each employer could hire at most two employees, so that the total number of jobs was less than the number of available employees. The employer's decision variable was t, holding constant w_l and w_h. There were 30 periods with market feedback. Employers used a bonus frame in some markets, and a penalty frame in other markets. A computer program simulated the employees' contract and effort decisions, on the basis of the median switchover points observed in the first step. In the bonus markets, an employee chose the offer with lowest t, and high effort, if $t \leq 8$, or fixed pay, and low effort, if $t > 8$. In the penalty markets, each employee's threshold for t was 7, other things equal. Observed levels of t in the employers' offers, and expected employer profit, were significantly higher for the bonus vs. penalty markets, overall and for the last five periods.

The third step tested whether a bonus preference occurs at equilibrium in a laboratory labor market. The procedure was the same as in the second step, except that "live" subjects were in the role of employees, instead of the computer program. The results revealed insignificant differences between the bonus and penalty markets for the levels of t in the employers' offers and expected employer profit. In contrast with the market setting in the second step, there was no significant bonus preference at equilibrium. Moreover, in contrast with the non-interactive setting in the first step, no bonus preference emerged at all in this labor market.

Orchard (2000) is an innovative study, because of the three-step approach. The first step replicated the basic finding of Luft (1994) in another non-interactive setting. The second step anticipated that market activity might over-whelm a bonus preference at the individual level, and demonstrated that even a small bonus preference, if consistently applied, significantly affected aggregate outcomes. Given the first two steps, the third step produced a meaningful test showing that a bonus preference did not occur at market equilibrium. A remaining concern, however, is that no-difference for the frame variable seems to be at odds with the high frequency of bonus vs. penalty contracts in practice. One possibility is that a persistent bonus preference depends on buyers' vs. sellers' market conditions. Orchard (2000) used a buyers' market setting, in that the total number of jobs was less than the number of available employees. In sellers' markets where employers are free to use either frame, the frequency of bonus contracts may be higher, as employers sweeten offers with the frame preferred by employees. As noted earlier, researchers should consider a variety of conditions under which market mechanisms, including psychological processes, induce or fail to induce rational decisions.

3.   GAME SETTINGS

3.1. Behavioral Game Theory

In David Mamet's screenplay for *The Untouchables*, the protagonist Eliot Ness feels exasperation at his inability to understand gangster behavior, and shouts the rhetorical question: "What is this . . . A GAME?" Like the movie viewer, behavioral accounting researchers would benefit from keeping this question in mind when observing economic decision-making in relation to accounting systems. Past behavioral accounting research has largely ignored strategic interaction. In contrast, mathematical modeling in accounting (cell M in Figure 1) has shifted to the almost exclusive use of non-cooperative game theory for understanding economic decision-making. In management accounting research, the shift was from using single-person decision theory to analyze the value of accounting information for belief revision about a state variable

(Demski & Feltham 1976), to using principal-agent theory to analyze the contracting value of accounting information for motivation and risk sharing (Baiman 1982). This move was complete by 1980. In auditing research, the shift was from characterizing the auditor as a Bayesian who collects and evaluates evidence in a parametric environment (Kinney 1975), to analyzing the best-response equilibrium strategies of auditors and auditees (Fellingham & Newman 1985; Shibano 1990). This move was complete by 1990.

Why are behavioral accounting researchers slow to adopt a strategic perspective? In overviews, behavioral accounting researchers make the point that a distinguishing feature of accounting settings is their multi-person aspect (Ashton & Ashton 1995; Libby 1989). In developing hypotheses and designing experiments, however, past behavioral accounting research rarely makes use of game theory. Several factors contribute to this omission. The training of doctoral students who specialize in behavioral accounting emphasizes psychology over economics including formal game theory. Behavioral accounting researchers often draw their inspiration from behavioral decision research, which traditionally employs a single-person framework. To attain adequate control, experiments that apply game theory normally require a high degree of abstraction in their design. Because of external validity concerns, some behavioral accounting researchers are hesitant to use abstract tasks and settings, and non-professional subjects, in their experiments. Most importantly, behavioral accounting researchers cannot accept the common knowledge assumption of unlimited rationality, and its implications for equilibrium strategies. None of the above is an insurmountable barrier to conducting behavioral accounting experiments in game settings. Indeed, the last point suggests a primary issue for behavioral accounting experiments: Extending prior applications of game theory in accounting, what are the implications of empirically valid behavioral assumptions for strategic decision-making?

At first blush, formal game theory may seem to be devoid of psychological or behavioral content. This conclusion is not true. Game-theoretic solution techniques depend critically on the assumption of how each player forms expectations about the opponent's behavior, i.e., common knowledge of rationality. Knowing one's own self-interest requires knowledge of the opponent's self-interest. Figure 2a shows a game in which players A and B move simultaneously (Kreps 1990). A decides to move up, middle, or down, and B decides to move left or right. The numbers represent the players' utilities for each combination of moves; e.g., if A moves up and B moves left, then A's utility is 3 and B's utility is 6. A dominance argument provides a solution to this game. A's utility is higher with middle instead of up, regardless of B's move. A should ignore up, and decide between middle and down. If B expects that A will ignore up, then B's utility is higher with right instead of left, regardless of A's decision between middle and down. B should ignore left. If A expects that B will ignore left, then A maximizes his utility with middle. Assuming that each

		Player B			
		Left		Right	
Player A	.	.	.	.	.
Up	.	3,6	.	7,1	.
Middle	.	5,1	.	8,2	.
Down	.	6,0	.	6,2	.

Figure 2a

		Player B			
		Left		Right	
Player A	.	.	.	.	.
Up	.	3,6	.	7,1	.
Middle	.	5,1	.	8,0	.
Down	.	6,0	.	6,2	.

Figure 2b

player forms expectations about the opponent's behavior in accord with the dominance argument, the game-theoretic prediction is that A moves middle and B moves right.

Whether actual players form expectations about others' behavior in this manner is a behavioral issue. The above prediction requires each player to ignore dominated moves, to expect that the opponent will ignore dominated moves, and to expect that the opponent will expect that he (the first player) will ignore dominated moves. With limited rationality, the chain of reasoning may be difficult to sustain. Also, dominance does not always yield a precise prediction with pure strategies (Figure 2b). Games with multiple equilibria, and the introduction of mixed strategies, add complications for the game theorist as well as players. Another behavioral issue is whether each player accurately estimates the opponent's utilities, as well as his own. Game theory assumes that each player shares the same game representation including the specified utilities. However, cognitive and affective factors may cause inaccurate expectations about the opponent's preferences. Further, individuals make social comparisons and react when they perceive lack of fairness in relative payoffs. Do the specified utilities reflect narrow self-interest (e.g., material gain) or expanded self-interest (e.g., material gain and fairness)? Analogous to Smith's (1991) question of how traders with limited rationality converge on competitive market equilibria, a basic issue in strategic settings is how players, each with limited rationality and expanded self-interest, succeed or fail to interact *as if* common knowledge of rationality holds (Plott 1996).

Behavioral game theory refers to a growing area of research that examines how actual individuals, with limited rationality and expanded self-interest, interact in game settings (Budescu et al. 1999; Camerer 1990, 1997; Rapoport 1999). The development of behavioral game theory parallels the earlier development of behavioral decision research. In behavioral decision research, experimenters observe deviations from single-person normative models, e.g., expected utility and Bayes' theorem, and explain the deviations in terms of psychological processes. In behavioral game theory, experimenters observe deviations from game-theoretic predictions, and explain the deviations in terms of realistic behavioral assumptions. The following list is a sample of issues addressed by recent studies in behavioral game theory:

(1) Levels of strategic reasoning (Nagel 1995; Thaler 1997). When game theory requires many levels of strategic reasoning, what level do actual players achieve? Do players adapt their behavior to the opponent's level of strategic reasoning?

(2) Fairness in bargaining (Bolton & Ockenfels 2000; Zwick & Chen 1999). How do actual players react when they perceive lack of fairness? How do they trade off material gain and fairness? What is the role of emotions, e.g., indignation and spite?

(3) Learning in games (Camerer & Ho 1999; Erev & Roth 1998). How do players revise their strategies given experience in a game? Does such revision involve adaptation to positive and negative reinforcement, or do players revise their beliefs about opponents' strategies?

(4) Equilibria with behavioral properties (Mukerji 1998; Yim 1999). How do equilibrium strategies change when modelers replace expected utility maximization with more realistic behavioral assumptions, e.g., ambiguity aversion?

3.2. Behavioral Accounting Experiments in Game Settings

Behavioral game theory is highly relevant for designing behavioral accounting experiments in game settings. At a fundamental level, both areas of research share the assumptions of limited rationality and expanded self-interest. In devising experimental procedures and interpreting results, behavioral accounting researchers will benefit greatly from the lessons of behavioral game theory. But, a warning is in order. A behavioral accounting study must include both *behavioral* and *accounting* elements. From the mid-1970s to mid-1980s, many behavioral studies appearing in accounting journals involved straightforward extensions of experiments in behavioral decision research, without much thought about the distinguishing features of accounting settings (Ashton & Ashton 1995). To avoid a similar mistake when relying on behavioral game theory, the new experiments must ensure that their settings involve significant accounting issues. Examples from cell M in Figure 1 include the contracting value of accounting information in principal-agent games and the extent of testing in auditor-auditee games. A close look at prior applications of game theory in accounting should uncover a large stock of behavioral issues for the new experiments to address. The rest of this section reviews several recent efforts along these lines.

3.2.1. Auditors' Risk Assessments and Strategic Dependence

An auditor's goal is to reduce, to an acceptably low level, his uncertainty about intentional or unintentional misstatements in an auditee's assertion (e.g., inventory as shown on the balance sheet is valued correctly). Professional auditing standards provide guidelines for structuring and performing audit tasks, including the audit risk model (AICPA 1999). Audit risk is the risk that the auditor fails to detect a misstatement that exists. Early in the audit, the auditor assesses the prior risk of misstatement. Based on this assessment and a target for audit risk, the auditor specifies a satisfactory level of detection risk, i.e., the risk that his tests fail to detect a misstatement that exists. The auditor applies a set of tests that are consistent with the specified detection risk. Given the test results, the auditor revises his prior risk into the posterior risk of misstatement, which is the basis for accepting or rejecting the auditee's assertion. Until recently, most applications of the audit risk model did not emphasize the distinction between intentional misstatements (e.g., fraudulent overstatement of inventory value) vs. unintentional misstatements (e.g., errors due to inadequate accounting systems). Although the risk of unintentional misstatements may be viewed parametrically, the risk of intentional misstatement requires a strategic perspective. In response to growing concern about fraud detection, a 1997 revision in the professional standards required separate prior risk assessments for intentional and unintentional misstatements.

Bloomfield (1995, 1997) examined the causes of inaccuracy in risk assessments when strategic dependence exists in an auditor-auditee game.[2] Strategic dependence is the degree to which the auditor's expectations about auditee behavior affects auditee behavior, given that the auditee responds optimally to the auditor's strategy. The game begins with the auditee receiving an imperfect signal from his accounting system about an account's true value. When the true value is low, there is a positive probability that the accounting system indicates a high value. Given his signal, the auditee asserts either a low or high account value. The auditor conducts a test that generates an imperfect signal conditional on the account's true value. Given his signal, the auditor accepts or rejects the auditee's assertion. Relative to the payoff for an honest assertion, the auditee's payoff for fraudulent overstatement is higher (lower) when the auditor accepts (rejects) his assertion. The auditor's payoffs include a cost for incorrect acceptance and a lower cost for incorrect rejection. The auditor's strategy involves detection risk, σ, i.e., the probability of incorrectly accepting an assertion of high value when the true value is low. The auditee's strategy is τ, i.e., the probability of asserting a high value when his accounting system indicates a low value. The best-response functions are $\sigma(\tau)$ for the auditor and $\tau(\sigma)$ for the auditee. The intersection of these functions determines the equilibrium strategies, $\sigma^*(\tau^*)$ and $\tau^*(\sigma^*)$, given common knowledge of unlimited rationality.

Bloomfield (1995) relaxed this assumption by employing the iterated elimination of dominated strategies. In special cases, this approach converges on $\sigma^*(\tau^*)$ and $\tau^*(\sigma^*)$. Generally, this approach reduces the set of plausible strategies to ranges for $\sigma(\tau)$ and $\tau(\sigma)$, so that each player remains uncertain about the opponent's strategy. This remaining uncertainty is positively related to strategic dependence, as measured by the product of the slopes of the players' best-response functions. Bloomfield (1995) derived a series of propositions that describe the relationship between strategic dependence and the rate of unintentional misstatements, reliability of auditor's signal, auditor's cost ratio, and upper bound on detection risk. Increases in strategic dependence due to these factors lower the accuracy of auditors' risk assessments about $\tau(\sigma)$, and lower the accuracy of game-theoretic predictions based on common knowledge of unlimited rationality.

Bloomfield (1997) reported an experiment that examined the effects of strategic dependence. Subjects were interacting auditors and auditees with asymmetric information, incentives, and strategies, corresponding to the above game. For control purposes, the instructions referred to auditees as "choosers" (i.e., choosing a fraudulent report or not), and auditors as "guessers" (i.e., guessing the report was fraudulent or not). Sixteen subjects were in fixed pairs throughout the experiment, and eight subjects were "re-paired" randomly and anonymously on each round. There were 25 rounds in each game, with comprehensive feedback after each round. Subjects also had a decision aid. Each subject entered his expectation for the opponent's behavior, and the aid computed his best response given risk neutrality. Subjects played four games, corresponding to a 2×2 within-subject design, with manipulations of the rate of unintentional misstatement and auditor's liability ratio. Strategic dependence was high given the combination of a low (high) rate of unintentional misstatement and high (low) auditor's cost ratio. Strategic dependence was low when both factors were either low or high.

Bloomfield (1997) hypothesized that high vs. low strategic dependence would decrease the accuracy of risk assessments and payoffs for both players, decrease the accuracy of game-theoretic predictions, and increase variability in strategy choice. The results supported all hypotheses. Focusing on the last five rounds of each game, higher strategic dependence produced higher average absolute errors in auditors' expectations about auditees' fraud rates, and in auditees' expectations about auditors' detection risk. Higher strategic dependence also produced larger deviations from game-theoretic predictions and more changes in strategy choice from round to round. Finally, there was no effect for the order of games, or using fixed pairs vs. re-pairing.

Bloomfield (1995, 1997) made an original contribution by examining a behavioral issue, i.e., effects of strategic dependence on the accuracy of player expectations, in a game setting. Relying on prior game-theoretic applications from cell M in Figure 1 (e.g., Shibano 1990) ensured the study's relevance to auditing. Relaxing the assumption of unlimited rationality with the iterated elimination of dominated strategies permitted clear predictions about the effects of strategic dependence. However, the hypothesized effects of strategic dependence did not depend on this approach. Bloomfield (1995, 1997) stressed that other approaches, e.g., evolutionary learning, can achieve similar outcomes. Analogous to the lens model (Hoffman 1960), the iterated elimination of dominated strategies served as a paramorphic representation of how players with limited rationality form expectations about opponents' behavior. The role of psychological processes in forming such expectations is left for subsequent research.

3.2.2. Extent of Auditing and Ambiguity Aversion

An effective strategy of experiments in behavioral decision research involves the between-group manipulation of a variable that, despite having no economic significance, often activates psychological processes. Systematic violations of a normative invariance principle highlight the role of cognition in decision-making (Tversky & Kahneman 1986). Behavioral experiments in game settings can employ a similar strategy. Consider ambiguity aversion. Let $P_k(m)$ and $P_{k'}(m)$ denote probability assessments based on different knowledge states, k and k'. When $P_k(m) = P_{k'}(m)$, choice should be invariant to the content or extent of k vs. k'. To test for such invariance, psychological experiments using non-interactive settings have manipulated the available information about a probability parameter, e.g., proportion of red balls in an urn, controlling for the parameter's expected value. Although the manipulation should not affect choice, subjects often exhibit *ambiguity aversion*, i.e., a preference for options with known vs. unknown probabilities (Camerer & Weber 1992; Frisch & Baron 1988). Many games include nature as a non-strategic player, and represent nature's move with a probability parameter, e.g., the probability that an account's true value is high vs. low in auditing games. By manipulating available information about the probability parameter, experimenters can observe the effects of ambiguity aversion on strategic interaction. Specifically, does ambiguity facing one player affect the opponent's behavior? A psychological variable with no economic significance in a non-interactive setting may be strategically relevant in a game setting.

Zimbelman & Waller (1999) experimentally investigated whether auditees are sensitive to the effects of auditors' ambiguity aversion on decisions about sampling and accepting or rejecting the auditee's assertion. Like prior applications of game theory in auditing (e.g., Newman & Noel 1989), the experiment involved a strategic setting defined by the players' information, decisions, and joint payoffs. Subjects in the role of auditee (i.e., "asserters") asserted an asset value, given knowledge of the true value. The asset was a portfolio consisting of items with low or high value. Subjects in the role of auditor (i.e., "verifiers") selected a costly sample of the items constituting the asset, and decided whether to accept or reject the asserted value. There were 15 rounds with feedback and re-pairing of subjects each round. The design included between-group manipulations of an economic variable (i.e., auditee pay for undetected overstatements) and a psychological variable (i.e., ambiguity facing auditors). The manipulation of ambiguity varied auditors' knowledge about the process that generated the true asset value. Imagine alternative populations differing in the proportion of items with low and high value. Nature selects a population, draws a random sample, and reveals the true sample value to the auditee. In the ambiguity condition, auditors knew neither the population that nature selected nor the probability distribution over alternative populations. In the no ambiguity condition, auditors knew the population that nature selected. In all conditions, auditees knew the extent of auditors' knowledge prior to sampling.

Zimbelman & Waller (1999) distinguished three levels of strategic thinking. In *zero-order* strategic thinking, a player considers conditions that directly affect his choice; e.g., auditors' ambiguity aversion increases their sampling. In *first-order* strategic thinking, a player considers conditions that directly affect the opponent; e.g., auditees' pay for undetected misstatements affects auditors' sampling. In *higher-order* strategic thinking, a player considers additional, potentially infinite, layers of complexity. Suppose an auditor (by zero-order thinking) increases sampling given ambiguity, and the auditee (by first-order thinking) responds by decreasing his tendency to misstate. Anticipating this decrease, the auditor (by higher-order thinking) moderates his sample size. To incorporate limited rationality, Zimbelman & Waller (1999) assumed that the behavior of auditors and auditees reflects zero- and first-order thinking, but not higher-order thinking.

Based on this assumption, Zimbelman & Waller's (1999) hypotheses included main and interactive effects of the manipulated variables. Regarding main effects, the incentive to misstate increases auditees' rate of misstatement and auditors' sample sizes, and ambiguity facing auditors increases sample sizes and decreases the rate of misstatement. The results were consistent with each main effect.[3] Regarding interactive effects, ambiguity has strategic implications that go beyond an individual preference for known vs. unknown probabilities. Ambiguity facing auditors, but not auditees, enhances the opportunity to misstate without detection. Whereas the *psychological* effect of ambiguity (due to ambiguity aversion) was expected to be robust, the *strategic* effect of ambiguity (due to the greater opportunity to misstate) was expected to depend on the incentive to misstate. Two hypotheses predicted interactive effects for ambiguity x the incentive to misstate: an amplifying interactive effect for auditors' sampling, and a dampening interactive effect for auditees' rate of misstatement. The results were consistent with the dampening interaction, but not the amplifying interaction. Auditees were more responsive to auditors' ambiguity aversion when the incentive to misstate was low vs. high, but auditors' sampling reflected only ambiguity aversion, without moderation for the auditee's incentive to misstate.

The problem of separating the psychological and strategic effects of ambiguity warrants more attention. Consider the role of ambiguity in a tax game (Graetz et al. 1986). The population of taxpayers includes strategic taxpayers with proportion ρ, who understate taxable income given the right incentive, and naïve taxpayers with proportion $1 - \rho$, who always report taxable income honestly. When a taxpayer reports low income, the tax auditor must decide whether to conduct a costly audit. If the audit reveals a false report of low income, then the taxpayer pays a fine as well as higher tax. Let α denote a strategic taxpayer's mixed strategy for understating when his true income is high, and β denote the tax auditor's mixed strategy for conducting an audit when reported income is low. The relationship between α and β depends on ρ. When $\rho < \rho'$ (where ρ' is the cutoff value for the "knife-edge" case), $\alpha = 1$ and $\beta = 0$. The tax auditor never audits, and the strategic taxpayer always reports low income. When $\rho > \rho'$, α varies inversely with ρ, and β is a positive constant. As long as the tax auditor knows that $\rho < \rho'$, or that $\rho > \rho'$, the audit decision is independent of α. Graetz et al.'s (1986) game-theoretic predictions assumed that the tax auditor knows ρ. A more realistic assumption is that the tax auditor faces ambiguity about ρ; e.g., he knows only that ρ is in the interval $[\rho_l, \rho_h]$. When $[\rho_l, \rho_h]$ excludes ρ', uncertainty about ρ normatively has no strategic relevance, but may have psychological relevance due to ambiguity aversion. When $[\rho_l, \rho_h]$ includes ρ', uncertainty about ρ acquires strategic as well as psychological relevance, and the audit decision depends how the tax auditor accommodates ambiguity. An experiment with a three-way manipulation of ambiguity (i.e., two conditions where $[\rho_l, \rho_h]$ either includes or excludes ρ', and a baseline condition where ρ is known) would help to separate the strategic and psychological effects of ambiguity in this game. Kim & Waller (2000) are investigating this issue.

3.2.3. Learning in Principal-Agent Games

In games as in markets, the experimental focus may be on equilibrium or process. Experiments focusing on equilibrium examine whether behavior deviates from game-theoretic predictions once the players' strategies stabilize. Experiments focusing on process examine the mechanisms by which players adjust their strategies before reaching equilibrium. Consistent with methodological individualism, game theorists derive their equilibrium predictions assuming players possess unlimited rationality, thus suppressing process issues. Realistically, players with limited rationality cannot intuit the equilibrium solutions of game theorists. Lacking immediate convergence, there must be a plausible mechanism that drives players' behavior. One such mechanism is learning from game experience (Camerer & Ho 1999; Erev & Roth 1998).[4] When game-theoretic predictions fail, the reason may be traceable to conditions that impair player learning. Even when game-theoretic predictions are successful, it is useful to know how players learn. Slow convergence may entail opportunity cost, which is minimized under the right learning conditions.

Many accounting settings involve games with an opportunity for learning over multiple periods. Consider a principal-agent game in which a risk-neutral employer hires a risk- and effort-averse employee to perform a task. The employer can observe output, but not effort or the state. The employer offers a contract that maximizes expected profit, subject to the employee's reservation wage and self-interested effort decision. An insight from principal-agent theory is that an optimal incentive contract balances motivation and risk sharing. For management accounting, another insight is that an imperfect, *ex post* state monitor has value through improved risk sharing, despite adding another element of uncertainty. This insight contradicts the naïve intuition that employees should not be held accountable for uncontrollable factors. To incorporate an imperfect monitor, players must avoid or abandon the naïve intuition and, implicitly or explicitly, replace it with the theoretical insight. For players with limited rationality, learning from repeated contracting is a plausible mechanism for adjusting the terms of incentive pay to include joint observations of output and the monitor's signal.

In general, learning depends on the task structure, as well as the nature or timing of feedback. Management accounting helps to structure the process of employment contracting, which may facilitate learning by players with limited rationality. In practice, accounting systems normally contain two steps: (1) *monitoring*, i.e., collecting direct or indirect observations of performance, and (2) *measurement*, i.e., mapping observations into a numerical scale. Assuming unlimited rationality, monitoring has contracting value, but measurement adds nothing. Consider a setting in which output is low (x_1) or high (x_2), and a monitor yields either of two signals (y_1 or y_2) that imperfectly reveal the state (Figure 3). Because the monitor reveals information about effort, beyond that revealed by output *per se*, the employee's pay function should include two terms:

$$w = f(x, y).$$

Monitor's
Signal

<pre>
               y₁   y₂
   Output . . .   .
           .   .   .
   x₁   . x₁, y₁   .   x₁, y₂ .
           .   .   .
           . . .   .
           .   .   .
   x₂   . x₂, y₁   .   x₂, y₂ .
           .   .   .
           . . .   .
</pre>

Figure 3. Observable Outcomes in Principal-Agent Game

The employer offers a contract with optimal values of w, conditional on x and y. Acting in self-interest, the employee accepts the contract and exerts the expected effort.

Given limited rationality, however, convergence on the optimal values of w may require learning. A step that simplifies the learning process is to express the contract in linear form (Milgrom & Roberts 1992):

$$w = a + bx + cy.$$

With the linear structure, the problem of incorporating the monitor reduces to specifying c. The linear contract depends on accounting measurement, i.e., mapping signals into a numerical scale, as well as monitoring. Further, accounting measurement is endogenous, in that an optimal linear contract must jointly specify c and the scale for y. Focusing on the learning process, a behavioral issue is whether convergence is faster, and opportunity cost is lower, when players with limited rationality use the linear vs. general contract form. Does a linear contract, which depends on accounting measurement, help players to incorporate an imperfect state monitor? If so, then one may conclude that limited rationality is necessary for accounting measurement in employment contracting. Frederickson & Waller (2000) are examining this issue.

4.   CONCLUSION

A prime goal of empirical science is valid causal inference, and a prime method for achieving this goal is experimentation (Cook & Campbell 1979). Through random assignment and other controls, experimentation eliminates many of the threats to validity that plague other empirical methods. Over the years, behavioral accounting experiments have improved greatly as to internal validity. Accordingly, one might expect an increased role for experimentation in accounting research. Instead, the response of non-behavioral colleagues to experimental evidence too often is crude criticism: "So what?" Slightly refined, there are two variants: (1) "So what? In competitive and strategic settings, decision-makers don't act like your subjects," (2) "So what? Even if decision-makers act like your subjects, other variables in competitive and strategic settings overwhelm the micro-effect that your experiment isolates."

Re-setting the setting of behavioral accounting experiments to include markets and games is a progressive response to both variants. The new experiments provide empirical evidence on whether individual behavior is different in interactive vs. non-interactive settings. External validity has multiple dimensions (i.e., person, task, setting, and time), and no experiment maximizes all dimensions simultaneously. Behavioral accounting experimenters can address criticism about external validity, in part, by extending their settings to include markets and games. The new experiments also permit assessments of the relative importance of psychological mechanisms involving limited rationality and expanded self-interest. "The exact course of events depends on the relative strength of different mechanisms at work" (Elster 1998, p. 60). Rather than strictly using non-interactive settings to demonstrate individual behavior in isolation, behavioral accounting experimenters can use market and game settings to demonstrate the extent to which individual behavior matters in determining aggregate outcomes.

NOTES

1. Since the mid-1980s, there have been many applications of experimental economics to accounting issues (Smith et al. 1987). For example, King & Wallin (1995) tested an economic model that predicted multiple disclosure equilibria in cases where a manager must balance the effects of disclosure on investors and an opponent. Such applications base their equilibrium predictions on orthodox assumptions about human behavior, i.e., unlimited rationality and narrow self-interest. Accordingly, I do not classify them as behavioral accounting research. In Figure 1, they occupy bottom cells in the last row.
2. Bloomfield's (1995, 1997) papers both came from his dissertation and share many features. Accordingly, I treat them as two parts of the same study.
3. Ambiguity facing auditors affected auditees' *rate* of misstatement, but not the *magnitude* of misstatement.
4. More subtly, another mechanism is teaching (Budescu et al. 1999). Each player, consciously or not, shapes the behavior of the opponent.

REFERENCES

American Institute of Certified Public Accountants (1999). *Professional Auditing Standards*. NY: American Institute of Certified Public Accountants.

Arkes, H. R., and C. Blumer (1985). "The Psychology of Sunk Cost." *Organizational Behavior and Human Decision Performance* 35, 124–40.

Ashton, R. H. (1976). "Cognitive Changes Induced by Accounting Changes: Experimental Evidence on the Functional Fixation Hypothesis." *Journal of Accounting Research* 14, 1–17.

Ashton, R. H., and A. H. Ashton (1995). *Judgment and Decision-Making Research in Accounting and Auditing*. Cambridge, UK: Cambridge University Press.

Baiman, S. (1982). "Agency Research in Managerial Accounting: A Survey." *Journal of Accounting Literature* 1, 154–213.

Baiman, S. (1990). "Agency Theory in Managerial Accounting: A Second Look." *Accounting, Organizations and Society* 15, 341–71.

Baker, G. P. et al. (1988). "Compensation and Incentives: Practice vs. Theory." *Journal of Finance* 43, 593–616.

Beaver, W. (1998). *Financial Reporting: An Accounting Revolution*. 3rd ed. Upper Saddle River, NJ: Prentice Hall.

Berg, J. et al. (1995). "The Individual versus the Aggregate." In *Judgment and Decision-Making Research in Accounting and Auditing*, edited by R. H. Ashton and A. H. Ashton, 102–34. Cambridge, UK: Cambridge University Press.

Blaug, M. (1992). *The Methodology of Economics*. 2nd ed. Cambridge, UK: Cambridge University Press.

Bloomfield, R. (1995). "Strategic Dependence and Inherent Risk Assessment." *The Accounting Review* 70, 71–90.

Bloomfield, R. (1997). "Strategic Dependence and the Assessment of Fraud Risk: A Laboratory Study." *The Accounting Review* 72, 517–38.

Bolton, G. E., and A. Ockenfels (2000). "ERC: A Theory of Equity, Reciprocity, and Competition." *American Economic Review* 90, 166–93.

Budescu, D. V. et al. (1999). *Games and Economic Behavior: Essays in Honor of Amnon Rapoport*. Mahwah, NJ: Lawrence Erlbaum Associates.

Camerer, C. F. (1987). "Do Biases in Probability Judgment Matter in Markets? Experimental Evidence." *American Economic Review* 77, 981–97.

Camerer, C. F. (1990). "Behavioral Game Theory." In *Insights in Decision Making: A Tribute to Hillel J. Einhorn*, edited by R. M. Hogarth, 311–42. Chicago: University of Chicago Press.

Camerer, C. F. (1997). "Progress in Behavioral Game Theory." *Journal of Economic Perspectives* 11, 167–88.

Camerer, C. F., and T. Ho (1999). "Experience-Weighted Attraction Learning in Normal Form Games." *Econometrica* 67, 827–74.

Camerer, C. F., and M. Weber (1992). "Recent Developments in Modeling Preferences: Uncertainty and Ambiguity." *Journal of Risk and Uncertainty* 5, 325–70.

Connolly, T. et al. (2000). *Judgment and Decision Making: An Interdisciplinary Reader*. 2nd ed. Cambridge, UK: Cambridge University Press.

Cook, T., and D. Campbell (1979). *Quasi-Experimentation: Design & Analysis Issues for Field Settings*. Boston: Houghton Mifflin.

Cox, J., and D. Grether (1996). "The Preference Reversal Phenomenon: Response Mode, Markets and Incentives." *Economic Theory* 34, 381–405.

Cyert, R. M., and J. G. March (1963). *A Behavioral Theory of the Firm*. Englewood Cliffs, NJ: Prentice Hall.

Demski, J. S., and G. A. Feltham (1976). *Cost Determination: A Conceptual Approach*. Ames, IA: Iowa State University Press.

Demski, J. S., and G. A. Feltham (1978). "Economic Incentives in Budgetary Control Systems." *The Accounting Review* 53, 336–59.

Dorward, N. (1987). *The Pricing Decision: Economic Theory and Business Practice.* London: Harper & Row.

Duh, R., and S. Sunder (1986). "Incentives, Learning and Processing of Information in a Market Environment: An Examination of the Base Rate Fallacy." In *Laboratory Market Research,* edited by S. Moriarty, 50–79. Norman, OK: University of Oklahoma.

Elster, J. (1998). "A Plea for Mechanisms." In *Social Mechanisms: An Analytical Approach to Social Theory,* edited by P. Hedstorm and R. Swedberg, 45–73. Cambridge, UK: Cambridge University Press.

Erev, I., and A. Roth (1998). "Predicting How People Play Games: Reinforcement Learning in Experimental Games with Unique, Mixed Strategy Equilibria." *American Economic Review* 88, 848–81.

Fellingham, J., and P. Newman (1985). "Strategic Considerations in Auditing." *Accounting Review* 60, 639–50.

Frederickson, J., and W. Waller (2000). "Contract Framing and Learning in a Principal-Agent Setting." Manuscript in process, Hong Kong University of Science & Technology.

Frisch, D., and J. Baron (1988). "Ambiguity and Rationality." *Journal of Behavioral Decision Making* 1, 149–57.

Gangully, A. et al. (1994). "The Effects of Biases in Probability Judgments on Market Prices." *Accounting, Organizations and Society* 19, 678–700.

Gode, D. K., and S. Sunder (1993). "Allocative Efficiency of Markets with Zero Intelligence Traders: Market as a Partial Substitute for Individual Rationality." *Journal of Political Economy* 111, 119–37.

Govindarajan, V., and R. Anthony (1983). "How Firms Use Cost Data in Price Decisions." *Management Accounting* 65, 30–36.

Graetz, M. J. et al. (1986). "The Tax Compliance Game: Toward an Interactive Theory of Law Enforcement." *Journal of Law, Economics, and Organization* 2, 1–32.

Hilton, R. W. et al. (1988). "Product Pricing, Accounting Costs, and Use of Product-Costing Systems." *Accounting Review* 53, 195–215.

Hoffman, P. J. (1960). "The Paramorphic Representation of Clinical Judgment." *Psychological Bulletin* 57, 116–31.

Hogarth, R. M., and M. W. Reder (1986). "Editors' Comments: Perspectives from Economics and Psychology." *Journal of Business* 59, S185–207.

Kachelmeier, S. (1996). "Do Cosmetic Reporting Variations Affect Market Behavior? A Laboratory Study of the Accounting Emphasis on Unavoidable Costs." *Review of Accounting Studies* 1, 115–40.

Kahneman, D., and A. Tversky (1972). "Subjective Probability: A Judgment of Representativeness." *Cognitive Psychology* 3, 430–54.

Kaplan, R. S., and A. A. Atkinson (1998). *Advanced Management Accounting.* 3rd ed. Upper Saddle River, NJ: Prentice Hall.

Kim, C., and W. Waller (2000). "Ambiguity Aversion and Strategic Interaction in Tax Setting." Manuscript in process, Hong Kong University of Science & Technology.

King, R., and D. Wallin (1995). "Experimental Tests of Disclosure with an Opponent." *Journal of Accounting and Economics* 19, 139–67.

Kinney, W. R. (1975). "A Decision Theory Approach to the Sampling Problem in Auditing." *Journal of Accounting Research* 13, 117–32.

Kreps, D. M. (1990). *Game Theory and Economic Modeling.* Oxford, UK: Oxford University Press.

Libby, R. (1989). "Experimental Research and the Distinctive Features of Accounting Settings." In *The State of Accounting Research as We Enter the 1990s,* edited by T. J. Frecka, 126–47. Urbana, IL: University of Illinois.

Lopes, L. (1994). "Psychology and Economics: Perspectives on Risk, Cooperation, and the Marketplace." *Annual Review of Psychology* 45, 197–227.

Luft, J. (1994). "Bonus and Penalty Incentives: Contract Choice by Employees." *Journal of Accounting and Economics* 18, 181–206.

Milgrom, S., and J. Roberts (1992). *Economics, Organization & Management.* Englewood Cliffs, NJ: Prentice Hall.

Mukerji, S. (1998). "Ambiguity Aversion and Incompleteness of Contractual Form." *American Economic Review* 88, 1207–31.

Nagel, R. (1995). "Unraveling in Guessing Games: An Experimental Study." *American Economic Review* 85, 1313–26.

Nelson, R. R., and S. G. Winter (1982). *An Evolutionary Theory of Economic Change.* Cambridge, MA: Belknap.

Newman, P., and J. Noel (1989). "Error Rates, Detection Rates, and Payoff Functions in Auditing." *Auditing: A Journal of Practice and Theory* 8, 50–63.

Orchard, L. (2000). "The Effects of Bonus vs. Penalty Incentives in a Laboratory Market Setting." Manuscript in process, University of Houston.

Oxenfeldt, A., and W. Baxter (1961). "Approaches to Pricing: Economist versus Accountant." *Business Horizons* 3, 77–90.

Plott, C. R. (1996). "Rational Individual Behavior in Markets and Social Choice Processes: The Discovered Preference Hypothesis." In *The Rational Foundations of Economic Behavior*, edited by K. Arrow et al., 225–50. London: Macmillan.

Prendergart, C. (1999). "The Provision of Incentives in Firms." *Journal of Economic Literature* 37, 7–63.

Rapoport, A. (1999). "Game Theory: Contributions to the Study of Human Cognition." *Cognitive Studies* 6, 142–67.

Shibano, T. (1990). "Assessing Audit Risk from Errors and Irregularities." *Journal of Accounting Research* 28, 110–40.

Simon, H. (1986). "Rationality in Psychology and Economics." *Journal of Business* 59, S209–24.

Slovic, P., and S. Lichtenstein (1983). "Preference Reversals: A Broader Perspective." *American Economic Review* 73, 596–605.

Smith, V. (1991). "Rational Choice: The Contrast between Economics and Psychology." *Journal of Political Economy* 99, 877–97.

Smith, V. et al. (1987). "Experimental Economics and Auditing." *Auditing: A Journal of Practice & Theory* 7, 71–93.

Smith, V., and J. Walker (1993). "Monetary Rewards and Decision Cost in Experimental Economics." *Economic Inquiry* 31, 245–61.

Swieringa, R. et al. (1979). "Empirical Evidence about the Effects of an Accounting Change on Information Processing." In *Behavioral Experiments in Accounting* 2, edited by T. Burns, 225–59. Columbus: Ohio State University.

Thaler, R. H. (1997). "Giving Markets a Human Dimension." *The Financial Times*, p. 6.

Tversky, A., and D. Kahneman (1986). "Rational Choice and the Framing of Decisions." *The Journal of Business* 59, S251–78.

Tversky, A., and D. Kahneman (1991). "Loss Aversion in Riskless Choice: A Reference-Dependent Model." *Quarterly Journal of Economics* 106, 1039–61.

Vera-Munoz, S. (1998). "The Effects of Accounting Knowledge and Context on the Omission of Opportunity Costs in Resource Allocation Decisions." *Accounting Review* 73, 47–72.

Waller, W. S. (1995). "Decision-Making Research in Managerial Accounting: Return to Behavioral-Economics Foundations." In *Judgment and Decision-Making Research in Accounting and Auditing*, edited by R. H. Ashton and A. H. Ashton, 29–54. Cambridge, UK: Cambridge University Press.

Waller, W. S. (2000). "Accounting as Behavioral Constraint: Effects of Alternative Costing Systems on Employee Behavior." Manuscript in process, Hong Kong University of Science & Technology.

Waller, W. S. et al. (1999). "Do Cost-Based Pricing Biases Persist in Laboratory Markets?" *Accounting, Organizations and Society* 24, 717–39.

Yim, A. T. (1999). "Reduced Cost of Law Enforcement: A Model with Ambiguity Aversion." Manuscript in process, Hong Kong University of Science & Technology.

Zimbelman, M. F., and W. S. Waller (1999). "An Experimental Investigation of Auditor-Auditee Interaction under Ambiguity." *Journal of Accounting Research* 37, 135–55.

Zwick, R., and X. Chen (1999). "What Price Fairness? A Bargaining Study." *Management Science* 45, 804–23.

Chapter 6

BEHAVIORAL STRATEGIES IN REPEATED PURE COORDINATION GAMES

Rami Zwick
Hong Kong University of Science and Technology

Amnon Rapoport
University of Arizona

Alison King Chung Lo
Duke University

1. INTRODUCTION

Consider the case where demand for some indivisible good exceeds the supply. In accordance with market forces prices typically go up and thereby decrease the excess demand[1]. However, in some cases, because of government regulation, custom, or social pressures applied by consumer groups, prices remain fixed. To meet the excess demand, alternative mechanisms have been devised to allocate the limited supply among the claimants. A commonly used mechanism allocates the goods according to the celebrated "first come, first served" principle. Seats in popular restaurants (where no reservations are taken) and newly introduced fashionable products (e.g., toys, records) are typically allocated in this manner. Although an argument can be made that this principle treats the claimants fairly, it has many disadvantages including, but not limited to, inefficient allocation of the good.

A second common mechanism is the priority list in which claimants are ranked according to some measure of need, contribution, power, or seniority.

EXPERIMENTAL BUSINESS RESEARCH. Copyright © 2002. Kluwer Academic Publishers. Boston. All rights reserved.

For example, kidneys in the US are allocated by criteria that are based on blood type, histologic match, and waiting time. These criteria are meant to be a compromise between delay of the surgery and graft success (histologic match). The problem with such mechanisms is that they cause endless debates about criteria of fairness that should underlie the construction of priority lists in different contexts. For example, who should get priority by the Hong Kong government while allocating the limited supply of housing, families seeking apartments or commercial investors seeking assets to resell? The criteria for determining priority lists must be socially accepted for the process to be perceived as fair.

A third mechanism, which is the focus of the present study, allocates the indivisible goods (hereafter referred to as "prizes") by lottery. For example, positions in some medical schools (Young, 1994), apartments in new development housing projects in Hong Kong, and prizes in state lotteries are allocated in this fashion. The principle underlying this mechanism, not shared by the former two mechanisms, is of no preferential treatment. Each claimant is assigned the same probability of receiving a prize regardless of time of arrival or assignment of priority. A major feature of the lottery mechanism is that the probability of receiving a prize is determined *endogenously*: the larger the number of claimants participating in the lottery, the smaller the probability that any one of them will receive one of the prizes.

Although determined endogenously, the probability of winning a prize is the outcome of some random device the properties of which are fully understood and commonly known. Rapoport, Lo, and Zwick (2000) noted that the lottery mechanism might also apply when the probability of winning a prize is *subjective* and commonly shared by all the players. For example, consider the case of n competing firms faced with a decision whether to enter a newly emerging market. Although no physical lotteries are involved in this case, each firm's decision is based on the probability it assigns to the event of successful entry that, in turn, depends on the number of entrants. If each firm estimates its probability of successful entry to be proportional to the number of entrants, then these commonly shared beliefs behave like a lottery.

Consider next the case where the demand for several independent indivisible goods exceeds the supply. If the principle of no preferential treatment is to be applied to this case, this situation can be modeled by *several independent lotteries* with endogenously determined probabilities, each offering a possibly different number of prizes at possibly different values. For example, households in Hong Kong seeking to relocate to public housing in one of the three non-urban areas (a commodity in short supply) can submit, if qualified, an application for re-housing (at a fixed rent). After the deadline, flats are allocated to the applicants by a lottery. Similarly, if they believe that their probability of being admitted to a certain program is proportional to the number of applicants for the same program, students applying for graduate studies are basically faced with multiple lotteries, each offering a different number of scholarships (prizes) at different values (e.g., prestige of the program, size of the scholarship). If the claimants can register to only one of the multiple lotteries because of regulation (as is the case in Hong Kong) or high application fees (as is sometimes the case in the graduate studies application example), the problem they face when trying to maximize their expected value is one of *tacit coordination*.

The study of tacit coordination under multiple lotteries with endogenously determined probabilities is part of a more general analysis of contingent behavior, which explores the relation between the behavior characteristics of the individuals who comprise some social aggregate and the characteristics of the aggregate (Schelling, 1978). The objectives of the members of the aggregate relate directly to other members, and these objectives are constrained by an environment that consists of other people who achieve their own objectives. Schelling pointed out that what makes the analysis interesting and difficult is that the entire aggregate outcome has to be evaluated, not merely how each member of the aggregate does within the constraints of his or her environment. As noted by many authors, an essential part of this analysis is empirical.

To study coordination in the presence of multiple and independent lotteries under the constraint (which may be relaxed) of a single entry[2] Rapoport et al. (2000) devised a non-cooperative n-person game, called the Consumers Choice of Prizes (CCP) game. This game was proposed to simulate the basic features of the tacit coordination problem when independent lotteries with endogenously determined probabilities are used simultaneously to allocate multiple goods (prizes), or the system of commonly shared beliefs behaves like a lottery.

The rest of this paper is organized as follows. Section 2 presents the CCP game and constructs its Nash equilibria. Section 3 first presents the experimental design for a special case of the CCP game in which the prizes offered by the different lotteries are all equal, and then summarizes the results. Section 4 tests and subsequently rejects two alternative models proposed to account for the behavioral regularities observed in the data. It then proposes a third model with perturbed choice probabilities that accounts for the major individual and aggregate findings. Section 5 concludes.

2.   THE CCP GAME

The CCP game is a non-cooperative n-person game with complete information. Formally, it presents to each of n symmetric players J alternatives (called *locations*) with m_j identical prizes in each location j (j = 1, 2, . . . , J). Each prize is worth g_j units. The values of n, J, m_j, and g_j are commonly known.

Each player i (i = 1, 2, . . . , n) must decide independently and anonymously which location to enter. Thus, the strategy set of each player includes J elements. Denote the number of entrants in location j by $n_j \left(\sum_{j=1}^{J} n_j = n \right)$. Once all the n players make their entry decisions, individual payoffs are determined for each player as follows:

- If $n_j \le m_j$, each player entering location j receives the prize g_j.
- If $n_j > m_j$, exactly each of the m_j (out of the n_j) entrants receives a prize of g_j. The remaining $n_j - m_j$ entrants receive nothing. Every subset $m_j \subset n_j$ is equally likely to be selected.

The CCP game imposes no cost of entry.

2.1. Pure Strategy Equilibria

There are $n!/(n_1^*! \ n_2^*! \ldots n_J^*!)$ pure strategy equilibria consisting of n_1^*, $n_2^*, \ldots, \ n_J^*$ players entering locations 1, 2, . . . , J, respectively $\left(\sum_{j=1}^{J} n_j^* = n \right)$, such that no single player benefits from unilaterally switching from location j to location j' (j ≠ j'). Given the multiplicity of equilibria, the subjects are faced with a coordination problem.

2.2. Mixed Strategy Equilibria

In the symmetric mixed strategy equilibrium each of the n players enters locations 1, 2, . . . , J with respective probabilities $q_1, q_2, \ldots, q_J$. In equilibrium, the expected value associated with entering each of the J locations, denoted by V, is the same. The equilibrium solution for risk-neutral players consists of the probabilities $q_1, q_2, \ldots, q_J$, that satisfy the following J + 1 equations in J + 1 unknown ($q_1, q_2, \ldots, q_J, V$):

$$g_j \sum_{k=0}^{m_j-1} \binom{n-1}{k} q_j^k (1-q_j)^{n-1-k} + g_j \sum_{k=m_j}^{n-1} \binom{n-1}{k} \left(\frac{m_j}{k+1} \right) q_j^k (1-q_j)^{n-1-k} = V, \qquad (1)$$

and

$$\sum_{j=1}^{J} q_j = 1, q_j > 0, \quad j = 1, 2, \ldots, J.$$

In the general case, these equations are solved numerically.

2.3. The Pure Coordination Game

The present study examines a special case of the CCP game where $J = 3$, the *number* of prizes differs from one lottery to another, but the *prize values* are equal, i.e., $g_j \equiv g \; \forall j$. Moreover, we impose the restriction $m_1 + m_2 + m_3 = n$. The pure strategy equilibrium is simply $n_j^* = m_j \forall j$. The game presents the following task to the group of n people: partition the group into J subgroups of m_j members each. If the task is successfully accomplished, and since $m_1 + m_2 + \ldots + m_J = n$ by construction, the outcome uncertainty is eliminated and each player is assured a prize of equal value. Note that in equilibrium subjects are indifferent to which subgroup they belong, hence a no-conflict pure coordination task is at hand. This, of course, might have significant implications to the dynamics of repeated play of the same game. Subjects may understand what is required of them to achieve successful coordination in this case, a fact that could facilitate their ability to tacitly coordinate expectations and behavior.

3. THE EXPERIMENT

3.1. Method

3.1.1. Subjects

Thirty-six subjects participated in two groups of eighteen subjects each. The subjects were Hong Kong University of Science and Technology students, mostly undergraduate students of Business Administration, who volunteered to take part in a single session of a decision making experiment with payoff contingent on performance. On the average, the subjects earned HK$172.56 (US$22.3) for their participation plus a HK$30.00 (US$3.9) show-up fee.

3.1.2. Design

The design consisted of six different games (Table 1) each of which iterated 16 times (blocks) for a total of 96 trials. The six games were constructed to span the way by which a group of 18 players can subdivide itself into three subgroups of almost equal number of members (Game 1), two small subgroups and one large (Game 6), and one small and two medium size subgroups (Game 4). The sum of the numbers of prizes was fixed at 18 for each game. Under pure strategy equilibrium play, the payoff per subject is $2.00 per trial for a total of HK$192.00 for the entire experiment.

3.1.3. Procedure

Upon arriving at the computer laboratory (which contains about 80 PCs), the subjects in each group were seated at eighteen computer terminals. These terminals were spread across the laboratory classroom. Communication between the subjects was strictly forbidden. The instructions were presented on the individual screens using PowerPoint slide show. The subjects read the instructions at their own pace with no time pressure. The text version of the instructions is presented in Appendix 1.

The subjects were instructed that they would participate in a series of games played repeatedly with the same group of eighteen subjects. Their task was to choose one of three lotteries, called (and marked on the screen) Yellow, Blue, and Red. At the beginning of each trial, the prize value (g) and number of prizes in each lottery (m_j) were displayed to the subjects, who were then required to choose one of the three lotteries. Appendix 2 presents screen shots for the decision task. The subjects were instructed that the game parameters would vary from trial to trial. Once all of them made their decision, the three values of n_j were displayed on the individual screens and the prizes were distributed.

After reading the information displayed on the first twelve screens, the subject's understanding of the procedure was tested through four hypothetical questions that varied the parameter values and number of entrants. The experiment commenced after all the subjects answered these questions correctly. The subjects were told that they would be paid their cumulative earnings at the end of the session plus a show-up fee.

Trials were arranged in 16 blocks of 6 trials each. In each block, Games 1 through 6 (Table 1) were presented in a possibly different random order. On the average, six trials separated two consecutive presentations (iterations) of the same game. To prevent response bias (e.g., color preference), the number of prizes for the same game was varied across colors in a balanced design. The entire experiment lasted about 75 minutes.

Table 1. Parameter Values and Equilibrium Solutions for the 6 games

	Prize Values			Number of Prizes			Pure Strategy Equilibrium			Mixed Strategy Equilibrium		
Game	g_1	g_2	g_3	m_1	m_2	m_3	n_1^*	n_2^*	n_3^*	q_1	q_2	q_3
1	2	2	2	7	6	5	7	6	5	.403	.333	.264
2	2	2	2	8	7	3	8	7	3	.470	.400	.130
3	2	2	2	9	5	4	9	5	4	.541	.263	.196
4	2	2	2	10	7	1	10	7	1	.596	.389	.015
5	2	2	2	12	4	2	12	4	2	.743	.191	.066
6	2	2	2	15	2	1	15	2	1	.928	.059	.013

3.2. Results

3.2.1. Individual Results

Tables 2A and 2B present the individual data from this study[3]. Each 18 × 16 row (subject) by column (iteration) matrix presents the raw data from one of the six games. Each cell in the matrix presents the (row) subject's choice in the (column's) replication (1 to 16). Black cells indicate a choice of j = 1, gray cells a choice of j = 2, and white cells a choice of j = 3. A cell with a dot on top of it indicates that the subject was *not* rewarded on the column's replication. Cells without dots indicate that a reward was given. The top row above each game matrix presents a coordination index that will be explained later.

Tables 2A and 2B can assist in identifying individual patterns of behavior and general trends. For example, cells with dots on top of them are rather sparse, indicating that not being rewarded was the exception rather than the rule. Out of a total of 192 (96 × 2) trials across the two groups, we observe 21 cases in which all 18 subjects received the prize – 6 in Group 1 (Table 2A) and 15 in Group 2 (Table 2B). These cases are marked with "0" at the top of the column. More than half of these cases occurred in Game 6. Across both groups, we find 6, 5, 5, 9, 6, and 18 subjects in Games 1, 2, 3, 4, 5, and 6, respectively, who received the prize on all 16 iterations of the game. Various subjects demonstrated consistent patterns of behavior. For example, subject 13 of Group 2 chose j = 1 on 95 of the 96 trials. Other subjects who almost always chose j = 1 on Games 3, 4, 5, and 6 are subjects 2, 3, and 7 of Group 1 and subjects 4, 7 and 12 of Group 2. Other subjects chose the same location almost always in one game but not in others (e.g., subject 12 of Group 1 in Game 6), and yet others varied their choices across replications. Table 3 presents the games in which a subject chose the same location on at least 14 of the 16 replications. These games are indicated by a circle if the persistent behavior

Table 2A. Observed Sequential Choices by Subjects, Games, and Trials – Group 1

Game 1

Game 2

Game 3

Table 2A. Continued

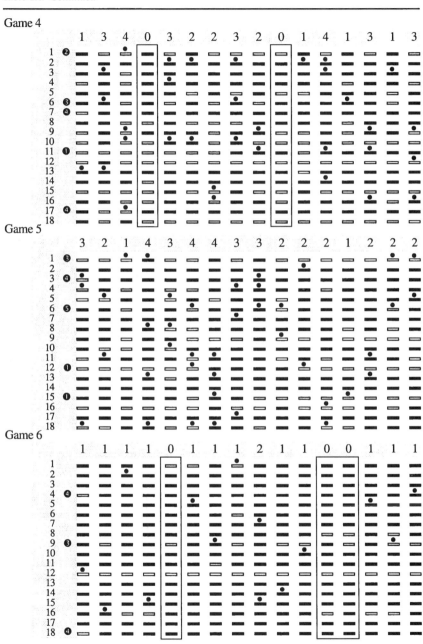

Table 2B. Observed Sequential Choices by Subjects, Games, and Trials – Group 2

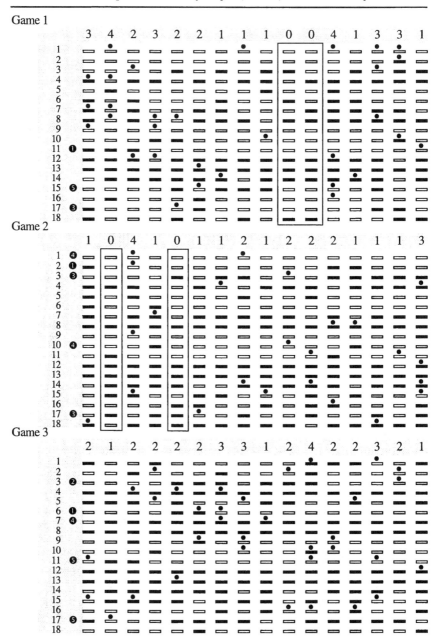

Table 2B. Continued

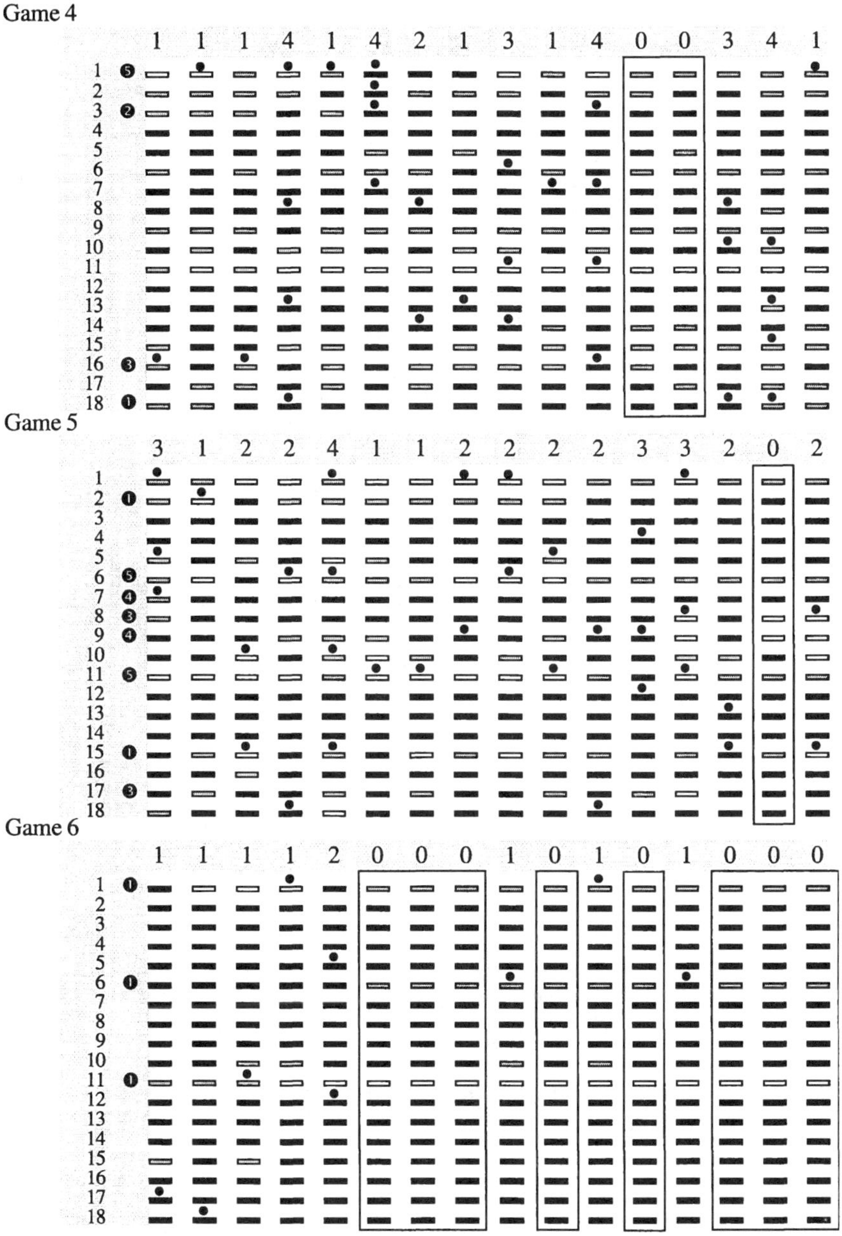

Game 4

	1	1	1	4	1	4	2	1	3	1	4	0	0	3	4	1

Game 5

	3	1	2	2	4	1	1	2	2	2	2	3	3	2	0	2

Game 6

	1	1	1	1	2	0	0	0	1	0	1	0	1	0	0	0

Table 3. Games with Consistent Behavior or Behavior that are Not Distinguishable from a Random Sequence

	Group 1							Group 2					
	Game							Game					
ID	1	2	3	4	5	6	ID	1	2	3	4	5	6
1		×	×			×	1	×		×		×	
2			◉	●	●	●	2	×		×	×		●
3	×		●	○	○	●	3	×				●	●
4		×		×	×	●	4	×	×	●	●	●	●
5		×	×	×	×	●	5	×	×	×	×	×	●
6	×	×				○	6	×	×		×		
7		○	○	○	●	●	7	×	×	○	●	○	●
8	×		×	×		×	8	×	×	●	○		●
9	×	×		×			9	×	◈	×	◈		●
10	×	×	×	×	×	●	10	×		×	×	×	×
11		×			×	○	11		▣		▣		
12		×		□		■	12	×	◉	○	●	●	●
13	×	×		○	○	●	13	●	●	●	○	●	●
14		×		○	●	●	14	×	×	×	×	●	●
15		◇	×	×		●	15		×	×	×	×	◉
16			×	×	×	×	16	×	×	×		○	●
17	◉	◉		◉	●	●	17				×		●
18	×		×	×	×	○	18	×	×	×		◉	●

Index
× - indistinguishable from a random sequence

No. of times observed	j = 1	j = 2	j = 3
16	●	◆	■
15	○	◈	□
14	◉	◇	▣

was choosing j = 1, a diamond for j = 2, and a square for j = 3. As may be expected, most of the subjects (27 out of 36) chose location j = 1 on Game 6 at least 14 times. Taken together, Tables 2A, 2B, and 3 show a very heterogenous pattern of the subjects' behavior between games and across iterations of the same game. Yet, as we show below, a high level of coordination was achieved in all games.

3.2.2. Aggregate Behavior

In studying aggregate behavior, the major dependent variable is the level of group coordination. We evaluate it by a proximity measure between observed and predicted (pure strategy equilibrium) number of entrants in each location. The proximity measure is simply the minimum number of subjects who have to switch their choices, given some distribution of choices, to achieve pure strategy equilibrium. For example, given a predicted equilibrium distribution of $m = (m_1, m_2, m_3) = (7, 6, 5)$ for Game 1 and an observed distribution of choices $n = (n_1, n_2, n_3) = (10, 7, 1)$, three subjects choosing location $j = 1$ and one choosing location $j = 2$ ought to switch their choices to location $j = 3$ to achieve equilibrium. Consequently, the measure of proximity in this case is 4.[4]

The minimum number of switches required for achieving perfect coordination, denoted MinS, was computed for each iteration t (t = 1, 2, . . . , 16). The resulting values are presented on the top of each game matrix in Tables 2A and 2B. Figure 1 displays a 5-trial moving average of the MinS scores by game and group. The MinS scores are seen to range between 1 and 3; they indicate a close proximity to the predicted pure strategy equilibrium.[5] Figure 1 indicates a group effect, with Group 2 exhibiting better coordination than Group 1 in Games 1, 2, and 6. There is also an indication of a systematic improvement in coordination over time for Group 1 in Games 1, 3, and 5.

To test for group, game, and replication effects, we divided the 96 trials of each group into 4 blocks of 24 trials each, with each block representing 4

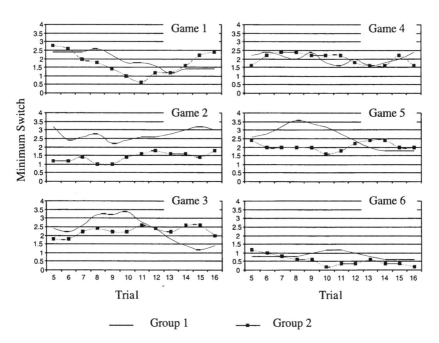

Figure 1. Five-Trial Moving Average of Deviation from Pure Strategy Equilibrium

replications of each of the 6 games. We then subjected the 192 MinS scores (96 for each group) to a $2 \times 4 \times 6$ group by block by game ANOVA with repeated measures on the block and game factors. The ANOVA yielded a significant group main effect ($F(1, 36) = 8.36$, $p < 0.001$). As suggested by Fig. 1, the mean MinS score of Group 2 (1.68) was significantly smaller than the mean of Group 1 (2.07). The ANOVA also yielded a significant game main effect ($F(5, 36) = 12.16$, $p < 0.001$). The Newman-Keuls post-hoc analysis shows no differences between Games 1, 2, 3, 4, and 5. The significant main game effect is entirely due to Game 6 for which the MinS score (0.719) is significantly smaller than the mean scores of the other five games (1.875, 2.187, 2.219, 2.000, 2.250, for Games 1 to 5, respectively). Although the mean MinS scores decreased across blocks (3.500, 2.063, 1.708, 1.667 for Blocks 1, 2, 3 and 4, respectively), the trend was not significant ($F(3, 34) = 2.32$, $p = 0.093$). The interaction between group and blocks was also not significant ($F(3, 34) = 2.40$, $p = 0.085$). Neither of the other two-way interaction effects nor the single three-way interaction effect were significant.

Table 4 presents the means and standard deviations of the number of entries in each location in the 16 iterations. The means and standard deviations of the MinS scores are presented on the two right-hand columns. The results are shown separately by game and group. Also presented in the table are the expected number of entries for both the pure and mixed strategy equilibria, the associated standard deviations under the mixed strategy equilibrium, and the expected numbers and standard deviations of the MinS score with respect to the mixed strategy equilibrium.

The results in Table 4 show a remarkable level of coordination. The null hypothesis that the observed and expected number of entries is equal cannot be rejected at the 0.05 level for all games and locations of Group 2. In Group 1, the only exceptions are locations 2 and 3 in Game 3 ($z = -3.135$ and 2.668, respectively, $p < 0.05$) and location 1 in Game 4 ($z = 2.328$, $p < 0.03$). Shifting attention to the MinS score, the hypothesis that the observed and expected (based on the mixed strategy equilibrium) scores are the same can not be rejected at the 0.05 level in both groups for Games, 3, 4, and 5. The MinS score is significantly smaller than expected in Games 1 and 6 of Group 1 ($z = 1.69$, $p < 0.05$, 4.77, $p < 0.01$, for Games 1 and 6, respectively), and higher in Game 3 ($z = -1.766$, $p < 0.04$). The MinS score is smaller than expected for Games 2 and 6 of Group 2 ($z = 2.531$, $p < 0.01$, 50.00, $p < 0.0001$, for Games 2 and 6, respectively).

4.   MODEL TESTING

This section reports the results of testing three individual level models that are designed to account for the high level of coordination observed in

Table 4. Means and Standard Deviations of Observed Number of Entries and Minimum Switch Deviation from Pure Equilibrium

Game		j = 1		j = 2		j = 3		MinS	
		Mean	SD	Mean	SD	Mean	SD	Mean	SD
1	Group 1	7.06	1.57	6.00	1.79	4.94	1.34	1.81	0.90
	Group 2	7.31	1.25	6.19	2.01	4.50	1.79	1.94	1.29
	Mixed Eq.	7.25	2.08	5.99	2.00	4.75	1.87	2.35	1.27
	Pure Eq.	7		6		5			
2	Group 1	9.19	2.37	5.69	2.63	3.12	1.20	2.88	1.19
	Group 2	8.56	1.09	6.25	1.73	3.19	1.05	1.50	1.15
	Mixed Eq.	8.46	2.12	7.20	2.08	2.34	1.43	2.31	1.28
	Pure Eq.	8		7		3			
3	Group 1	8.81	1.52	3.81	1.52	5.28	2.06	2.31	1.41
	Group 2	9.19	1.76	4.94	1.77	3.88	1.71	2.13	0.81
	Mixed Eq.	9.74	2.11	4.73	1.87	3.53	1.68	2.32	1.26
	Pure Eq.	9		5		4			
4	Group 1	11.19	2.04	5.75	2.05	1.06	0.57	2.06	1.33
	Group 2	10.75	2.05	6.06	2.29	1.19	0.54	1.94	1.48
	Mixed Eq.	10.73	2.08	7.00	2.07	0.27	0.52	2.08	1.27
	Pure Eq.	10		7		1			
5	Group 1	12.38	2.42	3.25	2.02	2.38	1.36	2.50	1.11
	Group 2	11.75	1.81	3.75	1.73	2.50	1.55	2.00	0.97
	Mixed Eq.	13.37	1.85	3.44	1.67	1.19	1.05	2.19	1.19
	Pure Eq.	12		4		2			
6	Group 1	15.56	0.81	1.38	0.81	1.06	0.25	0.88	1.33
	Group 2	15.12	0.81	1.87	0.81	1.00	0.37	0.56	0.63
	Mixed Eq.	16.70	1.10	1.06	1.00	0.23	0.48	1.88	0.84
	Pure Eq.	15		2		1			

both groups. The first model is based on a simple coordination convention, the second is the mixed strategy equilibrium, and the third postulates commonly shared choice probabilities that are individually perturbed.

4.1. A Coordination Model Based on Convention

We propose two variants of a model that can yield, in principle, a high level of coordination. For a given location j, denote by "+", "−", and "0" the cases where $n_j > m_j$, $n_j < m_j$, or $n_j = m_j$, respectively. If coordination is achieved (i.e., the location vector is characterized as 000), then all players are awarded the prize g. Deviation from equilibrium play results in one of three outcome patterns, namely, (+0−), (+−−), and (++−) up to permutation of these indices. Whenever $n_j \leq m_j$ (denoted by "−" or "0"), each of the n_j players receives the prize g. However, if $n_j > m_j$ (case "+"), only m_j players are awarded the prize g and the remaining $n_j - m_j$ players are awarded zero.

The model assumes that the allocation of prizes on iteration t (t = 1, 2, ..., 16) serves as a coordination device for the next time the *same* game G (G = 1, 2, ..., 6) is played (by the same players). It does so by identifying the subset of the subjects who are not rewarded as the "excess demand" in the game (Mehta et al., 1994). We propose two variants of the coordination model that impose different requirements on the subjects' memory of the outcome of the previously played game G. Since on the average, six trials separated two consecutive presentations (iterations) of the same game, it is reasonable to assume that not all aspects of the outcome of a game are available in memory the next time the game is played.

Version 1 – Memory is limited to the last iteration of game G. It assumes that a player can recall (with no error) his own choice and whether or not he was rewarded on that iteration.

Version 2 – In addition to the memory required by version 1, a player is assumed to recall the qualitative status of each of the other two locations in the previous iteration of game G as either "0", "−", or "+".

A reasonable convention would be for a player who was rewarded on entering location j of game G in iteration t to repeat entering the same location j on iteration t + 1[6], and for a player who was not rewarded on iteration t to enter a different location on iteration t + 1[7]. The two versions of the model differ as to the manner by which a non-rewarded subject chooses the entry location on iteration t + 1.

Version 1 – A non-rewarded subject on iteration t is equally likely to switch to any of the other two locations on iteration t + 1.

Version 2 – A non-rewarded subject on iteration t is more likely to switch to a "−" location on iteration t + 1. If, however, both other locations are of type "−", then version 1 holds.

4.1.1. Testable Implications

The convention model implies several testable hypotheses:

- Once perfect coordination is achieved, it will be preserved in all subsequent iterations of game G.
- Under a strong interpretation of the model (both versions), subjects will always switch location after not being rewarded and never switch after being rewarded. Under a weak interpretation, switching

is more likely to occur following no reward than reward on the previous iteration.
- Version 2 makes a specific prediction as to the exact location that will be chosen, given that a switch occurs.

These hypotheses are clearly rejected by the data. Turning to the first hypothesis, Tables 2A and 2B show that (perfect) coordination was achieved only six times in Group 1 (once in Game 3, twice in Game 4, and three times in Game 6) and fifteen times in Group 2 (twice in Games 1, 2, and 4, once in Game 4, and eight times in Game 6). However, only once in Group 1 (Game 6) and four times in Group 2 (Games 1, 4, and 6) was coordination achieved on at least two consecutive iterations of the same game. The longest string of coordination on successive iterations occurred on Game 6 of Group 2. However, this string was interrupted three times before the last iteration. Even in those cases where coordination was achieved twice in a row, it was not the case that all the 18 players chose the same location on the two successive presentations (see Ochs, 1990 for similar results). For example (Table 2B), we observe coordination on the 10th and 11th iterations of Game 1 played by Group 2. Yet, nine of the eighteen players changed their location choice between these two iterations of Game 1 (with switched decisions canceling one another).

Thus, we find no evidence for the prediction that players who were awarded the prize on game G would not switch their decisions on the next iteration of the same game. Even the considerably weaker prediction that subjects not awarded the prize on game G will be *more likely* to switch than stay on the same location the next time game G is presented is rejected for most subjects. Tables 5A and 5B present the relevant individual data for Groups 1 and 2, respectively. The two columns under the label "Not Rewarded" present the number of times, after not being rewarded on iteration t, a subject chose the same location on iteration t + 1 (=), and the number of times a different location was chosen (≠). The corresponding choice frequencies after a reward was provided on iteration t are presented under the "Rewarded" label (ignore for now the three subcategories, $n_t > m_t$, $n_t = m_t$, and $n_t < m_t$, and aggregate the frequencies for = and ≠). A square in the table indicates that the proportion of switching after no reward is significantly higher than after reward at the 0.1 significance level. The above hypothesis is supported by seven subjects of Group 1 and eight of Group 2. For other subjects, it is not even the case that switching is more likely to occur after no reward than after a reward. Note, however, that the frequency of not being rewarded was rather low. On average, subjects were rewarded on 88% and 91% of trials, for Groups 1 and 2, respectively. The lowest reward level was 79% for subject 5 of Group 1 and 78% for subject 1 of Group 2. Consequently, the test for equality of proportions at the individual level is based on relatively small frequencies. However, The overall

Table 5A. Frequency of Decisions on Time t + 1 – Group 1

ID	Not Rewarded $n_t > m_t$			Rewarded $n_t > m_t$			$n_t = m_t$		$n_t < m_t$		Switch		
	$=^1$	$\neq^2$		$=$	$\neq$		$=$	$\neq$	$=$	$\neq$	$\male$	$\female$	
1	0	8	■	17	23		7	12	9	14	28	14	◆
2	10	0		33	3		16	3	21	4	6	4	
3	6	4	■	42	4	●	15	0	19	0	4	1	◆
4	7	4		29	15		9	4	8	14	20	11	◆
5	7	11	■	19	13		13	2	13	12	9	23	◈
6	3	8		24	23		7	4	8	13	21	16	
7	5	0		39	3		15	1	23	4	5	3	
8	3	2		24	24		8	7	15	7	18	13	
9	7	10		12	22		6	10	8	15	24	23	
10	3	6		18	18		7	7	20	11	14	20	
11	9	4		23	16		10	3	15	10	12	11	
12	3	6	■	15	15	●	33	6	10	2	12	9	
13	6	5		36	10		11	5	11	6	15	5	◆
14	4	4	■	35	6		12	5	17	7	6	10	
15	6	6		20	10		8	4	28	8	12	9	
16	1	8	■	19	24		7	11	10	10	23	17	
17	3	6	■	39	4	●	16	1	20	1	5	2	
18	7	6		17	17		8	4	18	13	16	17	
ALL	90	98	■	461	250	●	208	89	273	151	250	208	◆

1 – stay

2 – Switch

■ – proportion of switching after no reward is significantly higher than after reward (0.1).

◆ – The hypothesis that given a switch-out from location a ($j_t = a$), if ($n_{b(t)} \leq m_b$ and $n_{c(t)} > m_c$) or ($n_{b(t)} < m_b$ and $n_{c(t)} = m_c$) then $P(j_{t+1} = b) > P(j_{t+1} = c)$ is supported (0.05).

● – The Hypothesis that $P(j_t \neq j_{t+1}|n_j > m_j) > P(j_t \neq j_{t+1}|n_j \leq m_j)$ is supported (0.05)

trend is as predicted: in Group 1 (2) 66% (70%) of the time the same location was chosen after receiving a reward compared to only 48% (47%) of the time after not receiving a reward.

Version 2 makes a specific prediction as to the exact location that is chosen if a switch occurs. The model predicts that given a switch-out from location a ($j_t = a$), then if ($n_{b(t)} \leq m_b$ and $n_{c(t)} > m_c$) or ($n_{b(t)} < m_b$ and $n_{c(t)} = m_c$) the switch is more likely to be made to location b; otherwise, it is as likely to be made to location b as to location c. The last two columns of Tables 5A and 5B present the frequencies of switches that either support (♂) or contradict (♀) the above hypothesis, given that one of the above conditions holds. A diamond indicates that the null hypothesis that the switch (under these conditions) is as likely to be to any of the other two locations is rejected at the 0.05

Table 5B. Frequency of Decisions on Time t + 1 – Group 2

	Not Rewarded			Rewarded						Switch	
	n > m			n > m		n = m		n < m			
ID	$=^1$	$\neq^2$		=	≠	=	≠	=	≠	♂	♀
1	9	11 ■		12	16 ●	22	3	12	5	21	10 ◆
2	1	6 ■		19	19 ●	16	5	18	6	18	8 ◆
3	5	1		24	15 ●	20	5	16	4	9	10
4	5	2		28	4	21	4	22	4	4	5
5	1	5 ■		19	16	15	11	15	8	20	10 ◆
6	4	4		17	22 ●	19	9	10	5	16	14
7	5	4 ■		28	8	21	3	18	3	6	6
8	5	5 ■		30	7 ●	24	0	18	1	5	4
9	3	6 ■		19	8 ●	15	8	28	3	13	4 ◆
10	2	8		11	17	10	16	14	12	24	18
11	7	5		13	11 ●	37	3	9	5	8	10
12	3	2 ■		33	3 ●	26	1	22	0	3	3
13	5	1 ■		34	1	26	0	23	0	2	0 ◆
14	4	2		25	12 ●	23	4	16	4	11	8
15	3	8		7	21 ●	16	13	7	15	26	23
16	3	5		16	15	16	9	16	10	21	10 ◆
17	2	2		22	19	13	12	8	12	25	11 ◆
18	5	3		27	7	21	8	11	8	10	9
ALL	72	80 ■		384	221 ●	361	114	283	105	242	163 ◆

level. Tables 5A and 5B indicate that only four subjects from Group 1 and seven from Group 2 rejected the null hypothesis. As before, the overall trend is as predicted.

The most troublesome finding for the coordination model is the relatively high frequency of switching after a reward. Why do subjects switch location after being rewarded for their choice on the previous iteration of the same game? One possible factor that might affect subjects' decision to switch out from location a ($j_t = a$) on iteration t + 1 is the qualitative relationship between n_j and m_j on time t. The rationale is as follows: if $n_j \leq m_j$, then the subject is rewarded and no luck is involved in the award. The subject may attribute his reward in this case to his "smart" choice. However, if $n_j > m_j$, even if a reward is awarded, the subject may attribute his reward to luck. Consequently, independent of the reward, $P(j_t \neq j_{t+1} \mid n_j > m_j) > P(j_t \neq j_{t+1} \mid n_j \leq m_j)$. Tables 5A and 5B present the relevant frequencies under the $n_t > m_t$, $n_t = m_t$, and $n_t < m_t$ labels (aggregate the frequencies for $n_t > m_t$ under both the reward and no reward columns for this analysis). A circle between the $n_t > m_t$ and $n_t = m_t$ columns indicates that the alternative hypothesis $P(j_t \neq j_{t+1} \mid n_j > m_j) \leq P(j_t \neq j_{t+1} \mid n_j \leq m_j)$ is rejected at the 0.05 level. Tables 5A and 5B show that the alternative hypothesis was rejected by three subjects of Group 1 and ten subjects of Group 2. However, as before, the overall trend is as predicted.

4.2. Mixed Strategy Equilibrium Play

Table 3 reveals that the mixed strategy equilibrium solution for risk-neutral players cannot account for our results. For example, six subjects of Group 1 and eight subjects of Group 2 chose location j = 1 in Game 5 at least 14 of 16 times (87.5%), in contrast to the equilibrium probability of play which is equal to 0.743. Similarly, six subjects of Group 1 and five subjects of Group 2 chose location j = 1 in Game 4 at least 14 out of 16 times, compared to the equilibrium probability of 0.596. The assumption that *all* the subjects followed the mixed strategy equilibrium under the assumption of risk-neutrality is not supported.

A considerably weaker hypothesis asserts that the subject's 16 decisions in the same game G constitute a random sequence generated by probabilities p_1, p_2, and p_3 ($p_1 + p_2 + p_3 = 1$) of entering locations j = 1, j = 2, and j = 3, respectively. We impose no further constraints on these three probabilities and allow them to vary from one player to another. The interpretation of this hypothesis is that each subject has stable propensities to enter each of the three locations in each of the six games, and that these propensities may vary across subjects and games, but for a given subject they are not adjusted over time. Table 6 presents cumulative probability distributions that a random sequence containing r_j elements of type j will generate R runs in a sequence of 16 decisions. With J = 3 and 16 replications, there are 30 possible sequences[8] presented as rows in Table 6. The non-shaded areas in the table present an 80% symmetric confidence interval for the hypothesis that the sequence is randomly generated.

The hypothesis of randomly generated sequences was tested separately on the individual level for each game. Tables 2A and 2B (second column) show the games for which the number of runs falls outside the confidence interval for a given subject. A (black) circle containing the number 1 indicates that the hypothesis of a randomly generated sequence is rejected at the 0.01 significance level. The numbers 2, 3, 4, and 5 correspond to significance levels of 0.10, 0.2, 0.3, and 0.4, respectively (all the tests are two-tailed). Even at the most liberal level of significance of 40%, that permits a relatively easy rejection of the null hypothesis, only 36 of the 108 (18 × 6) sequences in Group 1 and 28 of the sequences in Group 2 reject the null hypothesis. Using a wider and more common confidence interval of 90%, only 12 of the 108 choice sequences of Group 1 and 11 of the 108 sequences of Group 2 are rejected as non-random. Table 3 presents the choice sequences not rejected by the null hypothesis by subject and game (for a 60% confidence interval). It shows a

Table 6. Cumulative Probability Distributions that a Random Sequence Containing n1 Elements of Type 1, n2 of Type 2 and n3 of Type 3 will Contain R Number of Runs

n1	n2	n3	2	3	4	5	6	7	8	9	10	11	12	13	14	15	16
6	5	5	0.0	0.0	0.0	0.1	0.7	2.8	8.7	21.0	40.2	62.8	82.3	94.2	98.9	99.9	100.0
6	6	4	0.0	0.0	0.0	0.1	0.4	1.8	5.9	15.2	31.5	53.0	74.3	89.7	97.3	99.7	100.0
7	5	4	0.0	0.0	0.0	0.1	0.4	1.9	6.2	15.9	32.7	54.7	76.0	90.9	97.9	99.8	100.0
7	6	3	0.0	0.0	0.0	0.1	0.4	1.8	6.2	16.1	33.2	55.5	76.8	91.3	97.9	99.8	100.0
7	7	2	0.0	0.0	0.0	0.2	1.0	4.0	11.7	26.5	47.4	69.3	86.2	95.5	99.1	99.9	100.0
8	4	4	0.0	0.0	0.0	0.1	0.6	2.5	8.1	20.1	39.4	62.6	82.8	94.8	99.0	99.9	100.0
8	5	3	0.0	0.0	0.0	0.1	0.5	2.3	7.5	18.9	37.9	61.2	81.7	94.2	99.0	99.9	100.0
8	6	2	0.0	0.0	0.0	0.2	1.1	4.2	12.3	27.8	49.4	71.5	87.9	96.4	99.4	99.9	100.0
8	7	1	0.0	0.0	0.2	0.7	3.0	9.5	22.4	41.7	63.1	81.3	92.7	97.9	99.6	99.9	100.0
8	8	0	0.0	0.1	0.9	3.2	10.0	21.4	40.5	59.5	78.6	90.0	96.8	99.1	99.9	100.0	100.0
9	4	3	0.0	0.0	0.0	0.1	0.9	3.6	11.0	26.1	48.8	73.1	90.5	98.3	99.9	100.0	
9	5	2	0.0	0.0	0.0	0.3	1.5	5.7	16.0	34.5	58.0	79.7	93.2	98.7	99.9	100.0	
9	6	1	0.0	0.0	0.1	0.8	3.5	11.2	25.9	46.9	68.9	85.8	95.5	99.0	99.9	100.0	
9	7	0	0.0	0.1	1.0	3.5	10.8	23.1	42.7	62.2	80.6	91.6	97.5	99.4	99.9	100.0	
10	3	3	0.0	0.1	0.9	3.5	10.0	23.1	41.4	62.2	78.6	91.6	98.6	100.0			
10	4	2	0.0	0.0	0.3	1.8	7.0	19.5	41.4	68.4	89.4	98.6	99.9	100.0			
10	5	1	0.0	0.0	0.5	2.6	9.4	24.6	48.4	73.8	91.6	99.0	99.9	100.0			
10	6	0	0.0	0.2	1.3	4.7	13.7	28.7	49.7	70.6	86.4	95.8	99.0	100.0			
11	3	2	0.0	0.2	1.3	4.7	13.7	28.7	49.7	73.1	93.2	100.0					
11	4	1	0.0	0.2	1.2	5.4	15.8	34.7	58.0	80.1	93.2	100.0					
11	5	0	0.0	0.4	2.2	7.7	20.1	40.7	62.6	84.6	94.2	100.0					
12	2	2	0.0	0.4	2.2	7.7	22.9	58.0	84.6	100.0							
12	3	1	0.0	0.1	1.2	6.3	22.9	50.1	80.1	100.0							
12	4	0	0.1	0.9	4.5	15.4	33.5	63.7	81.9	100.0							
13	2	1	0.0	0.4	5.0	21.4	60.7	100.0									
13	3	0	0.4	2.9	11.4	37.1	60.7	100.0									
14	1	1	0.0	2.5	35.0	100.0											
14	2	0	1.7	13.3	35.0	100.0											
15	1	0	12.5	100.0													
16	0	0	100.0														

moderate degree of support for the very weak null hypothesis that most of the subjects randomized their location choices with probabilities p_1, p_2, and p_3 that might vary across games and within a game across subjects.

These findings give rise to three questions. First, how can such random behavior on the individual level generate the high level of coordination observed on the group level? Second, how sensitive is the group coordination to the heterogeneity of the subjects in their propensity to enter each location? Third, can an aggregation of random strategies account for the group level effects of reward and of over- and under-subscription on switching behavior?

4.3. A Choice Model with Randomly Perturbed Probabilities

The next model that we propose assumes that all the individual propensities to enter location j emerge from a single set of three probabilities, but differ from one another due to random perturbation. Our point of departure is the intuitive case where all 18 subjects enter each location with a probability that is proportional to the number of prizes: $p_j = m_j/\Sigma m_j^9$. The issue that we set to investigate is how much "noise" can we introduce and still achieve a satisfactory level of coordination. To answer this question, we perturbed these three probabilities in the following way. Denote the probability of player i choosing location j by p_{ij} (j = 1, 2, 3). We simulated the following process. First, for each simulated subject i we randomly selected three probabilities from the intervals [max(0, p_j – d), min(1, p_j + d)] such that $\Sigma p_{ij} = 1$. We used a uniform distribution for each interval. Next, a location was randomly selected for each subject based on his own individual probabilities. Given the 18 choices, the MinS scores were then computed (with respect to the pure strategy equilibrium). To find the expected MinS for a given d, the process was repeated 10,000 times. The larger the d, the larger the heterogeneity of the 18 simulated subjects. Further, as d approaches 1 the mean probability of entry in each location (across the 18 subjects) approaches 1/3.

Figure 2 presents the mean simulated MinS scores for various levels of d. As might be expected, the higher the heterogeneity of the simulated subjects, the larger is the expected deviation from coordination. Second, and again as might be expected, games with relatively flat distribution of prizes in the three locations are less sensitive to population heterogeneity. In particular, given 18 randomly selected probability distributions over the three locations in Game 1, good coordination is expected. The observed MinS scores for the six games (over the two groups) were between 0.56 and 2.88. Figure 2 shows that such results would be expected, given choice probabilities that deviate from the "intuitive" probabilities p_j by about ±0.2.

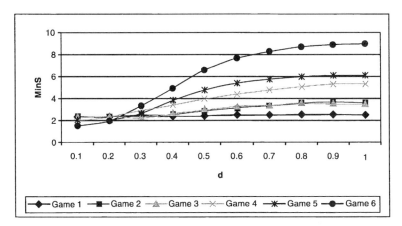

Figure 2. Expected MinS at Various Level of Population Heterogeneity in the Propensity to Enter each Location

Finally, we investigate the possibility that an aggregation of random strategies (with d = 0.2) would produce the group level regularities reported in Section 3. Recall that we found three significant group level effects:

- P(switch|reward) < P(switch | no reward).
- Given a switch-out from location a ($j_t = a$), if ($n_{b(t)} \leq m_b$ and $n_{c(t)} > m_c$) or ($n_{b(t)} < m_b$ and $n_{c(t)} = m_c$) then $P(j_{t+1} = b) > P(j_{t+1} = c)$.
- $P(j_t \neq j_{t+1} \mid n_j > m_j) > P(j_t \neq j_{t+1} \mid n_j \leq m_j)$.

To investigate this possibility, we simulated 10,000 group level results based on 18 simulated subjects (in each group) that enter each location with a perturbed probability of $p_j = m_j/\Sigma m_j \pm 0.2$ (under the restriction $\Sigma p_{ij} = 1$) for the 6 games and 96 trials as in our design.

Table 7 presents the proportions of simulated trials from replications 1 to 15 that were either rewarded or not rewarded by location[10]. Similar to our data, the frequency of no reward trials is rather low (11.6%). Note, however, that the probability of reward is a function of the exact location (% column). The probability of reward decreased from 0.921 to 0.852 to 0.801 for locations 1, 2, and 3, respectively. Given a reward observation, it is much more likely to come from j = 1 than from j = 2 or 3 (% row – the probabilities are 0.610 vs. 0.391). However, given a no reward observation, it is more likely to come from locations j = 2 or j = 3 (0.601) than from j = 1 (0.399). Given that the high propensity location is more likely to be repeated (randomly), this pattern demonstrates that an aggregation of random strategies can produce data that are consistent with the hypothesis that it is more likely to switch after no reward than after reward.

Table 7. Frequency of Reward / No-Reward by Location for a
Group Level Simulated Subjects

		j = 1	j = 2	j = 3
Rewarded	row	0.610	0.242	0.149
(88.4%)	column	0.921	0.852	0.801
	cell	0.539	0.214	0.131
Not Rewarded	row	0.399	0.319	0.282
(11.6%)	column	0.079	0.148	0.199
	cell	0.046	0.037	0.033

Table 8. Proportions of Games with Over- and Under-
Subscribers by Location for the Simulated Data

n_j vs. m_j	j = 1	j = 2	j = 3
<	0.267	0.656	0.189
=	0.156	0.144	0.489
>	0.578	0.200	0.322

Table 8 presents the results of the simulation with regard to the proportion of games on which capacity met (=), exceeded (<) or fell short of demand
(>) by location. Over all games, location 1 was over-subscribed 57.8% of the
time. The proportions of over-subscription in locations 2 and 3 were much
lower. However, the interesting pattern relates to the fact that in the simulation (as well as in our data) location 2 was much more likely to be under-
subscribed (65.6%) than the other two locations. Since location 1 was selected
most often, most of the switch-out observations occurred after location 1 was
chosen. Because a random switch (if it occurs) is more likely to occur to location 2 than location 3, coupled with the fact that location 2 was more often
under-subscribed, the observed pattern of switching to the under-subscribed
location is generated at the group level by our simulated subjects.

The only pattern of group behavior that could not be reproduced in
the simulation is the finding that subjects are more likely to switch on
iteration t + 1 after their location decision on iteration t was over-subscribed.
A random strategy that makes it more likely to select a high capacity location
($p_1 > p_2 > p_3$) will predict that switching will occur much more often after
selecting the low capacity compared to the high capacity location. However,
the simulation shows that the low capacity locations are the ones that are less
likely to be over-subscribed. Hence, the finding that switching decision is more
likely to occur after the location is over-subscribed was not replicated by the
simulation.

5. DISCUSSION

We set out to investigate large group coordination in six different pure coordination games that were repeated over time in a random order. For each of these games, perfect coordination would have eliminated the outcome uncertainty. Given the simplicity of the task, we expected that a high level of coordination would be achieved through some simple adaptation process. Our results seem to reject this hypothesis. Although a high level of coordination was achieved, we found no significant trends in the data across trials. Nor could we support the hypothesis that the frequent switching in choice of location was due to adaptation at the individual level. Rather, switching could be accounted for by commonly shared but individually perturbed choice probabilities. The important message is that the data should be carefully scrutinized in order not to fall into several possible traps, where a simple random process with "noise" can by its very nature produce what seems to be "sophisticated" adaptation behavior.

Our data suggest that the subjects in our task are not adaptive in the sense that is commonly used to describe subjects' behavior in experimental games. That is, they are neither belief (Selten 1986), nor reinforcement (Erev and Roth, 1999) nor adaptive EWA learners (Camerer and Ho, 1999). What are they than? Camerer and Ho (2000) argue in favor of going beyond simple adaptive and belief learning toward a model of sophisticated EWA learning and strategic teaching. We contend that our analysis demonstrates that it is often too easy to read too much sophistication into subjects' behavior, whereas a simple random process can account for the results. Rather than going outside simple adaptive and belief learning toward greater sophistication, we advocate more primordial models, the extreme of which is a completely random behavior. In our case, however, subjects did not select each location with equal probability but rather adopted unequal probabilities that are based on some intuitive notion of location attractiveness. In this respect their behavior is more sophisticated than completely random behavior, but not much more than that.

We do not argue that all the subjects behaved randomly all the time. The data clearly refute this statement. For example, we could not rule out as an artifact the finding that some subjects are more likely to switch out from a location for which demand exceeds supply. Further, it is quite clear that even across games, subjects did not exhibit consistent behavior, where in one game one pattern emerged but not in others. The question is at what level of detail should we explain the subjects' choices? Identifying clusters of subjects who behave similarly is probably the most practical approach (Stahl, Haruvy and Wilson, in press). We have tried unsuccessfully to follow this approach in our study. However, it turned out that this was not necessary because at the simplest level all subjects could be clustered into one group described by a mixed strategy with perturbed choice probabilities. We conjecture that although other adaptation processes might take place, in our task their contribution to explaining individual level behavior is negligible.

We only investigated heterogeneity of the group members at a very simple level of deviation from an underlying set of choice probabilities. The larger the group, the higher the heterogeneity that can be tolerated in our task. Such heterogeneity makes sense if the original choice probabilities are common to all players. We argue that this, indeed, is the case in our no-conflict coordination game. We do not expect this property to hold in all coordination games. On the contrary, whenever coordination elicits conflict, we believe that other considerations such as fairness and envy enter subjects' thoughts in different ways such that the assumption of common choice probabilities is probably no longer valid. This is why, for example, Zwick et al. (1999) found a low level of coordination in a market entry game that elicited conflict, whereas Rapoport et al. (in press) reported remarkably good coordination in a market entry game with no conflict.

ACKNOWLEDGEMENT

This research has been supported by a grant from the Hong Kong Research Grants Council (Project No. CA98/99.BM01).

NOTES

1. For various rationing rules discuss in the IO literature see Tirole (1997), pp. 212–214.
2. One may impose differential costs of entry for the different lotteries or different players. If the costs are relatively high in comparison to the prizes offered by the lotteries, then they may constrain the participants from entering all the lotteries.
3. The only non-reproducible information from these tables is the order by which the different 6 games were presented within each of the 16 blocks and the colors representing each location.
4. This measure is simply the sum of the number of over-subscribes. It is equivalent to $(1/2)\Sigma|n_j - m_j|$.
5. Given the parameters of the six games (Table 1), the mean MinS score over the six games is 15.3.
6. On the average, six trials separated any two iterations of the same game.
7. We propose this convention for a pure coordination game. If, for example, we change Game 5 from $g = (2, 2, 2)$ and $m = (12, 4, 2)$ to $g = (4, 5, 6)$ and $m = (12, 4, 2)$, the pure strategy equilibrium does not change and the task can again be interpreted as partitioning the group into three subgroups of 12, 4 and 2 members. However, if coordination is achieved, subjects do care to which subgroup they belong and may object to the convention suggested above. Rather, they may suggest an alternative convention where those who are rewarded are to switch to another location.
8. Note that types are interchangeable for this test. For the test purpose, the following two outcomes are equivalent: (11 in location 1, 3 in location 2, and 2 in location 3) and (3 in location 1, 11 in location 2, and 2 in location 3).

9. Note that these are the probabilities that minimize MinS, and not the probabilities that are prescribed by the mixed strategy equilibrium.
10. Replication 16 did not contribute data to the switching analysis.

REFERENCES

Camerer, C. F., and T. H. Ho (1999). "Experience-Weighted Attraction Learning in Games: Estimates from Weak-Link Games." In *Games and Human Behavior: Essays in Honor of Amnon Rapoport*, edited by D. Budescu, I. Erev, and R. Zwick, 31–52. Mahwah, NJ: Lawrence Erlbaum Associates.

Camerer, C. F., T. H. Ho, and J. K. Chong (2000). "Sophisticated EWA Learning and Strategic Teaching in Repeated Games." Wharton Working Paper No. 00-005.

Erev, I., and A. E. Roth (1999). "On the Rule of Reinforcement Learning in Experimental Games: The Cognitive Game-Theoretic Approach." In *Games and Human Behavior: Essays in Honor of Amnon Rapoport*, edited by D. Budescu, I. Erev, and R. Zwick, 53–77. Mahwah, NJ: Lawrence Erlbaum Associates.

Mehta, J., C. Starmer, and R. Sugden (1994). "Focal Points in Pure Coordination Games: An Experimental Investigation." *Theory and Decision* 36, 163–85.

Ochs, J. (1990). "The Coordination Problem in Decentralized Markets: An Experiment." *Quarterly Journal of Economics* 105, 545–59.

Rapoport, A., K. C. Lo, and R. Zwick (2000). "Choice of Prizes Allocated by Multiple Lotteries with Endogenously Determined Probabilities." Working Paper, Hong Kong University of Science & Technology.

Rapoport, A., D. A. Seale, and J. A. Parco (forthcoming). "Coordination in the Aggregate without Common Knowledge or Outcome Information." In *Experimental Business Research*, edited by R. Zwick and A. Rapoport. NY: Kluwer.

Schelling, T. (1978). *Micromotives and Macrobehavior*. NY: W. W. Norton.

Selten, R. (1986). "Anticipatory Learning in 2-Person Games." Discussion Paper Series B, University of Bonn.

Stahl, D. O., E. Haruvy, and P. Wilson (forthcoming). "Modeling and Testing for Heterogeneity in Observed Strategic Behavior." *Review of Economics and Statistics*.

Tirole, J. (1998). *The Theory of Industrial Organization*. Cambridge, MA: MIT Press.

Young, H. P. (1994). *Equity*. Princeton: Princeton University Press.

Zwick, R., and A. Rapoport (1999). "Tacit Coordination in a Decentralized Market Entry Game with Fixed Capacity." Working Paper, Hong Kong University of Science & Technology.

APPENDIX 1

Instructions to Subjects

Greetings!

You are about to participate in a decision making study. At the end of the session you will be paid according to your performance. A research foundation has contributed the funds to support this research.

Please read the instructions very carefully.

You are going to participate in many rounds of basically the same game. The game is very simple. If you make good decisions, you increase your chances of earning a considerable amount of money.

The game

The game is played by a group of 18 players (all those who are currently present at the PC Lab). You will repeatedly play the game (in rounds) with the same group of 18 players.

On each round, three lotteries will be conducted (called the YELLOW, BLUE and RED lotteries). You can participate in one and only one of these lotteries. You will be asked to choose participating in one of these lotteries without knowing the lotteries the other players in your group have selected.

At the beginning of each round, the information about the three lotteries will be presented in the following way:

Number of players in the group: 18 (you are one of them)

Prize	10	10	10
# prizes offered	2	4	12
# chosen			

In this round:

The YELLOW[1]	lottery offers	2	prize of	$10.
The RED	lottery offers	4	prize of	$10.
The BLUE	lottery offers	12	prize of	$10.

[1] Colors were represented by the actual colors on the screen.

Your task is to choose participating in one of these lotteries.

Because the number of prizes offered in each of the three lotteries may vary from round to round, you should pay close attention to them.

After all the members in your group choose which lottery to play, the computer will display the number of players who chose each of the three lotteries in the following manner:

Number of players in the group: 18 (you are one of them)

Prize	10	10	10
# prizes offered	2	4	12
# chosen	6	8	4

For example, in this round, 6 players chose to play the YELLOW lottery, 8 to play the RED lottery, and 4 to play the BLUE lottery (note that 6 + 8 + 4 = 18).

How winners are chosen in each lottery? If the number of players who choose to play in a given lottery is equal to or less than the number of prizes offered in this lottery then each one of them will win the prize.

If, however, the number of players who choose to play in a given lottery is more than the number of available prizes offered in this lottery then the computer will randomly select as many winners out of them as there are prizes this lottery.

For example, if 6 players chose the YELLOW lottery, 8 chose the RED lottery, and 4 chose the BLUE lottery, then the 4 players who had chosen the BLUE lottery wins $10 each because the number of players who chose the BLUE lottery (4) is less than the number of available prizes in this lottery (12).

Two of the 6 players who chose the YELLOW lottery will be randomly selected to win $10, and *four* of the 8 players who chose the RED lottery will be randomly selected to win $10.

Each of the 6 players who choose the YELLOW lottery is equally likely to be selected as one of the winners of the $10. Similarly, each of the 8 players who choose the RED lottery is equally likely to be selected as one of the winners of the $10.

Naturally, if no one choose any particular lottery, the prizes of this lottery are not awarded.

On each round, if you are not selected to win a prize in the lottery you chose, your payoff for this round is zero.

Summary

If the number of players who choose to play in a given lottery is equal to or less than the number of prizes offered in this lottery then each one of these players will win the offered prize in this lottery.

If, however, the number of players who choose to play in a given lottery is more than the number of available prizes offered in this lottery then the more players choose the same lottery the smaller the chances for each one of them to win that lottery prize.

We shall now test your understanding of the game. If your answers are incorrect, the computer will show you the correct answers and explain them.

.... Deleted..........

How do we pay you for your participation?
Your payoff for the session will equal your cumulative payoffs in all rounds. The highest possible take home pay is $222. This can happen if you always win the lottery on all rounds.

The lowest possible take home pay is $30. This can happen if you never win any prize in all rounds and you only get paid the show up fee.

The University regulation requires that all participants read and accept the conditions of the study.

For the consent form please press the consent form button.

.... Deleted..........

From now on you may not communicate with other participants or anyone else for that matter.

Please raise your hand to indicate to the monitor that you have finished reading the instructions. The Monitor will answer any questions you may have and will start the program for you.

APPENDIX 2

Screen Shots for the Decision Task[1]

Selection was done by pressing on the color corresponding for the choice

Screen 1

Round: 1

Prize	2	2	2
No. Available	7	6	5
No. Chosen			

Please choose one of the lotteries by pressing on the color corresponding to the lottery of your choice

After the selection subjects were instructed to confirm or cancel their choice

Screen 2

Round: 1

Prize	2	2	2
No. Available	7	6	5
No. Chosen			

You have Chosen to participate in the **RED** lottery, please confirm or cancel your choice

Confirm   Cancel

1 – In this example $m_{YELLOW} = 7$, $m_{RED} = 6$ and $m_{BLUE} = 5$. Colors were represented by the actual colors on the screen.

After confirmed choice, subjects were instructed to wait for the decision of all other players

```
Screen 3
                    Round: 1

         | Prize         | 2 | 2 | 2 |
         | No. Available | 7 | 6 | 5 |
         | No. Chosen    |   |   |   |

             You have Chosen to participate in the
             RED lottery, please wait for the outcome
                      of this round. . . .
```

After the outcome is presented, if $n_j > m_j$ for the selected location, subjects were instructed to wait for the random selection of winners

```
Screen 4
                    Round: 1

         | Prize         | 2  | 2  | 2 |
         | No. Available | 7  | 6  | 5 |
         | No. Chosen    | 4  | 10 | 4 |

             You have Chosen to participate in the
             RED lottery, Please wait for the random
             selection of 6 players out of the 10 who
             have chosen to participate in the RED
                        lottery. . . .
```

If the subject was randomly sleeted to win the prize

Screen 5

Round: 1

Prize	2	2	2
No. Available	7	6	5
No. Chosen	4	10	1

You have Chosen to participate in the
RED lottery. **You have been randomly
selected to win the $2 prize in this
round**
Press Continue for the next round

Continue

If the subject was not randomly sleeted to win the prize

Screen 6

Round: 1

Prize	2	2	2
No. Available	7	6	5
No. Chosen	4	10	4

You have Chosen to participate in the
RED lottery. **You have NOT been
randomly selected to win the $2 prize in
this round**
Press Continue for the next round

Continue

Part II

AUCTIONS

Chapter 7

EXTERNALITIES AND ALTERNATIVE AUCTION RULES FOR ACCESS TO RAIL NETWORKS: SOME EVIDENCE FROM THE LABORATORY

D44

L92

H41

Paul J. Brewer
Hong Kong University of Science and Technology

1. INTRODUCTION

Externalities involve an economic environment where the consumption of resources by a user may create benefits or costs for another user. Two types of externalities are key features of railroad scheduling: *conflict* externalities and *synergy* externalities.

Conflict externalities arise from potential crashes between trains or other violations of safety criteria and resource constraints – literally, one train getting too close to another train. These conflicts occur mainly in the scheduling of single-line rail in rural areas, where significant bottlenecks can occur as trains wait on sidetracks for oncoming traffic to pass. If operator 1 has a northbound train on a single line track, then operator 2 may be prohibited from having a southbound train on the same track, or may have to pull over at a sidetrack. Conflict externalities are not always negative for everyone. Operator 3 may wish to follow behind operator 1, and may gain a positive benefit from the operator 1's impact on train schedules.

Synergy externalities arise from an ability of trains to exchange passengers, cargo, or rolling stock at a station or other meeting point. That is, if one operator adjusts his schedule a bit, he may be able to meet another operator in such a way as to effect an easy transfer of passengers at a particular station, thus creating a gain for both railways.

These two types of externalities are a key issue in the developing literature. Market-based or auction-based mechanisms for deregulation of publicly owned railways will behave differently depending on what kinds of externalities the mechanism is designed, or not designed, to handle. Since market and auction mechanisms are known to have superior information aggregation and sorting capabilities when compared to old-fashioned, centralized schemes of command-and-control or assigned priority[1], one hope is that a market or auction-based mechanism can be designed to handle the most important types of externalities (e.g. avoiding crashes) while not performing too poorly on others (e.g. finding synergies). Unfortunately, creating such a mechanism is tricky, and by the end of this chapter we will have some partial success and an ability to understand some of the future challenges in this area.

Standard economic theory suggests that, in the absence of a property right tied to the existence or non-existence of the externality, ordinary markets and auctions will ignore the presence of externalities. Thus, one approach to dealing with externalities in a market setting is to create additional property rights and markets tied to the externalities, or to ensure that the market system acts as if these additional rights and markets have been created[2]. One problem with this is that markets for rights connected to externalities are often too thin to be considered competitive. For example, one train operator may benefit if another changes their schedule – a situation best described in terms of two-party bargaining rather than as a competitive market. This does introduce problems, and we will see that as a result of this and other problems, the techniques developed here for dealing with externalities are not perfect.

Coase [1960] suggested that in the absence of transactions costs, fully competitive markets might be unnecessary, provided there is a clear assignment of property rights. One of the conclusions from this chapter is that expending some efforts to properly organize commodity space can lower later transactions costs. Even so, to the extent that transactions costs are almost always non-zero in applications, we should not expect perfect allocations.

Laboratory researchers studying European railway deregulation have relied upon this preceding body of theory when creating prototype processes (more formally called economic allocation *mechanisms*) that are then tested via human subject experiments. Brewer [1995, 1999] and Brewer and Plott [1994, 1996] describe auctions where a rail network is modeled as an idealized *binary conflict network* (to be reviewed below) where property rights can be defined and auctioned in a way that guarantees the absence of conflict externalities. Within the network, it is assumed that the costs (or revenues) from running trains differ from operator to operator, and the role of the auction is to sort out both the question of an efficient network schedule as well as who should win the rights to run each train on the schedule. In Sweden, Nilsson [1999] follows a similar approach, the main difference being the replacement of Brewer and Plott's 1st price iterative auction with a 2nd price auction.

In contrast, Cox, Offerman, and Schram [1998] use a combination of *synergy* externalities and identical firms to demonstrate an opposing view being considered in The Netherlands. Their results are still consistent with standard theory, but involve different initial assumptions about the nature of rail firms and externalities. If the firms' costs for running trains and their demand curves for service are all identical, an auction for access to the track is not necessary to sort out efficient operators from the inefficient ones. By assumption, in this environment any operator is equally efficient: random choice would do as well as anything else. Their primary result is the criticism that an auction can produce schedules that fail to take account of the synergies of exchanging cargo or passengers. By comparing auctions "for the rails" and "on the rails" in this common-costs/values, synergy environment, these researchers conclude that a different auction, an auction for regional monopolies, would capture more synergies and be more efficient than an auction for accessing the tracks.

These various research efforts cannot be directly compared because while the laboratory methodologies are similar, critical assumptions about the *economic environment* (e.g. differences or similarities in firms' costs) are different. By investigating synergy externalities within the framework of the Brewer and Plott [1996] BICAP auction, it will be possible to understand what kinds of problems and issues these types of externalities create within a single consistent environment. Before delving into these topics, it is useful to briefly review existing laboratory techniques for those who may be unfamiliar with them.

The common laboratory methodology in these studies involves the use of cash-motivated human subjects, who compete according to the rules of a new mechanism within a controlled laboratory environment. The cash incentives, types of trains and tracks in the model environment, and the rules of the market or auction mechanism are parameters under the control of the experimenter, who sets these parameters and then observes the behavior of the human subjects as they compete in the mechanism. Plott [1994] calls this a *testbed approach*, and suggests that such a methodology can produce both a *proof of principle* and evidence for *design consistency*.

The *proof of principle* involves the creation of a prototype and its evaluation in the laboratory. The fact that a prototype can be constructed means that abstract ideas about how the mechanism should work have been reduced to practice, and incorporated both in the rules given to experimental participants and, quite often, within prototype trading software needed for the experiments. Evaluating the prototype is a question of showing that the mechanism will function. While it is impossible to know with certainty whether a mechanism that works in a controlled laboratory environment will work in a complex field environment, establishing the level of *design consistency* helps to bridge this gap.

Design consistency explores why it works – was it luck, or is the mechanism operating within the context of some theory that can suggest a way to better understand the capabilities and limits of the mechanism? Obtaining these answers is inexpensive when laboratory experimental methods are employed. Badly conceived, incompletely conceived, or internally inconsistent processes will reveal themselves when it is not costly. Processes based on unreliable principles can be exposed through inexpensive laboratory tests. Processes based on reliable principles are slowly and gradually identified, and after numerous laboratory tests may be ready for more testing and fine tuning in actual applications. The goal of this approach is not to provide instant answers to the question of which mechanism is best or most appropriate for a given application, but rather to provide a process for iterative improvement that incorporates the work of many researchers over time. As such, the research reported here is but a small step towards identifying a workably efficient allocation mechanism for environments where both combinatorics and externalities play a role.

Section 2 provides a number of examples of binary conflict networks, introduces issues of scheduling, efficiency, and computation, and introduces the Binary Conflict Ascending Price [BICAP] auction. BICAP was designed specifically to deal with the complexities, such as instabilities and non-existence of various equilibria, that can exist in network environments. The examples in Section 2 provide background and an introduction to some of the author's previously published works in this area.

Section 3 provides an example of a positive externality in a binary conflict network, and shows a relationship between certain kinds of positive externalities and the conflict externalities which the BICAP auction can already handle. Externalities might be handled – in theory – by minor changes in the way the network commodities are auctioned, so that agents can make their bids contingent on the presence or the absence of other network uses.

Section 4 explains the procedures used in the experiments designed to test this technique for handling the externalities. These procedures involve standard induced-value laboratory techniques. Basically, subjects are paid in cash the difference between the revenue values of projects they obtain in the auction and their winning bids. The experimenter sets the values of the projects and the rules of the auction, and observes the bids made by the subjects. As discussed above, these techniques are standard to laboratory practice in economics and almost identical to those employed in Brewer and Plott [1996] and Brewer [1999].

Section 5 presents the results of these experiments. The experiments show that the structure of the commodity space affects the ability of the BICAP auction to handle externalities. The observations are partially consistent with ideas embodied in Arrow-Debreu complete market theory as well as Coase's discussion of transactions costs. This paper does not focus on testing or comparing theories for why the incomplete market fails, but instead focuses on the potentials of complete markets for success or failure. The question is whether more efficient allocations are possible merely by restructuring the way access to the network is sold. The answer to this question, given the data, is positive.

Section 6 presents conclusions. The occasional difficulties encountered with the complete market design in the experiments suggest new areas for exploration in the development of mechanisms for allocating resources at shared network facilities.

2. THE BINARY CONFLICT NETWORK: NOTATION, DEFINITIONS AND EXAMPLES

In this chapter the focus is on environments where agents (from a set of agents $I = \{1, 2, 3, \ldots\}$) compete to run projects (from a set of projects $P = \{A, B, C, \ldots\}$) on a particular kind of network, where pairs of projects may conflict and any conflict results in an infeasibility. This network is called a binary conflict network. The purpose of this section is to introduce the concepts of scheduling, allocation, efficiency, and auctions on binary conflict networks through a series of examples. The notation[3] used is similar to previous work published in this area.

Definition: A *binary-conflict network* has three specific properties:
(1) *Exclusive Uses*. Each project is either run by a particular agent or it is not run at all. For example, if one agent is using the network for project A, then another agent may *not* use the network for project A.
(2) *Private Use Values*. Projects on the network generate private use values or revenues. The amounts involved are *not* public knowledge and may differ from agent to agent. For example, agent 1 will earn $5000 if he can use the network for project A but agent 2 will earn $8000 if she can use the network for project A. Agents do not know each other's values, and neither does the authority who wishes to sell access to the network.
(3) *Binary Conflicts between Projects*. Binary conflicts can arise between projects for many different reasons, but they always involve *pairs of projects*. A particular binary conflict c is a pair, e.g. $c = (A, B)$. A network's set of conflicts C can involve many such pairs; e.g. $C = \{(A, B),(A, C),(B, D), \ldots\}$. If the network is used for project A then no one may use the network for project B or project C, since C includes the pair (A, B) showing that project A conflicts with project B, and C includes the pair (A, C) showing that project A conflicts with project C. Note that the agents (or users) are not

important for determining conflicts – it is only the projects (or uses) that matter.

The distinguishing feature of a binary conflict network is the assumption that the feasible set is described by listing pairs of projects that conflict – pairs that are *not* feasible[4]. Otherwise, the approach adopted here is similar to the private-values environments discussed in the experimental and theoretical mechanism design literature, where each agent has a value for using the network resources and the question is how to structure a mechanism (such as an auction, market, or administrative process) so that the high-value agent is likely to win. Focusing on projects and conflicts allows one to ignore the various real commodities involved (safety along particular stretches of track, the number of gates at a train station, the load a bridge can withstand) because all of these issues have been summarized within the projects and conflicts.

The binary conflicts in the network can be considered to be extreme cases of negative externalities. For example, if the projects are trains, and if trains B and C are scheduled at such a time that they would crash into train A, then this is an important negative externality that must be avoided. We will refer to this type of externality as a *conflict externality*.

Brewer and Plott [1994] and Brewer [1995] resolve the conflict externalities by building constraints into the Binary Conflict Ascending Price (BICAP) auction such that conflicts are automatically resolved in a bid-revenue maximizing manner. Bidders in the BICAP auction can bid on a project knowing that no conflicting projects will be simultaneously allocated. Bids are evaluated continuously with a computer calculating the potential winners after each bid, given the conflicts that exist between the projects, and bidders receive feedback about who is winning. Bidding is closed when 60 seconds elapses with no bidding.

In an effort to more fully introduce the binary conflict networks and the BICAP auction, a series of four examples will provide a introduction to such concepts as "scheduling", "allocation", and "efficiency" within these environments.

The first example involves a model railroad environment used in previous experiments by Brewer and Plott [1996] and Brewer [1995]. This example is used as an introduction to such concepts as scheduling, allocation, efficiency, and the BICAP auction. The second example is a simplification, and involves what we would normally think of as pure private goods. It is seen that in this simplification BICAP reduces to a set of independent iterative 1st price auctions. The third example demonstrates a threshold public good in the form of a train or project that displaces several other projects. One-stage Nash equilibria of the BICAP auction are introduced and may be important to understanding how the auction will perform. The final example shows a type of flow network (such as an electric system or an oil pipeline) that is not easily characterized by binary conflict. This kind of example shows how many kinds of traditional networks would not fit into the binary conflict class, and helps delineate the limits of the class of networks under study.

Example 1: Binary Conflicts in a Model Railroad: Initial Concepts.

Figure 1A (below) shows a scheduling diagram for a hypothetical single track rail line connecting three cities in Sweden (Borlange, Uppsala, and Stockholm). Trains may choose to pull off the single main track at the Uppsala station, where a sidetrack exists. The single track creates a difficult constraint for scheduling purposes since it means there is no way for trains to safely pass each other or travel in opposite directions. It is therefore important to make sure that trains do not collide or come too close to each other on this single track, and this constraint is the primary constraint involved in allocating access to the track.

The axes of Figure 1A show time in the horizontal direction and location in the vertical direction. Thus, we can see that if trains A and C are both run, then A will hit C in a head on collision between Uppsala and Borlange. Therefore, trains A and C conflict with each other. Trains A and D do not conflict with each other, because D waits until A arrives before leaving. Train B, although it would wait in the Uppsala sidetrack for train C to pass, would conflict with train D further north. Train G is a very slow train, and it seems to preclude all the trains in {A..F} (they are either too fast and hit it from behind or hit it head on). Trains H and I are scheduled late at night, and do not conflict with any other trains. A number of other conflicts exist in the diagram that have not been mentioned. Additional conflicts also exist that do not occur on the track, but are due to safety or crew constraints; these additional conflicts are listed below the figure.

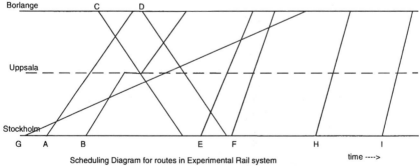

Scheduling Diagram for routes in Experimental Rail system   time ---->

Additional Safety Constraints (in addition to crashes indicated by the timetable): Trains A and B may not both be scheduled to run. Trains C and D may not both be scheduled to run. Trains E and F may not both be scheduled to run.

Figure 1A. Railroad Scheduling Diagram

Because all conflicts involve pairs of trains, it is possible to model this network as a binary conflict network. The binary conflict diagram is shown as Figure 1B below.

Here we will add some additional structure. Suppose various agents can operate the different trains, and their operating revenues from doing so are given in Table 1 below.

Here we have a set of agents $I = \{0, 1, 2, 3, 4, 5, 6, 7, 8, 9\}$, with each agent having different[5] values for each train. These values form a matrix given in the table above. Let V refer to the matrix of all the values, and let $V_j[p]$ refer to agent j's value for train p. For example, $V_3[C] = 307$. If agent 3 runs trains C and H, then her total revenue is the sum $V_3[C] + V_3[H] = 307 + 10 = 317$.

The existence of private values[6] for the projects (here the projects are trains) allows introducing the notions of optimal scheduling and allocation, as

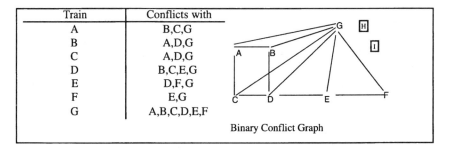

Train	Conflicts with
A	B,C,G
B	A,D,G
C	A,D,G
D	B,C,E,G
E	D,F,G
F	E,G
G	A,B,C,D,E,F

Binary Conflict Graph

Figure 1B. Binary Conflict Graph for Example 1

Table 1. Private Values for Trains

Agent id#	A	B	C	D	E	F	G	H	I
0	332	232	878	708	746	426	**2619**	127	127
1	946	521	321	241	739	265	2491	127	127
2	302	198	307	270	1013	645	1329	127	127
3	**1699**	**645**	307	206	306	217	509	10	2
4	1282	454	**1634**	**1447**	341	134	2543	68	173
5	801	354	933	465	936	561	2339	**430**	7
6	389	242	387	117	583	348	423	0	**1259**
7	320	132	1405	974	528	360	594	222	103
8	708	332	309	188	**1635**	**1421**	2005	24	28
9	372	277	341	138	395	284	1549	319	168

Bold denotes the highest private value for each train.

well as mechanisms for bidding on the projects. These concepts will now be formally defined, using Table 1 to illustrate examples. All of the definitions presented below are the standard ones.

Schedules and Allocation

Definition: A *schedule* $S \subseteq P$ is a set of uses of a network. The schedule is *feasible* if and only if S does not contain any conflict pairs. Feasibility of S is equivalent to $(S \otimes S) \cap C = \emptyset$.[7]

In terms of the binary conflict graph, a schedule is a subgraph, and a feasible schedule is a subgraph that contains no conflict lines. In example 1, the train schedule {A, D, F, H, I} is feasible. The schedule {A, B, C, D} is not feasible.

Definition: An *allocation* $\mathscr{A} = (S, i(s))$ is a schedule S together with a function $i(s)$: $S \rightarrow I$. The function identifies the agent who will operate each scheduled project.

For example, if $A = (S = \{A, D, F\}; i(A) = 1, i(D) = 3, i(F) = 5)$, then that means that trains A, D, and F are scheduled, and that furthermore, agent 1 runs train A, agent 3 runs train D, and agent 5 runs train F. No other trains are scheduled.

Feasibility of an allocation simply depends on the feasibility of the underlying schedule. Thus if S is feasible, then the allocation $A = (S, i(s))$ is feasible for any $i(s)$. If S is not feasible, then the allocation $A = (S, i(s))$ is not feasible regardless of the assignment function $i(s)$. Graphically, a feasible allocation is a subgraph with no conflict lines, where each project point is assigned to some agent.

Values of Schedules and Concepts of Efficiency

As defined above, the value of a project, say project A, to an individual agent j, is given by $V_j[A]$. One concept of efficiency is to choose an allocation that maximizes the sum of all such values.

Definition: The total value (*TV*) of an allocation $\mathscr{A}$ is the sum of revenues to the agents:

$$TV(\mathscr{A}) = \sum_{s \in S} V_{i(s)}[s].$$

In the example allocation involving {A, D, F} above, given the private values in Table 1, $TV(\mathscr{A}) = V_1[A] + V_3[D] + V_5[F] = 946 + 501 + 561 = 1713$.

Definition: An *optimal allocation* $\mathcal{A}^V$ is a feasible allocation that maximizes the total value *TV*.

Definition: *Efficiency of a feasible allocation* $\mathcal{A}$ is the ratio $TV(\mathcal{A})/TV(\mathcal{A}^V)$.

An efficiency of 1.0 (or 100%) means that a feasible allocation is optimal, and lower values show a departure from optimality. This is a standard measure.

From Table 1 and Figure 1 the optimal allocation is not immediately obvious, but it can be found as the solution to an integer programming problem or a graph-theoretic weighted-stable-set optimization problem. In this simple case, it reduces to comparing the schedules {A, D, F, H, I}, {B, C, E, H, I}, {A, E, H, I}, and {G, H, I}. The optimal allocation involves the schedule {A, D, F, H, I} with agent 3 running train A, agent 4 running train D, agent 8 running train F, agent 5 running train H, and agent 6 running train I. Here, the total value generated is $TV = 1699 + 1447 + 1421 + 430 + 1259 = 6256$.

Competitive Bidding by Agents

Suppose agents bid for the right to operate projects on the network. Let **B** denote the set of all bids and let $\mathbf{B}_k[p]$ denote agent k's bid on project p. Then, the total bid (*TB*) for an allocation is the sum of bids over the relevant agents receiving allocations:

$$TB(\mathcal{A}) = \sum_{s \in S} B_{i(s)}[s]$$

A *bid-maximizing allocation* $\mathcal{A}^B$ is a feasible allocation that maximizes the total bid *TB*.

For example, if agent 1 bids 200 on each train, and agent 4 bids 2200 for train G, then the bid-maximizing allocation will be to allocate train G to agent 4. Nothing is allocated to agent 1, because train G conflicts with all of agent 1's bids and produces higher bid revenue for network access. None of the other agents receive an allocation, as they did not bid.

Of course, this example might not be realistic in that some other profile of bids might be a more likely result. One might expect each agent to try to bid until they could no longer make a profit. This leads to the concept of a *one stage Nash equilibrium*, or NE1, where individual bidders cannot make themselves better off by raising their bids.

A particular auction that fits well with these concepts has been studied in laboratory experiments. It is the BICAP auction, defined below (and paraphrased slightly from Brewer and Plott [1996, p.869]).

Definition: The *Binary Conflict Ascending Price [BICAP] Auction* is an auction with the following rules:

(1) Each agent may submit bids for projects in a continuous time auction, whenever and however he wishes, until the auction closes.
(2) As agents bid, the highest bid for each project is made public. A new high bid for a project displaces any lower bids made on that project.
(3) At each moment in time a *potential allocation* is defined as the bid-maximizing allocation $\mathcal{A}^B$. This allocation is recalculated by the auctioneer after each bid and publicly announced.
(4) The process of bidding continues until some pre-specified time has elapsed with no bids taking place. When bidding has stopped, the potential allocation becomes the final allocation.

Theory suggests that agents with higher values will outbid agents with lower values. Experiments can be used to help answer this question. Brewer and Plott [1996] analyzed the BICAP auction in human subject experiments involving environments similar to the one in example 1. The results of these experiments indicate that BICAP can produce optimal allocations in environments like that in example 1, but do not always produce optimal allocation. The optimal allocation occurred in 18 of 21 test cases. In the three cases where the optimal allocation did not occur, the bids failed to be a one-stage Nash equilibrium and were inconsistent with rational profit maximization. That is, some agents bid too low or too high, or otherwise "left money on the table." Most of the optimal cases did involve convergence to a one-stage Nash equilibrium.

No theory currently exists to guarantee that optimal allocations will always be the result of the process. Although there is not much theory on complex bidding processes, a one-stage Nash equilibrium was observed in many cases. Although there are multiple NE1, many of which are suboptimal, the structure of bidding under BICAP seems to allow a way for agents to move away from bad equilibria towards optima. In Brewer and Plott [1996], the evidence for this involved *neutral bids* that were made by agents to move from one NE1 to another. These neutral bids do not change the allocation, and do not make the bidder immediately better off or worse off, but eventually lead to a region of instability between NE1. At a more practical level, the basic idea of how this works is revisited later on in example 3.

Experimental work by Brewer [1995, 1999] shows BICAP efficiency in certain more complex networks to be around 90%. However, that does not mean efficiency will always be so high in every type of network that one might imagine.

While a number of definitions have been made in this section regarding optimal scheduling and competitive bidding, there has been no attempt to explain which types of networks are more likely to be efficiently allocated under a competitive bidding system.

The next example explores how properties of the binary conflict network seem to translate into familiar economic notions of private and public goods. In the network of example 1 project G is problematic in that it creates a kind of public good or hold out problem. Projects H and I are independent of the rest of the network, and regardless of what happens in the network, it would be possible to auction the rights to run H and the rights to run I in isolation. H and I are closer to traditional private goods.

Before turning to new examples, which will be highly stylized and simplified, it is useful to briefly consider the problem of scaling up.

Computational Complexity and Determining Auction Winners

Computing the bid-maximizing allocations can become difficult when there are large numbers of feasible schedules. If there are only a few schedules, a person can do it. If there are a few million schedules, a computer could do it. But if there are 10^{100} or more schedules over which to optimize, it probably cannot be done unless there is a trick to eliminate most of the schedules from consideration. Because the problem of finding bid-maximizing allocations is a known[8] NP-complete integer optimization problem, we know that difficulty will scale exponentially in the problem variables, and so it is not so unusual to develop very difficult computations in the lab and impossible problems in the field.

The examples reported here involve only a few trains or projects. Consider what happens as we have more projects. For example, consider three disjoint copies of example 1 as a railroad with three tracks. The binary conflict network looks like three disjoint copies of Figure 1. In the interests of space, the resulting diagram is not shown. Suppose none of the train tracks interact with each other, so the scheduling problem of one track is separate from the scheduling problem of another track. Put another way, there are no conflicts between trains on different tracks. That would produce a binary conflict diagram that looks like three separate, disjoint copies of figure 1B, indicating that there are no dependencies between scheduling on one track and scheduling on another. It is not surprising that the bid maximization problem can be solved on each track separately.

Now, add some conflicts between the trains on the different tracks. This connects the binary conflict diagrams so that they can no longer be evaluated in isolation. By doing this, one can quickly go from a situation where there were a dozen or so possible schedules to a situation where there are hundreds or thousands of feasible schedules.

The optimization problem of finding the bid-maximizing allocations in the binary conflict network has a name in the operations research literature: the "stable set problem[9]." A little bit is known about what can make these problems hard or easy. The existence of a "claw" in the network can make it hard, and problems that do not have claws are solvable[10] in polynomial time. In our terminology, a claw involves a project that has at least three conflicting projects that do not conflict with each other. For example, in Figure 1, "G" is a claw, because it has three projects among its conflicts – A, D, and F – that do not conflict with each other. Project D involves a claw, because B, C, and E conflict with D and do not conflict with each other. It is not unusual for a network to have claws and become computationally complex as more and more projects are added.

Brewer [1999] suggested a means for dealing with complex optimizations within the BICAP auction. The idea is to admit that approximation is necessary, but to take the task of finding approximate bid-maximizing allocations away from the central computer. Agents in the auction would suggest allocations, and if these allocations increased the sum of bids, the agent would receive rewards that depended on an auction-like clock timer. Thus, this secondary institution was called the Computation Procuring Clock Auction [CPCA]. The combined institution was called the BICAP+CPCA mechanism.

Data from these previous experiments show that CPCA functioned effectively in providing bid-maximizing allocations as the result of decentralized suggestions or approximations from the agents.

Although the experiments to be described in this chapter do not involve complex environments, the BICAP+CPCA mechanism will be used in this paper as well. It provides an additional opportunity to obtain data on CPCA at the expense of producing a few periods where CPCA may fail to produce the outcome that would have been produced by a computerized optimization program. The CPCA data will be reported in a future work.

In some sense, we have started with the most complex examples, and have been mainly concerned about the mechanics of notation, setting up the problem, defining terms and the auction, and calculating the winner. It is useful to take a look at the economic details of smaller examples, to get a better feel for what is happening, and connect the world of binary conflict networks to more familiar economic examples.

Example 2: A Binary Conflict Network Involving Pure Private Goods.

A simple binary conflict network involving pure private goods is shown in Figure 2 below. In this case, $P = \{A, B, H, I\}$, $C = \{(A, B),(B, A)\}$, $I = \{1, 2, 3\}$ and V is given in the lower half of the figure. Notice that the only conflicts are between A and B. It is easily seen that this network involves 3 clearly distinct property rights. The property rights "right to run A or B but not both", "right to run H", and "right to run I" span all possible allocations of this network.

The efficient, value-maximizing allocation is the schedule $\{B, H, I\}$ with agent 1 running project B, agent 2 running project H, and agent 3 running project I.

This optimal allocation can be achieved as a NE1 of a BICAP auction. If agent 1 bids 376 for B, then agent 3 – who only has a value of 375 – cannot outbid him at a profit. Similarly, agent 2 could bid 301 on H and agent 3

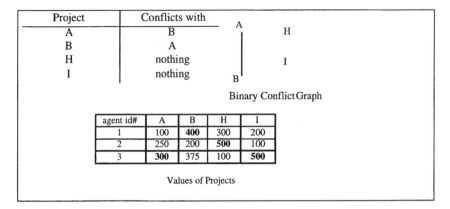

Figure 2. Easily Privatized Binary Conflict Environment

could bid 201 on I. These bids result in a NE1, since other agents cannot profitable exceed them, and would support the optimal allocation. Other schedules cannot be supported by bids consistent with competitive, one-shot profit maximization by all the agents. The optimal allocation is the unique likely result.

A more difficult environment for privatization is shown in Figure 3. This is a case in which a threshold public good is embedded as part of the allocation problem.

Example 3: A Binary Conflict Network Involving a Threshold Public Good.

Here the example is a simple network with a particular shape – involving a project that has many conflicts. In terms of trains, imagine that northbound trains A..F follow each other, and would all conflict with a southbound train G scheduled at the same time.

Because project G conflicts with all the other projects, the feasible schedules of interest are {A, B, C, D, E, F} or {G}. The total value TV{A..F} is 1200, while TV{G} is 1000, so the allocation of {A..F} to the agents 1–6 is optimal.

In this example, the value of G is such that {G} is not in the optimal (value-maximizing) allocation. However, {G} is a potential outcome of the auction. If agent 7 bids 800 (or 500, or 300, or 201) on G, and no one else bids, then the auction is at a one-stage Nash bidding equilibrium because no single bidder can bid enough to overturn G and make a profit. It is clear that

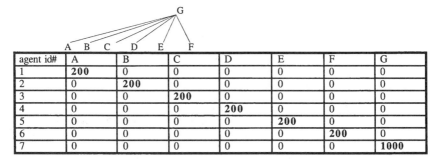

agent id#	A	B	C	D	E	F	G
1	200	0	0	0	0	0	0
2	0	200	0	0	0	0	0
3	0	0	200	0	0	0	0
4	0	0	0	200	0	0	0
5	0	0	0	0	200	0	0
6	0	0	0	0	0	200	0
7	0	0	0	0	0	0	1000

Figure 3. Bidding on This Network Involves a Threshold Public Good

unless all the other bidders cooperate, and together bid at least 1000, then agent 7 can outbid them and obtain G even though it is not optimal.

This situation involves what Ledyard [1995] calls a *threshold public good*. Displacing G is like a public good for the operators of A-F because if any one of them bids sufficiently high to displace G, then they all enjoy access to the track. Ledyard compares results of experiments with threshold public goods and pure public goods and concludes that the problems of allocating threshold public goods are much more manageable. In this context, because none of the operators of A-F pays their bid unless their sum exceeds the bid for G, negotiation is fairly cheap and quite often A-F may win when their values exceed the value of G. However, often is not the same as always, and it is true that if the value of G varies, then G may be allocated too often compared to what is optimal.

An alternative involves giving agents 1–6 the rights to run their projects, and requiring agent 7 to buy all of these rights if he should want to run train G. This eliminates the problem of G winning when it should not. But this also creates problems for agent 7 when his value for G is high enough to be optimal. Some of the agents could hold out. This would result in G being allocated on too few occasions.

Small changes in the rules of the bidding may have large effects on the outcome. It is unclear whether this environment is more or less difficult than the one in example 1. Here, there is no one to force agents 1–6 to bid up their favorite projects, whereas in example 1 many people might bid on each project. However, example 1 involves coordination problems that do not exist here. Here there are only two sensible allocations, whereas in example 1 there are many possible allocations.

The next example helps to define the limits of applicability of binary conflict networks by considering a type of resource that is *not* a binary conflict network.

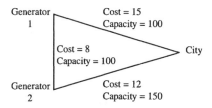

Figure 4. An Example of a Physical Network Diagram for a Simple Electric Grid

Example 4: A Network that does not involve Binary Conflicts.

Here the points are facilities at different physical locations. Supply facilities (generators) and demand facilities (a city) are connected to electrical
lines, which form a transportation network. The lines composing the network
involve certain transportation costs per unit and capacities.

Conflicts arising in this network can occur as a result of exceeding the
capacity constraints. However, these constraints do not involve conflicts
between pairs of projects. It might take 3 or 4 or 10 projects to violate the
capacity constraint in some part of the network. Thus, this is not a binary conflict network. However, when figures like this are drawn, usually the goal is
quite different from creating a place for competition to occur. Often when a
figure like this is drawn, it represents the operations of a single agent (either
a firm or government run entity) and there is a related cost minimization or
goal optimization problem.

Operations research specialists have categorized a number of management problems[11] into networks of the minimum cost or maximum flow variety,
simply by transforming appropriate parts of a problem into the elements of
the network, the capacities, or the costs. A diagram of such a network re-
sembles – in principle – Figure 4 above. Operations research often involves
how to mathematically solve for the best strategy of a single agent who faces
certain costs and benefits in the management of the network and all its components. The approach is very different from one where there are many agents,
each of whom want to use portions of the network, and who compete for access
through some decentralized mechanism[12].

3.   EXTERNALITIES IN BINARY
         CONFLICT NETWORKS

The purpose of this section is to show one way to add externalities into
the definition of binary conflict networks and explore how these externalities

might be resolved within an auction setting. The key contribution of this section is that certain *simple* types of externalities might, in theory, be resolved by extending the number of projects in the network. Adding certain virtual projects, together with conflicts to real projects, provides a means for restructuring the auction to allow the value of simple externalities to be communicated during competitive bidding.

Synergies between trains on a railway, can be introduced as a fourth property of binary conflict networks, in addition to the three properties offered at the beginning of section 2:

(4) *Externalities between Uses.* Externalities can arise between projects. A project may have a higher or lower value depending on what other projects exist in the network. For example, Project A might have a higher or lower value to agent i if project G is run by some agent (not necessarily i). Thus, an externality exists between A and G.

The interesting question, though, involves not the formal definition but the idea of *resolution* of externalities. How can we modify the environment so as to process externalities in a natural way? The answer to this question turns out to depend on the type of externality under consideration.

The idea is that once there are "complete markets" where agents can bid on projects contingent on the presence or absence of the externality, then efficient allocation may result. In contrast, in the case of "incomplete markets", agents cannot bid contingent on the externality – the market may not be able to account for whether or not the externality condition should occur, and suboptimal allocations will result. It is this idea that will be developed in this section and tested in the experiments described in section 4 and reported in section 5.

An externality in a binary conflict network is called *simple* if it can be resolved by adding at most one node to the network. The concepts of simple externalities and "resolving" externalities will be made clear in the following example. Essentially, resolving an externality means extending the commodity space so that the externality can be represented as an element of the commodity space and as an additive term in the revenue of agents.

Consider the network shown in Figure 5 below. It is similar to the network of example 1, except that Project G does not conflict with the other projects. By analogy to project H or I of example 1, here project G is like a private good that is completely independent of what happens in the rest of the network. In the following paragraphs, we will consider what happens when G has positive externalities with other projects in the network.

Suppose that a positive externality exists in the network of Figure 5. A positive externality increases the value of a project to various agents when certain conditions are satisifed. Unlike a conflict externality, it does not naturally show up in the binary conflict graph.

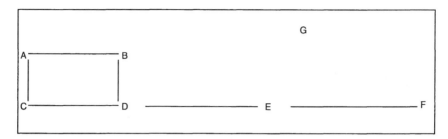

Figure 5. Binary Conflict Network with Unresolved Externality

For example, if the projects in Figure 5 are trains on a railroad network, perhaps train G is of higher value (to any operator) if it can meet with trains A and E and exchange cargo. It doesn't matter which agent(s) operate trains A and E – as long as these two trains are both on the network, the agent who operates train G has a higher revenue. We'll call this "Scenario 1".

Scenario 1: Project G is worth more to an agent if projects A and E are both allocated in the network.

How can the BICAP auction take the externality value into consideration? One way is by allowing bidding contingent on the presence of the externality. BICAP, as is, uses the conflicts in the network to select among allocations. Therefore, what is needed is to turn the positive constraint that A and E both be included into a set of negative constraints. These negative constraints say what must be excluded so that A and E have a guaranteed presence in the bid maximizing allocation. Note 1 states some conditions under which this is possible.

Note 1: Given demand for all projects, positive externalities involving AND-logic are equivalent to negative externalities involving AND-logic.

Rather than prove this formally, which would involve introducing some Boolean algebra, the principle will be illustrated with a second example. This should make clear what is at work. Consider that instead of scenario 1, we have scenario 2 below.

Scenario 2: Project G is worth more to an agent if projects B, C, D, and F are not allocated in the network.

Now re-examine the network of Figure 5. If projects B, C, D, and F are not allocated, then there will be nothing to conflict with A (only B and C conflict) and nothing to conflict with E (only D and F conflict). Thus, if B, C, D, and F are not allocated, then A and E will be allocated.

Similarly, if A and E are both allocated, then B, C, D, and F were not allocated, because these projects conflict with project A and/or project E.

Thus, the externalities in scenarios 1 and 2 result in identical economic environments and identical sets of outcome allocations, so long as some agents are guaranteed to bid on Project A and Project E.

Note 2: A positive externality involving AND-logic can be represented by an additional "project" with appropriate conflicts and values.

Consider the network of Figure 6 below, which adds a new virtual project G* to the network of Figure 5.

Note that G* conflicts with B, C, D, F, and G. Thus, if G* is allocated in a feasible manner, then B, C, D, and F are not allocated. As alluded to above, if B, C, D, and F are not allocated, then A and E will both be allocated. Thus, G* is allocated when A and E are both allocated and G* is not allocated when A and E are not both allocated. Also, G and G* cannot both be allocated at the same time. Thus, G* can be considered to be a version of G that can be allocated only when the externality condition is satisfied.

The project G* is an extension of the original network that includes the constraints of the environment of either externality scenario 1 or externality scenario 2 above. If an agent were to bid on G* in an auction, he would be assured of obtaining only the higher value that includes the effect of the positive externality should his bid be accepted.

It is important to note that the difference in the high bids between G* and G acts like a subsidy for agents bidding on complementary projects A and E. The sum of bids on A + E + G* is being compared to all other feasible sums of bids (involving G) in determining the allocation. Thus, the higher the bid on G* in relation to G, the lower the hurdle for agents bidding on A and E to receive an allocation.

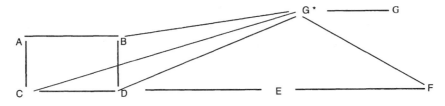

Figure 6. Splitting G into Projects G and G* Resolves the Network Externality

4.   EXPERIMENTAL PROCEDURES

Three series of experiments were conducted: CONTROL, COMPLETE, and INCOMPLETE. The three series are defined as follows:

- **CONTROL** These experiments use the network of Figure 5 together with the BICAP+CPCA auction. There are no positive externalities. These experiments can be considered to be software and procedure tests. The question is whether the auction will perform as well as it did in Brewer [1999], where BICAP+CPCA was also studied. If it does, then we will assume throughout the series that the software is working and that agents understand the instructions and screens.
- **COMPLETE MARKETS** These experiments use the network with externalities with the bidding structure of Figure 6 in the BICAP+CPCA auction. The term "complete" indicates that G* was present in the network, so that agents could make their bids for G contingent on the presence of the externality if they so desired: Agents bidding on G* know the externality must occur for their bid to be accepted, but agents choosing to bid on G accept the risk that the externality may or may not occur.
- **INCOMPLETE MARKETS** These experiments use the network with externalities with the bidding structure of Figure 5 in the BICAP+CPCA auction. Thus agents could not bid on project "G*". Agents bidding on G cannot condition their bids on whether or not the externality conditions will be satisfied. In some sense, when agents bid on G they do not know whether the externality will occur. While the externality exists in their revenue function, the conditions to bring about an enhanced value for G may or may not occur. Thus, markets are incomplete.

Each experiment consisted of three separate repetitions called periods. A period involved a replication of the network with the same set of subjects and different revenue values for the projects. Subjects earned the sum of their profits for all three periods. Values, bids, and profits in the experiment were denominated in "francs" and later changed to dollars by multiplying by a scale factor that varied over subjects. Subjects knew their franc to dollar ratio at the beginning of each experiment, but did not know others' ratios. Subjects kept their trading profits, plus a small show up fee. Total payments to subjects were ranged from US$10 to US$60 per subject for a 2 hour session.

5.   EXPERIMENTAL RESULTS

Data from the series of the experiments support four results. Result 1 shows that COMPLETE MARKETS yield a highly efficient identification of positive externalities. In the case of INCOMPLETE MARKETS, Result 2 shows that the market never identifies positive externalities. The INCOMPLETE MARKETS treatment always estimates the value of the externality as zero, for the trivial reason that agents cannot bid contingent on the externality outcome. Result 3 shows that the errors that occur under the COMPLETE vs. INCOMPLETE MARKETS treatments tend to be in opposite directions. This occurs because the COMPLETE market treatment sometimes results in an overestimate of the size of the externality. Result 4 demonstrates that exposure-related losses can occur when a strong positive externality exists under INCOMPLETE MARKETS. Exposure losses can occur because an agent who tries to assemble a package of projects that benefit from the positive externality must commit high bids on some projects before knowing whether she can win the others and take advantage of the externality between them[13].

Result 1: COMPLETE MARKETS result in efficient identification of externalities.
Support: There are 5 experiments, with 3 periods in each experiment, and 3 separate "train tracks" of projects for each period. This results in $5 * 3 * 3 = 45$ separate network environments. The **V** matrices were varied in these environments, and given the particular parameter values used [not shown], G* was optimal in 23 cases and G was optimal in 22 cases. The table below classifies the resulting observations, or auction outcome allocations, from the laboratory. Of the cases where G* was optimal, G* was always (100%) the result of the bidding mechanism. Of the cases where G was optimal, G was the result of the bidding in 82% (18) of the cases and G* was the result of the bidding in 18% of the cases.

	Optimal Allocation $\mathscr{A}^V$	
	G* $\in \mathscr{A}^V$ [23 total]	G* $\notin \mathscr{A}^V$ [22 total]
Auction Outcome G* $\in \mathscr{A}^{FINAL}$	23 or 100% [optimal]	4 or 18% [false positives]
G* $\notin \mathscr{A}^{FINAL}$	0 [omissions]	18 or 82% [optimal]

Result 2: INCOMPLETE MARKETS result in never identifying the positive externalities.
Support: There are 2 experiments, with 3 periods in each experiment, and 2 separate "train tracks" of projects for each period that satisfy the incomplete

market condition (no bidding on G*). This results in 12 separate network environments. The V matrices were varied in these environments, and given the particular parameter values used, G* was optimal in 8 cases and G in 4 cases. The outcomes from the laboratory experiments are shown in the table below. Of the cases where G* was optimal, G* was never (0%) the result of the bidding mechanism. Of the cases where G was optimal, G was always the result of the bidding. Thus, the mechanism neglects the value of the externality.

	Optimal Allocation $\mathscr{A}^V$	
	$G^* \in \mathscr{A}^V$ [8 total]	$G^* \notin \mathscr{A}^V$ [4 total]
Auction Outcome		
$G^* \in \mathscr{A}^{FINAL}$	0 [0% optimal]	0 [0% false positives]
$G^* \notin \mathscr{A}^{FINAL}$	8 [100% omissions]	4 [100% optimal]

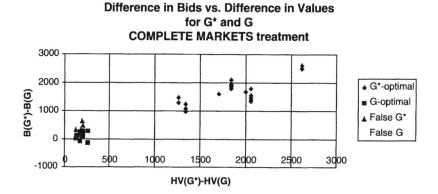

Difference in Bids vs. Difference in Values for G* and G COMPLETE MARKETS treatment

Result 3: Errors that occur under the COMPLETE vs. INCOMPLETE MARKETS treatments tend to be in opposite directions. The COMPLETE market treatment sometimes results in an overestimate of the size of the externality. The INCOMPLETE MARKETS treatment always estimates the value of the externality as zero, for the trivial reason that agents cannot bid on the externality outcome.

Support: The tables for Results 1 and 2 (above) already confirm this trend. In addition, the graph above shows more detail regarding what is happening in the COMPLETE MARKET case. The difference in revenue values for G and G* for the high value agent is plotted on the horizontal axis, with the difference in bid on the vertical axis. It is seen that exaggeration of externality values do occur in BICAP+CPCA, although not in the majority of cases. These exaggerations in value can lead to *false positives* where the allocation is changed as though there were a stronger externality condition.

One cause for these false positives can be found by a cursory examination of agent's bidding behavior. It appears that many of the agents who bid on G* do not also bid on G. If the highest value agent for G is also the highest value agent for G*, and that agent bids only on G*, then some other agent (not the high value agent) will hold the high bid for G. In such a situation, the difference in bids will be larger than the difference in values.

Result 4: A strong positive externality, coupled with INCOMPLETE MARKETS, can result in loss exposure and actual losses to *package risk-takers*. These are agents who try to assemble synergistic packages of projects that benefit from the positive externality.
Support: An example of this effect occurred in an experiment held on 02/07/97. Agent #1 overbid on A, E, and G, in an attempt to create the externality condition. The agent was unable to secure one of the projects, and lost money on the other 2.

Although an example does exist, this is the only observed example. Nothing is known about how common or rare the losses might be. The example does illustrate how exposure in aggregating a package of goods in multiple auctions can contribute to a kind of transactions cost. The high value agent for G* does not reveal the value of the externality, because to do so he must engage in a very risky strategy of trying to win A and/or E.

6.   CONCLUSIONS

A number of experimental researchers have shown that markets can produce optimal allocations from an initial state of disbursed private information. As shown by the initial Brewer and Plott [1996] BICAP experiments, the presence of large scale indivisibility, non-convexity, and complex patterns of interdependency that are found within a network environment need not preclude the information aggregation needed for efficient auction operations. This paper has shown how to extend these results to include certain types of externalities.

Experiments by previous researchers have confirmed theories that classical markets do not take into account the value of an externality. The research presented here both affirms this view and shows a possible solution. Typically, markets being tested are not complete – so there is no way for the externality to be priced and traded among the agents. In a complete and properly structured mechanism, efficient allocation can be restored. The experiments presented here demonstrate this principle in action, within the environment of a binary conflict network.

Starting with scattered private information about the values of the various projects and the value of the externality, this paper shows that market structure determines whether the value of the externality can be revealed and compared to the cost of aligning several projects that are required for the externality to occur. If the markets are not structured correctly, then the value of the externality cannot be revealed, and its value will never be reflected in the allocation that occurs. If the markets are structured correctly, optimal allocation can occur – although it does not always occur.

BICAP can address the thin-markets problem involved with externalities by connecting the auction for the presence or absence of the externality to the auctions for the rights to run the rest of the trains, and thereby rendering these auctions interdependent. In this way, bids on other trains can also be bids for [e.g., A, E] or against [B, C, D, F] the existence of the externality.

However, the thin markets problem may also offer some clues for why BICAP sometimes overestimates the value of the externality, because in our test design the same agent who had the high value for G often also had the high value for G* but only had the high bid for one or the other. Efficient information aggregation needs for this agent to reveal their values, but it is not in their strategic interests to do so. This may explain why BICAP tended to overestimate the value of the externality in some cases. The degree of error in the overestimate is limited by other agents who are willing to bid on G while the high value agent only bids on G*.

As it is not yet clear how to make the decision of whether a genuine externality exists, the role of regulators in a binary conflict network might be in identifying which projects truly involve externalities and ought to be set up for contingent bidding rather than normal bidding. If we left these structural decisions to the agents in the market, it is not clear what would happen – but it is clear that the contingent bidding creates a bias towards the externality while the absence of contingent bidding creates a bias in the market against the externality.

A future research agenda involving binary conflict networks is warranted. Several questions remain which require theoretical and experimental work. First of all, if the externality is a negative externality ("congestion") instead of a positive externality ("synergy"), do the biases involved in complete and incomplete markets change or do they stay the same? What other sorts of externalities can be solved by properly augmenting the commodity space?

The ease of visually communicating complex patterns of interdependency to human subjects, the ability to include classical problems (public goods, coordination, externalities, etc.) into the network in an obvious way, and the diversity of possible applications make binary conflict networks an interesting class of networks. It is hoped that the initial work with these models and mechanisms like the BICAP auction will encourage a conversation between theorists and experimentalists as to what properties of networks are economically significant and what mechanisms – whether they are centralized or decentralized – are most likely to produce efficient network allocations.

ACKNOWLEDGEMENT

The research reported here was made possible by the financial support of the Hong Kong SAR Research Grants Council (CA98/99.BM01) and the Research Investment Grant program of Georgia State University.

NOTES

1. A number of authors argue this point. While a full review is beyond the scope of this paper, some highlights include: Hayek [1945], who discusses the nature of market planning vs. central planning in terms of *knowledge of the peculiar circumstances of time and place*; the attempt by Hurwicz [1972] to formalize the idea of decentralized economic systems; a number of contributions to the theory of *mechanism design*, as reviewd by Groves and Ledyard [1987]; early laboratory work by Smith [1962] and Grether, Isaac and Plott [1989] (the work was done in the 1970s but published later) establishing the efficiency of markets; and more recent laboratory work on application-specific smart markets and auctions, including Rassenti, Smith, and Bulfin [1982] (airport slots), Banks, Ledyard and Porter [1989] (contingency planning), Plott and Porter [1990,1996] (space missions), Olson and Porter [1994] (1:1 assignment), and McCabe, Rassenti and Smith [1987, 1989] (electricity and oil pipelines).
2. Arrow [1969; pp. 145–148] gives an interesting example of externalities whereby '. . . suitable and indeed not unnatural reinterpretation of the commodity space, externalities can be regarded as ordinary commodities, and all the formal theory of competitive equilibrium is valid, including its optimality. [p. 146]' Plott and Meyer [1975] take a similar view towards externalities and production. In some sense the binary conflict model described in this chapter is another means for reorganizing the commodity space so that simple auction mechanisms, such as BICAP, can be applied.
3. **Bold face** letters usually identify a set, such as the set of agents **I**, the set of projects **P**, or the set of conflicts **C**. Normal face capital letters A, B, C, . . . are usually projects (or uses) of the network. As this paper concentrates on rail networks in particular, the projects A, B, C may occasionally be called trains A, B, C. Lower case letters are generally elements of sets – an agent i, or an agent j, or a conflict **c**. Particular agents are numbered, e.g. Agent 1. In some of the more complex examples to follow, there are enough

trains that the notation can get a bit confusing in places. Questions about the notation can hopefully be resolved by the typeface and context: for instance, I is a train while **I** is the set of agents, i ∈ **I** represents an agent generically, and a particular agent would be numbered, e.g. agent 3 has a value of $7000 for running train I.

4. For example, in a rail network, we might define feasibility as stating that no pairs of trains can crash or violate other safety constraints. Besides rail, other application areas exist, e.g., specialized land rights and radio spectrum rights. Some projects involving land or radio spectrum can occur no closer than a certain range of certain other projects. For example, city planners may decide that heavy industry should be at least 2 miles from residences, or spectrum planners may decide that certain kinds of radio towers need to be a minimum distance apart or have special antennae patterns to focus the signal into disjoint regions and reduce interference.

5. If the agents are railroad operators, differences in values might involve differences in managerial ability, technology or other factors differentiating these firms. In the laboratory experiments, these values are set by the experimenter.

6. Here, the term *private values* refers to the standard induced-values economic framework of Smith [1982]. In particular, it means *both* (i) that agent's have different realizable values for a project rather than a common value *and* (ii) that values are private information in the sense that each agent knows only his or her own values. Private values imply that (i) some particular set of projects and agents should "win" from a value maximization point of view, (ii) none of the agents individually has enough knowledge to calculate this set, but instead the sum of agents' knowledge is needed. The research revolves around whether an auction with a particular set of bidding rules can extract this information.

7. The symbol ⊗ is the standard Cartesian set product that constructs a set of pairs from two sets of elements, i.e., for sets **X** and **Y**, $\mathbf{X} \otimes \mathbf{Y} = \{(x, y): x \in \mathbf{X} \text{ and } y \in \mathbf{Y}\}$. Thus **S**⊗**S** is the set of all project pairs $\{(s_1, s_2)\}$ that can be constructed from the projects operating in schedule **S**. If **S**⊗**S** does not contain any conflicting pairs defined in **C**, then the schedule **S** is feasible. Written in mathematical notation, this feasibility condition becomes $(\mathbf{S} \otimes \mathbf{S}) \cap \mathbf{C} = \emptyset$.

8. Maximizing the sum of bids subject to the constraint of no conflicts is mathematically identical to the weighted stable set problem. Karp [1972] proves that the stable set problem is among the hardest group of computational problems, known as the NP-complete class of problems.

9. The stable set problem is briefly discussed by Gerards [1995; pp. 154, 158] who is primarily concerned with matching problems. Matching involves the lines in a graph having a positive value, whereas in the stable set problem the nodes have value and one wishes to avoid the lines in the graph. There are mathematical relationships between the two classes of problems. See also the discussion of independence systems by Korte and Vygen [2000, pp. 280–281].

10. See, for instance, Minty [1980].

11. See Ahuja, Magnati, Orlin, and Reddy (1995) for a list of 42 applied examples of this technique.

12. A notable exception is the work of Vernon Smith and his colleagues, who have investigated smart market mechanisms for the distribution of electricity and natural gas. They assume that all units input and output from the network are identical in quality and that agents only care about network and cash flows, and not whose units they are getting (buyers) or where units go (sellers). Therefore, the nature of competition does not involve a binary conflict network as it does in a railway, where agents are interested in navigating the network without collision. Instead, the smart markets resemble a series of multiple unit auctions that allocate goods that exist at various nodes in the network.

13. The complementarities involved in assembling packages from items sold in separate auctions, and the exposure risk it generates, are described in Rassenti, Smith, and Bulfin [1982] in the context of a criticism of the separate-auctions proposal by Grether, Isaac, and Plott [1970s, published 1989] for deregulating US airports. To eliminate the exposure risk, Rassenti, et.al., proposed one of the first combinatorial auction systems. Their design involved 1st price sealed bids for packages of airport slots, but was unwieldy in the amount of information required for efficient bidding.

REFERENCES

Ahuja, R. K., T. L. Magnati, J. B. Orlin, and M. R. Reddy (1995). "Applications of Network Optimization." In *Handbooks in Operations Research and Management Science: Volume 7 Network Models*, edited by M. O. Ball et al. Amsterdam: Elsevier.

Arrow, K. J. (1983). "The Organization of Economic Activity: Issues Pertinent to the Choice of Market vs. Nonmarket Allocation." In *Collected Papers of Kenneth J. Arrow: Volume 2 – General Equilibrium*. Cambridge: Harvard University Press. First published by Joint Economic Committee, United States Congress. *The Analysis and Evaluation of Public Expenditures: The PPB system*. Vol. 1 Washington, DC: GPO, 1969.

Banks, J. S., J. O. Ledyard, and D. P. Porter (1989). "Allocating Uncertain and Unresponsive Resources: An Experimental Approach." *Rand Journal of Economics* 20, 1–25.

Brewer, P. J. (1995). "Allocation and Computation in Rail Networks: A Binary Conflicts Ascending Price Mechanism (BICAP) for the Allocation of the Right To Use Railroad Tracks." Ph.D. Thesis, California Institute of Technology.

Brewer, P. J., and C. R. Plott (1996). "A Binary Conflict Ascending Price (BICAP) Mechanism for the Decentralized Allocation of the Right to Use Railroad Tracks." *International Journal of Industrial Organization* 14, 857–86.

Brewer, P. J. (1999). "Decentralized Computation Procurement and Computational Robustness in a Smart Market." *Economic Theory* 13, 41–92.

Brewer, P. J., and C. R. Plott (2000). "A Smart Market Solution to a Class of Back-Haul Transportation Problems: Concept and Experimental Testbeds." Caltech Social Science Working Paper No.1082.

Coase, R. H. (1960). "The Problem of Social Cost." *Journal of Law and Economics* 3, 1–44.

Cox, James C., T. Offerman, M. A. Olson, and Arthur J. H. C. Schram (1998). "Competition for vs. on the Rail: A Laboratory Experiment." Mimeo.

Gerards, A. M. H. (1995). "Matching." In *Handbooks in Operations Research and Management Science: Volume 7 Network Models*, edited by M. O. Ball et al. Amsterdam: Elsevier.

Grether, D., M. Isaac, and C. Plott (1989). *The Allocation of Scarce Resources: Experimental Economics and the Problem of Allocations of Airport Slots*. San Diego: Westview Press.

Groves, T., and J. Ledyard (1987). "Incentive Compatibility Since 1972." In *Informaiton, Incentives, and Economic Mechanisms: Essays in Honor of Leonid Hurwicz*, edited by T. Groves, R. Radner, and S. Reiter, 48–111. Minneapolis: University of Minnesota Press.

Hayek, Friedrich A. (1945). "The Use of Knowledge in Society." *American Economic Review* 35, 519–30.

Hurwicz, L. (1972). "On Informationally Decentralized Systems." In *Decision and Organization*, edited by C. B. McGuire and R. Radner, 297–336. Amsterdam: North-Holland.

Hurwicz, L. (1995). "What is the Coase Theorem?" *Japan and the World Economy* 7, 49–74.

Karp, R. M. (1972). "Reducibility among Combinatorial Problems." In *Complexity of Computer Computations*, edited by R. E. Miller and J. W. Thatcher. NY: Plenum Press.

Korte, B., and J. Vygen (2000). *Combinatorial Optimization*. Berlin: Springer-Verlag.

Ledyard, J. O. (1995). "Public Goods: A Survey of Experimental Research." In *The Handbook of Experimental Economics*, edited by J. H. Kagel and A. E. Roth. Princeton: Princeton University Press.

McCabe, K. A., S. J. Rassenti, and V. L. Smith (1987). "An Experimental Mechanism for the Simultaneous Auction of Gas and Pipeline Rights in a Transmission Network." Report Prepared for the Federal Energy Regulatory Commission, Economic Science Laboratory, University of Arizona.

McCabe, K. A., S. J. Rassenti, and V. L. Smith (1988). "A New Market Institution for the Exchange of Composite Goods." Discussion Paper 88–13, University of Arizona.

McCabe, K. A., S. J. Rassenti, and V. L. Smith (1989). "Designing 'Smart' Computer Assisted Markets: An Experimental Auction for Gas Networks." *European Journal of Political Economy* 5, 259–83.

Minty, G. J. (1980). "On Maximal Independent Sets of Vertices in Claw-Free Graphs." *Journal of Combinatonial Theory*, Series B 28, 284–304.

Nilsson, J.-E. (1999). "Allocation of Track Capacity: Experimental Evidence on the Use of Priority Auctioning in the Railway Industry." *International Journal of Industrial Organization* 17, 1139–62.

Olson, M., and D. Porter (1994). "An Experimental Examination into the Design of Decentralized Methods to Solve the Assignment Problem with and without Money." *Economic Theory* 4, 11–40.

Plott, C. R. (1994). "Market Architectures, Institutional Landscapes and Testbed Experiments." *Economic Theory* 4, 3–10.

Plott, C. R., and R. A. Meyer (1975). "The Technology of Public Goods, Externalities, and the Exclusion Principle." In *Economic Analysis of Environmental Problems*, edited by E. S. Mills. NY: Columbia University Press.

Plott, C. R., and D. Porter (1990). "An Experiment with Space Station Pricing Policies." Caltech Social Science Working Paper No. 704.

Plott, C. R., and D. Porter (1996). "Market Architectures and Institutional Testbedding: An Experiment with Space Station Pricing Policies." *Journal of Economic Behavior and Organization* 31, 237–72.

Rassenti, S. J., V. L. Smith, and R. L. Bulfin (1982). "A Combinatorial Auction Mechanism for Airport Time Slot Allocation." *Bell Journal of Economics* 5, 402–17.

Smith, V. L. (1962). "An Experimental Study of Competitive Market Behavior." *Journal of Political Economy* 70, 111–37.

Chapter 8

EQUILIBRIUM BIDDING STRATEGIES UNDER THE ENGLISH AND THE SECOND-PRICE AUCTIONS

D44

Soo Hong Chew
Hong Kong University of Science and Technology

Naoko Nishimura
Shinshu University

1. INTRODUCTION

When bidders have independent private valuations of a deterministic auctioned object, the revenue equivalence between the English auction and the second-price auction, is known in the auction literature.[1] Several papers investigated bidding behavior when there is uncertainty in the value of the auctioned object. Chew (1989) observes that the symmetric Nash equilibrium bid under the second-price auction may not be demand revealing when bidders do not possess expected utility preferences. He further provides condition on bidders whose preferences exhibit the betweenness property to optimally bid less than their reservation values. Karni and Safra (1989) show that the Nash equilibrium bidding behavior under the English auction is demand revealing if and only if bidders' preferences satisfy betweenness.

Neilson (1994) derives the equilibrium bidding behavior under the second-price auction and show that equilibrium bids are lower than bidders' reservation values when their preferences satisfy Machina's (1982) Hypothesis II. In a similar modeling setting, we obtain Nash equilibrium bidding behavior for the second-price auction. Based on a weaker behavioral condition, which is motivated by an empirical finding in Harless and Camerer (1994),[2] we show that equilibrium bids will be bounded from above by bidders' reservation values. In conjunction with the result of Karni and Safra, it follows that equilibrium revenue under the English auction is higher than under the second-price auction. This result provides the theoretical setting for an experimental test of the revenue equivalence theorem reported in Chew and Nishimura (2001).

Section 2 presents the preference mode. Section 3 derives equilibrium bidding behavior for the second-price and the English auctions. A summary of results and some discussions on the experimental applications are provided in Section 4.

2.   BETWEENNESS-CONFORMING PREFERENCES

Consider an individual facing risks, represented by elements of the set D_J of cumulative probability distributions with outcomes in an interval $J \subset \Re$. A riskless payoff y is denoted by the degenerate distribution $\delta_y \in D_J$. Suppose the individual has a complete and transitive preference relation $\geq$ over D_J satisfying continuity in terms of convergence in distribution (see Billingsley, 1968). Then there is a utility functional U on D_J representing $\geq$ (Debreu, 1964).

Consider the following intuitively appealing property of $\geq$, called *betweenness*, which weakens the independence axiom.

Definition 1 (Betweenness): A preference relation $\geq$ satisfies *betweenness* if for any

$$F, G \in D_J, F \geq G \text{ implies that } F \geq \beta F + (1-\beta)G \geq G \text{ for all } \beta \in (0,1).$$

The betweenness-conforming class of preferences, which generalizes expected utility, was axiomatized in Chew (1983, 1989), Fishburn (1983), and Dekel (1986). The utility of a risky prospect $F \in D_J$ for a betweenness-conforming preference relation is given by the solution to

$$\int_J \phi(x,\alpha)dF(x) = 0, \tag{1}$$

in which the *deviation function* $\phi: J \times Rng(U) \to \Re$ is bounded and continuous in both x and α, and decreasing in the second argument (see Chew 1989).

This class of preferences coincides with weighted utility (Chew, 1983; Fishburn, 1983) when $\phi(x,\alpha) \equiv w(x)[v(x) - \alpha]$. Expected utility results when the weight function w is constant. Consistency with *first order stochastic dominance* corresponds to the case where ϕ is increasing in x, while consistency with *second order stochastic dominance* corresponds to the concavity of ϕ in α (Chew and Mao, 1995). We assume that ϕ is differentiable with respect to both x and α, and that U is *path differentiable* in the sense of Chew and Nishimura (1992). To be consistent with *first order stochastic dominance*, we require ϕ to be increasing in its first argument.

The *Allais paradox* (Allais, 1953; Harless and Camerer, 1994) refers to a frequently observed choice pattern that violates the implications of expected utility theory. For Frechet differentiable preference functionals, Machina (1982) offers *Hypothesis II* to account for the Allais type behavior. For betweenness-conforming preferences, we can state Hypothesis II as: For any $\alpha \in Rng(U)$, $\phi(\cdot,\alpha)$ is at least as concave as $\phi(\cdot,\alpha')$ for $\alpha \geq \alpha'$.

Hypothesis II requires the indifference curves to fan out over the entire probability simplex for any three outcomes. In a recent paper by Harless and Camerer (1994), the empirical validity of fanning out choice pattern was confirmed only when the outcomes of the lotteries are restricted to be gains, but not when they are perceived as losses relative to the status quo payoff. This motivates our adoption of a weaker and descriptively appealing condition called the *Allais hypothesis*.

Definition 2 (Allais Hypothesis): A betweenness-conforming utility functional U with a deviation function ϕ satisfies the *Allais hypothesis*, if for any $y \in J$, for any $\alpha > U(\delta_y)$, and for any $x_1, x_2 \in J$ with $x_1 < y < x_2$,

$$\frac{\phi(x_2,\alpha)-\phi(y,\alpha)}{\phi(y,\alpha)-\phi(x_1,\alpha)} \leq \frac{\phi(x_2,U(\delta_y))-\phi(y,U(\delta_y))}{\phi(y,U(\delta_y))-\phi(x_1,U(\delta_y))} \tag{2}$$

When ϕ satisfies the above Allais hypothesis, the consumer is at the present wealth level y not more averse to an increase in risk in the sense of Diamond and Stiglitz (1974) than at any higher wealth level. In a probability simplex, this property requires the indifference curves, in the area with higher utilities than $U(\delta_y)$, to be at least as steep as indifference curves through the intermediate vertex δ_y.

3. EQUILIBRIUM BIDDING STRATEGIES

In this section, we derive and compare individuals' bidding strategies employed in the English auctions and the second-price sealed bid auctions.

Specifically, we consider an auction where bidder i ($= 1, 2, \ldots, n$) competes for a single risky auctioned object, which yields possible outcomes (x_1^i, $x_2^i, \ldots, x_k^i$) with common probabilities ($p_1, p_2, \ldots, p_k$). The following are common knowledge:

(i) The probabilities $\{p_j\}_{j=1}^k$.
(ii) For bidder i ($= 1, 2, \ldots, n$), each possible outcome x_j ($j = 1, 2, \ldots, k$) is independently drawn from an interval $[\underline{x}_j, \bar{x}_j]$.
(iii) Bidders have betweenness-conforming preferences represented by utility functionals $\{U^i\}$, $i = 1, 2, \ldots, n$.

For a realization $\mathbf{x}^i$ of the private values of the possible outcomes, we represent the auctioned object for player i as a distribution $F_\mathbf{x}^i = \Sigma_{j=1}^k p_j \delta_{x_j^i}$. Let $F_{\mathbf{x}-b}^i$ denote the situation where player i wins the auctioned object $F_\mathbf{x}^i$ and pays the dollar amount b. When the auctioned object is deterministic, i.e., $k = 1$, it is known that bidding one's private value is a dominant strategy for both the English and the second-price auction. It is straightforward to verify that this remains a dominant strategy under our risky independent private value model for expected utility maximizing bidders.

For a given betweenness-conforming U^i, we can identify bidder i's private value θ^i for $F_\mathbf{x}^i$ with the reservation implicitly by the solution to:

$$U^i\left(F_{\mathbf{x}-\theta^i}^i\right) = U^i\left(\delta_{y^i}\right), \tag{3}$$

where y^i refers to the bidder i's current wealth level. Omitting the superscript i, we may rewrite expression (3) as:

$$\int_J \phi(t, U(\delta_y)) d[F_{\mathbf{x}-\theta}(t) - \delta_y(t)] = 0 \tag{4}$$

English Auction

Based on the information commonly available, a representative player constructs the probability distribution $Q(\cdot)$ of the highest bid s amidst possible bids made by others. Assume that $Q(\cdot)$ has a density function $q(\cdot)$ with support $[\underline{s}, \bar{s}]$. Let b^e be an English auction bid level of player i. Bidding is assumed to take place continuously with no chance of a tie. Every time the auctioneer calls out the new price level $r \in [\underline{s}, \bar{s}]$, each agent revises her assessment of s using Bayes' Rule. Then, for a given auctioned object $F_\mathbf{x}$, the payoff from planning to withdraw from bidding at b^e, when the current floor price is r, can be given by the expression $H(b^e; r)$:

$$H(b^e;r) = \int_r^{b^e} F_{\mathbf{x}-s}(t) \frac{q(s)}{1-Q(r)} ds + \int_{b^e}^{\bar{z}} \left[\frac{q(s)}{1-Q(r)} ds \right] \cdot \delta_y(t). \tag{5}$$

Withdrawal occurs when the floor price reaches the planned bid level, i.e., $r = b^e$, and the payoff expected at the withdrawal point corresponds to δ_y. Among non-expected utility preferences satisfying some smoothness property, Karni and Safra (1989) established that bidding one's reservation value in an English auction for a risky auctioned object remains a dominant strategy if and only if players' preferences satisfy betweenness. Thus, the optimal bid b^{*e} in the English auction equals θ.

Second-Price Auction

Define $G(\cdot)$ to be the distribution of the highest bid z submitted by bidders other than i. $G(\cdot)$ has a density function $g(\cdot)$ and $Supp[G] = [z,\bar{z}]$. Bidding strategy b^S gives a payoff distribution, $H(b^S)$:

$$H(b^s) = \int_z^{b^s} F_{\mathbf{x}-s}(t)g(z)dz + \int_{b^s}^{\bar{z}} [g(z)dz] \cdot \delta_y(t). \tag{6}$$

Thus the auction mechanism is identified with a complete information game $\langle I, \{B^i\}, \{U^i\}\rangle$, where $I = \{1, 2, \ldots, n\}$ is an index set of players, and the real interval B^i is a bidding strategy set for bidder i. In contrast with the case where an auctioned object is deterministic, we no longer have dominant strategies. Nash equilibrium provides the natural solution concept in this setting. Since U^i is quasi-concave in probability mixtures, a Nash equilibrium exists in mixed strategies.[3] Given betweenness, such equilibrium consists of component pure strategies that are individually indifferent to the equilibrium mixed strategy for each bidder.

Assuming $U[H(b^S)]$ is smooth with respect to bidding strategy b^S, the optimal b^{*S} satisfies the first order condition, which depends on the deviation function ϕ evaluated at the utility level $U[H(b^{*S})]$. At the same time, individually rationality implies

$$U\left[H\left(b^{*S}\right)\right] \geq U(\delta_y). \tag{7}$$

Thus, the optimal bidding decision based on $\phi(\cdot, U[H(b^{*S})])$ is, in general, different from the one based on $\phi(\cdot, U(\delta_y))$ which arises at the decision point in the English auction.

Under expected utility, the optimal bidding decision based on ϕ at $U[H(b^{*S})]$ coincides with the one at $U(\delta_y)$. Therefore (as observed in Karni and Safra (1989)), this is the only case where bidding one's reservation price is a dominant strategy in the second-price auction. For betweenness-conforming bidders satisfying the Allais hypothesis, bidding is more aggressive at $U(\delta_y)$ than at $U[H(b^{*S})]$, so that the optimal bid in the second-price auction is no higher than the one in the English auction.

Theorem: *Let $U^i : D_J \to \Re$, $i \in I$, be bidder i's betweenness-conforming utility functional, with deviation function $\phi^i : J \times Rng(U) \to \Re$, where ϕ^i is strictly increasing in its first argument, and strictly decreasing and differentiable in its second argument. Suppose each bidder's utility functional U^i satisfies the Allais hypothesis (resp: counter Allais hypothesis). Then the equilibrium price in the second-price auction is bounded from above (resp: below) by the equilibrium price in the English auction for a non-deterministic auctioned object.*

Proof: See Appendix.

This result provides the theoretical basis for an experimental test of the revenue equivalence hypothesis investigated in Chew and Nishimura (2001). They report price data from 155 rounds in which two identical objects are sold sequentially. The first object is sold by a second-price auction. The second object is sold by an English auction before revealing the winner and the price from the preceding second-price auction. In each round, this procedure generates a pair of prices, one from the English auction and the other from the second-price auction. For riskless auctioned objects, the observed paired price data support the revenue equivalence theorem. For risky auctioned objects, however, they find that English auction generates significantly higher prices than the second-price auction.

4.   CONCLUDING REMARKS

We derive equilibrium bidding strategies for betweenness-conforming bidders under the English and the second-price auctions when bidders have independent private valuations of a risky auctioned object. Under a behavioral condition, requiring fanning-out of indifference curves on the upper half of the probability simplex, we show that the equilibrium revenue under the second-price auction does not exceed the corresponding equilibrium revenue under the English auction. This provides a theoretical rationale for the prevalence of English auctions over the second-price auctions.

There have been experimental studies on the revenue equivalence among various auction forms for riskless objects since the experiments by Coppinger, Smith, and Titus (1980). Overall the literature supports the equivalence between the English and the second-price auction in the revenue for a riskless object (see, e.g., Kagel, 1995). Our theoretical results provide the basis for the formulation of test hypotheses for an experimental test of the revenue equivalence theorem for risky auctioned objects in the study of Chew and Nishimura (2001). They find that the English auction generates significantly higher prices than the second-price auction, which is consistent with the behavior of the Nash equilibrium bidding behavior of betweenness-conforming bidders under the Allais hypothesis.

A natural follow up experimental study is to incorporate a within-subject direct test of whether bidders exhibit Allais preference in individual choice settings. In this setting, we can test a sharper implication of this paper. Revenue equivalence continues to hold for risky auctioned objects when bidders conform to expected utility. When bidders exhibit strict Allais preferences, revenues from English auctions would exceed those from the second-price auctions.

APPENDIX

Proof of Theorem:
Since the optimal bid in an English auction coincides with one's reservation price θ, it suffices to compare the optimal bid in the second-price auction, b^{*S}, with θ. Let

$$A = \{i | x_i - \theta \geq y\} \text{ and } B = \{j | x_j - \theta < y\}.$$

Given $F_x = \Sigma_{j=1}^k p_j \delta_{x_j}$, let $\varphi : J \times Rng(U) \rightarrow \Re$ be defined by

$$\varphi(h,\alpha) = \frac{\sum_{i \in A} p_i [\phi(x_i - h, \alpha) - \phi(y, \alpha)]}{\sum_{j \in B} p_j [\phi(y, \alpha) - \phi(x_j - h, \alpha)]} - 1. \tag{8}$$

Observe the following two properties of φ.

    (i) φ is strictly decreasing in h.
    (ii) If φ satisfies the Allais hypothesis, then $\varphi(h,\alpha) \leq \varphi(h,U(\delta_y))$, for $\alpha > U(\delta_y)$.

From (4), the reservation price θ for $F_x = \Sigma_{j=1}^k p_j \delta_{x_j}$ satisfies

$$0 = \int_J \phi(t, U(\delta_y)) \, d[F_{x-\theta}(t) - \delta_y(t)]$$

$$= \sum_{i \in A} p_i [\phi(x_i - \theta, U(\delta_y)) - \phi(y, U(\delta_y))] + \sum_{j \in B} p_j [\phi(x_j - \theta, U(\delta_y)) - \phi(y, U(\delta_y))]$$

$$= \left\{ \sum_{j \in B} p_j [\phi(y, U(\delta_y)) - \phi(x_j - \theta, U(\delta_y))] \right\} \varphi(\theta, U(\delta_y)). \tag{9}$$

It follows that $\varphi(\theta, U(\delta_y)) = 0$.

In the second-price auction, using the expression for the payoff distribution in (6), the marginal utility at bid level b is given by:

$$\frac{dU(H(b))}{db} = -g(b)\left\{\int_J \phi(t,U(H(b)))d[F_{x-b}(t) - \delta_y(t)]\right\}\bigg/\int_J \phi_2(t,U(H(b)))d\,H(b)(t).$$

Since ϕ_2 is negative by assumption, the above expression has the same sign as

$$\int_J \phi(t,U(H(b)))\,d[F_{x-b}(t) - \delta_y(t)], \tag{10}$$

which in turn has the same sign as $\varphi(b,U(H(b)))$.

Suppose the optimal bid level $\hat{b} > \theta$. By Property (i) of φ, for $\hat{b} > \theta$, $\varphi(\hat{b},U(\delta_y)) < \varphi(\theta, U(\delta_y)) = 0$. Moreover, $U(H(\hat{b})) > U(\delta_y)$, since $U(H(\hat{b})) \geq U(H(\theta))$ from the optimality of $\hat{b}$ and $U(H(\theta)) > U(\delta_y)$. By Property (ii) of φ, $\varphi(\hat{b},U(H(\hat{b})) \leq \varphi(\hat{b},U(\delta_y))$. Consequently, $\varphi(\hat{b},U(H(\hat{b})) < 0$, which contradicts the optimality of $\hat{b} > \theta$. Therefore, the optimal bid level in the second-price auction is bounded from above by θ.

We omit details of the proof for the case of counter Allais hypothesis, which are similar.□

ACKNOWLEDGEMENT

The authors would like to thank Greg Engl and Stergios Skaperdas for their helpful comments. Financial support from the Research Grants Council of Hong Kong (HKUST6234/97H), National Science Foundation (SES 8810833), Seimeikai 1992 as well as the Grant-in-Aide for Scientific Research by Japanese Education Ministry (1999–2000) is gratefully acknowledged.

NOTES

1. The reader is referred to McAfee and McMillan (1987) for a survey of the auctions literature.
2. Harless and Camerer (1994) find that the fanning out pattern in the probability simplex is supported when outcomes are positive relative to the status quo, but not when they are negative.
3. This has been observed in Crawford (1990) for the case where pure strategy sets are finite. This result for more general settings of continuous pure strategy sets follows, for example, from modifying the classical result of Glicksberg (1952) by observing that quasi-concavity implies that the best response correspondences are convex-valued. See Dekel, Safra, and Segal (1991) for the case of two-person games.

REFERENCES

Billingsley, P. (1968). *Convergence of Probability Measures*. NY: Wiley.
Chew, S. H. (1983). "A Generalization of the Quasilinear Mean with Applications to the Measurement of Income Inequality and Decision Theory Resolving the Allais Paradox." *Econometrica* 51, 1065–92.

Chew, S. H. (1989). "Axiomatic Utility Theories with the Betweenness Property." *Annals of Operations Research* 19, 273–98.

Chew, S. H. and J. Mao (1995). "A Schur-Concave Characterization of Risk Aversion for Non-Expected Utility Preferences." *Journal of Economic Theory* 67, 402–35.

Chew, S. H. and N. Nishimura (1992). "Differentiability, Comparative Statics, and Non-Expected Utility Preferences." *Journal of Economic Theory* 56, 294–312.

Chew, S. H. and N. Nishimura (2001). "Revenue Non-Equivalence between the English and the Second-Price Auctions: Experimental Evidence." *Journal of Economic Behavior and Organization.* Tentatively accepted.

Coppinger, V., Smith, V., and J. Titus (1980). "Incentives and Behavior in English, Dutch, and Sealed-Bid Auctions." *Economic Inquiry* 1–22.

Crawford, V. (1990). "Equilibrium without Independence." *Journal of Economic Theory* 50, 127–54.

Debreu, G. (1964). "Continuity Properties of Paretian Utility." *International Economic Review* 5, 285–93.

Dekel, E. (1986). "An Axiomatic Characterization of Choice under Uncertainty." *Journal of Economic Theory* 40, 304–18.

Dekel, E., Safra, Z., and U. Segal (1991). "Existence and Dynamic Consistency of Nash Equilibrium with Non-Expected Utility Preferences." *Journal of Economic Theory* 55, 229–46.

Diamond, P. and J. Stiglitz (1974). "Increase in Risk and in Risk Aversion." *Journal of Economic Theory* 3, 308–60.

Fishburn, P. (1983). "Transitive Measurable Utility." *Journal of Economic Theory* 31, 297–317.

Glicksberg, I. L. (1952). "A Further Generalization of the Kakutani Fixed Point Theorem, with Application to Nash Equilibrium Points," *Proceedings of the American Mathematical Society* 3, 170–4.

Harless, D. W., and C. F. Camerer (1994). "The Predictive Utility of Generalized Expected Utility Theories." *Econometrica* 62, 1251–89.

Kagel, J. H. (1995). "Auctions: A Survey of Experimental Research." In *The Handbook of Experimental Economics*, edited by J. H. Kagel and A. E. Roth. Princeton: Princeton University Press.

Karni, E., and Z. Safra (1989). "Dynamic Consistency, Revelations in Auctions, and the Structure of Preferences." *Review of Economic Studies* 56, 421–34.

Machina, M. (1982). "Expected Utility Analysis without the Independence Axiom." *Econometrica* 50, 277–323.

McAfee, R. P., and J. McMillan (1987). "Auctions and Bidding," *Journal of Economic Literature* 25, 699–738.

Neilson, W. (1994). "Second Price Auctions without Expected Utility." *Journal of Economic Theory* 62, 136–51.

Vickery, W. (1961). "Counterspeculation, Auctions, and Competitive Sealed Tenders." *Journal of Finance* 16, 8–37.

Chapter 9 | J5|

PHYSIOLOGICAL ANTICIPATION AND ENDOWMENT EFFECTS: INFERRED BRAIN FUNCTION IN THE FORMATION OF ALLOCATIONS IN AN ENGLISH AUCTION

John Dickhaut
University of Minnesota

Kip C. S. Smith
Kansas State University

Kevin McCabe
George Mason University

Nicole R. Peck
Kansas State University

Vijay Rajan
University of Minnesota

1. INTRODUCTION

Among economic theorists, proving the existence of a competitive general equilibrium and then evaluating the equilibrium allocation of goods and services has been a major endeavor. The pile of papers on existence and attributes of the general equilibrium is Everest-like, while comparatively, the pile of papers on getting to equilibrium is like a ski-slope in Florida. Some of the papers in the smaller pile are motivated by the desire to avoid the problems of employing the mythical archetypal Walrasian auctioneer (see Hahn, 1988). That desire, while understood, requires the difficult activity of specifying the price-setting process and determining if that process leads to equilibrium. We consider an alternative premise: that using electrocardiograms to infer brain function of players in an English Auction yields a more complete sketch of how a simple economy gets to equilibrium. We make this proposal fully aware that this attempt is a small first step in discovering the processes employed in getting to equilibrium in more complicated institutions.

Recently (Cason and Friedman, 1993, 1996; Easley and Ledyard, 1993; Gjerstad and Dickhaut, 1998), there has been an interest in seeing if there exists an iterative or updated signal-response model of the market behavior of individuals that produces the price sequences generated by double auctions. Gjerstad and Dickhaut report success in using a signal response (or non-Bayesian "learning") model which converts public data seen by each market participant to some action such as bid, ask, take, or hold on the part of that participant. Using their model, they were able to replicate the type of price sequences in data from double auctions provided by A. Williams and V. Smith.

Doing what Gjerstad and Dickhaut report having done is something, but, for those acquainted with neuroscience, not enough. That discipline leads us to believe that much behavior during auctions is preconscious processing; in particular, neuroscience informs us that visible stimuli to the participant transmit signals to the occipital lobe and then the lobe sends signals to at least both the frontal lobe and amygdala. To date, however, none of those doing economic experiments have attempted to find out if inferring what is hidden from sight bears on observed behavior in an experimental setting. The current paper uses physiological data in the form of heart rate and heart-rate variability to infer different emotional and cognitive effort levels in relation to the arrival of information in the market. We regard our research as a first step in the effort to isolate brain functions in continuous time in economic settings.

In this research, we confine ourselves to the English auction. In the English auction signals (the start, withdrawals, and end) are readily identified. Moreover, the time of occurrence of the heartbeat metrics can be relatively easily matched with time of signals. Contrasted with the typical double auction, the English auction has but a few novel information stimuli in a specific run of the auction. Matching and interpreting the timing of double auction market signals and physiological measures is overly ambitious at this time.

We have three fundamental findings to date. First, for the two participants remaining in the auction, heartbeats per unit time tend to reach a maximum prior to the second withdrawal. Thus there appears to be a physiological anticipation of the withdrawal of that participant by the two participants who will remain in the auction, which (based on the appropriate literature) we attribute to being an emotional anticipation. The second finding is a physiological habituation effect. Participants' maximum heart rate and cognitive effort levels become further removed from other participants' withdrawals as participants engage in more auctions. This effect can be attributed to participants discovering through time the dominant strategy (withdrawing from the auction at one's value) and therefore learning to ignore other participants' withdrawals. Finally, between auctions it is possible to isolate a physiological endowment effect that distinguishes the person that obtains the good (the winner) versus those for whom there is no change in endowment. We consider this phenomenon a cognitive effort endowment effect.

1.1. Organization of the Paper

Making the argument requires several steps. We first briefly review the stimuli our participants see during an experimental auction. We then elucidate a stylized account of how the brain modulates autonomic and cognitive functions during an English auction. The account melds findings from experimental economics, cognitive psychology, and neuroscience. Third, we use this account to explain the behavioral and psychophysiological responses we expect to see during an English auction. Fourth, we develop a set of hypotheses that apply to signals in the electrocardiogram and to retrospective assessments of emotions experienced during the auctions. Fifth, our discussion of our experimental method emphasizes technical aspects of the measurement and analysis of heart rate and heart-rate variability. Sixth, we present data that reveal the general characteristics of the price data and the emotional and effort metrics and suggest that both the price and psychophysiological data are consistent with what one would expect. Seventh, we present evidence for (1) systematic anticipation of public information during the auction, (2) habituation to that information, and (3) evidence of a physiological endowment effect at the end of an auction. Finally, we explore how the observed physiological data relate to questionnaire data on emotions experienced during the auctions.

1.2. Stimuli in the Experimental Auction

Our participants are seated at separate computer terminals. At the beginning of an English auction, the screen reveals the participant's reservation value (i.e. the maximum amount the experimenter will pay the participant for owning the asset at the end of the auction). Throughout the experiment, the bottom right corner of the screen displays the participant's profits to date. Reservation values and profits are private knowledge. In contrast, prices and the number of bidders are public knowledge. The top right corner of the screen displays the number of the bidders remaining in the auction. The current price for bids is shown both numerically and graphically. Each tick of the clock simultaneously changes both the numerical and graphical representations of price. At the start of the auction the outstanding bid price is $0. The price then rises steadily until all but one bidder drops out. The remaining bidder wins the auction. The predicted economic behavior is for each participant to follow what is called a dominant strategy, namely stay in the auction until the price reaches that participant's value. In a four person auction this means the predicted price in the auction will be the third highest reservation price in the auction.

1.3. Brain Response

Our description of brain function as it applies to the English auction is an informed sketch. Many processes are left out because we believe they do not affect the behaviors we observe and their description would require detail that would obscure the fruits of our labor.

The participants see the public and private information displayed on their computer terminals. We assume that this (strictly visual) information is transferred from the retina to visual centers in the occipital lobe where it is partially reassembled and then sent to various associative areas of occipital cortex (Kandel, Schwartz, & Jessell, 1995). From there, the information follows two projection paths, one to prefrontal cortex and the other to the limbic system. The former leads to, in ways that we do not pretend to understand or to address, a representation of the auction that becomes the focus of controlled "cognitive" information processing. We assume that it is the participant's conscious awareness of this representation that contributes to behavior that is invariably consistent with the dominant strategy.

Our focus is on the pathway through the limbic and autonomic systems to the cardiovascular system. Information travels from associative areas in the occipital lobe to the thalamus to the amygdala to the hypothalamus and, finally, to the pituitary gland and the brain stem. The hypothalamus acts both directly and indirectly on the autonomic nervous system. The autonomic system has two major divisions: the sympathetic division which marshals the body's resources for action and the parasympathetic system which maintains basal metabolism under normal conditions. The direct connection from the hypothalamus triggers the vagus nerve and other parasympathetic neurons in the brain stem. The indirect connection acts on the endocrine system through the pituitary to release hormones that influence sympathetic function.

The multiple connections between the limbic system and the autonomic system interact to regulate both heart rate and heart-rate variability (and other homeostatic and alerting mechanisms). The sympathetic division has a dominant effect on heart rate; the parasympathetic division has a dominant effect on heart-rate variability (Andreassi, 1980). The two divisions are often reciprocally active but are not necessarily so; they may be coactive or coinhibited (Berntson, Cacioppo, & Quigley, 1995). For example, sympathetic activation coupled with reciprocal parasympathetic inhibition speeds the heart and diminishes the variability with which it beats. Coactivation speeds the heart but allows its rate to vary. As discussed below, the electrocardiogram, one of our sources of data, contains information about both heart rate and heart-rate variability.

At the same time as messages project downward from the hypothalamus to the heart, messages pass upward from the heart, viscera, and other organs to ventral medial frontal cortex (Damasio, 1994). The ventral medial cortex organizes these signals and makes them available for preconscious processing. Information from the ventral medial cortex is occasionally but not necessarily transmitted into a conscious representation of emotional state. We do not claim to understand or address the neural process that supports the representation of emotions.

1.4. Links between Behavioral and Physiologic Responses

1.4.1. The Link between Heart-Rate Variability and Cognitive Effort

We assume the human information processing system has a limited capacity for cognitive processing (Kahneman, 1973). We further assume that cognitive effort can be operationally defined as a function of the total amount of controlled information processing in which the participant is engaged (Mulder, 1980). That is, controlled information processing consumes the limited resource and is, accordingly, inherently effortful. Exemplars of controlled processing relevant to the auction task are search and maintenance of information in short-term memory, retrieval of information and action agenda from long-term memory, and decision making (Shiffrin & Schneider, 1977).

The relative level of controlled processing during the execution of a task can be inferred from changes in cardiovascular state (Backs, Ryan, & Wilson, 1994; Berntson, Cacioppo & Quigley, 1991). The variability with which the heart beats over a period of roughly 10 seconds is regulated by the interaction of the sympathetic and parasympathetic divisions of the autonomic system. Sympathetic control facilitates controlled processing by marshaling the body's physical and cognitive resources. As the task demand for controlled processing increases, sympathetic control (coupled with parasympathetic inhibition) causes the heart to beat more regularly (over a 10 second period). In contrast, parasympathetic (vagal) control (coupled with sympathetic inhibition) allows the mind and body to "relax" and the heart to beat relatively irregularly.

Heart-rate variability in the 0.07 to 0.14 Hz window (covering the 10 second period) reflects the net action of the two components of the autonomic system on the cardiovascular system in response to task demand. A reduction in the power in the 0.07 to 0.14 Hz window reveals sympathetic control and can be inferred to reflect relatively high levels of cognitive effort. In contrast, surges in power in the 0.07 to 0.14 Hz window are indicative of parasympathetic control and can be inferred to reflect relatively low levels of cognitive effort. The interaction of sympathetic and parasympathetic control makes the power in the 0.07 to 0.14 Hz window a proxy for the current level of controlled information processing.

Spectral analysis of heart-rate variability has been successfully used in both laboratory and operational environments to infer changes in task-relevant controlled information processing (Aasman, Mulder, & Mulder, 1987; Smith, 1996; Vicente, Thornton, & Moray, 1987). For example, in a study of spot currency traders, Smith (1996) found that heart-rate variability consistently fell (effort rose) when traders read headlines that they inferred would lead the market to drive prices in a direction disadvantageous to their holdings. Traders' effort fell when they read headlines that promised to boost their profits. Similarly, Backs (1995) found that effort rose when commercial airline pilots (either the captain or the first officer) took control of the aircraft and fell when they relinquished control.

1.4.2. The Link between Heart Rate and Elicited Emotions

Through cross-cultural and cross-species research, scientists have determined a list of six basic emotions that are evident across mammals throughout the world. The basic emotions include anger, anxiety, disgust, joy, sadness, and surprise. These emotions appear to have neural substrates, universal expression, and specific yet common experiential-motivational-behavioral links (Collet, Vernet-Maury, Delhomme, & Dittmar, 1997; Lane & Schwartz, 1990). Each emotion is relevant to goal-driven behavior; for instance, joy is an emotion related to the achievement of a goal or subgoal, leading the organism to continue with the behavior, modifying if necessary, while anger denotes a frustration of a goal, resulting possibly in aggressive behavior. Furthermore, emotions quickly identify a plan of action for the animal; this exists as an affective bias that often is genetically programmed for the survival of the animal, such as the autonomic "fight or flight" response, or as an acquired bias, such as an endowment effect.

Examining the role of autonomic activity in emotions is a relatively new concept, although several researchers have investigated how emotions are reflected in arousal (Collet et al., 1996; Ekman, Levenson, & Friesen, 1983; Kojima, Ogomori, Mori, Hirata, Kinukawa, & Tashiro, 1996; Levenson, Ekman, & Friesen, 1990; Pasternac & Talajic, 1991; Sinha, Lovallo, & Parsons, 1992). In the present experiment, we are interested in how specific affective responses alter heart rate in humans. One of the earliest studies in the current area was conducted by Ekman, Levenson, and Friesen (1983). Through asking the participants to contract certain facial muscles, associated with universal expressions of emotions, the researchers elicited emotions in the participants and measured the change in their heart rates. The experiment showed that anger and fear increased heart rate by approximately 7.9 beats per minute (bpm), sadness by 6.4 bpm, joy and surprise by 1.9 bpm, and a

−0.3 bpm change for disgust. The changes in heart rate for sadness, anger, and anxiety were significantly greater than those for joy, surprise, and disgust ($p < 0.05$).

Levenson, Ekman, and Friesen replicated their study in 1990. They used a similar experimental procedure, although the separate sections of the experiment included actors and researchers as participants, presumably individuals who would not feel much variable emotion in response to the awkward nature of the task, in addition to non-actors and non-researchers. Inspecting all the data in addition to only the data in which the participants most closely produced the target emotions, Levenson, Ekman, and Friesen (1990) reproduced their previous results. Across the data, sadness changed bpm by approximately 4.2, fear by 5.3, anger by 5.1, joy by 2.3, and disgust and surprise by 0.4. Results were more pronounced yet obtained similar directional statistics in the data where the expression was close to the intended emotion: 7.0 bpm change for anger, 4.6–5.5 bpm change for fear and sadness, 2.3 change for joy, and 0.1 change for disgust and surprise. Sadness, anger, and fear had significantly higher changes in bpm than did disgust and surprise; anger and fear produced greater physiologic changes than joy.

Sinha, Lovallo, and Parsons (1992) examined the emotions of joy, sadness, fear, and anger in a related study on the contrast of specific emotions on cardiovascular systems. The participants were asked to reconstruct and then imagine certain events in their lives in which one of the four target emotions was experienced. In the study, the researchers found that joy and sadness produced a positive change of approximately 8.20 bpm, while fear and anger actualized changes of 12.45–13.15 bpm. Their neutral condition, not eliciting a target emotion, resulted in a change of 2.12 bpm, significantly lower than the other conditions ($p < 0.05$).

It is important to note that different emotions can produce a heart rate elevation, thus when we see changes in heart rate in the data some attempt will be made to identify what types of emotion are involved.

1.5. Hypotheses to Be Examined

- The introduction of heart-rate monitoring equipment will not significantly distort previous findings regarding the relative ability of economic theory to predict the prices of the auction.
- Participants with low values will generally exhibit lower emotional levels than participants with high values in an auction, and participants with low values will tend to generally exhibit lower effort levels than participants with high values in an auction.
- The distribution of physiological responses will track public information about exits from the auction, i.e. an unusual number of maximum emotional levels will occur for people with high values

before the second exiter exits the auction, relative to the assumption
that the maximum levels are uniformly distributed.

- The distribution of responses to public information across auctions
  will indicate that participants habituate to that information.
- There will be an unusual clustering of maximum values of cognitive effort and of emotional response immediately following an
  auction relative to the assumption that the maximum levels are
  uniformly distributed.
- Results with respect to physiologic indicators of emotion will be
  corroborated by post-experimental questionnaire responses.

2.   METHOD

2.1. Participants

In the first run of the experiment, participants were 4 graduate students
attending the University of Minnesota, Twin Cities. Two groups of four undergraduate students participated in the next two runs of the experiment. Of
the 8 undergraduates, 7 were female and 1 male. The undergraduates were students at colleges across the United States and Puerto Rico attending a summer
research opportunities program sponsored by the Cognitive Science Center at
the University of Minnesota, Twin Cities. All participants were selected on a
volunteer basis.

2.2. Experimental Platform

A computer program was created to administer 96 four-person auctions:
48 English and 48 Dutch. The computer program and experimental procedure parallels the process described in Kagel (1995). The type of auction
presented was randomized throughout the 96 trials. In each auction, the four
participants bid against one another to purchase and resell to the experimenter
the asset being auctioned, in order to earn a profit. The price at which a
particular participant could resell the asset was randomly determined by the
program at the beginning of each auction. This was the individual's "redemption value." In the trials emulating the English clock procedure, the price
steadily rose by either $0.02 or $0.06 until the third person exited the auction,
at which time the remaining person purchased the asset for the price at which
the third person exited. Once a bidder exited the auction, he or she could not
return.

Throughout an auction, participants were informed on the computer
screen of the number of bidders in the auction. The number of bidders

was explicitly represented at all times and was, public knowledge. A change in the number of bidders implicitly disclosed the time when a bidder exited the auction. The identities of the bidders remaining in the auction were not disclosed.

Depending on the price paid for the asset compared to the redemption value of the asset, the winner of each auction had either a profit or a loss. After the first 48 auctions, each participant was shown his or her total profit for the first half of the experiment; after the second 48 auctions, the participant was shown his or her profit for the second half of the experiment. The sum of the two profit values determined the participant's total profits for the experiment.

2.3. Auction Procedure

At the assigned time, participants arrived and were randomly assigned to a station, where they read and signed a consent form briefly describing the experimental process and assuring confidentiality. Each station was surrounded by a screen to ensure privacy and prevent participants from uncontrolled interactions with one another. Every participant received a $5.00 attendance payment, which was not at risk during the experiment. The participants received detailed instructions concerning the two types of auctions and how profits would be calculated. After signing consent forms, the participants were prepared for and connected to an electrocardiogram (EKG) monitor. Three electrodes were placed on the body, one immediately under the left collarbone, and two on the torso, between the ninth and tenth ribs on either side.

After participating in four practice auctions, the participants bid in 96 auction trials, randomly alternating between English and Dutch auctions. Each auction lasted approximately 40 seconds and the participants were given a 15 second pause between auctions. After the first 48 auctions, the participants were requested to participate in a two minute subtraction calculation task. We then resumed with the second and final block of 48 auction trials. Following the trials, the participants completed a questionnaire on their emotional responses to events in the English auctions. They were then privately paid the amount of their individual profits.

2.4. Measures

2.4.1. Behavioral Data

The computer program that presented the auctions captured the following data: the bidders' reservation values, the time (price) when each bidder exited, and the bidders' earnings.

2.4.2. Time Series of Interbeat Intervals

Our approach to heart-rate data acquisition and analysis adopts many of the techniques used by Mulder (1980) and Smith (1996). The raw psychophysiologic data are the electrical signals associated with the high-amplitude R-wave spike of the electrocardiogram. The signal is collected by three unobtrusive biopotential electrodes placed on the participant's torso. The signal is fed through a pre-amplifier to an analog-to-digital converter in an MS-DOS-based computer. Post-processing subtracts the times of adjacent R-wave spikes for the entire experimental session to yield a (90+ minute long) time series of interbeat intervals (seconds/beat). The time series of interbeat intervals forms the raw data for spectral analysis. Data were collected continuously throughout the two blocks of auctions and while participants relaxed before, after and between blocks of auctions.

2.4.3. Physiological Metric of Effort

To condition the time series for fast Fourier analysis (FFT), a fifth-order fitting algorithm is used to create an equivalent time series consisting of pseudo-observations every half second. This time series is chopped into a set of overlapping segments. For this study, the segments were 20 seconds long and adjacent segments two seconds apart. Each segment was further conditioned using a Hamming window to remove high frequency artifact and least squares regression to remove low frequency artifact. The tapered regression residuals formed the input to the FFT. The algorithm generates a periodogram containing 5 estimates of power in the 0.07 to 0.14 Hz window.

The metric of effort is calculated from the periodogram. The periodogram is smoothed and the area under the curve between 0.07 and 0.14 Hz estimated by numerical integration. The area under the curve represents the total power (variability) in the original interbeat time series in the window modulated by the autonomic system. The estimate of total power is subtracted from an arbitrary constant. The subtraction yields an index that varies directly with the level of cognitive effort. High values of the index indicate sympathetic control, relatively high levels of controlled processing, and low variability in the interbeat time series.

To facilitate comparison across participants, the indices are normalized within participants. For this study, more than 2000 segments were processed and values of the index calculated for each participant. Each index value is assigned to the midpoint of the segment of the time series from which it was calculated. Centering the index within its segment locates changes that reflect transition in the level of cognitive effort. It is important to stress that the index is not an absolute measure of cognitive effort or of controlled information processing. Rather, the index is a consistent monotonic scale for comparing levels of cognitive effort across participants and auctions.

2.4.4. Physiological Metric of Emotion

As discussed above, a least squares regression equation was calculated for each segment of the interbeat interval data. We used standardized values (z-scores) of the intercept of this regression as our metric of emotion. Like the metric of effort, the metric of emotion was centered at the middle of its segment of data. Note that the intercept and, hence, this metric have the property that as heart rate goes up, the time between heart beats goes down. Thus, the metric varies inversely with heart rate and emotional response.

2.4.5. Questionnaire

At the end of the experiment, the participants completed a questionnaire concerning the emotions they experienced during the English auction trials. Each of the questions identified a particular event that occurred during the auction. Events included the instances when the first person dropped out of the auction and the participant was still involved, instances when the second person dropped out and the participant was still involved, when the participant won the auction, and when the participant did not win the auction. Each question asked the participant to rate on a scale from 1 (no feeling) to 8 (strong feeling), how much he or she experienced each of the 6 basic emotions (anger, anxiety, disgust, joy, sadness, and surprise). The 1 to 8 Likert rating scale resembled that of Ekman, Levenson, and Friesen (1983) and Levenson, Ekman, and Friesen (1990). The order in which the emotions were listed under each question was randomly chosen for each participant.

3. RESULTS

Only data from the 48 English auctions are discussed here. Since there were no significant differences across participant groups, their results are combined.

3.1. Price Data

Although it was not a central issue of the study, we want to establish that the functioning of the auction was not affected in a fundamental way simply

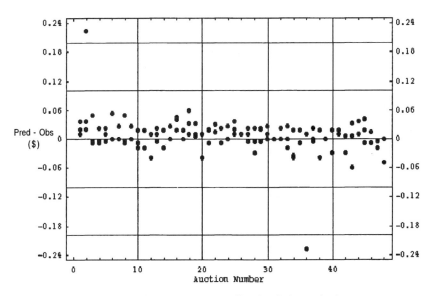

Figure 1. Difference between predicted and observed price

because participants' hearts were being monitored. Generally the theory of English Auctions predicts quite well in the sense that the time at which the third participant exits is very close to the time of exit predicted using the dominant strategy. We would then expect that difference between predicted price and observed price should be near zero.

Figure 1 illustrates the results of the auction for the three groups of four participants. The graphs plot the difference between predicted and actual winning price per auction for the 48 English auctions in the experiment. With the exception of two outliers, most exits from the auction were within one second of the predicted exit. We consider these data as being consistent with earlier results on the English Auction (Kagel, 1995).

3.2. Physiological Metric of Emotion

It is intuitively plausible to expect people who remain in the auction until the end (participants with the first and second highest values) to exhibit higher levels of emotion than people who exit the auction before it finishes (participants with the lowest and second to lowest values). As a check for the emotion metric, we compare the distributions of the metric of emotion across participants grouped by exit order. Figure 2 is a barchart comparing the metric of emotion for early exiters (the first and second bidders to exit) and for late

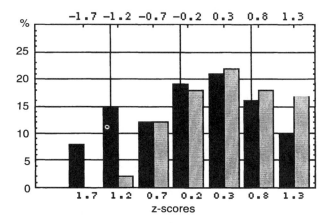

Figure 2. Bar chart of z-scores of the median value of the emotion metric for early exiters (gray) and late (black) exiters

exiters (the third bidder to exit and the winner). The early exiters are shown in gray and the late exiters in black. The distribution of bars indicates the distribution of median values of the metric of emotion during an auction.

We expect the distribution for bidders who remained in the auction to reflect greater emotional responses, that is, to be shifted *left*. The overall median z-scores are −0.16 for participants who exited late, and −0.05 for participants who exited early. The distributions are significantly different at the 0.07 level using a sum of the ranks test.

3.3. Physiological Metric of Effort

Similarly, we expect people who remain in the auction until the end to exhibit higher levels of cognitive effort during the auction than people who exit the auction before it finishes. As a validity check for the effort metric, we compare the distributions of the effort metric across participants grouped by exit order. Figure 3 is a barchart showing the distribution of the metric for participants who exited early and late. Early exiters are shown in gray and the late exiters in black. Note, the higher the value (z-score), the higher the cognitive effort. The data are the median effort metrics during an auction.

We expect to see the distribution for bidders who remained in the auction to reflect increased levels of cognitive effort, that is, to be shifted *right*. The overall median z-scores are −0.045 for participants who exited early and 0.14 for participants who exited late. The distributions are significantly different at the 0.07 (again) level using a sum of the ranks test.

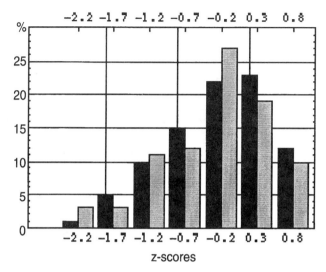

Figure 3. Bar chart of z-scores of median value of the effort metric for early exiters (gray) and late (black) exiters

3.3.1. Autocorrelation

Both our metrics are time series. Time series often display systematic cyclicity – autocorrelation – that violates the assumption of independence that underlies traditional statistical analyses. Our observed data – interbeat intervals – are no exception. In fact, the metric of effort is predicated on the presence of a fundamental cyclicity at 0.10 Hz that reflects the action of the autonomic system on the action of the heart. The presence of this cyclicity in the observed data raises the specter of unanticipated cyclicity in the metrics derived from them. To test for hidden cycles in the metrics, we constructed correlograms for both metrics and tested for autocorrelations beyond the Bartlett band (Gottman, 1981).

The emotion metrics (both median and maximum heart rate in an auction) for two undergraduate participants violated the null hypothesis of no auto-correlation. Both exhibited a pronounced linear trend with positive slope. The correlograms indicated strongly positive autocorrelations for the first half dozen or so lags. These observations suggest that these two participants may have become increasingly disenfranchised with the experiment as it progressed. The effort data for these two individuals and both metrics for the other nine participants exhibit no extraneous autocorrelation or trends. All other time series of metrics (median and maximum, effort and emotion) are free of hidden autocorrelations and other effects that might bias statistical tests.

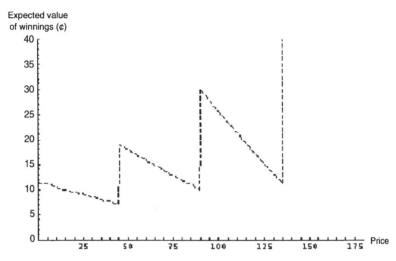

Figure 4. Expected value of winnings as a function of price during an average auction

3.4. Emotional Anticipation of Information

Figure 4 depicts the expected value of a winner in an "average auction" while the auction is in progress. By average auction we mean the average set of redemption values drawn from a uniform distribution 1 to 225 (45, 90, 135 and 180). Figure 4 assumes these four redemption values and, further, that each participant exited at his or her value. We see that there are sharp discontinuities in expectations for the eventual winner as other bidders leave the auction. We are in search of information to document that the emotional level anticipates these discontinuities. Note that for both the eventual winner and the third person out of the auction (late exiters), there is a sharp discontinuity when the second person leaves the auction.

Using data of late exiters we attempt to determine if the behavior of the maximum emotional level is consistent with the notion that those people with high redemption values emotionally anticipate the exit by the second person out of the auction. We merge the late exiters' data to see if there are an unusual number of maxima in the emotion metric preceding the actual exit time of the second person out. Figure 5 is a barchart depicting the time of the maximum value of the emotion metric during an auction for late exiters with respect to the time of the second person's exit. Negative values indicate emotional maxima prior to the second person's exit. The distribution is skewed to the left.

While the barchart in Figure 5 is relatively easy to construct and interpret, conclusions drawn from it can be misleading because of the variable end

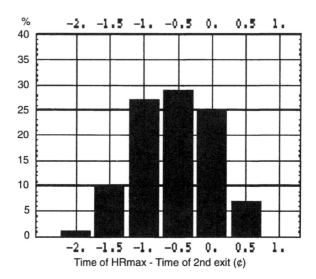

Figure 5. Difference in cents between the time of the maximum value of the emotion metric for winners and third exiters and the time when the second exiter exited

point of the auction. Note that an auction with a low end point will almost of necessity tend to push the point the maximum emotion closer to the time of the second person's exit even if we assume that the maximum level of emotion is achieved at any point during the auction. To control for sampling variation of endpoints and to avoid an erroneous inference, we used Monte Carlo Methods to simulate the sampling distribution of the number of observations in the interval from $-.99$ to $-.29$ cents (immediately preceding the second participant's exit) under the assumption that the maximum emotional level would occur at any point between the beginning and end of the auction for each participant. Using 10000 such draws we found for the those remaining in the auction observations of 72 or more maxima in the interval $-.99$ to $-.29$ cents was significant at the 0.01 level. This result is consistent with the interpretation that late exiters physiologically anticipate the exit of the second exiter. Thus, the unusual number of maxima in the emotional metric for late exiters prior to the second bidder's exit (Figure 5) is consistent with the proposition that late exiters anticipate the release of public information.

The questionnaire data showed that the second bidder's exit from the auction inspired more anxiety, joy, and surprise in the third person out and the eventual winner than it did anger, sadness, and disgust ($p < 0.01$). Thus for late exiters there is consistency between the questionnaire data and the heart-rate response in the auctions.

3.5. Cognitive Effort and Public Information

We attempted to determine if the distribution of the maximum values of the effort metric during the auctions was consistent with the notion that those individuals with high values (late exiters) cognitively anticipate the exit by the second person out of the auction. We compared the data from late exiters and early exiters and found no evidence for differential cognitive effort during the auctions. Therefore, those graphs, along with the related statistical tests, are not presented.

3.5.1. Habituation with Respect to Public Information

The English Auction has a dominant strategy – exit at your value. Information about when others leave the auction should play no role in executing this strategy. Nevertheless, in the beginning of the experimental trials, public information about when others exit the auction may serve as a novel stimulus that provides a basis for participants to learn more about the environmental setting. Through time, this effect may wear off; that is, participants may habituate, cease to respond, to public information. We examined this possibility by looking for a differential response to information in the first 24 and last 24 experimental trials. The measure we used was the distance in cents between (a) the time of peak values of a participant's emotional and effort metrics during an auction and (b) the nearest person's exit prior to the participant's exit. For example, when we examined the third person out, we calculated the distance between that participant's peak emotional and effort metrics and the time of the first and second persons' exits. Whichever was smaller became the measure of sensitivity to public information for that participant in that auction.

In the first 24 auctions, the average distance between emotional maxima and the nearest information event was 15 cents. In the second half it was 21 cents. The sum of ranks tests indicates this difference was significant at the 0.04 level. Similarly, the average distance for effort maxima shifted from 15 cents to 20 cents, a difference significant at the 0.08 level. We conclude that these data are consistent with habituation. Habituation of emotional response appears to be stronger than habituation of cognitive effort.

3.5.2. Between Auction Measurements

Years of work in psychology and cognitive science suggest that there are many mental phenomena that may occur in economic settings after an exchange has occurred. For example, in his research in cognitive dissonance,

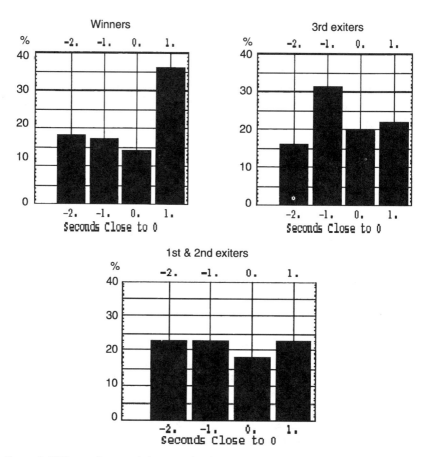

Figure 6. Difference in seconds between the time of the maximum value of the effort metric and the time when the auction ended (0)

Leon Festinger studied the fact that people felt better about a car after they bought the car than before they purchased the very same car (Festinger, 1957). More recently, Kahneman and his colleagues have found that the gift of a mug could create an unexpected unwillingness to resell the mug under the weak assumption on average 50% of those receiving the mug would prefer it less than 50% of the people who did not receive a mug (e.g., Kahneman, Knetsch, & Thaler, 1990). This latter phenomenon is part of a larger set of findings called the endowment effect, an effect from ownership beyond what is usually assumed in economics.

In this study, we infer what happens in auctions from heartbeat data after the auction has ended. Figure 6 shows the time in seconds between the peak

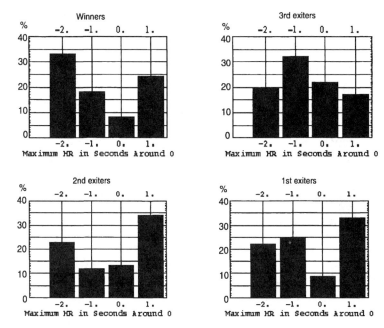

Figure 7. Difference in seconds between the time of the maximum value of the emotion metric and the time when the auction ended (0)

values of the effort metric and the end of the auction for winners, for the third persons out, and for the two early exiters. The data reflect a physiological endowment effect in that winners' cognitive effort goes up significantly immediately after the auction ends ($p = 0.01$, under the null hypothesis that the maximums are equally likely to fall in each second interval). In contrast, for the first, second and third persons out there is no change in cognitive effort immediately after the auction. For the third person, although the difference is not statistically significant, there is a slight increase in cognitive effort for the third person prior to exiting the auction; this is consistent with the participant trying to time his or her exit from the auction.

Figure 7 shows the time in seconds between the peak values of the emotion metric and the end of the auction for all four participants. The data at the end of the auction are consistent with a change in emotional level for three of the four bidders. We compare the observed distributions of peak values of the emotion metric to the null hypothesis that a maximum emotional level was just as likely to occur at any one of the seconds surrounding the end of the auction. For a winner, second person out, and first person out, the distributions of maximum emotion were significantly different at the 0.005 level. For winners, the emotional peak may reflect the elation of winning the auction.

For the early exiters, it may indicate elation that their wait is over or anxiety about the next auction. For the third exiter, the emotional peak just before the end of the auction (his or her exit) may represent disappointment, sadness, or anger at missing the opportunity to win.

3.6. Questionnaire on Emotional Reaction to Events

We mainly focus on the questionnaire data concerning reaction at the end of the auction. Joy dominated over the other five emotions when an individual won an auction ($p < 0.001$); however, participants also felt high levels of surprise ($p < 0.01$) and anxiety ($p < 0.05$). Not winning an auction produced opposite experiences; anxiety, sadness, and anger were experienced more than the other emotions. Over four events (the first person exiting, the second person exiting, not winning an auction, and winning an auction), anxiety, joy, and surprise were significantly greater than feelings of anger, sadness, and disgust ($p < 0.001$). Thus, the results with the heart-rate metric are very consistent with the hypothesis that a change in heart rate can be associated with the different types of emotions that we would expect for winners and losers.

4.   CONCLUSION

The results outlined in this paper are part of an initial investigation of cognitive effort and emotional involvement in economic settings. We make several observations based on the present experiment. First, given the existing concern over the viability of expected utility and many of its replacements (see Camerer, 1995), we appear to have found a method of gathering data that has no precommitment to how people do (or should) make choices while the economy is in operation. Second, our data appear to corroborate the notion that an individual's expectations are not independent of affect. High emotional levels appear to be consistent with anticipating when the second person will leave the auction. Third, our data appear to isolate a unique endowment effect associated with the winner of the auction. that implies that different cognitive effort is occurring for winners rather than other participants. In addition, the data reveal consistent changes in heart rate that can be associated with questionnaire data concerning the emotional responses to the release of public information.

We have taken an initial step toward understanding the interaction of cognition and emotion in the processes employed in attaining equilibrium. As with all exploratory studies, this study suggests as many hypotheses as it has tested. Here, we offer two such hypotheses about cognitive and emotional involvement for future research in experimental economics.

First, while there has been much active interest in learning in experimental economics, there is a continuing development of learning (habituation) at the neuronal level that appears to be in parallel with the type of learning observed in this experiment and this type of learning has not been specifically measured previously. Given that neuroscientists have also mapped out conditioned response at the neural level, it would appear likely that we can refine our ideas of learning in experiments further using this methodology. For example, rather than high emotional levels being associated with a divergence away from an information event, conditioned response should lead maximum emotional levels to be closer to an information event.

Second, the presence of information cues per se in the English auction may possibly be the explanation of why it outperforms the second price sealed bid auction, even though the game theoretic prediction is the same (Kagel, 1995). Currently, we are examining the implications of the present study by replicating it with more refined methodology and measurement and a wider variety of auction settings. With time we may discover that the understanding of brain function in relation to economic institutions can be the source of building better institutions.

ACKNOWLEDGEMENTS

We acknowledge the comments of Patricia Pardo and Jose Pardo as well as other members of the Cognitive Neuroimaging Unit at the V. A. Medical Center in Minneapolis. We also acknowledge the comments of Judy Rayburn, Chandra Kanodia, Brian Shapiro, Arijit Mukherji and other members of the University of Minnesota Accounting workshop series. Furthermore, we are indebted to David Grether, Jim Cox, Jason Shachat and Tom Rietz for comments on earlier drafts of the paper. We are extremely grateful to Jack Kareken for continued criticism, encouragement and useful insights in explicating the fundamental ideas of the paper.

REFERENCES

Aasman, J., G. Mulder, and L. J. M. Mulder (1987). "Operator Effort and the Measurement of Heart-Rate Variability." *Human Factors* 19, 111–70.
Andreassi, J. L. (1980). *Psychophysiology: Human Behavior and Physiological Response.* NY: Oxford University Press.
Backs, R. W. (1995). "Going beyond Heart Rate: Modes of Autonomic Control in the Cardiovascular Assessment of Mental Workload." *The International Journal of Aviation Psychology* 5, 25–48.
Backs, R. W., A. M. Ryan, and G. F. Wilson (1994). "Psychophysiological Measures of Workload during Continuous Manual Performance." *Human Factors* 36, 514–31.

Berntson, G. G., J. T. Cacioppo, and K. S. Quigley (1995). "Autonomic Determinism: The Modes of Autonomic Control, the Doctrine of Autonomic Space, and the Laws of Autonomic Constraint." *Psychological Review* 98, 459–87.

Camerer, C. (1995). "Auctions: Individual Decision Making." In *The Handbook of Experimental Economics* edited by J. H. Kagel and A. E. Roth, 587–683. Princeton, NJ: Princeton University Press.

Cason, T. N., and D. Friedman (1993). "An Empirical Analysis of Price Formation In Double Auction Markets." In *The Double Auction Market: Institutions, Theories, and Evidence*, edited by D. Friedman and J. Rust, 253–83. Reading, MA: Addison-Wesley.

Cason, T. N., and D. Friedman (1996). "Price Formation in Double Auction Markets." *Journal of Economic Dynamics and Control* 20, 1307–37.

Collet, C., E. Vernet-Maury, G. Delhomme, and A. Dittmar (1997). "Autonomic Nervous System Response Patterns Specificity to Basic Emotions." *Journal of the Autonomic Nervous System*, 62, 45–7.

Damasio, A. R. (1994). *Descartes' Error: Emotion, Reason, and the Human Brain.* NY: Putnam.

Easley, D., and J. Ledyard (1993). "Theories of Price Formation and Exchange in Double Oral Auctions." In *The Double Auction Market: Institutions, Theories, and Evidence*, edited by D. Friedman and J. Rust, 63–97. Reading, MA: Addison-Wesley.

Ekman, P., R. W. Levenson, and W. V. Friesen (1983). "Autonomic Nervous System Activity Distinguishes among Emotions." *Science* 221, 1208–10.

Festinger, L. (1957). *A Theory of Cognitive Dissonence.* Stanford, CA: Stanford University Press.

Gjerstad, S., and J. Dickhaut (1998). "Price Formation in Double Auctions." *Games and Economic Behavior* 22, 1–29.

Gottman, J. M. (1981). *Time Series Analysis: A Comprehensive Introduction for Social Scientists.* Cambridge Press.

Hahn, F. (1988). "Auctioneer." In *The New Palgrave: A Dictionary of Economics*, 136–8. The Macmillan Press Limited.

Kagel, J. H. (1995). "Auctions: A Survey of Experimental Research." In *The Handbook of Experimental Economics* edited by J. H. Kagel and A. E. Roth, 501–85. Princeton, NJ: Princeton University Press.

Kahneman, D. (1973). *Attention and Effort.* Englewood Cliffs, NJ: Prentice-Hall.

Kahneman, D., J. L. Knetsch, and R. H. Thaler (1990). "Experimental Tests of the Endowment Effect and the Coase Theorem." *Journal of Political Economy* 98, 1325–48.

Kandel, E. R., J. H. Schwartz, and T. M. Jessell (1995). *Essentials of Neural Science and Behavior.* Stamford, CT: Appleton & Lange.

Kojima, K., K. Ogomori, Y. Mori, K. Hirata, N. Kinukawa, and N. Tashiro (1996). "Relationship of Emotional Behaviors Induced by Electrical Stimulation of the Hypothalamus to Changes in EKG, Heart, Stomach, Adrenal Glands, and Thymus." *Psychosomatic Medicine* 58, 383–91.

Lane, R. D., and G. E. Schwartz (1990). "The Neuropsychophysiology of Emotion." *Functional Neurology* 5, 263–6.

Levenson, R. W., P. Ekman, and W. V. Friesen (1990). "Voluntary Facial Action Generates Emotion-Specific Autonomic Nervous System Activity." *Psychophysiology* 27, 363–84.

Mulder, G. (1980). "The Heart of Cognitive Effort. Studies in the Cardiovascular Psychophysiology of Mental Work." Ph.D. Thesis, University of Groningen, Groningen, Netherlands.

Pasternac, A., and M. Talajic (1991). "The Effects of Stress, Emotion, and Behavior on the Heart." *Methods and Achievements in Experimental Pathology* 15, 47–57.

Shiffrin, R. M., and W. Schneider (1977). "Controlled and Automatic Human Information Processing: II. Perceptual Learning, Automatic Attending, and a General Theory." *Psychological Review* 84, 127–90.

Sinha, R., W. R. Lovallo, and O. A. Parsons (1992). "Cardiovascular Differentiation of Emotions." *Psychosomatic Medicine* 54, 422–35.

Smith, K. (1996). "Decision Making in Rapidly Changing Environments: Trading in the Spot Currency Markets." Ph.D. Thesis, University of Minnesota, Minneapolis, Minnesota.

Vicente, K. J., D. C. Thornton, and N. Moray (1987). "Spectral Analysis of Sinus Arrhythmia: A Measure of Cognitive Effort." *Human Factors* 19, 171–82.

Chapter 10

(Japan)

PRICE DISCLOSURE, MARGINAL ABATEMENT COST INFORMATION AND MARKET POWER IN A BILATERAL GHG EMISSIONS TRADING EXPERIMENT

D44
Q25

Yoichi Hizen
University of Pennsylvania

Tatsuyoshi Saijo
Institute of Social and Economic Research, Osaka University
CREST, Japan Science and Technology Corporation

1.   INTRODUCTION

Against the global warming, the discussion on how to control the total amount of greenhouse gases (GHG's) has started among countries in the late of 1980's. At the third session of the Conference of the Parties (COP3) to the United Nations Framework Convention on Climate Change (UNFCCC) at Kyoto in December, 1997, the Kyoto Protocol was adopted, which was the first agreement on the quantified GHG emission limitation. It assigns each Annex B country (an advanced country or a country undergoing the process of transition to market economy) the quantity she should comply with, and calls for these countries to reduce their overall emissions by at least five percent below the 1990 level in the commitment period 2008 to 2012. To assist the countries in achieving compliance, the Protocol authorizes three major mechanisms, that is, emissions trading, joint implementation, and the Clean

EXPERIMENTAL BUSINESS RESEARCH. Copyright © 2002. Kluwer Academic Publishers. Boston.
All rights reserved.

Development Mechanism. The details of mechanisms, however, remained to be elaborated. Designing these mechanisms is an urgent task since they should start working by 2008 at the latest. Among them, this paper focuses on designing desirable institutions for GHG emissions trading through the use of experimental economics.[1]

Although we know "roughly" that introducing a market for GHG emissions achieves the lowest cost to reduce them, we do not know how the emissions should be traded in the market. As a first step toward designing the GHG emissions trading institution, this paper deals with bilateral trading. There are two main backgrounds to start with bilateral trading. First, the participants in the GHG emissions trading in the Kyoto Protocol are countries. Thus, bilateral negotiations between the government officials of two countries can be the major style of trading. Second, we already have an example of bilateral trading used as an emissions trading institution. In the U.S.A., the acid-rain control program in the Clean Air Act Amendments of 1990 introduced tradable emission allowances for sulfur dioxide, and most of the trades have been carried out through bilateral trading. This program attained the greater reduction of sulfur dioxide emissions than the assigned amount. However, we cannot conclude from this observation that bilateral trading works best as an emissions trading institution because there were other factors which might lead to this great reduction, for example, the permission for banking, the existence of technologies reducing marginal abatement costs, and the combined use of annual auctions.[2] We cannot compare the results of this program with the case of competitive equilibrium or the case of other institutions, without the firms' abatement cost information or the data from other institutions. The experiment on bilateral trading provides a means for study in a controlled environment isolated from these complicating factors. The experiment will also help to provide insight on emissions trading policy under alternative policies for which no field data exist. Such data may be useful for evaluating existing schemes, such as those used in the U.S.A., and provide suggestions for further improvement.[3]

The bilateral trading examined in this paper has a special feature, which we call the *dual role property* of a trader. That is, each participant in the institution can be a buyer and a seller depending on the allowance price. This is a natural property of real emissions trading, but each subject is assigned to be either a buyer or a seller in most previous experiments in emissions trading. Recently, Bohm (1997) employed this property, and reported a bilateral trading experiment among four teams consisting of experienced public officials or experts appointed by the Energy Ministries. Each team represented one of four Nordic countries, and had some information on the marginal abatement cost curves of all teams.[4] The asks and bids were exchanged by fax without revealing this information to other teams. It took four days to complete this experiment. The resulting prices were very close to the competitive equilibrium price and its efficiency was 97%, which was very high.

Following Bohm's experiment, we designed a bilateral trading experiment with two controls: (i) open or closed information of contracted prices, and (ii) open or closed information of marginal abatement cost curves. Thus, there are four different treatments. In this way, we can understand which information treatment would be effective for bilateral trading to work as a GHG emissions trading institution.

We conducted two experimental sessions for each treatment. The first finding is that the efficiency of the eight sessions is very high, regardless of open or closed information. That is, open information of contracted prices and/or marginal abatement costs does not improve efficiency. It was more than 99% in 6 sessions, and 98% and 92% in the remaining two sessions. This finding contrasts with the widely accepted views on bilateral trading, that is, (i) it would be inefficient in the sense that some dissatisfied traders could not be eliminated due to mismatching, and (ii) the revelation of contracted prices would improve its efficiency.[5] Second, marginal abatement costs are equalized in most of the sessions except for the 92% efficiency session. Third, the contracted prices did not converge to the competitive equilibrium price. This observation is different from Bohm's. Fourth, subjects who could exercise market power did not use that power. In each session, we had six subjects who were supposed to represent Russia, Ukraine, U.S.A., Poland, EU, and Japan.[6] In our setting, only the U.S.A. had market power, and the subjects who were assigned this role did not reduce their quantity demanded in order to lower the price.

The paper is organized as follows. In the next section, we describe the experimental design in detail, and section 3 presents the results. In section 4, we discuss why efficiency is so high. Section 5 discusses the future agenda.

2. EXPERIMENTAL DESIGN

The experiment has two controls: (i) open or closed information of contracted prices, and (ii) open or closed information of marginal abatement cost curves. Therefore, there are four treatments. Repeating the same treatment twice yields eight sessions. In what follows, "O" represents " open" information and "C" represents "closed" information. For example, "OC2" indicates session 2 in the treatment of open information of contracted prices and closed information of marginal abatement cost curves. That is, the first digit indicates price information, the second digit marginal cost curve information, and the last the session number.

At least six students were recruited for each session by campus-wide advertisement at Osaka University, Japan, during October, 1998. These students were told that there would be an opportunity to earn money in a research experiment. None of them had prior experience in a bilateral trading experiment. Each session lasted approximately 160 minutes. The mean payoff per

234

subject was \$31.25 (\$1 = 115 yen). The maximum payoff was \$66.09, and the minimum payoff was \$17.39.

Let us describe an "OO" session. Eight subjects were seated at desks in a relatively large room and listened to a tape-recorded instructions. This instruction part took about 45 minutes. In this part, each subject received a sample graph (see Figure 1). The upper half is a sample marginal abatement

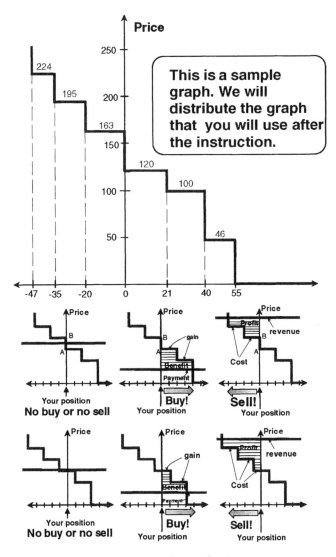

Figure 1. A Sample Graph

cost curve. Each subject was told that the initial position is at 0. If the subject moves to the right, she buys the allowance and earns benefits, and if she moves to the left, she sells the allowance and obtains a profit.[7] All possible situations were depicted in the lower half of Figure 1. After receiving instructions on how to transact with other subjects, all subjects were examined in order to check their understanding of the instructions. The best six subjects continued the experiment, and the rest were paid $13 and asked to leave the room.[8] Then each subject was assigned an identification number from 1 to 6 and, at the same time, each subject received her own marginal abatement cost curve. In the "OO" session, each subject received Figure 2 with all six abatement cost curves, and had fifteen minutes to examine it (i.e., open information of marginal abatement cost curves).[9] Then bilateral trading started. Since every subject had a tag with an identification number, subjects could identify other subjects' marginal abatement cost curves. Every subject could move around the room freely to find a subject with whom to transact. During negotiations, subjects were not allowed to talk. Only numbers (price and quantity), and "yes" and "no" symbols on their negotiation sheets were exchanged in order to avoid information leakage. Once a pair reached an agreement, they reported the price and quantity to an experimenter, who announced these numbers on the blackboard (i.e., open information of contracted prices). The maximum time for negotiations was 60 minutes, and subjects could end their negotiations early if all agreed to it. The full 60 minutes was used in all sessions except "CO2." In this session subjects quit at 58:30.

During the experiment, we did not use any country names or the term "emissions trading." That is, subjects faced a situation where trading of an abstract commodity was conducted with an abstract price.

3. EXPERIMENTAL RESULTS

3.1. Efficiency of Bilateral Trading

Define the efficiency of bilateral trading as follows:

$$\frac{\text{Surplus extracted in the experiment}}{\text{Surplus extracted at competitive equilibrium}}$$

This is a standard measure of efficiency. Efficiency in experiments is usually measured as the percentage of the maximum possible surplus extracted from the institution. Since our institution includes no externality, the maximum is attained at the competitive equilibrium.[10] In our design, the competitive equilibrium price ranges from 118 to 120. We regard 119, which is the midpoint

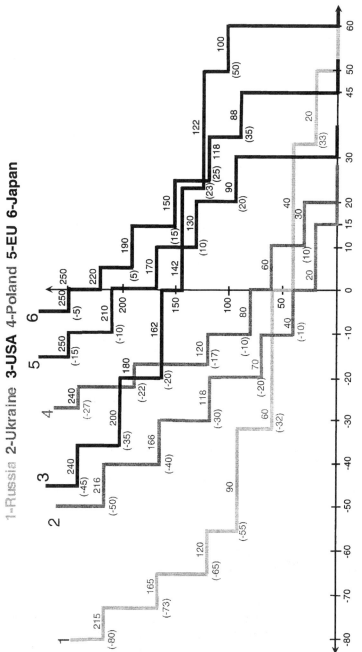

Figure 2. All Marginal Abatement Cost Curves

Table 1. Efficiency of Bilateral Trading

Subject No.	OO1	OO2	OC1	OC2	CO1	CO2	CC1	CC2
1 (2555)	1420	1870	960	1710	1510	1100	1460	1600
(Russia)	0.556	0.732	0.376	0.669	0.591	0.431	0.571	0.626
2 (1290)	1140	914	360	1665	1320	940	1536	2370
(Ukraine)	0.884	0.709	0.279	1.291	1.023	0.729	1.191	1.837
3 (610)	685	683	2060	372	1846	615	583	550
(U.S.A.)	1.123	1.120	3.377	0.610	3.026	1.008	0.956	0.902
4 (390)	520	570	850	530	500	555	910	500
(Poland)	1.333	1.462	2.179	1.359	1.282	1.423	2.333	1.282
5 (620)	800	1105	1300	755	−150	1080	81	150
(EU)	1.290	1.782	2.097	1.218	−0.242	1.742	0.131	0.242
6 (1525)	2425	1800	1450	1844	1400	2700	2390	1800
(Japan)	1.590	1.180	0.951	1.209	0.918	1.770	1.567	1.180
Sum (6990)	6990	6942	6980	6876	6426	6990	6960	6970
	1	0.993	0.999	0.984	0.919	1	0.996	0.997

between 118 and 120, as the competitive equilibrium price. At this price, the surplus is 6990. In Table 1, the top row indicates the name of the sessions, the left column shows the I.D. numbers of subjects, and the numbers in parentheses are their individual surplus at the competitive equilibrium price. In each cell, the upper figure is the actual individual surplus the subject earned, and the lower figure is the efficiency of this subject. For example, the figure of 0.732 for subject 1 in the "OO2" session is the ratio between 1870 and 2555, which we call individual efficiency.

As Table 1 shows, the efficiency of each session is quite high except "CO1." The reason for the low efficiency level in this session is that subject 5 traded with other subjects even though she suffered a loss. Individual efficiencies are quite different even for the same subject number. Statistical tests show that Russia consistently earned a much lower surplus than that of the competitive equilibrium and Poland earned a greater surplus than that of the competitive equilibrium. The efficiency of the other countries is close to one. As we discuss later, the only country that had some market power was the U.S.A. We still do not understand why Russia and Poland deviated from the competitive equilibrium efficiency and why the U.S.A. did not exploit its market power.

Figure 3 shows efficiency changes over time. After sixteen minutes, the efficiency in all sessions except session "CC2" was greater than 80%, and it was more than 90% in 6 sessions of 8 after 25 minutes. Efficiency usually is monotonically increasing, but in session "OC2" efficiency moved up and down. This was due to the fact that one subject bought allowances at a loss, but sold them at a relatively high price. Summarizing these findings, we have:

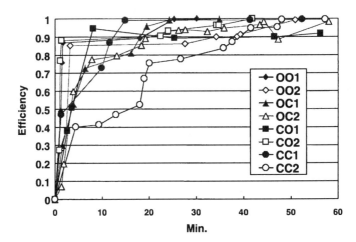

Figure 3. Efficiency Over Time

Observation 1. (i) *The efficiency of bilateral trading is almost one, regardless of open or closed information of contracted prices and marginal abatement cost curves.*

(ii) *Russia's efficiency is low, Poland's efficiency is high, and the efficiency of the other countries is close to one.*

(iii) *The efficiency in 6 sessions out of 8 was more than 90% after 25 minutes.*

Support. To verify whether each country's efficiency is higher than, lower than or close to one, we conducted a t test for the mean. Ignoring the treatment, we have eight observations for each country's efficiency. Since the treatments are different among these observations, and the data size is small, we also conducted a sign test. The null hypothesis is that the efficiency of the country is one. The t-statistics of Russia, Poland and Japan were significantly different from 0; they were -10.35, 3.89 and 2.68 respectively. The p-values of the sign test for these three countries were 0.01, 0.01 and 0.29 respectively. The high p-value of the sign test for Japan means that her relatively high efficiency in the experiment could have happened by accident with probability 0.29 even if her efficiency was in fact close to one. Thus, we conclude that the efficiency of Japan cannot be said to be higher than one. For the efficiency of each session, we did not use statistics because it cannot rise beyond one and so the distribution is not symmetric with regard to one. However, as Table 1 shows, the efficiency is almost one in all sessions except "CO1", whose efficiency is 0.919 and still high. Observation 1-(iii) comes from Figure 3.

From this observation, high efficiency seems to be an intrinsic property of bilateral trading under the dual role property.

3.2. Contracted Prices in Bilateral Trading

Figures 4-1 and 4-2 show contracted prices and quantities over time. The gray horizontal line in each small graph shows the competitive equilibrium price range of 118–120. The left-hand side number of a square is the seller's subject number, the right-hand side number is the buyer's subject number, and the number under the square is the contracted quantity. If the variance of the last three contracted prices is significantly smaller than the variance of the first three contracted prices, then we say that the contracted price sequence converges. We find convergence of contracted prices in five of eight sessions, but no information disclosure effect is observed. Similarly, Figures 5-1 and 5-2 show bids and asks over time. A white symbol denotes an ask, and a gray symbol a bid.

Observation 2. (i) *Contracted average prices in the "CC" sessions (under closed information of contracted prices and marginal abatement cost curves) roughly equal the competitive equilibrium price, but the variances of prices in the "CC" sessions are larger than those of the rest except "OC1".*

(ii) *Average prices cannot be said to equal the competitive equilibrium price in sessions other than the "CC" sessions.*

(iii) *The average price of the last three contracts is not equal to the competitive equilibrium price in any session.*

(iv) *The convergence of contracted prices is found in five of eight sessions, but no information disclosure effect on convergence is observed.*

Support. To verify whether the average price of each session is equal to the competitive price, we conducted a t test for the mean. However, since more than one unit of allowances were traded at the same price between two subjects at once, observations are not independent. Thus, we also conducted a sign test. The null hypothesis is that the average price of the session is equal to the competitive price. The t-statistics of only "CC1" and "CC2" were not significantly different from 0; they were -1.40 and -1.64 respectively. The sign test obtained high p-values in "CO1", "CC1" and "CC2"; they were 0.08, 0.27 and 0.65, respectively. Since t-statistic of "CO1" was significantly different from zero (-4.65), and the p-value of the sign test for this session was relatively small, we conclude that the average price of "CO1" is not equal to the competitive price while those of "CC1" and "CC2" are. Similarly, we conducted the same t test on the average price of the last three contracts for each session, and in every session it was significantly different from the competitive price (we did not use a sign test here because the number of price levels was only three and so a sign test cannot provide any strong evidence). To compare the variances of contracted prices between sessions, we conducted an F test for equal variances. The null hypothesis is that there is no difference of variances between two sessions. The F-statistics are summarized in Table 2. In each cell, the upper figure is the F-statistic between sessions in the row and column. The lower figure in parentheses is its one-side p-value. The

240

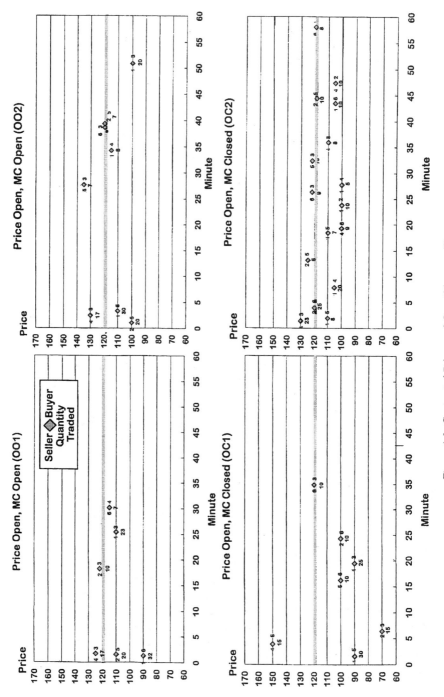

Figure 4-1. Contracted Prices and Quantities over Time

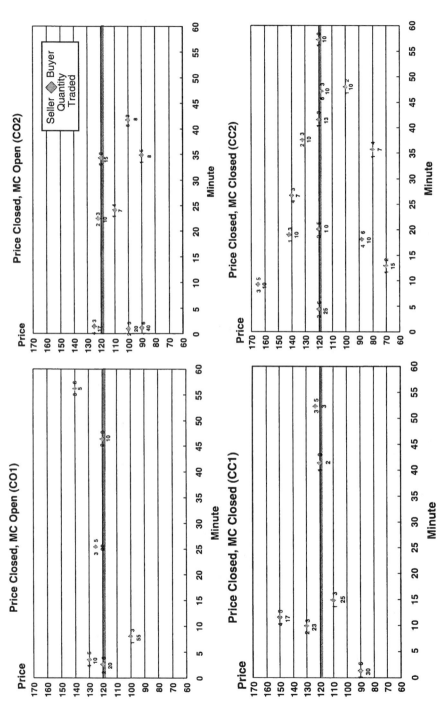

Figure 4-2. Contracted Prices and Quantities over Time

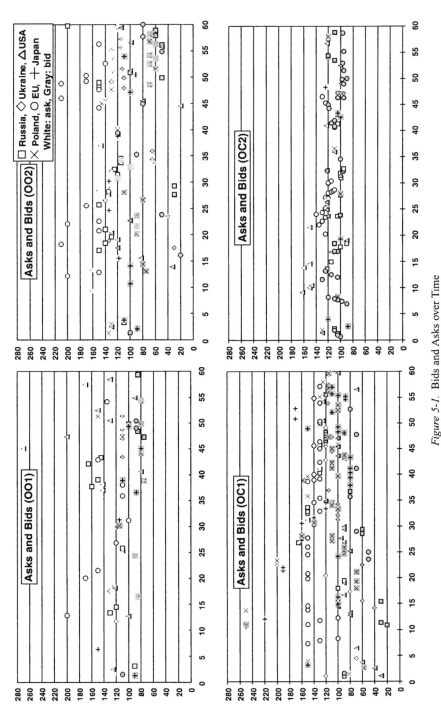

Figure 5-1. Bids and Asks over Time

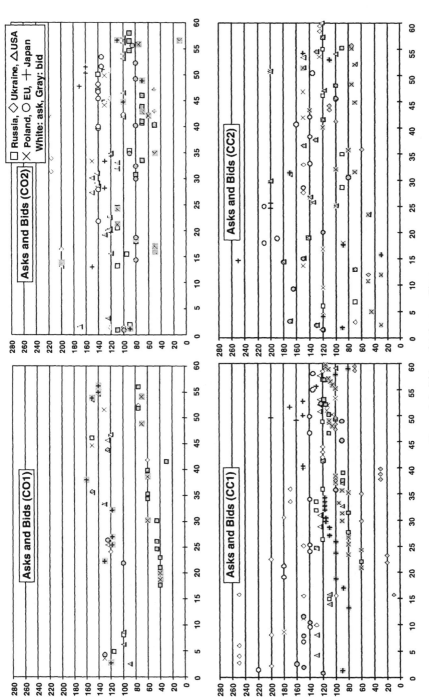

Figure 5-2. Bids and Asks over Time

Table 2. F-statistics (P-values) for Equal Variance of Contracted Prices

	OO2	OC1	OC2	CO1	CO2	CC1	CC2
OO1	1.17	3.23	1.66	1.03	1.21	2.80	3.73
	(0.21)	(0.00)	(0.00)	(0.44)	(0.15)	(0.00)	(0.00)
OO2		3.77	1.42	1.20	1.41	3.27	4.35
		(0.00)	(0.02)	(0.16)	(0.03)	(0.00)	(0.00)
OC1			5.35	3.14	2.67	1.15	1.16
			(0.00)	(0.00)	(0.00)	(0.23)	(0.21)
OC2				1.70	2.01	4.64	6.18
				(0.00)	(0.00)	(0.00)	(0.00)
CO1					1.18	2.72	3.63
					(0.18)	(0.00)	(0.00)
CO2						2.31	3.08
						(0.00)	(0.00)
CC1							1.33
							(0.06)

variances of prices in "CC1" and "CC2" were 459.79 and 613.18 respectively, which were greater than those of other sessions except "OC1", in which it was 530.51. Table 2 shows that the variance difference is significantly large between the "CC" sessions and others except "OC1". We also conducted the same test on the variance between the first three and the last three contracted prices within each session. The F-statistics (one-side p-values) of "OO2", "OC2" and "CO2" were 1.33 (0.19), 1.02 (0.47) and 1.10 (0.39) respectively, while those of other sessions were so large that the p-values were almost 0.

By the nature of bilateral trading, the price contracted by a pair of subjects is determined by negotiation. Even though several other contracted prices have already been announced, a pair of subjects cannot reach an agreement if either of them rejects these prices. For this reason, the competitive equilibrium price cannot play the role of the standard of trade. The step-function nature of marginal abatement cost curves can be a supplementary reason why contracted prices did not converge to the competitive price. For example, in session "CO2", Russia sold 8 allowances at price 90 at 35 minutes and her marginal abatement cost reached the kink which includes the competitive price (see Figures 4-2 and 2). Since her marginal cost from −32 to −55 is constant and it is 90, she did not suffer any loss in this trade. However, this made the average price of the last three contracts significantly lower than the competitive price in this session. If her marginal abatement cost curve were smooth, she should have suffered loss and so would not have accepted such a low price.

3.3. The Effect of Disclosure of Contracted Price and Marginal Abatement Cost Curve Information

The effect of disclosure of contracted prices can be calculated by comparing the "OO" and "CO" sessions, and the "OC" and "CC" sessions. However, since the variances of contracted prices in sessions "OC1" and "OC2" cannot be said to be the same, we omitted these sessions from the comparison. Under this constraint, we compare the "OO" sessions with the "CO" sessions. No differences are observed among the variances of these sessions.

For the same reason mentioned in the above paragraph, we compare the "CO" sessions with the "CC" sessions to measure the effect of disclosure of marginal abatement cost curve information. We find that the variance of contracted prices in the "CO" sessions is smaller than in the "CC" sessions. Summarizing these facts, we have:

Observation 3. (i) *Assuming that each subject knows the other subjects' marginal abatement cost curves well, the disclosure of contracted prices does not have any impact on the variance of contracted prices.*

(ii) *Under closed information of contracted prices, the disclosure of marginal abatement cost curves reduces the variance of contracted prices.*

Support. Comparing two sessions within the same treatment, we find the F-statistic for equal variance between "OC1" and "OC2" to be significantly large, which is 5.35 (see Table 2). This implies that the variances are different between these sessions. The F-statistics between "OO" sessions and "CO" sessions are small except between "OO2" and "CO2", for which it is 1.41. If we employ a two-side F test between these two sessions, however, the null hypothesis cannot be rejected with the 5% significance level. Therefore, we conclude that the variances of the "OO" and "CO" sessions are not different. On the other hand, the F-statistics between the "CO" and "CC" sessions are significantly large, and so their variances are different.

3.4. Equalization of Marginal Abatement Costs over Time

Behind efficiency, we can see how marginal abatement costs changed over time. Figures 6-1 and 6-2 show their change in each session. If a subject sells allowances and reaches the kink on the marginal cost curve, we choose the right-hand side cost figure, and if a subject buys allowances and reaches the kink on the marginal cost curve, we choose the left-hand side cost figure. Due to the step-function nature of our marginal abatement cost curve, we must be careful when evaluating marginal costs. For example, the marginal abatement cost of Russia in session "OO1" was 90 after 25 minutes. Checking the raw data, we find that Russia sold exactly 55 units of emissions allowance in 25 minutes. Therefore, if the subject wanted to sell one more unit, its marginal abatement cost would have been 120 (see Figure 2). Taking account of this fact, we have:

Observation 4. *Except for the EU subject in session "CO1," the marginal abatement costs of all subjects approach the competitive equilibrium price.*

Support. The step-function nature of our marginal abatement cost curves allows the data to take only some particular values. For example, the EU's marginal cost can be only 0, 90, 130, 170, 210 or 250. Thus, instead of using statistics, we drew Figures 6-1 and 6-2, examined them taking the step-function nature into account, and reached Observation 4.

3.5. Market Power Issues

We define market power as follows. Given that all other countries behave as price takers, if a country can increase her surplus by changing her behavior, that is, how many allowances she sells or buys at each price, then we say that she has market power. This is called unilateral market power.[11] Each country's marginal abatement cost curve can be regarded as her excess demand curve. To understand how much market power a particular country has, we first aggregate these excess demand curves of all countries other than this country. Given the aggregate excess demand curve of other countries, by changing how many allowances this country sells or buys at each price, we obtain a different market-clearing price. Using the new price, we calculate this country's surplus and compare it with her surplus at the competitive equilibrium. This procedure shows that the only country that has market power in our design is the U.S.A. Note that the U.S.A. subject can find her market power before the actual trade only in marginal abatement cost disclosure sessions. In sessions with closed information of marginal cost curves, she can only guess it negotiating with other subjects. Although the surplus of the U.S.A. was more than three times her surplus at the competitive equilibrium in two sessions of eight, the statistical tests used in Observation 1 showed that they were not different as a whole. That is, the U.S.A did not exercise market power to increase her surplus. Most probably, the subjects could not exploit the marginal abatement cost curve information to use such market power.

4.   DISCUSSION

Let us think about how high efficiency can be promoted by the dual role property, that is, each country can buy *and* sell the allowance depending on

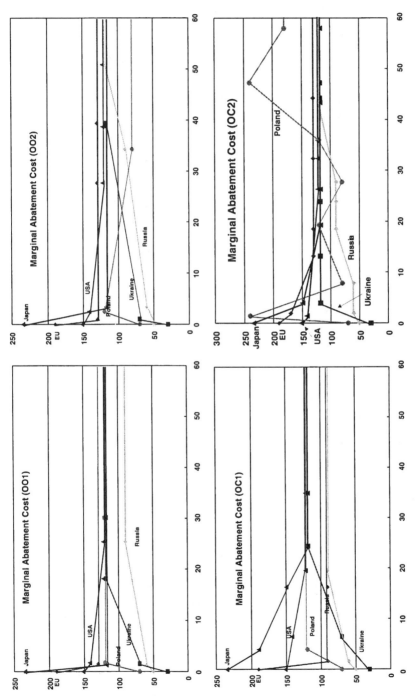

Figure 6-1. Marginal Abatement Cost over Time

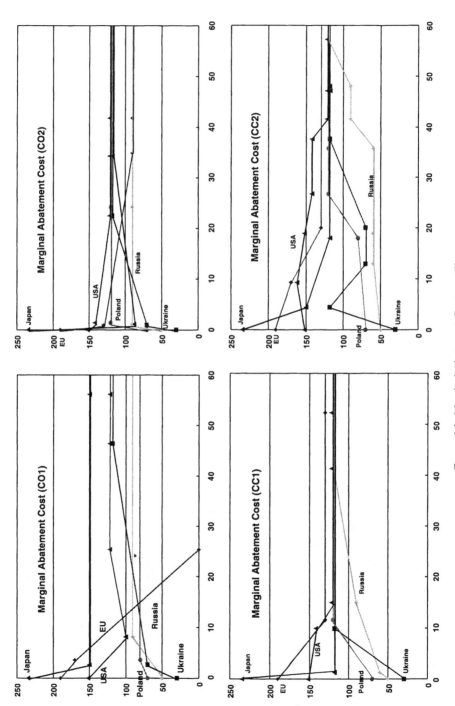

Figure 6-2. Marginal Abatement Cost over Time

Price

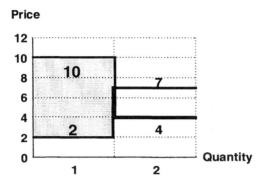

Figure 7. Efficiency of Bilateral Trading

the price. Consider the following simple demand and supply curves with two sellers and two buyers drawn in Figure 7. Each seller has just one unit of a good. On the other hand, each buyer wants to buy just one unit of the good. Apparently the competitive equilibrium price must be between 4 and 7, and the social surplus becomes 8. If buyers can only buy and sellers can only sell, a mismatch can easily occur. Consider a pair in which the buyer's value is 10 and the seller's cost is 7. If they trade with each other, the surplus is 3. Consider another pair in which the buyer's value is 4 and the seller's cost is 2. The surplus of this pair is 2 and hence the sum of the surplus is 5, which is less than 8. After these trades, no mutually beneficial trade will occur. Now consider the case in which everyone can buy and sell. After these trades, the buyer whose value is 4 has one unit of the good and hence she can sell it. Since the seller whose cost is 7 does not have any good, he can buy it. If this pair trades with each other, they can enjoy 3 units of surplus, so that the total surplus becomes 8. Actually, starting from any trading pair, we can find a path that leads to a Pareto efficient allocation.[12]

Thus, the dual role property seems to be an important factor in achieving high efficiency. In order to confirm this statement, we need to conduct a bilateral trading experiment with the *uni*-role property where the role of a buyer or a seller is fixed. In an experiment that studies electronic bulletin board trading for emission permits, Cason and Gangadharan (1998) investigated bilateral negotiation with the uni-role property. The efficiencies of three sessions with bilateral negotiation are 57 percent, 77 percent, and 68 percent, which are less than those of the continuous double auction. Since the experiment of Cason and Gangadharan is quite different from our experiment, further study is needed to obtain new insights about the dual role and uni-role properties.

5.   CONCLUDING REMARKS

In this experiment, it was found that first, the efficiency of bilateral trading is quite high, regardless of open or closed information of contracted prices and/or marginal abatement cost curves. That is, high efficiency seems to be an intrinsic property of bilateral trading under the dual role property. Second, marginal abatement costs are equalized over time. Third, on the other hand, contracted prices did not converge to the competitive price over time. Fourth, subjects who had market power did not use it.

We used just six subjects in each session. If the number of participants increases, the number of possible matchings increases with the square order of the number of participants. That is, if there are many participants in bilateral trading, they cannot communicate well through matching. Therefore, the number of subjects is an open question to be explored.

Our experiment is a prelude to several more experiments that aim at designing the entire emissions trading institutions. In order to provide a solid basis for such a design, we plan to conduct the following: (1) Oral double auction experiment, (2) Banking experiment, (3) Non-compliance experiment, (4) Liability experiment and (5) Market power experiment.

ACKNOWLEDGEMENT

This research was partially supported by CREST (Core Research for Evolutional Science and Technology) of the Japan Science and Technology Corporation (JST). We also thank an anonymous reviewer, Professor James C. Cox and participants of the CREST workshop for helpful comments and discussions, and Dr. Yasuko Kawashima of the National Institute for Environmental Studies in Japan for providing marginal abatement cost information.

NOTES

1. For recent experimental results in emissions trading, see Cason and Plott (1996), Godby, Mestelman and Muller (1998), and Muller and Mestelman (1998).
2. 2.8% of annual total allowances is auctioned once a year.
3. Some evaluation of sulfur dioxide emissions trading has just started. See, for example, Schmalensee et al. (1998) and Stavins (1998).
4. Bohm distinguished two concepts of marginal abatement cost curves. *Technical* marginal cost curves are based upon scientific knowledge. He assumed that each team knew the others' technical cost curves very well, but did not know *social* marginal abatement cost curves. Social abatement costs include considerations of real-world political constraints concerning employment and distribution effects. Cost curves used in his experiment were social ones. In our experiment, these two concepts coincide.

5. These views are not based upon either economic theory or empirical evidence. Feldman (1973) shows that allocations through bilateral trading can attain Pareto efficiency in a finite number of steps.

6. Although we designed our experiment supposing that subjects represent these countries, we used abstract terms during the experiment to avoid any effect of country names or the term "emissions trading" on subjects' behavior.

7. We implicitly presume that position 0 is the position where each country attains the goal required by the Kyoto Protocol without emissions trading. Since subjects can never move away from this position without emissions trading, the goal is always achieved. That is, our experimental setting does not address the non-compliance issue but focuses on what kind of trading should be done in the world where non-compliance never happens.

8. The number of subjects who actually participated in bilateral trading was 6. Sessions where 8 subjects participated at the outset were "OO1", "OO2", and "CO2", sessions with 7 subjects were "OC2", "CC1", and "CC2", and sessions with 6 subjects were "OC1" and "CO1".

9. Since information on the marginal abatement cost curves around 2010 is hard to obtain, we draw these curves based upon some information provided by Dr. Kawashima.

10. For the efficiency concept, see Davis and Holt (1993).

11. For the definitions of market power, see Holt (1995).

12. See Feldman (1973).

REFERENCES

Bohm, Peter (1997). "A Joint Implementation as Emission Quota Trade: An Experiment among Four Nordic Countries." Nord vol. 4. Nordic Council of Ministers.

Cason, Timothy N., and Lata Gangadharan (1998). "An Experimental Study of Electronic Bulletin Board Trading for Emission Permits." *Journal of Regulatory Economics* 14, 55–73.

Cason, Timothy N., and Charles R. Plott (1996). "EPA's New Emissions Trading Mechanism: A Laboratory Evaluation." *Journal of Environmental Economics and Management* 30, 133–60.

Davis, Douglas D., and Charles A. Holt (1993). *Experimental Economics*. Princeton, NJ: Princeton University Press.

Feldman, Allan M. (1973). "Bilateral Trading, Processes, Pairwise Optimality, and Pareto Optimality." *Review of Economic Studies* 40, 463–73.

Godby, Robert W., Stuart Mestelman, and R. Andrew Muller (1998). "Experimental Tests of Market Power in Emission Trading Markets." Mimeo.

Holt, Charles A. (1995). "Industrial Organization: A Survey of Laboratory Research." In *The Handbook of Experimental Economics*, edited by John H. Kagel and Alvin E. Roth. Princeton, NJ: Princeton University Press.

Muller, R. Andrew, and Stuart Mestelman (1998). "What Have We Learned from Emissions Trading Experiments?" *Managerial and Decision Economics* 19, 225–38.

Schmalensee, Richard, Paul L. Joskow, A. Denny Ellerman, Juan Pablo Montero, and Elizabeth M. Bailey (1998). "An Interim Evaluation of Sulfur Dioxide Emissions Trading." *Journal of Economic Perspectives* 12, 53–68.

Stavins, Robert N. (1998). "What Can We Learn from the Grand Policy Experiment? Lessons from SO_2 Allowance Trading." *Journal of Economic Perspectives* 12, 69–88.

Part III

LEARNING AND CONSTRUCTION

Chapter 11

EWA LEARNING IN BILATERAL
CALL MARKETS

Colin F. Camerer
Caltech

David Hsia
Citicorp

Teck-Hua Ho
University of Pennsylvania

1.   INTRODUCTION

This paper is about learning in bilateral call markets. In these markets, a buyer and a seller are privately informed of their values and submit their bids anonymously. If the buyer's bid is (weakly) more than the seller's ask, they trade at the midpoint of their bids. Understanding learning in bilateral call markets serves as a foundation for studying learning in more complex market institutions such as posted offers and double auctions. It also forces a generalization of learning models developed for simpler games to environments in which learning contingent on one realized random variable, such as a buyer's valuation in one trial. Similarity-based generalization is a natural way to extend what is learned locally, which is undoubtedly important when people learn in very complex environments (which has not been thoroughly explored experimentally).

Studying learning in games is important because most of game theory revolves around the analysis of different equilibria of a wide range of games.

The question of how, and whether, equilibrium actually arises was not thoroughly explored until recently. Now theorists actively study the dynamic properties of various models of evolution and learning, with a special focus on which types of equilibria these dynamics converge to (e.g., Weibull, 1998; Fudenberg and Levine, 1998). However, less attention has been paid to how well these dynamic models fit and predict data. The natural place to start is with data from laboratory experiments, where we have good control over the subjects' incentives and perceptions of the game they are playing, and the information they receive which helps them learn. Eventually, of course, these models should be extended to explain and predict learning in field settings (e.g., Ho and Chong, 1999).

Many of these models – though not all – have traditionally been classified into two groups: reinforcement, and belief learning. Reinforcement models update some unobserved propensity, reinforcement level, or attraction, according to what a chosen strategy actually earned (perhaps relative to some reference point, which might adapt). Belief models form beliefs based on some weighted average of previous observations of what other players have done. Beliefs are then used to compute expected payoffs of different strategies, and those with a higher expected payoff are chosen with a higher probability. Camerer and Ho (1999) created a more general model, experience-weighted attraction (EWA) learning, which hybridizes the main features of reinforcement and belief learning. In EWA, strategies have attractions which are updated by decaying lagged attractions and multiplying them by an experience weight (which is also updated), and adding either the payoff received from choosing a strategy, or δ times the foregone payoff from unchosen strategies. Attractions are then divided by the experience weight, which controls whether attractions are averages or cumulations of past payoffs. More details of this model are given below.

This paper extends the EWA approach to bilateral call markets. In these markets, a single buyer and seller are each privately informed about their own value and cost, denoted V and C, respectively. The probability distributions of possible values and costs, f(V) and g(C), are commonly known. They submit bids, denoted v(V) and c(C). If the buyer is willing to pay at least as much as the seller demands, $v(V) \geq c(C)$, they trade at a price which is the midpoint of their bids, $(v(V) + c(C))/2$; otherwise they do not trade.

These are bilateral call markets because they are two-agent examples of general call markets. In call markets, many traders submit demand and supply schedules, and the market is "called" at the price where supply meets demand. The mechanism used to determine prices in the two-agent case is also called the sealed-bid mechanism.

We investigate bilateral call markets for two reasons. First, there is an enormous amount of experimental evidence about the way in which market institutions influence prices and quantities, and the speed and nature of convergence, when there are many traders (see Holt, 1995, for a review). Very few of the learning models developed to carefully explore learning in simpler strategic games have been applied to market data. The only exceptions we know of are two studies of call markets with many buyers and sellers. Cason and Friedman (1999) applied a form of direction learning to a laboratory call market with four buyers and four sellers and random supply and demand each period. They found that partial adjustment toward ex post optimal bids explained a significant portion of the observed behavior. In addition, there is strong asymmetry in the adjustment and significant 'observational learning' taking place. The result shows that actual received payoffs are not the only information traders use to guide their decisions. Hsia (1999) applied EWA (and some models which are extreme special cases of it) to the same data and found that EWA did significantly better than both reinforcement and belief based models.

In the call markets studied by Cason, Friedman, and Hsia, Bayesian Nash equilibrium strategies require markdowns or markups of valuations (i.e., a buyer should bid some fraction of her value), which are approximately constant for all valuations, and small compared to markdowns in the bilateral call markets. This relatively weak incentive to optimize may have contributed to the asymmetry in traders' adjustment and the inability to observe significant learning parameters in some cases. By extending EWA from games to bilateral call markets, we hope to learn something about how the model can be applied to more complicated market institutions, in which bidding strategies are complex (nonlinear) and there is a torrent of information (bids, asks, and acceptances) which influences learning.

Second, it is cognitively plausible to think that when a buyer draws a valuation V, bids $v(V)$, and either makes a trade or doesn't, she learns something about how she should bid for valuations similar to V. This effect can be captured in a model which "learns less" about events that are far from V and $v(V)$, or less similar to V and $v(V)$, in a sense that we make precise later. Similarity-based generalization of learning is well-established in cognitive psychology and heuristics like these are used in machine learning in computer science (see Kaelbling, Littman, and Moore, 1996, for a summary). Similarity-based learning is also arguably a "cognitively economical" heuristic because scarce attention is allocated where it is likely to be most useful – namely, in the vicinity of the current valuation and bid. Our approach is closely related to the approach of Sarin and Vahid (1997). These authors showed that "spillover" of reinforcement from a chosen strategy to neighboring strategies could explain why players actually converge to equilibrium much more rapidly than they are predicted to solely by choice reinforcement, in order-statistic experiments conducted by Van Huyck, Battalio and Rankin (1996).

The long-run goal of the approach we take in this paper is a general theory of learning in markets and other complex economic environments. Such a theory would be a scientific breakthrough if it could connect game-theoretic learning models to approaches in psychology and computer science. A theory of market learning would also be useful in practice. Theorists are now actively engaged in designing more and more complex incentive systems, or "mechanisms", to help societies and firms incentivize agents to act in ways which maximize some objective function. Business firms are also designing more ambitious trading systems – e.g., internet auction companies Ebay and Ubid. These mechanisms are usually discovered by trial-and-error learning or managerial hunches, or by theorists searching for sets of rules which balance "incentive compatibility" and "individual rationality". However, the definition of rationality in mechanism design ignores the cognitive difficulty of computing how to behave under the rules, or the difficulty of learning from experience. In practice, every applied mechanism designer has an intuitive sense that some mechanisms work beautifully in theory, but will fail in practice because they are too opaque for agents to figure out or learn (e.g., Ledyard, 1993). A theory of learning could formalize the designers' intuitions by suggesting precise "learnability" constraints. Adding these constraints would inform which mechanisms would be easiest to learn, and hence most likely to work well in practice (e.g., Friedman, 1998).

The EWA learning approach posits that there is a general rule of learning that is applicable across all games and individuals. Differences across games and heterogeneity in player learning behaviors are captured by differences in EWA learning parameters[2]. Since the EWA rule nests reinforcement and belief learning as special cases, the theory allows for some subjects to be reinforcement learners while others to be belief learners (although our prior research suggests they are neither of these special cases when one allows for heterogeneity (see Camerer and Ho, 1998)). The main virtue of the EWA approach is that one can apply the same model to study any game. The empirical work reported in the next section suggests that the model is capable of capturing learning behaviors in 32 data sets spanning a wide variety of games. The same approach can also be applied to predict behaviors in brand new games if learning parameters can be sensibly determined ex ante (perhaps inferring from learning parameters estimated in similar games).

The paper proceeds as follows. The next section describes the EWA approach (and alternative theories) and summarizes results from earlier studies comparing them. Section 3 describes previous experimental results on bilateral call markets. Section 4 shows how EWA learning can be extended to study behaviors in bilateral call markets. Section 5 reports the estimation results and Section 6 examines an alternative model of learning specifically developed for studying learning in bilateral call markets by Daniel et al. (1998). Section 7 concludes.

2.   PRIOR RESEARCH IN LEARNING IN GAMES

There have been dozens of studies fitting different learning models to experimental data. Rather than summarize this large and growing literature, we will only mention some highlights and dwell on precursors which motivate our analysis of the call market data. We start with notation. We study n-person normal-form games. Players are indexed by i ($i = 1, \ldots, n$), and the strategy space of player i, S_i consists of m_i discrete choices, that is, $S_i = \{s_i^1, s_i^2, \ldots, s_i^{mi-1}, s_i^{mi}\}$. $S = S_1 \times \ldots \times S_n$ is the Cartesian product of the individual strategy spaces and is the strategy space of the game. $s_i \in S_i$ denotes a strategy of player i, and is therefore an element of S_i. $s = (s_1, \ldots, s_n) \in S$ is a strategy combination, and it consists of n strategies, one for each player. $s_{-i} = (s_1, \ldots, s_{i-1}, s_{i+1}, \ldots, s_n)$ is a strategy combination of all players except i. S_{-i} has a cardinality of $m_{-i} = \Pi^n_{j=1, j\neq i} m_j$. The scalar-valued payoff function of player i is $\pi_i(s_i, s_{-i})$. Denote the actual strategy chosen by player i in period t by $s_i(t)$, and the strategy (vector) chosen by all other players by $s_{-i}(t)$. Denote player i's payoff in a period t by $\pi_i(s_i(t), s_{-i}(t))$. Many theories assume that each strategy has a numerical attraction, which determines the probability of choosing that strategy. Learning consists of changes in attractions based on experience. (In "rule learning" the strategies are rules which map history into choices, and players update the attractions of these rules; e.g., Salmon, 2000a and Stahl, 1999.)

Learning models of this sort require a specification of initial attractions, how attractions are updated by experience, and how choice probabilities depend on attractions. The core of the EWA model is two variables which are updated after each round. The first variable is $N(t)$, which we interpret as the number of "observation-equivalents" of past experience. The second variable is $A_i^j(t)$, player i's attraction of strategy j *after* period t has taken place.

Updating is governed by two rules. The experience weight $N(t)$ is updated according to $N(t) = \phi(1 - \kappa)N(t - 1) + 1$. Attractions are updated according to

$$A_i^j(t) = \frac{\phi \cdot N(t-1) \cdot A_i^j(t-1) + [\delta + (1 - \delta) \cdot I(s_i^j, s_i(t))] \cdot \pi_i(s_i^j(t), s_{-i}(t))}{\phi(1 - \kappa)N(t-1) + 1}$$

where $I(x, y)$ is an indicator function which is one when $x = y$ and 0 otherwise. Intuitively, attractions are equal to decayed (by ϕ), experience-weighted ($N(t - 1)$) lagged attractions, plus reinforcement for the received payoff (if $s_i^j = s_i(t)$) or δ times the reinforcement for a foregone payoff.[3] This numerator is then quasi-normalized by dividing by $\phi(1 - \kappa)N(t - 1) + 1$. Previously we denote the term $\phi(1 - \kappa)$ by ρ and estimate ρ instead of κ (see for example Camerer and Ho, 1999). The free parameters δ, ϕ, and κ all have intuitive interpretations.

The weight on foregone payoffs δ is a kind of "imagination" of foregone payoffs, or "simulation" of outcomes under alternative competitive scenarios; it might also be considered responsiveness to opportunity costs or regret. The decay parameter ϕ is naturally interpreted as the degree to which players realize other players are adapting, so that old observations on what others did become less and less useful. The parameter κ determines the growth rate of attractions, which reflects how quickly players lock in to a strategy or, in machine learning terms, how quickly players shift from "exploring" an environment to "exploiting" what they have learned. When $\kappa = 0$, attractions are weighted averages of lagged attractions and past (δ-weighted) payoffs, where the averaging weights are $\phi N(t-1)/(\phi N(t-1)+1)$ and $1/(\phi N(t-1)+1)$. When $\kappa = 1$, the denominator becomes one and attractions are (decayed) cumulations of past payoffs. When attractions are cumulations, a strategy which is chosen frequently and yields positive payoffs can build up a large "lead" over unchosen strategies, so that exploration is brief and a player quickly turns to exploiting their historical information by locking in to one strategy rapidly.

Note that while we have not subscripted the key parameters δ, κ, and ϕ, they obviously could be different across players or games. Attractions must determine probabilities of choosing strategies in some way. We generally use

the logit form, $P_i^j(a, t+1) = \dfrac{e^{\lambda \cdot A_i^j(t)}}{\sum_{k=1}^{m} e^{\lambda \cdot A_i^k(t)}}$, but a power form fits about equally

well (Camerer and Ho, 1998).

Figure 1 shows a cube with axes representing the imagination parameter δ, the change parameter ϕ, and exploration/exploitation parameter κ. Many existing theories are simply extreme cases of EWA learning which are represented by points or edges of the cube. For example, cumulative reinforcement, average reinforcement, weighted fictitious play are edges and Cournot and fictitious play are vertices of this cube.

When $\delta = 0$, $\kappa = 1$ (and $N(0) = 1$), then $N(t) = 1$ and the attraction updating equation becomes $A_i^j(t) = \phi \cdot N(t-1) \cdot A_i^j(t-1) + [\delta + (1-\delta) \cdot I(s_i^j, s_i(t))] \cdot \pi_i(s_i^j(t), s_{-i}(t))$. This is the simplest form of cumulative choice reinforcement (e.g., Roth and Erev, 1995, with some features left out). When $\delta = 0$, $\kappa = 0$ (and $N(0) = 1/(1-\phi)$), the attraction updating equation becomes $A_i^j(t) = \phi \cdot A_i^j(t-1) + (1-\phi) \cdot I(s_i^j, s_i(t)) \cdot \pi_i(s_i^j(t), s_{-i}(t))$. This is a form of averaged choice reinforcement (attractions are averages of previous attractions and incremental reinforcement). The most surprising extreme case is weighted fictitious play. When $\delta = 1$, $\kappa = 0$, then the attractions are updated according to

$$A_i^j(t) = \frac{\phi * N(t-1) * A_i^j(t-1) + \pi_i\left(s_i^j(t), s_{-1}(t)\right)}{\phi \cdot N(t-1) + 1}$$

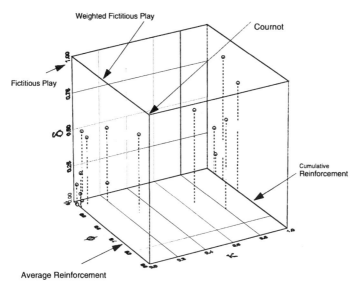

Figure 1. EWA cube

This updating rule corresponds exactly to updating of expected payoffs according to "weighted fictitious play", in which players' weight the last observation of what others did by one, and from t periods ago by ϕ^{t-1}, form a belief which is a normalized average of these weighted observations, and use those beliefs to calculate expected payoffs. Weighted fictitious play includes fictitious play ($\phi = 1$) and Cournot best-response dynamics ($\phi = 0$) as special cases.

Seen as vertices of the EWA parameter cube, it is obvious that reinforcement and belief learning models are closely related rather than fundamentally different (as many people have suggested). Belief learning (of the weighted fictitious play sort) is simply a kind of generalized reinforcement in which unchosen strategies are reinforced by foregone payoffs, as strongly as chosen strategies are, and reinforcements are averages rather than cumulations.

The EWA cube also suggests that there is no good *empirical* reason to think that players' parameter configurations would necessarily cluster on the vertices corresponding to reinforcement and belief learning. Indeed, early studies did not consider a wide range of parameter values and hence, have never found clustering on particular vertices. (Instead, the typical study simply chose an edge or vertex and asked how well that specific learning rule matched the data, compared to a benchmark like Nash equilibrium or random choice.) Furthermore, the intuition behind reinforcement is compelling – namely, chosen strategies are reinforced more strongly – and the intuition behind belief learning is compelling too – unchosen strategies should be strongly reinforced too. There is no scientific reason to choose one intuition or the other, when one can respect both intuitions with a value of δ between 0 and 1 (i.e., a learning model in the interior of the cube).

More generally, empirical results comparing reinforcement and belief models have been mixed. Many direct comparisons of the two favored reinforcement models (Mookerjhee and Sopher, 1994, 1997; Erev and Roth, 1998). However, when weighted linear combinations of reinforcements and expected payoffs are used to fit data, the weight on expected payoffs is about ten times higher than on reinforcements (Erev and Roth, 1998; Battalio, Samuelson and Van Huyck, 1997; Munro, 1999). The mixed results could be due to use of games and techniques which do not have enough power to distinguish between models (Salmon, 2000b).

Studies which estimate the EWA model provide an easy way to compare the extreme special cases to one another, and to EWA, by testing the implied restrictions on parameter values. Table 1a summarizes results of model estimation from 32 data sets, including our earlier papers, call markets (Hsia, 1998), cost allocation processes (Chen and Khoroshilov, 2000), extensive-form centipede (Camerer, Ho and Wang, 1999), continental divide games (Camerer, Ho and Chong, 1999), "unprofitable" games (Morgan and Sefton, 1998), signaling games (Anderson and Camerer, 2000), patent race games with iteratively dominated strategies (Rapoport and Amaldoss, 2000), and 5 × 5 matrix games (Stahl, 1999).

The goodness-of-fit statistic, summarized in Table 1b, is −1 times log likelihood except in Chen (1999). The column "EWA" reports the -*LL* of the EWA model. The reinforcement and belief models report the *difference* between the -*LL*'s of those models and the EWA statistic. (Positive differences mean that EWA fits better.)

Values of δ tend to be between .5 and 1 in most studies except those in which games have only mixed-strategy equilibria, where δ is close to zero. The value of ϕ is reliably around .9 or so, with a couple of exceptions.

What about model comparisons? The fairest comparisons estimate parameters on part of a sample of data and forecast choices out-of-sample, so that models with more parameters will not necessarily fit better.[4] (Indeed, if they succeed in-sample by overfitting, they will do particularly badly when predicting out-of-sample.) In those 11 comparisons (denoted "OUT" in the third column from the right), EWA predicts better than reinforcement in every case, although usually modestly. EWA predicts better than belief learning in 9 of 11 cases, by a large margin in some data sets, and does worse in two constant-sum games.

Of course, EWA necessarily fits better in the other 20 in-sample comparisons than reinforcement and belief models because the latter are special cases. But it also does better in almost all cases when penalizing EWA for

Table 1a. A Summary of EWA Parameter Estimates in Various Games

CITATION	GAME	EWA estimates (standard error)				Comments
		δ	ϕ	ρ	N(0)	
Camerer, Hsia and Ho (this chapter)	Sealed bid mechanism	n.a.	1.00	0.91	11.2	ψ, ω & κ replace δ, ρ
Camerer, Ho and Chong (1999) Hsia (1999)	"Continental divide" Call markets	0.750 0.47 (0.32)	0.611 0.97 (0.01)	0.001 0.74 (0.06)	0.762 3.80 (0.88)	
Amaldoss et al. (2000)	Same function alliance – equal profit sharing	0.000 0.000 0.070	0.952 0.985 0.892	0.889 0.986 0.867	3.732 1.773 0.110	High reward Med. reward Low reward
	Same function alliance – proportional sharing	0.000 0.000 0.000	0.988 0.923 0.969	0.996 0.959 0.959	15.176 6.401 3.438	High reward Med. reward Low reward
	Parallel development of product – equal sharing	0.000 0.168 0.2112	0.911 0.903 0.883	0.585 0.934 0.645	0.406 4.910 0.236	High reward Med. reward Low reward
Rapoport and Amaldoss (2000)	Patent race game – symmetric players	0.000 0.000	0.940 0.970	0.929 0.984	4.613 15.747	Low reward High reward
	Patent race game – asymmetric players	0.475 0.137	0.901 0.959	0.857 0.973	1.418 12.454	Strong player Weak player
Anderson and Camerer (2000)	Signaling games (game 3) (95% confidence interval) Signaling games (game 5) (95% confidence interval)	0.69 (.47, 1.00) 0.54 (.45, .63)	1.02 (.99, 1.04) 0.65 (.59, .71)	1.00 (.98, 1.00) 0.46 (.39, .54)	32.9 32.8, 32.9 3.37 (3.4.3.4)	
Camerer and Ho (1999)	Median-action coordination	0.853 (0.005)	0.800 (0.018)	0.000 (0.000)	0.647 (0.059)	

Table 1a. Continued

CITATION	GAME	EWA estimates (standard error)				Comments
		δ	φ	ρ	N(0)	
	4 × 4 Mixed-strategy games payoff = 5 rupees	0.000 (0.035)	1.04 (0.010)	0.961 (0.014)	19.63 (0.065)	
	4 × 4 Mixed-strategy games payoff = 10 rupees	0.73 (0.103)	1.005 (0.009)	0.946 (0.011)	18.391 (0.713)	
	6 × 6 Mixed-strategy games payoff = 5 rupees	0.413 (0.082)	0.986 (0.005)	0.935 (0.006)	15.276 (0.009)	
	6 × 6 Mixed-strategy games payoff = 10 rupees	0.547 (0.054)	0.991 (0.011)	0.926 (0.024)	9.937 (0.017)	
	p-beauty contest	0.232 (0.013)	1.330 (0.004)	0.941 (0.000)	16.815 (0.000)	
Camerer, Ho and Wang (1999)	Normal form centipede (odd player)	0.3190 (0.3157)	0.9092 (0.1414)	.0010	1.001 (2.2278)	Clairvoyance full update, κ
	Normal form centipede (even player)	0.239 (0.3218)	0.902 (0.1370)	.946	12.744 (4.9620)	Clairvoyance full update, κ
Chen and Khoroshilov (2000)	Cost allocation	.80 ~ 1.0	1 (fixed)	.1 ~ .3	0 (fixed)	
Morgan and Sefton (1999)	"Unprofitable" games (baseline games)	0.084 (0.074)	0.925 (0.014)	0.916 (0.026)	3.632 (1.255)	
	"Unprofitable" games (upside games)	0.142 (0.064)	0.893 (0.012)	0.000 (0.004)	0.374 (0.343)	
Stahl (1999)	5 × 5 matrix games	.663 (.0211)	.337 (.0439)	.085 (.0821)	0.000 (0.000)	
Camerer and Ho (1998)	Weak-link coordination	0.652	0.582	0.198	2.187	

Table 1b. A Summary of EWA Forecast Accuracy in Various Games

CITATION	GAME	Model accuracy					Comments
		EWA	Choice reinforce – EWA	Belief – EWA	In/ Out of sample	Fit tech- nique	
Camerer, Hsia and Ho (this chapter)	Sealed bid mechanism	1102	30.84	65.46	IN	-LL	ψ, ω & κ replace δ & ρ
Camerer, Ho and Chong (1999)	"Continental divide"	1189.85	248.81	180.09	IN	-LL	
Hsia (1999)	Call markets	1915	0	403	IN	-LL	
Amaldoss et al. (2000)	Same function alliance – equal profit sharing	886.314	1.545	529.616	IN	-LL	High reward
		767.491	30.065	390.379	IN	-LL	Med. Reward
		1399.71	9.44	541.47	IN	-LL	Low reward
	Same function alliance – proportional sharing	910.777	36.432	812.953	IN	-LL	High reward
		1054.99	18.33	615.9	IN	-LL	Med. Reward
		1013.73	13.33	1095.61	IN	-LL	Low reward
	Parallel development of product – equal sharing	1194.15	0.11	566.31	IN	-LL	High reward
		1321.45	9.49	497.19	IN	-LL	Med. Reward
		1297.71	4.51	484.08	IN	-LL	Low reward
Rapoport and Amaldoss (2000)	Patent race game – symmetric players	3551.70	12.06	1097.69	IN	-LL	Low reward
		2908.08	20.21	725.94	IN	-LL	High reward
	Patent race game – asymmetric players	3031.54	89.06	706.77	IN	-LL	Strong player
		2835.51	15.65	610.98	IN	-LL	Weak player
Anderson and Camerer (2000)	Signaling games (game 3)	72.16	6.48	10.08	OUT	-LL	
	Signaling games (game 5)	139.52	14.08	23.68	OUT	-LL	

Table 1b. Continued

CITATION	GAME	Model accuracy			In/ Out of sample	Fit technique	Comments
		EWA	Choice reinforce – EWA	Belief – EWA			
Camerer and Ho (1999)	Median-action coordination	41.05	39.22	72.85	OUT	-LL	
	4 × 4 Mixed-strategy games payoff = 5 rupees	326.38	9.12	–40.78	OUT	-LL	
	4 × 4 Mixed-strategy games payoff = 10 rupees	341.71	18.03	8.38	OUT	-LL	
	6 × 6 Mixed-strategy games payoff = 5 rupees	301.70	6.77	–5.42	OUT	-LL	
	6 × 6 Mixed-strategy games payoff = 10 rupees	362.26	13.68	8.92	OUT	-LL	
	p-beauty contest	2381.28	213.09	172.93	OUT	-LL	
Camerer, Ho and Wang (1999)	Normal form centipede (odd player)	1016.84	57.61	536.25	OUT	-LL	Clairvoyance, full update, κ
	Normal form centipede (even player)	951.30	46.42	604.7	OUT	-LL	Clairvoyance, full update, κ
Chen and Khoroshilov (2000)	Cost allocation	.73 ~ .88	–.01 ~ .07	n.a.	IN	MSD	
Morgan and Sefton (1999)	"Unprofitable" games (baseline games)	1729.47	0.59	n.a.	IN	-LL	
	"Unprofitable" games (upside games)	1906.45	16.15	n.a.	IN	-LL	
Stahl (1999)	5 × 5 matrix games	4803.73	64.68	n.a.	OUT	-LL	
Camerer and Ho (1998)	Weak-link coordination	358.058	29.105	438.546	IN	-LL	

extra degrees of freedom using a standard *chi-squared* test, or the Akaike or Bayesian criteria. For example, if the difference in LL is 4 points or more then the special-case restriction will be rejected by the *chi-squared* test. By this criterion, EWA fits more accurately than belief learning in all in-sample comparisons, and fits more accurately than reinforcement in 16 out of 20 comparisons.

Figure 1 shows estimates of EWA parameters for 20 of the 32 studies in Table 1a.[5] Each point represents the results of one study. There is no strong tendency for parameter estimates to cluster in any particular corner or vertex, although there are quite a few points in the lower corner corresponding to averaged-reinforcement learning ($\delta = 0$, $\kappa = 0$) with high ϕ. We are not sure why points are different for different games, although we note that every study which has looked for cross-game variation has found statistically significant variation. Eventually, of course, it would be good to have a theory which specifies parameter values in advance, from empirical regularity or the structural properties of a game Ho, Camerer and Chong (2001) present such a theory, with one parameter, and apply it to seven data sets.

Figure 1 also allows us to diagnose why certain special cases of EWA model perform poorly. For example, reinforcement models perform poorly in games where most players earn zero payoffs, such as market games (Roth and Erev, 1995), tournaments, auctions, or beauty-contests (Camerer and Ho, 1999). They also perform poorly when behavior starts in one region of a strategy space and drifts steadily toward another region whose support is not overlapping with the initial choices (such as continental divide games). The problem in these games with shifting support is that strategies, which are eventually played, are not played early on frequently enough to "get them started." One can see EWA as, among other things, simply fixing these two weaknesses in reinforcement models with a single repair. By including responsiveness to foregone payoffs, players who earn zero can still learn rapidly, and players can shift strategies to parts of the strategy space they have not explored before. It is conceivable that these regularities could also be explained by supplementing choice reinforcement with a variety of ad-hoc cognitive strategies, but EWA is able to explain both classes of regularities with a single parameter.

3.   BILATERAL CALL MARKET EXPERIMENTS

There have been several experiments on bilateral call markets (see Roth, 1995, pp. 253–348; Camerer, 2002, for reviews.) The earliest work is by Radner and Schotter (1989). They studied the case in which values and costs are uniformly distributed from 0 to 100. In this case, the equilibrium bid functions for risk-neutral agents are piecewise linear, which require buyers to underbid their values and sellers to overbid their costs. For example, the buyer should bid her value (v(V) = V) up to 25, and bid v(V) = (25 + 2V)/3 for higher values. In some sessions, they use non-uniform value distributions, which predict bid functions with lower slopes. They find that empirical bid functions, estimated by regressions of actual bids on values, have slopes and slope differences (reflecting the piecewise linearity) which are rather close to those predicted by theory, and which change with the value distribution in the predicted way. Linhart, Radner, and Schotter (1990) extended their study by forcing players to submit reservation prices to agents, who bargained on their behalf (see also Schotter, Snyder and Zheng, 2000).

Radner and Schotter (1989) found that when players bargained face-to-face, rather than by submitting bids, that efficiency was quite high. In fact, efficiency was higher than predicted by any equilibrium bid functions, so the players were violating individual rationality constraints for the sake of joint gain. The variance of prices was also high (compared to the sealed-bid control), which suggests that some players were much better bargainers than others and were able to put their skill to use when bargaining face-to-face. Players were able to jointly create more surplus than predicted by theory. Valley et al. (1998) unpacked this finding by comparing the sealed-bid mechanism with treatments in which players passed written bids back and forth, and communicated face-to-face, before submitting sealed bids. They found that while subject pairs did not typically reveal both of their values to one during the pre-bidding communication, they were frequently able to coordinate on a single price, which they then both bid. As in Radner and Schotter (1989), efficiency was higher than predicted by any equilibrium in the communication conditions, particularly for face-to-face communication.

Several studies by Rapoport and colleagues extended the work of Radner and Schotter (using no pre-bid communication). Rapoport and Fuller (1995 used the "strategy method", eliciting the entire v(V) function. They used symmetric uniform [0,100] values in one experiment. In a second experiment the seller's cost was uniform from [0,100] but the buyer's value was uniform from [0,200]. In that case, there is a piecewise linear equilibrium in which buyers make a constant bid of 116.7 for values above 150. From a learning point of view, these bid functions with flat portions are interesting because it is an open question whether bidders can learn to bid a constant rather than a function which increases monotonically with value.

Rapoport and Fuller found reasonable conformity with the piecewise-linear functions, except that subjects tended toward more full revelation of values over time (i.e., in the opposite direction of equilibrium).

Daniel, Seale, and Rapoport (1998) replicated the asymmetric-value experiment with similar results.[6] They also ran two experiments in which the seller's costs are uniforms from [0,100] and [0,20] respectively, and the buyer's value is uniform from [0,200]. We analyze their data in experiment 2 because the equilibrium bid functions are farthest from fully-revealing bidding, so there is more room to observe learning. The extreme asymmetry in values produces a (piecewise) linear equilibrium solution (LES) of

$$B = \begin{cases} V & \text{if } V < 50 \\ 50/3 + (2/3)V & \text{if } 50 < V \leq 70 \quad \text{for all } V(\text{buyers}) \\ 190/3 & \text{if } V > 70 \end{cases}$$

and

$$A = 50 + (2/3)C \quad \text{for all } C \ (\text{Sellers})$$

where V and B are the buyers' values and bids and C and A are the sellers' costs and asks.

Most call market experiments have been done with symmetric uniform distributions, which produce linear equilibrium bid functions as Bayesian Nash equilibrium bidding strategies. (There usually are other nonlinear equilibria, such as "one-price" equilibria and others.) When we usually observe approximately linear bid functions in these markets, it is not clear whether traders "learned" to bid linearly or just happen to use a constant markdown ratio as a convenient strategy. The extreme asymmetry of the linear equilibrium in this case provides the buyers with the opportunity and incentive to learn a more complicated strategic behavior, since the optimal markdown ratios vary from 0% to almost 70% over the range of possible values.

In their experiment, there were 10 pairs of randomly matched buyers and sellers each period. They were rematched each period but did not change roles as buyers or sellers. The same sets of 50 values and costs were used in different order for each of the 10 pairs. Figure 2 shows all the bids in experiment 2 (circles) compared to the linear equilibrium (squares) and Figure 3 shows the same bids over time as bidders modify their behavior. There is clearly a change in bidding behavior over time as buyers learn the optimal bid function. Next we will look at buyers' learning behavior in this market.

4. SIMILARITY-BASED GENERALIZATION OF EWA LEARNING

We are interested in using EWA learning as a more general alternative to adaptive behavior in this market. In contrast to a customized learning model developed by Daniel et al. (1998) (labeled the DSL model for short) (to be discussed later), EWA learning does not a priori assume a direction of adjustment for each outcome, nor an identical adjustment for all values. Rather it considers the foregone payoffs for all possible value/strategy combinations and

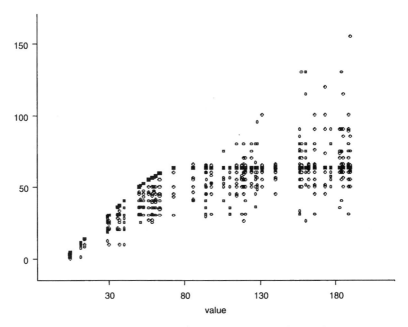

Figure 2. Comparison of Actual Bids vs. LES Bid Function

updates the propensities for each strategy individually depending on the local impact of a choice. As we will see later, EWA model does a comparable job in fitting the data at a cost of complexity for the sake of generality (i.e., the same EWA model can be applied to many other games while the DSL model can only be used to study bilateral call markets).

4.1. Buyer's Adaptive Learning Behavior

To use the EWA learning model for describing buyer's adaptive learning behavior, we first discretize the values into 10 equal increments from 0 to 200[7]. Corresponding to the middle of each value increment, there are 16 strategies of evenly spaced markdown ratios from 0% to 75%. Thus we have 10 values with 16 possible strategies each, making a total of 160 value dependent strategies. Assuming that the value dependent initial attractions for a bidder i are given by normal distributions of given means and variances, they can be written as, $A_i^{b/v}(0) = v\text{max} * v * N(b_i(0), \mu_i|v, \sigma_i|v)$, where v is the random value draw, $\mu_i|v = \alpha_i + \beta_i v + \gamma_i v^2$, the mean absolute markdown conditional on realized values, and $\sigma_i|v = \eta_i v$, the variance of absolute markdowns conditional on realized values, or

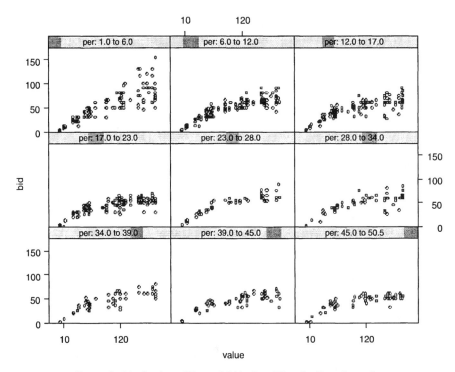

Figure 3. Distribution of Buyers' Bids Over Time for Experiment 2

$$A_i^{b/v}(0) = v \max * v * \frac{1}{\sqrt{2\pi}\eta_i v} \exp\left\{-[b_i(0)-(\alpha_i + \beta_i v + \gamma_i v^2)]\big/[2(\eta_i v)^2]\right\} \quad (1)$$

In this particular specification, the distribution of average markdown (in absolute price rather than in percentage) is assumed to be a quadratic (which includes linear bid function as a special case) function of values. The initial attractions are assumed to be normally distributed around this mean at each of the 10 value with the standard deviation proportional to the private values for that distribution. Thus we scale the normal probability density function by private value, v, to put initial attractions for different values on similar absolute levels. The parameter vmax scales initial attractions to maximize the likelihood function in a way similar to setting an initial attraction to zero to achieve identification in earlier models.

Given the initial attractions, attractions are updated according to,

$$A_i^{b/v}(t) = \frac{\phi^\tau N(t-1)\cdot A_i^{b/v}(t-1) + \tau\pi_i^{b/v}(b_i,v_i,b_{-i}(t))}{\phi^\tau(1-\kappa)^\tau \cdot N(t-1)+\tau}, \quad t\geq 1 \quad (2)$$

$$N_i^{b/v}(t) = \phi^{\tau}(1-\kappa)^{\tau} \cdot N_i^{b/v}(t-1) + \tau, \quad t \geq 1 \tag{3}$$

for subject $i = 1$ to n, strategy $S^{b/v}$ and value draw v.

where $\tau = e^{-\psi|v - v_i(t)| - \omega|b - b_i(t)|}$

Parameters ϕ, $N_i^{b/v}(t)$ and κ have the same interpretations as in Camerer and Ho (1999), denoting discount in attractions, experience equivalent count and whether the experience weight depreciates faster than the attractions respectively. In equation (3), the experience weight for each value dependent strategy is increased by τ each period, rather than by 1 in Camerer and Ho to reflect the partial generalization of experience to neighboring values and strategies. The parameter τ takes on values between 0 and 1 and indicates the "similarity" between strategies. The variables ψ and ω decay the spillover of experience from values and bids using the distances between realized and hypothetical values and bids, $v - v_i(t)$ and $b - b_i(t)$, respectively. The distance between bids measures the "closeness" in strategies and the distance between values measures the "similarity" in experience. In bilateral call markets, they both take the form of difference in prices. The two parameters allow us to separate the effect of the two distances qualitatively. For example, τ for a chosen value/strategy combination will be 1 since both $v - v_i(t)$ and $b - b_i(t)$ are equal to zero. On the other hand, if there is little generalization in values or strategies for a particular game, both ψ and ω will be relatively large, causing τ to fall very quickly away from the chosen value/strategy pair, resulting in little increase in the experience count.

Foregone payoffs, $\pi_i^{b/v}$, are easily calculated by profits from hypothetical bids since a buyer knows the opposing seller's ask from the price after the market closes. Finally we use the logit model to convert the attractions for each strategy to probabilities of choosing one, given by, $P_i^{b/v}(t) = \dfrac{e^{\lambda A_i^{b/v(t)}}}{\sum_{k=1}^{mi} e^{\lambda A_i^k(t)}}$.

4.2. Seller's Adaptive Learning Behavior

The sellers in Daniel et al. (1998)'s experiment also appear to modify their asks over time as shown in Figure 4, although the change is not as dramatic as in buyers' case. We use the same EWA learning developed for the buyers to study sellers' adaptive behavior to further generalizes the application of EWA learning model to different learning environments. The sellers' costs are drawn from a uniform (0, 20) and observed asks are in the range of (9, 100) with one ask at 150. The discrete costs in the models are (2, 6, 10, 14, 18) and the strategies are (5, 10, 15, 20, . . . , 85, 90, 95, 100). This evenly spaced 5 by 20 grid covers all the value/strategy combinations in the data

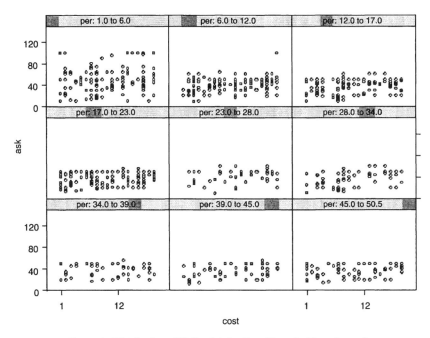

Figure 4. Distribution of Sellers' Asks Over Time for Experiment 2

except one at 150, which is approximated in the estimation by the closest strategy at 100. The sellers' strategies are simply prices, rather than absolute markups as in the case of buyers for simplicity. An absolute markup over cost should produced very similar results since the range of costs is from 0 to 20 and the optimal ask function is A = 50 + 2/3* (cost), resulting in a maximum difference of 13.3 in strategy space based on the optimal bid function. On the other hand, a model of markup ratios will miss many asks unless a very large number of strategies are used in the model because the intercept of the optimal ask function and the limited range. In addition, players did not appear to use markup ratio as strategies in the experiment.

The initial attraction profile is modeled as normal distributions centered around a linear function defined by ($\alpha + \beta$* cost). A linear function rather than a quadratic is used for simplicity since the optimal bid function is linear and there is little evidence of quadratic bid function by the sellers in the experiment. Vmax scales the initial attraction from standard normal distribution with standard deviations (η) estimated by the optimization procedure as noted before.

Given the initial attractions, attractions for a strategy, $S^{a/c}$, are updated just like the buyers before according to,

$$A_i^{a/c}(t) = \frac{\phi^\tau N(t-1) \cdot A_i^{a/c}(t-1) + \tau \pi_i^{a/c}(a_i, c_i, a_{-i}(t))}{\phi^\tau (1-\kappa)^\tau \cdot N(t-1) + \tau}, \quad t \geq 1,$$

and,

$$N_i^{a/c}(t) = \phi^\tau (1-\kappa)^\tau \cdot N_i^{a/c}(t-1) + \tau, \quad t \geq 1$$

where subject $i = 1$ *to* n, with strategy $S^{a/c}$ for an ask, a, given a cost draw c, and

$$\tau = e^{-\psi|c-c_i(t)| - \omega|a-a_i(t)|}$$

The parameter ψ is the decay for cost distance and ω is the decay for ask distance. Together they measure the spillover or generalization of learning from one ask/cost combination to another similar to the buyers' model. All the other parameters have similar interpretations as corresponding ones in the buyers' model.

5.   ESTIMATION RESULTS

The nonlinear optimization was done with SAS Proc NLP using a large number of starting points to ensure a global maximum was achieved. Table 2 shows estimated parameters for experiment 2 using a one-segment and a two-segment EWA learning model. We focus on the results for experiment 2

Table 2. Summary of EWA Learning Parameter Estimates for Buyers in Experiment 2

Parameters	Parameter estimates (standard errors from SAS)		
	One-segment model (SE)	Two-segment model	
N(0)	11.2 (67.4)	13.7 (6.8)	
Vmax	1.46 (14.2)	1.79 (1.4)	
α	0.04 (1.10)	0.09 (0.053)	−0.26 (0.106)
β	0.126 (0.73)	0.238 (0.125)	0.256 (0.065)
γ	0.072 (0.12)	0.048 (0.027)	0.052 (0.012)
η	0.219 (1.21)	0.210 (0.084)	0.208 (0.104)
Proportion		39.8%	60.2%
κ	0.09 (0.27)	0.07 (0.03)	
ψ	0.02 (0.05)	0.01 (0.01)	
ω	0.08 (0.12)	0.10 (0.03)	
ϕ	1.00 (constrained)	1.00	
-LL	1102.2	1071.1 ($\chi^2 = 62.2, p < .005$)	

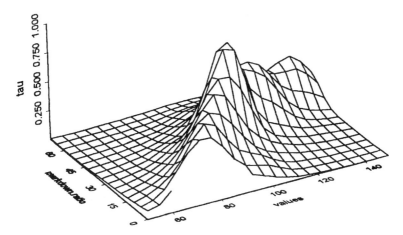

Figure 5. Distribution of Generalization Parameter, τ, for Buyers with v = 100, s = 30% in Experiment 2

Table 3. Summary of Bootstrap Parameter Distribution for Buyers in Experiment 2 with λ and ϕ fixed at 1.0. (500 iterations)

	N(0)	VMAX	α	β	γ	η	κ	ψ	ω
Average	3.987	1.101	−0.028	0.152	0.081	0.168	0.156	0.046	0.099
std dev.	0.104	0.473	0.194	0.134	0.106	0.062	0.066	0.040	0.056

because of the greater asymmetry in value distributions produce stronger incentive for a nonlinear bid function and more dramatic adaptive behaviors. Estimated parameters for ψ and ω are quite small, indicating significant spillover of reinforcement to other values and strategies. A typical distribution of the generalization parameter, τ, is shown in Figure 5 for a value draw of 100 and a markdown ratio of 30%. The value of τ falls off from $\tau = 1$ quickly as we move away from the realized value/choice combination but there is still substantial learning for some strategies with values as low as 50. There is no discounting of attractions ($\phi = 1$) and a small κ means that choices are based more on average attractions rather than cumulative ones. The two-segment model seems to fit the data better but does not produce noticeably different initial attractions between the two segments. Table 3 gives the bootstrapped standard errors of estimated parameters. They are generally smaller than the ones calculated using the covariance matrix in SAS.

Figure 6 shows simulated bids using estimated parameters and Figure 7 shows the average bids for 30 such simulations. The individual simulation displays a transition of bids over time which is similar to the actual bids in the experiment. The most prominent feature is the reduction in bid variance away

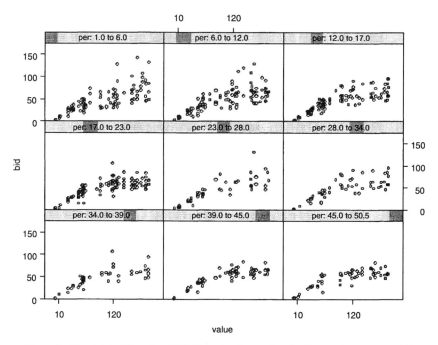

Figure 6. Simulated Bids using EWA Learning Parameters for Buyers in Experiment 2

from the LES bid function. The average of 30 simulations did a relatively poor job of capturing the magnitude of reduction in dispersion in asks.

Table 4 summarizes the estimated EWA learning parameters for sellers from experiment 2 using both the one- and two-segment models. The one-segment estimates indicate that initial attraction profile is approximately normal around a constant ask of $20, with a standard deviation of 6.48. In contrast to the estimates for buyers, the decay parameters for cost and ask are similar in magnitude with more generalization for different strategies than for different costs. This is expected because the optimal bid function is very non-linear for the buyers, resulting in little benefit to generalize the experience from different values. On the other hand, the bidding strategies for sellers are quite constant across costs, allowing for more useful generalization. The esti-mated value for ϕ is approximately one. The standard deviations of the one-segment model parameters are calculated from a bootstrap of 500 iterations with the results summarized in Table 5. Standard deviations obtained from this method are generally larger than the ones from the covariance matrix but of similar magnitude. A two segment model shows significant heterogeneity in the distribution of initial attractions as evidenced by the values of the log like-lihood function, with a $\chi^2 = 39.17$ (p < .005). The two segments differ mostly

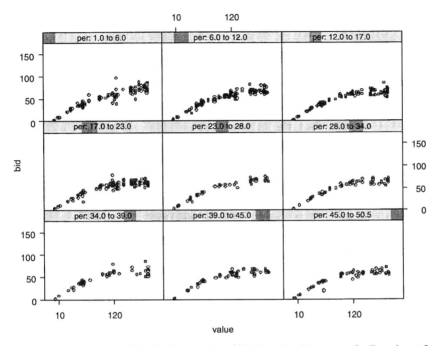

Figure 7. Average Bids of 30 Simulations using EWA Learning Parameters for Experiment 2

Table 4. Summary of EWA Learning Parameters for Sellers in Experiment 2

Parameters	Parameter estimates (standard errors from SAS)		
	One-segment model	Two-segment model	
N(0)	3.29 (0.69)	3.27 (1.72)	
Vmax	19.24 (3.18)	14.43 (42.90)	
α	20.09 (2.59)	15.52 (34.90)	23.55 (8.66)
β	0.04 (0.19)	0.31 (2.20)	0.42 (0.22)
η	6.48 (1.12)	3.75 (17.85)	3.56 (7.39)
Proportion		78.3%	21.7%
κ	0.312 (0.022)	0.315 (0.071)	
ψ	0.091 (0.026)	0.089 (0.034)	
ω	0.059 (0.009)	0.048 (0.028)	
ϕ	1.011 (0.012)	1.014 (0.038)	
-LL	942.754	923.167	
		$\chi^2 = 39.17$ (p < .005)	

Table 5. Summary of Bootstrap Parameter Distribution for Sellers in Experiment 2 with $\alpha = 20$ and $\beta = 0$. (500 iterations)

	N(0)	VMAX	STD	κ	ψ	ω	ϕ	LL
Avgerage	3.155	19.348	7.575	0.313	0.087	0.061	1.013	−943.08
Std. Dev.	0.973	4.256	5.196	0.046	0.046	0.024	0.025	308.62

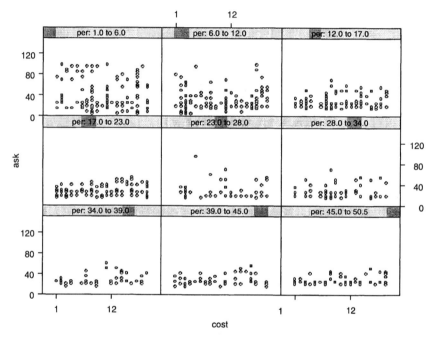

Figure 8. Simulated Sellers' Asks Using Estimated EWA Learning Parameters for Experiment 2

in the level of the linear ask function. Figure 8 shows the simulation of sellers' asks using estimated parameters from the one-segment model. We see tightening of asks over the periods similar to the observed pattern in the experiment.

6.   A CUSTOMIZED MODEL OF LEARNING

Daniel et al. (1998) looked at learning in this experiment and developed a customized model of learning (labeled as DSL model) where a buyer increases or lower her bid in the form a one parameter family of exponential functions[8],

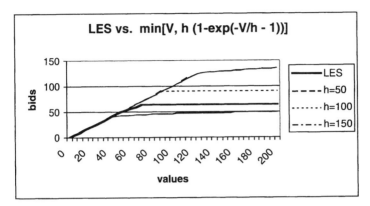

Figure 9. Comparison of LES Bid Function with DSR's One Parameter Exponential Bid Function with Different Values for Parameter h

$$\text{Min}[\text{V}, h*(1-\exp(-V/h-1))].$$

We can see from Figure 9 that this bid function is approximated by two linear segments, a full revelation strategy followed by an almost flat exponential function with the point of transition determined by the parameter of choice, h. Higher h produces bidding closer to values and a longer range of fully revealing bids. The right choice of parameter h fits the linear equilibrium quite well. In their adaptive model, successful trades lead buyers to lower their bids in the form of lower h and potentially profitable but unsuccessful bids lead to higher bids next period. In DSR's model, the strength of adjustment is proportional to either actual payoff when trade takes place or potential profit when a buyer misses a trade. Their learning model is described by,

$$B_t = \min[V_t, h_{t-1}(1-\exp(-V_t/h_{t-1}))] \quad t = 1, 2, \ldots$$

where

$$h_t = h_{t-1} \cdot [1 - w_t^+(V_t - P_t)] \quad \text{if } B_t \geq A_t$$
$$h_t = h_{t-1} \cdot \max[1, 1 + w_t^-(V_t - A_t)] \quad \text{if } B_t < A_t$$

The strength of adjustment, w_t^+ and w_t^- are discounted by $w_t^+ = (1-d)w_{t-1}^+$ and $w_t^- = (1-d)w_{t-1}^-$, where d is a discount factor that depreciates the impact of outcomes.

They used a rule similar to the one used for the buyers to explain the observed behavior of sellers in this market,

$$a_t = \max[C_t, c_{t-1} + m_{t-1}C_t], \quad t = 1, 2, \ldots$$

where $m_t = \max(0, c_t/k - 1)$ is the slope of the (linear) ask function. The constant, k is chosen to minimize the RMSE of the model relative to observed choices and c_t is the parameter that determines the aggressiveness of the ask function by controlling both its intercept and slope. The principle of adjustment is analogous to the buyers' case, given by,

$$c_t = c_{t-1}[1 + w_{s,t}^+(p_t - C_t)], \text{ when there is a trade and}$$
$$c_t = c_{t-1}\min(1, 1 - w_{s,t}^-)(b_t - C_t), \text{ when there is no trade,}$$

where $w_{s,t}^+ = (1 - d)w_{s,t-1}^+$ and $w_{s,t}^- = (1 - d)w_{s,t-1}^-$ are the incremental adjustment parameters that produce the optimal magnitude of adjustment with a constant discount of d. Thus after s a trade, a seller will bid more aggressively by increasing both the intercept and slope of the linear function in direct proportion to her trading profit. When she missed a potentially profitable trade, she will bid less aggressively next period by adjusting the linear function down using the difference between buyer's bid and her own cost.

They estimated individual parameters for each subject using the first 30 periods, then predicted the last 20 periods based on the estimated parameters. The average RMSEs for the first 30 and the last 20 periods are 9.31 and 8.73, respectively for the buyers and 13.39 and 7.54, respectively for the sellers in experiment 2. If we estimate the one-segment EWA learning model using the first 30 periods only, we get the parameters for buyers and sellers given in Table 6.

The RMSE of EWA predicted choices for the first 30 and last 20 periods based on the estimates are 12.66 and 10.27 for the buyers and 17.24 and 12.03 for the sellers. The numbers are based on average choices from 30 simulations of the model since EWA is a stochastic choice model, whereas DSR's is a deterministic model. Clearly these numbers are not directly comparable because the EWA learning model was estimated for an "average" buyer and seller, but DSR's learning model is optimized for individual subjects[9]. Using the averages of the individually estimated parameters given in DSR's paper produced RMSEs of 18.38 and 20.91 for the buyers and 19.24 and 10.86 for the sellers. There is not a clear preference for one model vs. another based on numerical comparison of predicted choices alone.

Table 6. Estimated EWA Learning Parameters for Bilateral Call Market using Period 1–30

Parameters	N(0)	vmax	α	β	γ	η	κ	ψ	ω	ϕ
Buyers	6.328	1.346	−.318	.393	.026	.191	.158	.012	.064	1.0
Sellers	3.418	36.761	15.515	2.107		12.941	.293	.036	.088	1.0

Now we look at the learning mechanisms driving both models. In the bilateral call market, a good learning model needs to predict the direction and strength of adjustment each period. The DSR model is particularly well suited to fit the bidding behavior of individual buyers in this institution because of the optimal two-segment bid function and the simple ordered strategy space. If a buyer makes a trade, the foregone payoffs will be less than the profit for all higher bids and higher than the realized profit for all lower bids down to the point of the actual ask. Thus the direction of modification, if any, should be to lower bids next period. On the other hand, if a buyer misses a trade but has a value higher than the seller's asking price, the direction is clearly to bid higher next period.

Once the direction of change is determined, DSR's model uses the data to determine the optimal discount rate to fit the observed speed of adjustment. The discount rate makes sure that the rate of adjustment diminishes continuously until it becomes negligible. An odd feature is that as bids fall and profit rises, the rate of learning *increases*; but this acceleration is choked off by the discount rate which is estimated to be quite high. We can see that DSR's learning model is a very parsimonious way of fitting the observed adaptive behavior in this institution. However, it makes more sense to use foregone profit rather than actual profit to fit the strength of the adjustment when there is a trade because foregone profit was used when one misses a potentially profitable trade.

The same concern regarding buyers' adaptive behavior can be said about sellers in DSR model. Namely, there is an asymmetry in information usage in that actual payoff is used to motivate adaptive behavior when there is a trade but foregone payoff when there is no trade. EWA learning considers both actual and foregone payoffs for all choice adjustments. In addition, DSR's functional form is rather specific to the institution involved and the deterministic model does not allow for any stochastic property in subjects' choices. The convergence of choices is primarily driven by the discount parameter even as the actual payoffs increase with experience.

7. CONCLUSION

The application of EWA learning model to bilateral call markets extends a general learning model to market-like institutions with more complex strategies. Subjects in this market learn to partially generalize experience from one value/cost condition to another in response to the incentives from nonlinear optimal bid functions. The same learning model can be applied to other market institutions where subjects economize on learning by taking into consideration similarity between past experience and a new environment while still recognizing the difference in market incentives between them.

This application also demonstrated that when we use EWA learning in markets institutions with simple price strategies, the foregone payoffs from each choice produce the correct direction of adjustment without the ad-hoc assumption on the direction of optimal strategies. In addition, EWA learning will also produce the strength of adjustment from foregone payoffs. The generality of EWA learning can further capture the confidence and extent with which subjects utilize the foregone payoffs to adjust their choices from period to period when the payoff information may be too complex or not fully realized.

Overall, EWA learning produces a generalized adaptive model of behavior that includes elements of reinforcement and belief-based as special cases at some cost of complexity for the benefit of generality and logical consistency. It is a good foundation to build upon to extend our understanding of adaptive behaviors in more general games and market institutions. In future works, we should investigate the similarity parameters, ψ and ω, to better characterize their magnitude and significance in different market institutions.

NOTES

1. Thanks to James Walker and Terry Daniel for supplying data and to Amnon Rapoport for valuable comments on an earlier version of this manuscript. This research has been supported by NSF grant SBR 9730364 and a MacArthur Foundation Preferences Network postdoctoral fellowship to David Hsia.
2. Even if players have the same set of learning parameters, their behaviors are different as long as they have different experiences (e.g., faced a different opponent or received a different actual or foregone payoff).
3. Note well that while we assume players are reinforced by their monetary payoffs, the reinforcement function could easily be altered to account for loss-aversion, concave or convex utility for payoffs, or fairness.
4. More precisely, if the special-case restriction is true, then the more general model will necessarily fit better in-sample, but will generally fit worse out-of-sample. Furthermore, criteria like the Bayesian information criterion, which penalizes a more complex theory for extra degrees of freedom, are carefully constructed so that even when sample sizes grow large, so that conventional test statistics appear to favor more complex theories, the extra-parameter penalty grows and there is no such bias.
5. Chen's results are excluded because she did not estimate all parameters precisely. Results from the same game played at different stakes levels are collapsed together, and estimates are averaged across stakes levels. This reduces the 32 observations in Table 1 to 20 in Figure 1.
6. Rapoport, Daniel and Seale (1999) replicated the DSR experiment 1. They also ran an experiment in which the buyer's values are uniform [100,200] and seller costs are uniform from [0,200]. These parameters flip around the bid functions so they are the opposite of those (i.e., buyer and seller bid functions switch) from experiment 1.
7. We experimented with different discretizations of the strategies space. The results are quite robust as long as there are at least 10 divisions.

8.   The same authors later replaced this model with another one where buyers and sellers are treated in a symmetric way (see Seale et al., in press).
9.   The data do not allow us to reliably estimate the EWA model at the individual level.

REFERENCES

Amaldoss, Wilfred, Robert J. Meyer, Jagmohan S. Raju, and Amnon Rapoport (2000). "Collaborating to Compete." *Marketing Science* 19, 105–26.

Anderson, Christopher M., and Colin F. Camerer. "Experience-Weighted Attraction in Sender-Receiver Signaling Games." *Economic Theory*.

Battalio, Raymond, Larry Samuelson, and John van Huyck (1997). "Optimization Incentives and Coordination Failure in Laboratory Stag Hunt Games." Texas A&M Working Paper.

Camerer, Colin F. (2002). Behavioral Game Theory. Princeton: Princeton University Press.

Camerer, Colin, and Teck-Hua Ho (1998). "Experience-Weighted Attraction Learning in Coordination Games: Probability Rules, Heterogeneity and Time-Variation." *Journal of Mathematical Psychology* 42, 305–26.

Camerer, Colin, and Teck-Hua Ho (1999). "Experience Weighted Attraction Learning in Normal Form Games." *Econometrica* 67, 827–73.

Camerer, Colin, Teck-Hua Ho, and Juin-Kuan Chong (in press). "Sophisticated EWA Learning and Strategic Teaching in Repeated Games." *Journal of Economic Theory*.

Camerer, Colin, Teck-Hua Ho, and Xin Wang (1999). "Individual Differences in EWA Learning with Partial Payoff Information." Working Paper, Marketing Department, University of Pennsylvania.

Cason, Timothy N., and Daniel Friedman (1999). "Learning in a Laboratory Market with Random Supply and Demand." *Experimental Economics* 2, 77–98.

Chen, Yan, and Yuri Khoroshilov (2000). "Learning under Limited Information." Working Paper, Economics Department, University of Michigan.

Daniel, Terry, Darryl Seale, and Amnon Rapoport (1998). "Strategic Play and Adaptive Learning in the Sealed-Bid Bargaining Mechanism." *Journal of Mathematical Psychology* 42, 133–66.

Erev, Ido, and Alvin E. Roth (1998). "Predicting How People Play Games: Reinforcement Learning in Experimental Games with Unique, Mixed Strategy Equilibria." *American Economic Review* 88, 848–81.

Friedman, Eric J. (1998). "Learnability in a Class on Non-Atomic Games Arising on the Internet." Working Paper, Economics Department, Rutgers University.

Fudenberg, Drew, and David K. Levine (1998). *The Theory of Learning in Games*. Cambridge: MIT Press.

Ho, Teck-Hua, and Juin-Kuan Chong (1999). "A Parsimonious Model of SKU Choice." Working Paper, Marketing Department, University of Pennsylvania.

Ho, Teck-Hua, Colin Camerer, and Juin-Kuan Chong (2001). "Functional EWA Learning in Games: A Parameter-Free Approach." Working Paper, Marketing Department, University of Pennsylvania.

Holt, Charles A. (1995). "Industrial Organization: A Survey of Laboratory Research." In *The Handbook of Experimental Economics*, edited by John H. Kagel and Alvin E. Roth, 349–443. Princeton: Princeton University Press.

Hsia, David (1999). "Learning in Single Call Markets." Working Paper, University of Southern California.

Kaelbling, Leslie Pack, Michael L. Litman, and Andrew W. Moore (1996). "Reinforcement Learning: A Survey." *Journal of Artificial Intelligence Research* 4, 237–85.

Ledyard, John O. (1993). "The Design of Coordination Mechanisms and Organizational Computing." *Journal of Organizational Computing* 3, 121–34.

Linhart, P. S., Roy Radner, and Andrew Schotter (1990). "Behavior and Efficiency in the Sealed-Bid Mechanism: An Experimental Study." C. V. Starr Center Research Report 90-51, New York University.

Mookerjhee, D., and B. Sopher (1994). "Learning Behavior in an Experimental Matching Pennies Game." *Games and Economic Behavior* 7, 62–91.

Mookerjhee, D., and B. Sopher (1997). "Learning and Decision Costs in Experimental Constant-Sum Games." *Games and Economic Behavior* 19, 97–132.

Morgan, John, and Martin Sefton (1998). "An Experimental Investigation of Unprofitable Games." Working Paper, Princeton University.

Munro, Alistair (1999). "Rules of Thumb in Cycling Coordination Games." Working Paper, University of East Anglia.

Radner, Roy, and Andrew Schotter (1989). "The Sealed-Bid Mechanism: An Experimental Study." *Journal of Economic Theory* 48, 179–220.

Rapoport, Amnon, and Mark A. Fuller (1995). "Bidding Strategies in a Bilateral Monopoly with Two-Sided Incomplete Information." *Journal of Mathematical Psychology* 39, 179–96.

Rapoport, Amnon, and Wilfred Amaldoss (2000). "Mixed Strategies and Iterative Elimination of Strongly Dominated Strategies: An Experimental Investigation of States of Knowledge." *Journal of Economic Behavior and Organization* 42, 483–521.

Roth, Alvin E. (1995). "Bargaining Experiments." In *The Handbook of Experimental Economics*, edited by John H. Kagel and Alvin E. Roth. Princeton: Princeton University Press.

Roth, Alvin E., and Ido Erev (1995). "Learning in Extensive-Form Games: Experimental Data and Simple Dynamic Models in the Intermediate Term." *Games and Economic Behavior* 8, 164–212.

Salmon, Tim (2000a). "Evidence for Learning to Learn Behavior in Normal Form Games." Caltech Working Paper.

Salmon, Tim (forthcoming). "An Evaluation of Econometric Models of Adaptive Learning." *Econometrica*.

Sarin, Rajiv, and Farshid Vahid (1997). "Payoff Assessments without Probabilities: Incorporating 'Similarity' among Strategies." Working Paper, Texas A&M University.

Seale, Darryl A., Terry E. Daniel, and Amnon Rapoport (forthcoming). "Information Advantage in Two-Person Bargaining with Incomplete Information." *Journal of Economic Behavior and Organization*.

Schotter, Andrew, Blaine Snyder, and Wei Zheng (2000). "Bargaining through Agents: An Experimental Study of Delegation and Commitment." *Games and Economic Behavior* 30, 248–92.

Stahl, Dale (1999). "Evidence Based Rules and Learning in Symmetric Normal-Form Games." *International Journal of Game Theory* 28, 111–30.

van Huyck, John, Joseph Cook, and Raymond C. Battalio (1997). "Adaptive Behavior and Coordination Failure." *Journal of Economic Behavior and Organization* 32, 483–503.

van Huyck, John, Raymond C. Battalio, and Frederick W. Rankin (1996). "Selection Dynamics and Adaptive Behavior without Much Information." Working Paper, Texas A&M University.

Valley, Kathleen, Leigh Thompson, Robert Gibbons, and Max H. Bazerman (1998). "Using Dyadic Strategies to Outperform Equilibrium Models of Communication in Bargaining Games." Working Paper 99-080, Harvard Business School.

Weibull, Jorgen W. (1998). "Evolution, Rationality and Equilibrium in Games." *European Economic Review* 42, 641–49.

Chapter 12

ON THE APPLICATION AND INTERPRETATION
OF LEARNING MODELS

D83

Ernan Haruvy
University of Texas at Dallas

Ido Erev
Technion – Israel Institute of Technology

1. INTRODUCTION

Recent research in experimental economics suggests that simple models of learning can have nontrivial practical implications. For example, our research suggests that learning models can be used to design optimal pricing policy (Haruvy & Erev, 2000), efficient rule enforcement rules (Perry, Erev & Haruvy, 2000; Shany & Erev, 2000), efficient bonus systems (Haruvy, Erev, and Perry, 2000) and even optimal gambling devices (Haruvy, Erev, and Sonsino, 2000).

Although these and similar examples of applications appear promising, examination of the mainstream learning literature seems to suggest that the evidence in support of each application is limited. Specifically, the studies that were used to derive the various applications appear contradictory. Whereas some studies favor reinforcement learning models (e.g., Erev & Roth, 1998; Sarin & Vahid, 1999), other studies demonstrate the superiority of belief-based models (e.g., Stahl, 2000), or a combination of the two approaches (e.g., Camerer and Ho, 1999b).

In a recent paper, Erev and Haruvy (2000) argued that these apparent contradictions do not reflect a true inconsistent finding. Rather, they proposed, apparent contradictions merely reflect different research constraints derived from the distinct short-term research goals. Under this optimistic argument, the apparent inconsistencies do not weaken the practical implications of learning research. They simply suggest that different research methods are needed to address different practical problems. The main goal of the current research is to review, extend and emphasize the practical implications of this argument. Since many of the business related applications were derived from simulation-based reinforcement learning models, the present research focuses on the evidence that appear to contradict this line of research.

2.   THE DIFFERENT APPROACHES TO STUDY LEARNING AND THE APPARENT CONTRADICTIONS

The basic argument of Erev and Haruvy (2000) is that the different conclusions reached by different learning studies are artifacts of the different research constraints. Since learning models cannot be well specified (because human behavior is sensitive to interactions between billions of neurons and many environmental variables), the different constraints are expected to lead to different conclusions. To clarify these confusing constraints, it is convenient to think about a two-dimensional classification of the basic learning research.

2.1.   A Two-Dimensional Classification of Learning Research

Approaches to learning can be classified along two dimensions: (1) the time horizon used in estimation and prediction, and (2) the generality of parameters across games. The first dimension deals with whether one-period-ahead approaches are preferred to longer-run simulations, and the second deals with the question of whether to restrict parameter values to be identical over games. These dimensions are critical to the strategic implementation of learning theory.

2.1.1. Time-Horizon

The purest approach to analyze data calls for using all the observations and for testing all the assumptions that can be tested. In the context of learning research this approach implies a focus on one-period-ahead (predicting each observation based on all the data that could affect it), and statistical tests of the significance of all the relevant variables and interactions. The one-period-ahead prediction maximizes a likelihood function that is constructed by fitting one-period-ahead predictions to observed actions. Camerer and Ho (1997, 1998, 1999a, 1999b) provide some of the most prominent examples of data driven analyses of this type. They propose a general model of learning, *experience weighted attraction* (EWA), and use one-period-ahead econometric analysis to estimate its parameters and select the significant explanatory variables. Their results were instrumental in showing that decision-makers were affected by forgone payoff (in violation of reinforcement learning models), but that this effect of forgone payoffs tended to be weaker than the effect of realized payoffs (in violation of belief-learning models). Another influential finding of the Camerer and Ho research agenda was that the assumption of general parameters across games could be statistically rejected.

Under the alternative time horizon approach, computer simulations help to find the model that best predicts the observed learning curves (T-periods-ahead) in a set of games. This approach appears inefficient as it ignores individual period-to-period interdependencies in the data. However, given that models are misspecified, this approach is not at all unreasonable. In a misspecified model, since the model is a rough approximation of behavior, minimizing predictive error one-period-ahead does not necessarily guarantee a minimization of a T-periods-ahead prediction.

Erev, Bereby-Meyer, and Roth (1999; also see previous research by Roth and Erev, 1995) pursued the T-periods-ahead minimum mean squared distance (MSD) approach with their two-parameter reinforcement learning model, hereafter referred to as REL (for REinforcement Learning). This line of research demonstrates the potential usefulness of simple models. For example, Roth et al. (2000), who studied randomly selected constant sum games, found that the *predictive value* of REL (and a of a similar stochastic fictitious play model) in predicting choice probabilities in blocks of 100 trials is around 7.[1] A review by Barron and Erev (2000) shows that this result is not limited to normal-form games. With the two parameters estimated by Erev et al. (1999), REL provides useful predictions for 82 distinct experimental tasks.

2.1.2. Generality of Parameters Over Games

A fairly common statistical finding is that games cannot be pooled (e.g., Stahl, 1996; Camerer and Ho, 1999b). Yet, as demonstrated by the T-periods-ahead research reviewed above, it is nevertheless not unreasonable to analyze data sets under the constraint of general parameters over games. This constraint is often imposed to facilitate ex-ante predictive ability (for examples of using this approach in one-period-ahead analysis see Stahl, 2000; Cheung

& Friedman, 1998). If games have different parameters, one's ability to predict ex-ante dynamic play in a new setting is limited. Generality allows estimating one set of parameters on a large number of games and using this set of parameters for ex ante predictions in similar games.

In the framework of this essay, another motivation arises of great importance to the interpretation of parameters: Not pooling over games, we run the risk of overfitting curves. In that sense, pooling provides somewhat of a safeguard against overfitting, which gives more salience to the interpretation assigned to parameters.

2.2. The Implications of the Different Approaches to Model Comparison

Under the assumption of well-specified research models, the different approaches to evaluate models are expected to lead to the same conclusions. Yet, if the models are not well specified, the different approaches may lead to seemingly contradicting findings. Thus, the apparent contradictions in the learning literature could be explained by the hypothesis of misspecified research models. Erev and Haruvy (2000) present evidence in support of this assertion. Their evidence comes from an experimental study demonstrating that different model comparison criteria lead to different conclusions concerning the model that best fits a single data set. Applying different criteria to the Erev-Haruvy (2000) data, the criterion used by Erev et al. (1999) appears to favor their model, whereas the criterion used by Stahl (2000) favors his model and the criterion used by Camerer and Ho (1999) favors the EWA model. Implicit in this observation is the suggestion that each of the three research constraints can lead to robust applications. And, that there is no one absolutely "correct" research constraint. To clarify this point the following sections demonstrate two examples in which T-periods-ahead-simulations-based analysis provides robust predictions (of T-periods-ahead behavior) even when it appears to be inconsistent with the result of one period ahead maximum likelihood analysis.

3. HAZARDS OF INTERPRETATION WITH MISSPECIFICATION – THE EXAMPLE OF AGGREGATION

Though we know of strong systematic evidence of individual differences in economic behavior, from demographic effects in consumer populations to industry effects in production, aggregation is one of the most common practices in empirical economics. One example is traditional macroeconomic analysis, where one imposes the existence of a stable model among aggregates. One criticism of old-school macroeconomic regression approaches is that they are purely statistical and not grounded in any model of individual behavior. To counter that criticism (following the critique by Lucas, 1976), dry statistical approaches to measure relationships between aggregate variables have been increasingly replaced by representative agent models. These are essentially models of a single decision-maker obeying the constraints of rational choice or other behavioral foundations. Though this appears to resolve the behavioral criticism, the problem of imposing homogeneity in large populations is a critical one.

The problems inherent to such aggregation and homogeneity assumptions are beyond the scope of this paper, although many works have addressed such problems and attempted to suggest solutions. For a comprehensive review of these problems, we suggest Stoker (1993). A known survey which focuses on the flaws of the representative agent approach is Kirman (1992).

In learning models, we often find aggregation in one of two forms: aggregation over games and aggregation over players. Section 2.2. reviewed the hazards of pooling over games. Just as behavior differs across different games, so it does across different players. Studies such as Daniel, Seale, and Rapoport (1998), Cheung and Friedman (1997), Stahl (1996), and Camerer and Ho (2000) concluded that individuals are sufficiently different that pooling them together implies a grave misspecification. One approach suggested by Stahl and Wilson (1994, 1995) is to divide players into sub-populations of similar characteristics. Even then, Haruvy, Stahl, and Wilson (2000) suggest that heterogeneity within each sub-population should be modeled with extreme caution.

Despite our ability to occasionally capture heterogeneity with clever models, such models can easily get out of hand and lose robustness, particularly when the complexity of learning behavior is added. Hence, despite convincing evidence in Cheung and Friedman (1997), Stahl (1996), and Camerer and Ho (2000) against aggregation over individuals, subsequent studies such as Cheung and Friedman (1998), Stahl (2000, 2001), and Camerer and Ho (1999b) succumb to the need for parsimony and pool individuals.

Given the misspecification inherent in models which pool players or games, the different criteria and interpretation assigned to parameters take on new importance. To demonstrate the need for caution in choosing evaluation criteria and parameter interpretation it is constructive to examine a simplified example presented of a binary choice task: Assume that the probability of choice A by player i at trial t is:

$$P_i(t) = \alpha F_i(t-1) + (1-\alpha)(0.3 + \varepsilon_i) \tag{1}$$

where $P_i(1) = F_i(1) = 0.5$, and for $t > 1$, $F_i(t) = [F_i(t-1) \cdot (t-1) + \chi_i(t)]/t$, $\chi_i(t)$ takes on the value of 1 if A is chosen by i at time t and 0 otherwise, and ε_i is uniformly distributed between -0.3 and 0.3. In other words, a player i adjusts sluggishly towards the propensity of his type, where types are uniformly drawn between 0 and 0.6. Suppose we know that the average player will eventually choose A with a probability of 0.3, but we don't know the value of the parameter α. Theoretically, the natural interpretation is that $(1 - \alpha)$ is *the speed of adjustment*. When α equals 1, the player never adjusts, and when alpha equals 0, the player adjusts immediately to the final propensity corresponding to his type. The (albeit artificially generated) problem now is that even though we are aware of heterogeneity, we are not able to estimate the epsilon parameter for each player, due to computation intensity, data limitations, or desire for less parameters motivated by parsimony considerations. Since we know that epsilon is on average 0, we eliminate epsilon from the estimated model. We then estimate alpha. Will α retain its original interpretation? To examine this question, we first generate an artificial data set using simulation with a true value of $\alpha = 0.3$. The left-hand side of Figure 1 presents the proportion of A choices of subjects in this data set.

The parameter α is then estimated using the two common estimation methods in learning research. The first estimation method, denoted as TPAM, is a T-periods-ahead simulation approach with the minimum mean squared distance criterion. By that approach, one simulates hundreds of players under

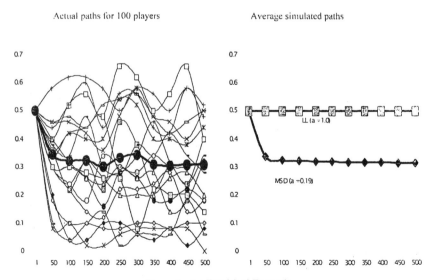

Figure 1. An Empirical Example

different sets of parameter values, aggregates the results, and compares aggregates. The second method, denoted OPAL, is a one-period-ahead likelihood approach. Under that approach, each period, based on the player-specific past, the model produces a player-specific prediction for the following period, which is then compared to the actual player choice, thereby constructing a likelihood function.

The estimated values are $\alpha = 0.19$ under the TPAM method and $\alpha = 1$ under the OPAL method. The right-hand side of Figure 1 presents the aggregated predictions of the model, derived using computer simulations, using these two estimates.

The results clearly show that the OPAL estimate clearly fails to reproduce the adjustment process though both estimates are incorrect. Nevertheless, it is important to see that both estimates are informative. Specifically, the OPAL result ($\alpha = 1$) implies that given the heterogeneity in the population, an individual player's past frequency of choice is the best predictor of his or her next period choice. This finding is informative and useful, though α can no longer be thought of as the speed of adjustment parameter.

Looking at the longer-horizon TPAM approach, we see that α is estimated at 0.19. Since the TPAM approach in essence aggregates over individuals (a simulation approach ignores individual histories), α could conceivably be interpreted as the speed of adjustment parameter for the representative player. Yet, the probability that this estimate is correct for a randomly picked individual would be nearly nil.

Although aggregation over players, as well as the method of estimation chosen, were shown to be consequential for the interpretation of parameters, the lack of aggregation may be no less perilous for interpretation. Individual player estimates may carry little information for prediction about the population. Similarly, individual game estimates may carry little predictive power and reek of overfitting.

4.   HAZARDS IN INTERPRETATION –
AN EXPERIMENTAL DEMONSTRATION

4.1. Experimental Design

Erev and Haruvy (2000) studied a set of four simple binary choice tasks for which the popular learning models have different predictions. In their study, the feedback provided after each trial included the obtained payoff as well as the forgone payoff (the payoff to the unchosen alternative). To facilitate examination of the interpretation of the different parameters, the current paper replicates these four conditions without the presentation of the forgone payoffs. Thus, the current section examines four decision tasks under two information conditions. We refer to the information condition run by Erev and Haruvy (2000) as "F," for full information, and to the new condition as "P," for partial information.

The first task we consider is a choice between two sure gains: 10 tokens versus 11 tokens (100 tokens = 1 shekel). Since the different models address losses differently we also study a loss version of this task: a choice between a sure loss of −10 and a sure loss of −11. To allow evaluation of the effect of payoff variance (another important difference between the models), two noisy variants of the two basic decision tasks are added. Noise is introduced by replacing the outcome of 11 (−11) with a gamble that pays 1 and 21 (−1 and −21) with equal probabilities. In the F condition, subjects see the payoffs for both the button they chose and for the one they did not choose. In the P condition, only obtained payoffs for the chosen button are presented.

We name the treatments by the payoff to the button that is different between all treatments (11; −11; −1, −21; 1, 21) as well as by the information content (partial of full). Hence we have conditions (11 P), (11 F), (−11 P), (−11 F), (1, 21 P), (1, 21 F), (−1, −21 P) and (−1, −21 F).

A total of 76 subjects participated in the study (10 in each of the original conditions and 9 in each of the new conditions). Subjects were recruited by ads posted around the Technion campus that promised a substantial amount of money for a participation in a short decision making experiment. Subjects were randomly assigned to one of the eight experimental conditions, were seated at separate terminals and presented with two buttons on the computer screen. Subjects were told that the experiment consisted of 200 trials and their task was to select between the two buttons. In the F information design, a number, corresponding to token payoffs, would appear on each button after a subject made a selection. The number on the selected button would be added to the cumulative payoff shown at the bottom of the screen. In contrast to the F information design, where both the realized and foregone payoffs are displayed each period, in the P information design, the foregone payoff were not shown on the button not selected.

4.2. Predictive Value and Interpreting Parameters

The main experimental results are presented in Figure 2. The y-axis represents the proportion of choices of the alternative with the expected payoff of 11 (or −11). Each curve presents the average choices (over 9–10 subjects) in 5 blocks of 40 trials each. To reflect the fact that subjects did not receive prior information, we start all the curves from an initial probability distribution of 0.5 at time 0.

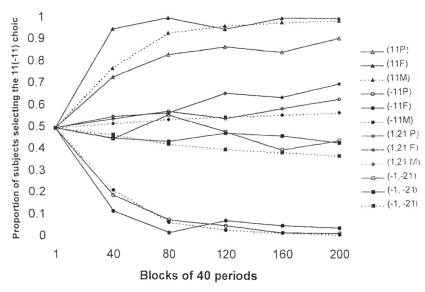

Figure 2. Different Treatments under Full Information and Partial Information Design
P = Partial Information; F = Full Information; M = Model Prediction

In addition to the eight experimental conditions, Figure 2 presents the predictions of the REL model (Erev et al., 1999) for each condition. The predictions were derived using computer simulations with the parameters of the model estimated by Erev et al. on different experimental tasks. The results reveal a surprisingly good predictive power. Over the eight conditions the mean squared deviation of the model (when predicting choice proportions in blocks of 40 trials) is lower than the corresponding variance over individuals (MSD = 0.0523; S^2 = 0.0545). This implies (see Roth et al., 2000) that the model is far more informative for prediction than observing 9 subjects in each condition.

The main criticism toward applying models like REL (i.e., validated using TPAM analysis) comes from advocates of OPAL analysis. The argument is that the TPAM method ignores most of the data and for that reason leads to possibly biased and clearly inefficient predictions. The main goal of the current analysis is to demonstrate that in the current example, using more data does not insure better understanding of the relevant behavior. To achieve this goal we selected to reexamine the data using the OPAL method and Camerer and Ho's (1997) Experience Weighted Attraction (EWA) model. This model was selected because it is a leading model in the learning literature with interesting and meaningful parameters. In that model, several simple belief learning and reinforcement learning models are nested as special cases. The idea behind the EWA model is simple and intuitive: players evaluate the performance of each possible action in the last period and update their propensities to use each action accordingly. However, the action actually played by each player receives greater attention in the evaluation process and consequently greater propensity than warranted if only relative performances were evaluated. Hence, actions are reinforced according to past performance, but actions actually played receive some additional reinforcement.

Player i's choice probabilities over the J possible strategies in period t, denoted by the J × 1 vector $P_i(t)$, are expressed as logistic functions of the "attraction" of each strategy, $A_i^j(t)$, where i indexes the individual and j the strategy:

$$P_i^j(t) = \frac{\exp(\lambda A_i^j(t))}{\sum_{k=1}^J \exp(\lambda A_i^j(t))}, \tag{2}$$

where λ can be thought of as a precision parameter, or the sensitivity of players to attractions. The attractions are updated according to the following two dynamics:

$$A_i^j(t+1) = \{\phi N(t) A_i^j(t) + [\delta + (1-\delta)\chi^i(j,t)]e_j U_i(t)\}/N(t) \tag{3}$$

and

$$N(t+1) = \rho N(t) + 1, \tag{4}$$

where $U_i(t)$ is the J × 1 vector of payoffs to decision maker i in period t for the J possible strategies, e_j is a vector with 1 in the jth place and 0 elsewhere, $\chi^i(j,t)$ a characteristic function that takes the value of 1 if player i played action j in period t and 0 otherwise, and δ is *an 'imagination parameter'* which determines the ability of a player to consider foregone payoffs. There are two decay parameters, ϕ and ρ. The parameter ϕ is thought of as depreciation of past attractions and the parameter ρ is thought of as decay in strength of experience. Also, the following initial conditions are imposed: $A_i^j(0) = A_0^j$ and $N(0) = N_0$, where N_0 and A_0^j are scalar parameters.

Our focus in this section is the 'imagination parameter' δ. The interpretation assigned by Camerer and Ho (1999b) is that δ measures the extent to which the representative player pays attention to foregone payoffs. Camerer and Ho (1999b) show that δ generally takes on intermediate values between 0 and 1 and significantly different from both 0 and 1. Hence, Camerer and Ho (1999b) conclude that belief and reinforcement learning models are essentially "corners" of a true hybrid model – in this case EWA. In contrast, other schools of thought argue that belief and reinforcement learning models are not generally at odds, and that ultimately they provide the same qualitative direction (e.g., Erev and Roth, 1998). By that argument, the δ parameter is likely to be a fine-tuning parameter to 'better fit the curve,' rather than a pivotal link between "contradicting philosophies." The empirical fact that δ fluctuates wildly across similar games (Camerer and Ho, 1999b) appears to support this assertion. Alternative explanations for why delta significantly contributes to fit are many.

Stahl (2000) suggests a plausible alternative to the interpretation of $\delta <$ 1 as "lack of imagination." According to Stahl, the substantive effect of $\delta < 1$ is to increase the relative impact of recent history on current propensities.[2]

A second possible explanation is that a $\delta < 1$ better captures the flattening over time of the learning curve. Either explanation has little to do with a player paying partial attention to foregone payoffs and everything to do with curve fitting.

All we need to do to see whether the significance of δ is related to attention to foregone payoffs, as Camerer and Ho (1999b) interpret it to be, is to compare the experimental treatments which provide information on foregone payoffs to those that provide no such information.

A cursory look at Figure 2 reveals that the curves corresponding to the different treatments are not so different. Treatment-by-treatment t-tests (Table 1) confirm this finding. We proceed to estimate EWA parameters for each of the eight treatments (Table 1). We cap N_0 at an upper limit of 100 periods and λ at an upper bound of 10. We find these computationally necessary for identification.[3] We see that δ tends to fluctuate a great deal – a finding that is consistent with that of Camerer and Ho (1999b). Surprisingly, however, we find that the estimated δ is larger in the partial information design relative to the full information design in conditions (11) and (−1, −21). In other words, the Camerer-Ho interpretation of δ would seem to imply that subjects in these games make *greater* use of information on foregone payoffs, though in reality no such information on foregone payoffs is given to them! Using the

Table 1. Parameter Estimates for Eight Treatments – EWA

	11 Full	11 Partial	−11 Full	−11 Partial	1, 21 Full	1, 21 Partial	−1, −21 Full	−1, −21 Partial
ρ	1.000	0.944	0.703	0.718	0.800	0.760	0.967	0.000
ϕ	0.000	0.456	0.488	1.000	0.011	0.069	1.000	0.000
δ	0.104	0.723	1.000	1.000	0.738	0.000	0.000	1.000
N_0	2.959	49.76	100.0	100	100.0	0.000	100	9.776
λ	0.450	6.874	5.159	10	0.018	0.067	0.639	0.002
Log-likelihood	−360.432	−548.044	−397.120	−424.708	−1205.19	−923.760	−1236.72	−1192.41

Table 2. t-tests Between Different Information Contents: Treatment-By-Treatment

	P-value
(11)	0.106
(−11)	0.314
(1, 21)	0.652
(−1, −21)	0.914

Table 3. Parameter Estimates for Testing H_0: $\delta_1 = \delta_2$, where δ_1 is the Imagination Parameter under the Full Info Design and δ_2 is the Imagination Parameter under the Partial Info Design

	11 Pooled $\delta_1 = \delta_2$	11 Pooled $\delta_1 \neq \delta_2$	11 Pooled $\delta_1 > \delta_2$	−11 Pooled $\delta_1 = \delta_2$	−11 Pooled $\delta_1 \neq \delta_2$	−11 Pooled $\delta_1 > \delta_2$
ρ	0.980	0.983	0.980	0.703	0.703	0.703
ϕ	0.254	0.241	0.254	1.000	1.000	1.000
δ_1	0.631	0.532	0.631	1.000	1.000	1.000
δ_2	0.631	0.621	0.631	1.000	1.000	1.000
N_0	76.517	87.410	76.517	100	100	100
λ	10.0	10.0	10.0	10	10	10
Log-likelihood	−950.536	−946.114	−950.536	−824.403	−824.403	−824.403
	1, 21 Pooled $\delta_1 = \delta_2$	1, 21 Pooled $\delta_1 \neq \delta_2$	1, 21 Pooled $\delta_1 > \delta_2$	−1, −21 Pooled $\delta_1 = \delta_2$	−1, −21 Pooled $\delta_1 \neq \delta_2$	−1, −21 Pooled $\delta_1 > \delta_2$
ρ	0.967	0.969	0.969	1.000	1.000	1.000
ϕ	0.088	0.086	0.086	1.000	1.000	1.000
δ_1	0.000	0.155	0.155	0.000	0.000	0.000
δ_2	0.000	0.000	0.000	0.000	0.000	0.000
N_0	22.468	22.779	22.779	100.0	100.0	100.0
λ	0.540	0.588	0.588	0.000	0.000	0.000
Log-likelihood	−2070.07	−2067.34	−2067.34	−2633.96	−2633.96	−2633.96

likelihood ratio test, we tested significance of the difference in delta across designs (Table 2). We further ran a conditional test. In that test, we pooled the treatments across designs and forced all parameters for a given condition, except delta, equal for both the full information and partial information designs. Results are shown in table 3. The results clearly show that whereas in condition (-11), δ clearly equals 1 for both designs,[4] and in condition $(-1, -21)$, δ is not significantly different from 0 under either design, in conditions (11) and $(1, 21)$, δ is significantly different between designs. In fact, in treatment (11), δ_1 is significantly smaller than δ_2, a finding not easily explained by the EWA interpretation of δ.

5.   CONCLUSIONS

At first glance, the results summarized here appear to be discouraging: They demonstrate that common techniques used in learning research are likely to lead to incorrect conclusions. The statistical methods used in learning works to find the "best model," or the "correct" interpretation of parameters, yield biased results. Nevertheless, we believe that the current findings may have constructive implications as they clarify some of the apparent inconsistencies in the learning literature. When the unrealistic and confusing assumption of well-specified research models is removed, it is easy to see that the apparent contradictions reflect different yet robust and potentially compatible findings.

To evaluate possible alternatives to the assumption of well-specified research models it is useful to start by asking why this confusing assumption was introduced in the first place. There are many answers, but one in particular seems relevant to the direction of research we have chosen to pursue. By this reasoning, the long-horizon TPAM approach, though more in-line with the need for prediction in economics, is nonetheless far more expensive. To illustrate, imagine a typical experiment involving N players repeatedly matched for T periods using a matching protocol such that every player affects every other player directly or indirectly in at least one period. At the end of the experiment (a typical learning experiment lasts from 20 minutes to 3 hours), the N subjects must be paid a fair amount of money. In return, the TPAM follower has obtained only one observation! This is because, according to TPAM, the entire path is the relevant observation to be compared with simulations. In essence, the TPAM approach, due to its reliance on simulations, "throws away" relevant historical individual data.

The OPAL approach, on the other hand, treats this data set as $N \times T$ observations. This is because, looking at each player's history up to period t, we can derive a prediction for that player's action in period $t + 1$. This prediction is then matched with the player's actual choice to arrive at the likelihood relevant to that player in period t + 1, resulting in N × T such matches. With this number of observations, asymptotic results generally apply, giving the experimenter the ability to use powerful econometric techniques. The only restriction on the follower of OPAL wishing to use OPAL estimates and results for long horizon predictions is the need to make the one "simple" assumption that the model is well-specified. Under that assumption, OPAL estimates would make sense in long-horizon predictions.

Alternatively, in the context of experimental business research, where observations are relatively cheap and data sets quickly accumulate, it may be possible to replace the perfect specification assumption by using larger data sets and by focusing on the *predictive value* of the models (see Roth et al., 2000). If a model is shown to have high predictive value in a wide set of tasks, it is clear that it can also advance our understanding of economic behavior. Ultimately, we hope that the accumulation of large data sets and the analysis of the accumulated data will improve our ability to identify better-specified models as well.

ACKNOWLEDGEMENT

This research was supported by the Israel-USA Binational Science Fund and the National Science Foundation. We thank Al Roth and Bob Slonim for useful comments.

NOTES

1. The predictive value of a model is defined (see Roth et al., 2000) as the size of the experiment that needs to be run to derive predictions that are more accurate than the ex ante predictions of the model.
2. This conclusion is based on an examination of a population version of EWA. The flavor of this conclusion nonetheless applies to the standard EWA.
3. Not doing so does not result in an improvement in the log likelihood (to the third decimal point).
4. This in itself is an interesting finding: In its present form, EWA is not suitable for games with negative payoffs. Since unplayed actions receive a reinforcement of zero, played actions which receive a negative payoff, even when that payoff is the best obtainable, are penalized relative to unplayed actions and will be discouraged according to EWA, whereas these actions are best and should increase in observed frequency.

REFERENCES

Barron, G., and I. Erev (2000). "Toward a General Descriptive Model of One-Shot and Repeated Decision Making under Risk and Uncertainty." Technion Working Paper.

Bereby-Meyer, Y., and I. Erev (1998). "On Learning To Become a Successful Loser: A Comparison of Alternative Abstractions of Learning Processes in the Loss Domain." *Journal of Mathematical Psychology* 42, 266–86.

Camerer, C., and T. Ho (1997). "EWA Learning in Games: Preliminary Estimates from Weak-Link Games." In *Games and Human Behavior: Essays in Honor of Amnon Rapoport*, edited by David V. Budescu, I. Erev, and Rami Zwick. Mahwah, NJ: Lawrence Erlbaum Associates.

Camerer, C., and T. Ho (1998). "EWA Learning in Coordination Games: Probability Rules, Heterogeneity, and Time-Variation." *Journal of Mathematical Psychology* 42, 305–26.

Camerer, C., and T. Ho (1999a). "Experience-Weighted Attraction Learning in Games: Estimates from Weak-Link Games." Chap. 3 in *Games and Human Behavior*, edited by David V. Budescu, Ido Erev, and Rami Zwick, 31–52. Mahwah, NJ: Lawrence Erlbaum Associates.

Camerer, C., and T. Ho (1999b). "Experience-Weighted Attraction Learning in Normal Form Games." *Econometrica* 67, 827–74.

Camerer, C., T. Ho, and X. Wang (2000). "Individual Differences in the EWA Learning with Partial Payoff Information." Working Paper.

Cheung, Y.-W., and D. Friedman (1994). "Learning in Evolutionary Games: Some Laboratory Results." Working Paper No. 303, Economics, UCSC.

Cheung, Y.-W., and D. Friedman (1997). "Individual Learning in Normal Form Games: Some Laboratory Results." *Games and Economic Behavior* 19, 46–76.

Cheung, Y.-W., and D. Friedman (1998). "Comparison of Learning and Replicator Dynamics Using Experimental Data." *Journal of Economic Behavior and Organization* 35, 263–80.

Daniel, T. E., D. A. Seale, and A. Rapoport (1998). "Strategic Play and Adaptive Learning in Sealed Bid Bargaining Mechanism." *Journal of Mathematical Psychology* 42, 133–66.

Erev, I., and E. Haruvy (2000). "On the Potential Uses and Current Limitations of Data Driven Learning Models." Technion Working Paper.

Erev, I., and A. Roth (1998). "Predicting How People Play Games: Reinforcement Learning in Experimental Games with Unique Mixed Strategy Equilibria." *American Economic Review* 88, 848–81.

Erev, I., Y. Bereby-Meyer, and A. Roth (1999). "The Effect of Adding a Constant to All Payoffs: Experimental Investigation, and Implications for Reinforcement Learning Models." *Journal of Economic Behavior and Organization* 39, 111–28.

Fudenberg, D., and D. K. Levine (1998). *The Theory of Learning in Games*. Cambridge: MIT Press.

Haruvy, E., and I. Erev (2000). "When to Pursue Variable Pricing: The Relationship Between Price Format and Quality." Mimeo.

Haruvy, E., I. Erev, and O. Perry (2000). "Probabilistic Employee Incentives." Mimeo.

Haruvy, E., I. Erev, and D. Sonsino (2000). "The Medium Prizes Paradox: Evidence From a Simulated Casino." Mimeo.

Haruvy, E., D. O. Stahl, and P. W. Wilson (forthcoming). "Modeling and Testing for Heterogeneity in Observed Strategic Behavior." *Review of Economics and Statistics*.

Kirman, A. P. (1992). "Whom or What Does the Representative Individual Represent?" *Journal of Economic Perspectives* 6, 117–36.

Lucas, R. E. Jr. (1976). "Econometric Policy Evaluation: A Critique." *Carnegie-Rochester Conference Series on Public Policy* 1, 19–46.

Nerlove, M. (1958). "Distributed Lags and Demand Analysis." USDA Handbook No. 141, Government Printing Office.

Roth, A., and I. Erev (1995). "Learning in Extensive Form Games: Experimental Data and Simple Dynamic Models in the Intermediate Term." *Games and Economic Behavior* 8, 164–212.

Roth, A. E., I. Erev, R. L. Slonim, and G. Barron (2000). "Learning and Equilibrium as Useful Approximations: Accuracy of Prediction on Randomly Selected Constant Sum Games." Working Paper, Harvard University.

Sarin, R., and F. Vahid (1999). "Payoff Assessments without Probabilities: A Simple Dynamic Model of Choice." *Games and Economic Behavior* 28, 294–309.

Stahl, D. O. (1996). "Boundedly Rational Rule Learning in a Guessing Game." *Games and Economic Behavior* 16, 303–30.

Stahl, D. O. (2000). "Action Reinforcement Learning versus Rule Learning." Working Paper, University of Texas.

Stahl, D. O. (2001). "Population Rule Learning in Symmetric Normal-Form Games: Theory and Evidence." *Journal of Economic Behavior and Organization* 45, 19–35.

Stahl, D. O., and P. W. Wilson (1994). "Experimental Evidence on Players' Models of Other Players." *Journal of Economic Behavior and Organization* 25, 309–27.

Stahl, D. O., and P. W. Wilson (1995). "On Players' Models of Other Players-Theory and Experimental Evidence." *Games and Economic Behavior* 10, 213–54.

Stoker, T. M. (1993). "Empirical Approaches to the Problem of Aggregation over Individuals." *Journal of Economic Literature* 31, 1827–74.

Chapter 13

PREFERENCE CONSTRUCTION AND RECONSTRUCTION

Frank R. Kardes
University of Cincinnati

Murali Chandrashekaran
University of Cincinnati

James J. Kellaris
University of Cincinnati

Preferences are frequently used to predict choice and to shape marketing strategy. Market surveys and experiments assessing consumers' preferences are frequently used to design new products, forecast sales, set prices, and guide promotion and advertising strategy. Most commonly-used procedures to elicit and analyze consumers' preferences – such as conjoint analysis and other forms of multiattribute evaluation modeling (e.g., Green and Srinivasan 1990; Lynch 1985) – assume that consumers' preferences are well-defined, articulated, and stable. However, recent research suggests that well-defined, articulated preferences are not always available in memory to serve as a basis for decision making (Coupey, Irwin, and Payne 1998; Payne, Bettman, and Johnson 1992, 1993; Slovic 1995). Instead of consulting a master list of previously-formed preferences stored in memory, decision makers are sometimes required to construct or generate preferences on-line while responding to preference measures (Hastie and Park 1986). The distinction between previously-formed, memory-based preferences versus constructed, on-line

EXPERIMENTAL BUSINESS RESEARCH. Copyright © 2002. Kluwer Academic Publishers. Boston.
All rights reserved.

preferences is important, because, theoretically, only the former type is predictive of subsequent behavior (Feldman and Lynch 1988; Fischhoff 1991). The goal of the present set of studies is to investigate the conditions under which previously-formed preferences are retrieved from memory, and the conditions under which newly-formed preferences are constructed on-line. We also examine the role of metacognitive processes in reconstructing previously-formed preferences from newly-formed preferences.

1. IDENTIFYING MEMORY-BASED VERSUS CONSTRUCTED PREFERENCES

The principle of invariance is the hallmark of memory-based preference (Tversky and Kahneman 1986; Tversky, Sattath, and Slovic 1988). Normative theories of rational choice assume that decision makers have well-defined and stable preference orderings: observed preferences should not differ as a function of the manner in which choice options are framed or described (description invariance) or the manner in which preferences are elicited or measured (procedure invariance).

Contrary to the invariance principle, empirical evidence indicates that preferences are often unstable, inconsistent, and highly malleable (Coupey et al. 1998; Payne et al. 1992, 1993; Slovic 1995). Much of this instability stems from preference construction processes in which decision makers generate values and rules for forming preferences while making choices and decisions. Decision makers have a wide variety of inferential rules for constructing preferences (Kruglanski 1989; Nisbett 1993) and are sensitive to a wide variety of task-related and contextual variables that influence rule selection and use (Payne et al. 1992, 1993). However, sensitivity to surface details and insensitivity to underlying structure lead decision makers to view each choice problem as unique (Kahneman and Lovallo 1993). Consequently, rules for generating preferences are selected and applied inconsistently across situations, and this often results in labile preferences.

One important implication of the constructive perspective is that, contrary to the description invariance principle, preferences can be influenced by subtle variations in the wording or framing of choice options. Research on the framing effect has shown that preferences differ reliably and systematically as a function of the manner in which choice outcomes are described or framed (e.g., Bettman and Sujan 1987; Fischhoff 1983; Levin and Gaeth 1988; Linville and Fischer 1991; Maheswaran and Meyers-Levy 1990; Puto 1987; Qualls and Puto 1989; Schneider 1992; Tversky and Kahneman 1981, 1986). The most well-known example of the framing effect is the "Asian disease problem," in which respondents are told that an outbreak of an unusual Asian disease in the U.S. is expected to result in 600 deaths (Tversky and Kahneman 1981). When asked to choose between two programs, one of which was expected to save 200 lives for certain ($p = 1.00$) and the other was expected to save either 600 (with $p = .33$) or zero lives (with $p = .67$), most respondents prefer the no-risk ($p = 1.00$) option. When outcomes are reframed in terms of losses – i.e., 400 will die for certain vs. a risky option (either zero [$p = .33$] or 600 [$p = .67$] will die – most respondents prefer the risky option. Prospect theory suggests that losses are more influential than equivalent gains, and, consequently, people respond very differently to losses versus gains (Tversky and Kahneman 1981, 1986). People are often risk averse when they focus on gains, and risk seeking when they focus on losses.

2. BETWEEN-SUBJECTS VERSUS WITHIN-SUBJECT FRAMING EFFECTS

Prior research on framing has focused on between-subjects framing effects. That is, one group of subjects typically receives a pair of choice options framed in terms of gains, whereas an independent group of subjects receives a pair of equivalent options framed in terms of losses. Although aggregated data is informative and useful, between-subjects designs mask individual differences by summarizing data in terms of group averages. Conversely, within-subject designs permit the investigation of individual differences but mask the quantitative regularities provided by aggregated data. Consequently, it is desirable to examine the robustness of judgmental phenomena using both between-subjects and within-subject designs (Hershey and Schoemaker 1980; Hirt and Castellan 1988). Because design manipulations do not alter the weighting and value functions of prospect theory, the model suggests that both types of framing effects should be observed. Within-subject framing effects are observed when the same individuals prefer a no-risk option when outcomes are framed in terms of gains and a risky option when outcomes are framed in terms of losses.

> *H1*: Decision makers should exhibit risk aversion when choice outcomes are framed in terms of gains, and risk seeking when choice outcomes are framed in terms of losses. This pattern should be observed for both between-subjects (*H1a*) and within-subject (*H1b*) framing effects.

Although between-subjects framing effects are consistent with the constructive perspective, within-subject framing effects provide even stronger evidence for preference construction. If the same individuals prefer one option in one context, and the opposite option in another context, dramatic preference instability would be exhibited. A preference reversal (i.e., preferring A to B in one context, and B to A in another) represents the most extreme form of preference inconsistency. Furthermore, a preference reversal induced by subtle wording or framing manipulations reflects extreme preference instability.

3.   THE ROLE OF FAMILIARITY IN PREFERENCE CONSTRUCTION

Another important implication of the constructive perspective is that all preferences may not be equally susceptible to framing effects (Payne et al. 1992, 1993). In some domains, decision makers may have relatively stable and consistent preferences. Well-defined, articulated preferences should be more likely to be observed in familiar (vs. unfamiliar) domains. Familiarity is determined by the amount of relevant experience accumulated by the decision maker (Alba and Hutchinson 1987; Coupey et al. 1998). Decision makers familiar with a particular domain are likely to have a large store of relevant knowledge and experience to draw on when attempting to solve a decision problem. The knowledge store may include some relatively well-articulated preferences that were formed previously while attempting to solve similar choice problems in the past.

Consistent with this hypothesis, recent research has shown that the principle of procedure invariance is less likely to be violated in familiar (vs. unfamiliar) domains (Coupey et al. 1998). When previously-formed preferences are well-defined and stored in memory, different elicitation procedures (i.e., choice versus matching) reveal stable preferences. Although prior research has examined the moderating influence of familiarity on procedure invariance, prior research has not investigated the moderating influence of familiarity on description invariance. Strong evidence for preference construction would be obtained if familiarity moderates both procedure invariance and description invariance.

> *H2*: Framing effects should be less pronounced for preferences elicited in familiar (vs. unfamiliar) choice contexts. This pattern should be observed for both between-subjects (*H2a*) and within-subject (*H2b*) framing effects.

4.   MEMORY RECONSTRUCTION AND THE ILLUSION OF PREFERENCE STABILITY

When information stored in memory is poorly-articulated or difficult to retrieve, people often use currently available information as a basis for drawing inferences about the past (Loftus, Coan, and Pickrell 1996; Ross 1989).

Memory for the past is often reconstructed from the present. Misleading questions, suggestions, exaggerations, and other types of misinformation available in the present can lead people to manufacture memories of the past that seem plausible but that have no basis in reality. Misinformation effects and the construction of false memories have important implications for any situation requiring accurate memory for past events (e.g., eyewitness testimony, susceptibility of childhood memories to suggestions occurring during psychotherapy).

Although reconstructive memory processes have rich and important implications for a remarkably wide range of topics and issues, these processes have been neglected in preference research. This is unfortunate because memory plays a crucial role in judgment and choice (Lynch and Srull 1982; Weber, Goldstein, and Barlas 1995). We suggest that preferences can be reconstructed as well as constructed. Preference reconstruction involves inferring past preferences on the basis of present preferences and inferences about the relationship between past and present preferences. If preferences are first constructed and later reconstructed, using preferences to predict choice and to shape marketing strategy becomes a very risky enterprise. Preferences may differ dramatically depending on the timing of preference elicitation. Moreover, recall accuracy for past preferences is likely to be highly inaccurate when different cues and rules are used for preference construction in the past versus preference reconstruction in the present.

Memory reconstruction does not always lead to memory distortion or to the creation of false memories, however. Reconstruction can either reduce or enhance recall accuracy depending on the relationship between the currently available information and the past event that one is attempting to recall (Hirt 1990; Hirt, Erickson, and McDonald 1993). When memory representations are difficult to retrieve directly, currently available information is used as an anchor, and adjustments are performed based on intuitive theories, schemata, or expectations concerning stability or change (Ross 1989). Little or no adjustment occurs if stability is expected, whereas substantial adjustment is performed if change is expected. If adjustment occurs, the amount and the direction of the adjustment is consistent with the implications of the individual's intuitive theory.

Many people assume that their skills and abilities improve with age and experience (Ross 1989). Advanced students recall their early study skills (e.g., freshman-year skills) as being markedly inferior to their current skills; advanced managers recall their early decision making skills as much less effective (and less valuable to the firm), relative to their current skills. Memory reconstruction processes are likely to sharpen the contrast between the past and the present where skills and abilities are concerned.

Conversely, many people assume that their personal traits and dispositions are quite stable over time (Ross 1989). Personal traits and opinions are often expected to be persistent and resistant to change. We suggest that this expectation is likely to extend to personal preferences, and we refer to this expectation as the "illusion of preference stability." If this illusion exists, current preferences should be used as an anchor or benchmark for drawing inferences about past preferences. Moreover, to the extent that decision makers believe that their preferences are consistent and stable over time, recall for past preferences should be distorted to align with current preferences. Because the degree of perceived consistency between past and present preferences is likely to be exaggerated, recall accuracy should be greater when past and present preferences are similar as opposed to dissimilar.

H3: Recalled past preferences should be consistent with present preferences regardless of the level of preference stability that is observed.
H4: Recall accuracy for past preferences should be greater when preferences are stable as opposed to unstable.

5. STUDY 1

5.1. Procedure

Subjects were 164 undergraduate business students at a large midwestern university (69 females and 95 males). Their ages ranged from 18 to 47 years (median = 21). Sixteen subjects failed to participate in one of the two sessions and were excluded from the analyses.

5.1.1. Session 1

Subjects received a booklet presenting two decision scenarios: one pertaining to a choice task familiar to most students (the class scheduling scenario) and one pertaining to a choice task unfamiliar to most students (the account management scenario). Hence, task familiarity was manipulated as a within-subject factor.

Two choice options, a no-risk option and a risky option, followed each scenario. Subjects were asked to choose one option for each scenario. Half of the subjects received choice option outcomes framed in terms of gains (for both scenarios), and half received choice option outcomes framed in terms of losses (for both scenarios). Subjects were randomly assigned to framing conditions, and in session 1, framing was manipulated as a between-subjects factor.

5.1.2. Session 2

Three weeks later, subjects received another booklet containing the familiar and the unfamiliar choice task scenarios. Again, a no-risk and a risky option followed each scenario. Subjects who were assigned to gain frame conditions in session 1 were assigned to loss frame conditions in session 2. Conversely, subjects who were assigned to loss frame conditions in session 1 were assigned to the gain frame conditions in session 2. Hence, across sessions, framing was manipulated as a within-subjects factor.

5.2. The Class Scheduling Scenario

Imagine that you are trying to plan a class schedule for next quarter. Some of the classes you need are offered at the same time, and there are other problems you must work around. After studying your options, you have narrowed your choices down to two alternative schedules. Both are fairly convenient, involve reasonable professors, and offer five courses that you need. The only practical difference between the two schedules is the grades you can expect to make.

In gain frame conditions, the choice options were described as follows:

SCHEDULE X: If you select this combination of courses, you will *definitely* make an "A" in two of the classes.
SCHEDULE Y: If you select this combination of courses, there is a 35% chance you will make all A's this quarter, and a 65% probability that none of your grades will be A's.

In loss frame conditions, the choice options were described as follows:

SCHEDULE X: If you select this combination of courses, you will definitely *not* make an "A" in three of the classes.
SCHEDULE Y: If you select this combination of courses, there is a 35% chance that none of your grades will be below an A this quarter, and a 65% probability that all of your grades will be below an A.

5.3. The Account Management Scenario

Imagine that you are an account executive for a large company. You just found out that a major competitor will be entering your market. Reliable forecasts estimate that you will lose 600 profitable accounts to this new competitor. You must choose a plan to deal with this threat. You have narrowed your choices down to two alternatives.

In gain frame conditions, the choice options were described as follows:

PLAN A: If this plan is adopted, 200 accounts will be retained.
PLAN B: If this plan is adopted, there is a 1/3 probability that 600 accounts will be retained, and a 2/3 probability that no accounts will be retained.

In loss frame conditions, the choice options were described as follows:

PLAN A: If this plan is adopted, 400 accounts will be lost.
PLAN B: If this plan is adopted, there is a 1/3 probability that no accounts will be lost, and a 2/3 probability that 600 accounts will be lost.

5.4. The Estimation Framework

5.4.1. Structure of the Data and Definitions

The data from the experiment consists of information on a sample of size N from the population of interest, for each of T choice situations (in our case N = 148 and T = 4). For every individual i, i = 1, 2, . . . , N, the following will be observed:

1.   whether the no-risk or risky option was chosen in each of the four choice decisions, denoted by Y_{it}, t = 1, . . . , T, and
2.   the vectors $X_{it} = [X_{it1}, . . . , X_{itp}]$ describing the experimental treatments at each choice decision.

The discrete outcome Y_{it} can be defined as follows:

$Y_{it} = 1$, if the no-risk option was chosen in condition X_{it}
      $= 0$, if the risky option was chosen in condition X_{it}, t = 1, . . . , T.

5.4.2. Model Specification for Within-Subjects Discrete Choice Data

Because the dependent variable, Y_{it}, is discrete in nature, the probit model framework can serve as the basis for estimation. Following standard probit analysis (Greene 1990), Y_{it} can be considered a reflection of a continuous latent random variable, Y_{it}^*. In general, estimation of the impact of the independent variables then is based on the following equations (Greene 1990):

$$Y_{it}^* = \beta_0 + X_{it}\beta + \varepsilon_{it}, \; i = 1, \ldots, N; \; t = 1, \ldots, T; \; \beta = [\beta_1, \ldots \beta_p], \qquad (1)$$

$$Y_{it} = 1, \text{ if } Y_{it}^* \geq 0 \qquad\qquad\qquad\qquad\qquad\qquad\qquad (2)$$
$$\quad = 0, \text{ otherwise.}$$

The standard probit model, however, is inappropriate because the design involves within-subjects factors and each subject provides more than one data-point. In such cases, as in repeated-measures designs, unobserved "temporally" correlated error components need to be explicitly considered. Consequently, following Butler and Moffitt (1982) and similar to standard within-subjects "random-block" effects ANOVA specification, we decompose the error term, ε_{it} in equation (1) as follows:

$$\varepsilon_{it} = \tau_i + \delta_{it}, \; i = 1, \ldots, N; \; t = 1, \ldots, T, \qquad\qquad\qquad (3)$$

where $\tau_i \sim N(0, \sigma_\tau^2)$, $\delta_{it} \sim N(0, \sigma_\delta^2)$. Further, we define the interclass correlation coefficient (i.e., corr($\varepsilon_{it}, \varepsilon_{is}$), $\tau \neq s$) as $\rho = \sigma_\tau/(\sigma_\tau^2 + \sigma_\delta^2)^{1/2}$.

5.4.3. Parameter estimation – The likelihood function

Estimating the impact (**b**) of independent variables on dynamic choice proceeds by maximizing the sample likelihood function given the above structural framework. To motivate the development of the likelihood function, we define (a) the sequence of Y_{it} with a vector $Y_i = [Y_{i1}, Y_{i2}, \ldots Y_{iT}]$, $t = 1, \ldots,$ T, where Y_{it} is the discrete choice variable for the ith individual at the tth time period, and (b) a super vector $X_i = [X_{i1}, X_{i2}, \ldots, X_{iT}]$ that contains all the independent variables for all individuals and for all T time periods.

The likelihood function can now be specified by deriving the probability of observing Y_i given X_i. The Appendix (see equation A10) provides a discussion and derivation for the following expression for the likelihood function:

$$L = \Pi_i \int_{-\infty}^{\infty} \Pi_i \Phi\{J_{it}(2Y_{it} - 1)\} \times \varphi(\tilde{\tau}_i) d\tilde{\tau}_i \qquad\qquad (4)$$

where:

$$J_{it} = \beta_0 + X_{it}\beta + \tilde{\tau}_{it}\rho(1 - \rho^2)^{-1/2} \qquad\qquad\qquad (4a)$$

$$\tilde{\tau}_1 = \tau_i/\sigma_\tau, \text{ and} \qquad\qquad\qquad\qquad\qquad\qquad (4b)$$

Π_i and Π_t denote, respectively, the continuous product over all observations and time periods, and Φ [.] and $\varphi(.)$ denote, respectively, the c.d.f. and p.d.f. of the standard normal.

Maximizing L will yield consistent and efficient estimates for b_0 and $\mathbf{b} = [b_1, \ldots, b_p]$, the impact of the independent variables on dynamic choice (Heckman 1990). Involving one numerical integration, per observation, of products of cumulative normal error functions, maximization is straightforward in LIMDEP (Greene 1991).

5.5. Results

In this section, we present findings from the test of hypotheses based on the estimation of the repeated-measures probit model presented in equation (4). The discrete choice variable served as the dependent variable and the experimental design conditions served as the independent variables. In addition, we defined a dummy variable GROUP with two levels: the gain-loss group received the gain frame in session 1 and the loss frame in session 2, whereas the loss-gain group received the loss frame in session 1 and the gain frame in session 2. Because frames differed across sessions, interactions involving GROUP will allow us to test hypotheses regarding within-subject preference reversals over time.

5.5.1. Between-Subjects and Within-Subject Framing Effects

Table 1 presents the results from the estimation based on a sample size of $N = 148$ and each subject providing data on four choice decisions ($T = 4$). A likelihood ratio test reveals that the hypothesis H_0: $\boldsymbol{\beta} = \mathbf{0}$ was rejected ($\chi_5^2 = 98.04$, $p < 0.0001$). Thus, the independent variables explained a significant portion of the variance in the choice data. Observe in Table 1 that the risky option was less likely to be chosen when the decision problem was framed in terms of gains versus losses ($b = -1.297$, $p < 0.0001$). This finding indicates that decision makers exhibit risk aversion when choice outcomes are framed in terms of gains and supports hypothesis *H1a*.

Note in Table 1 that a significant GROUP X FRAME interaction was found ($b = -0.327$, $p < 0.01$). This within-subject preference reversal was very similar to the commonly observed between-subjects preference revearsal: subjects made risky choices in loss frames and risk averse choices in gain frames ($t = 8.59$, $p < 0.0001$ in gain-loss conditions, and $t = 5.13$, $p < 0.0001$ in loss-gain conditions). Thus, *H1b* is supported.

5.5.2. Moderating Effects of Familiarity

The effect of framing on choice, however, was moderated by the familiarity of the choice context. A significant FRAME X FAMILIARITY

Table 1. Results of estimating the repeated-measures probit model – Study 1

Independent Variables (IVs)	Parameter Estimates[a] (N = 148, T = 4)
Constant	0.749**
	(0.111)
FRAME	−1.297**
	(0.156)
GROUP'FRAME	−0.327*
	(0.109)
FAMILIARITY	−0.625**
	(0.152)
FRAME'FAMILIARITY	0.597*
	(0.216)
FRAME'FAMILIARITY'GROUP	0.111
	(0.154)
Descriptive performance	
Log-likelihood	−355.86
Log-likelihood under no impact of IVs	−404.88
Likelihood ratio (χ^2_5)	98.04**
Predictive performance	
Proportion correct	0.662
C_{pro}	0.501
C_{max}	0.524

** $p < 0.0001$; * $p < 0.01$.
[a] Standard errors are in parentheses.

interaction was found ($b = 0.597$, $p < 0.01$), supporting the hypothesis that familiarity reduces between-subjects framing effects (*H2a*). The proportion of subjects choosing the risky option decreased with task familiarity in loss frame conditions (0.73 vs. 0.54); no simple main effect of task familiarity is evident in gain frame conditions. Similar significant interactions were found in each group, supporting the hypothesis that familiarity reduces within-subject framing effects (*H2b*), $t = 2.66$, $p < 0.01$ in gain-loss conditions, and $t = 1.89$, $p < 0.06$ in loss-gain conditions. Finally, observe in Table 1 that a main effect of familiarity emerged ($b = -0.625$, $p < 0.01$), indicating that the risky option is less likely to be chosen in familiar (vs. unfamiliar) choice contexts.

5.5.3. Predictive Performance

While the likelihood ratio test provides evidence for the descriptive performance of the model structure, it is also important to assess the predictive ability of the model. Consequently, using estimates from the within-subjects probit model, a discriminant (classification) exercise was performed and the proportion of correct predictions noted. Observe in Table 1 that the model correctly predicted choice in 392 out of 592 choice decisions, yielding a predictive index of 66.2%. The proportion of correct classification exceeds both the proportional chance criterion (C_{pro}) and the maximum chance criterion (C_{max}) – two benchmarks advocated by Morrison (1969) to assess predictive performance.

5.5.4. Discussion

As predicted, both between-subjects and within-subject framing effects were observed. Decision makers exhibited risk aversion (a preference for the no-risk option) when choice outcomes were framed in terms of gains, and risk taking (a for the risky option) when identical choice outcomes were framed in terms of losses. This pattern was observed whether decision makers were exposed to gain frames only, loss frames only, or both frames. Furthermore, both between-subjects and within-subject framing effects were reduced (but not eliminated) when the choice task was familiar as opposed to unfamiliar.

Consistent with the constructive perspective, decision makers respond differently to different descriptions of the same choice problem. The manner in which choice outcomes are described or framed influences the selection of inferential rules for preference construction. Gain frames highlight benefits and encourage decision makers to seek potential opportunities (Schneider 1992). Loss frames emphasize costs and threats that motivate decision makers to seek security or protection. Different goals activate different inferential rules which then yield different preferences and patterns of choice.

6. STUDY 2

Study 1 demonstrated that constructive processes result in dramatic shifts in preference over time as a function of relatively subtle contextual variations. Study 2 was designed to explore reconstructive memory processes and to investigate whether preference shifts are accompanied by perceptions of preference instability. If people believe that their preferences are stable and consistent, they may be unlikely to detect shifts in preference even when within-subject preference reversals are induced. If this illusion of preference stability exists, and if present preferences are used to infer past preferences, recall accuracy should be greater when past preferences are consistent as opposed to inconsistent with present preferences.

6.1. Experimental Design

The design for Study 2 was motivated by two main considerations. First, a test of the hypotheses requires at least two time periods. Second, preference consistency must vary over time. Following Study 1, preference consistency was manipulated via intertemporal framing. Different frames induce within-subject preference reversals and low preference consistency. By contrast, repeated exposure to the same frame over time should produce high preference consistency.

An organizational buying scenario was developed and no-risk and risky choice options were provided. In session 1, subjects were randomly assigned to framing (gain or loss) conditions. In session 2, three weeks later, subjects were randomly assigned to one of four conditions. In the *different frame* condition, subjects who received the gain frame in session 1 received the loss frame in session 2 (gain-loss); subjects who received the loss frame in session 1 received the gain frame in session 2 (loss-gain). In the *different frame plus incentive* condition, subjects received different frames across sessions and were offered a chance to win a monetary prize if and only if they could recall their past preferences accurately. In the *same frame* condition, subjects who received the gain frame in session 1 also received the gain frame in session 2 (gain-gain); subjects who received the loss frame in session 1 also received the loss frame in session 2 (loss-loss). In the *recall only* control condition, subjects were asked to recall their session 1 preferences.

6.2. Procedure

Subjects were 153 undergraduate business students at a large midwestern university. One subject failed to participate in the second session and was excluded from the analyses.

6.2.1. Session 1

Subjects received a booklet presenting an organizational buying scenario and a choice task. As in experiment 1, subjects were asked to select one of two choice options (a no-risk option or a risky option). Half of the subjects received choice option outcomes framed in terms of gains, and half received choice option outcomes framed in terms of losses. Subjects were randomly assigned to framing conditions. Framing was manipulated as a between-subjects factor in session 1.

6.2.2. Session 2

Three weeks later, subjects were randomly assigned to one of four conditions: different frame, different frame plus incentive, same frame, or recall only. In the *different frame* condition, subjects who received the gain (loss) frame in session 1 received the loss (gain) frame in session 2. In the *different frame plus incentive* condition, opposite frames were presented across sessions and an incentive was offered for accurate recall. Specifically, subjects were told that if their recalled preferences matched their earlier preferences, their names would be entered in a lottery for a $25 cash prize. In the *same frame* condition, subjects received the gain (loss) frame in both sessions. In the *recall only* condition, subjects were asked to recall their session 1 preferences. No new (session 2) scenarios or preference measures were presented.

6.3. The Organizational Buying Scenario

Imagine that you are in the process of selecting a vendor from whom you will buy construction materials for your firm. There is a price advantage to buying all twelve items your firm needs for this project from a single source. After ample consideration you have narrowed your choices down to just two potential suppliers. The two suppliers are equivalent in most respects (e.g., prices, terms, reliability, service, reputation). All twelve items are available from both suppliers. The only notable difference between the two suppliers is variability in the quality of their materials. (For the purposes of this decision, assume that the following estimates are reliable and accurate.)

In gain frame conditions, the choice options were described as follows:

VENDOR X: If you buy from this supplier, 8 of the 12 items will definitely be above quality specifications.
VENDOR Y: If you buy from this supplier, there is a 2/3 probability that all 12 items will be above quality specifications, and 1/3 probability that none of the 12 items will be above quality specifications.

In loss frame conditions, the choice options were described as follows:

VENDOR X: If you buy from this supplier, 4 of the 12 items will definitely be below quality specifications.
VENDOR Y: If you buy from this supplier, there is a 1/3 probability that all 12 items will be below quality specifications, and a 2/3 probability that none of the 12 items will be below quality specifications.

6.4. Recall for Past Preferences

In different frame, different frame plus incentive, and same frame conditions, subjects first indicated their current (session 2) preferences and were then asked to recall their past (session 1) preferences. In the recall only control condition, only memory for past preferences was assessed. The recall instructions stated:

> Several weeks ago, you completed an earlier version of this survey in which you were asked to choose between two suppliers: Vendor X and Vendor Y. Only one outcome was possible with Vendor X. For Vendor Y, one of two outcomes was possible and the probability for each outcome was provided. Your task is to remember which vendor you selected [in the prior session]. Which vendor did you choose three weeks ago?

Finally, confidence in recall accuracy was assessed on a scale ranging from "not at all confident" (1) to "very confident" (7).

6.5. Results

6.5.1. Preference Consistency

First, we provide a replication of the within-subjects preference reversal observed in Study 1. Because we observe preferences at two points in time in different frame, different frame plus incentive, and same frame conditions, we can assess preference consistency in these three groups. Accordingly, we define three effects-coded dummy variables (gain-gain, gain-loss, loss-gain) to reflect the frames subjects were exposed to in seesion 1 and session 2. In turn, we analyze these data with the repeated-measures probit model presented in equation (4) with $N = 114$ and $T = 2$.

Table 2 presents the results of the estimation. A likelihood ratio test reveals that the independent variables explained a significant portion of the variance in the choice data ($\chi^2_4 = 52.28$, $p < 0.0001$). Observe that the risky option was less likely to be chosen when the decision problem was framed in terms of gains versus losses ($b = -2.23$, $p < 0.0001$). As in experiment 1, we obtained significant within-subject preference reversals in different frame and different frame plus incentive conditions ($p = 0.834$, $p < 0.0001$ for gain-loss and $b = -0.635$, $p < 0.0001$ for loss-gain).

No shifts in preference were found in same frame conditions ($b = 0.072$, *ns*, for gain-gain). Preference consistency was high because the decision frame did not vary over time. Hence, preference consistency varied reliably as a

Table 2. Results of estimating the repeated-measures probit
model – Study 2

Independent Variables[a] (IVs)	Parameter Estimates[b] (N = 114, T = 2)
Constant	0.716*
	(0.058)
FRAME	−2.230*
	(0.114)
Gain-Loss'TIME	0.834*
	(0.069)
Loss-Gain'TIME	−0.645*
	(0.072)
Gain-Gain'TIME	0.072
	(0.057)
Descriptive performance	
Log-likelihood	−118.47
Log-likelihood under no impact of IVs	−144.61
Likelihood ratio (χ_5^2)	52.28*
Predictive performance	
Proportion correct	0.719
C_{pro}	0.530
C_{max}	0.620

* $p < 0.0001$.
[a] In defining the three dummy variables (Gain-Loss, Loss-Gain
and Gain-Gain), the Loss-Loss condition served as the base;
TIME was simple 2-level dummy variable reflecting the session
(first or second) of the study.
[b] Standard errors are in parentheses.

function of intertemporal framing. In different frame and different frame plus
incentive conditions, robust preference reversals were observed. By contrast,
in same frame conditions, no changes in preference were observed.

Finally, note in Table 2 that the model correctly predicts choice in 164
out of 228 choice decisions, yielding a predictive index of 71.9% compared
to $C_{pro} = 0.53$ and $C_{max} = 0.62$.

6.5.2. Recall for Earlier Preferences

We estimate a probit model to test the hypothesis that current preferences
influence recall for past preferences (*H3*). Using data from different frame,
different frame plus incentive, and same frame conditions, the dependent
variable in this analysis was the actual discrete recall variable while $PREF_2$

Table 3. Recall of Earlier Preferences and Recall Accuracy –
Study 2

Covariates	Dependent Variable[a]	
	Recall of earlier preferences	Recall accuracy
Constant	−0.827*** (0.181)	−0.180 (0.213)
PREF$_2$	0.789** (0.274)	−
PREF$_1$	0.512* (0.269)	−
Consistency	−	0.885** (0.263)
Descriptive performance		
Log-likelihood	−66.57	−67.48
Log-likelihood under no impact of covariates	−75.55	−73.24
Likelihood ratio	$\chi^2_2 = 17.96$**	$\chi^2_1 = 11.52$**
Predictive performance		
Proportion correct	0.728	0.702
C_{pro}	0.530	0.550
C_{max}	0.623	0.658

*** $p < 0.0001$; ** $p < 0.01$; * $p < 0.10$; N = 114.
[a] Entries are parameter estimates (standard errors in parentheses); a dash in a column indicates that the covariate was not included in the probit analysis.

(preference in session 2) and PREF$_1$ (preference in session 1) served as the independent variables. Results are presented in Table 3. As Table 3 indicates, the independent variables explain significant variation in the pattern of recall ($\chi^2_2 = 17.96, p < 0.01$).

Note in Table 3 that current preferences (PREF$_2$) are significant determinants of recall of earlier preferences ($b = 0.789, p < 0.01$), consistent with *H3*. Subjects who preferred the risky option in session 2 believed that they also preferred the risky option in session 1; subjects who preferred the no-risk option in session 2 believed that they also preferred the no-risk option in session 1. Interestingly, the memory representation of earlier preferences (PREF$_1$) is only marginally significant in explaining recall patterns ($b = 0.512, p < 0.07$).

Observe in Table 3 that the model correctly predicted recall in 83 out of 114 cases, yielding a predictive index of 72.8% compared to $C_{pro} = 0.53$ and $C_{max} = 0.623$.

6.5.3. Recall Accuracy

To test the hypothesis that accuracy of recall for past preferences increases with preference consistency (*H4*), we first compare (using 1-tailed *z* tests) aggregate recall accuracy in each group to a naive recall accuracy of 0.50. Subsequently, we estimate a probit model to assess the impact of consistency in preferences on recall accuracy.

In the different frame condition, recall accuracy did not differ significantly from chance performance (0.58 vs. 0.50, $z = 1.02$, *ns*). Recall accuracy is low when preference consistency is low. Interestingly, recall accuracy improved in the different frame plus incentive condition (0.66 vs. 0.50, $z = 2.04$, $p < 0.01$). Recall accuracy was also high in the same frame condition (0.71 vs. 0.50, $z = 2.59$, $p < 0.01$). Recall accuracy is high when incentives for accuracy are present or when preference consistency is high. Finally, in the recall only control condition, recall accuracy was only marginally greater than chance performance (0.63 vs. 0.50, $z = 1.61$, $p < 0.06$).

To shed light on the determinants of recall accuracy, we estimated a probit model with recall accuracy (accurate vs. inaccurate) as the dependent variable and preference consistency as the independent variable. The independent variable was constructed as follows: if the same preference at both sessions was observed ($PREF_1 = PREF_2$), preference consistency $= 1$, 0 otherwise. Table 3 presents the results of this analysis and indicates that preference consistency significantly enhanced recall accuracy ($b = 0.885$, $p < 0.01$). The overall model fit was significant ($\chi_1^2 = 11.52$, $p < 0.01$) and correct prediction rate was 70.2% compared to $C_{pro} = 0.55$ and $C_{max} = 0.658$. Hence, support was found for the hypothesis that recall accuracy increases with preference consistency (*H4*).

Finally, recall confidence was greater in the different frame condition than in the recall only control condition ($Ms = 5.05$ vs. 3.92, $t_{77} = 2.64$, $p < 0.01$). Recall confidence was also greater in the same frame condition than in the recall only condition ($Ms = 5.37$ vs. 3.92, $t_{74} = 3.54$, $p < 0.01$). However, recall confidence in the different frame plus incentive condition did not differ from confidence in the recall only condition ($Ms = 4.61$ vs. 3.92, $t_{72} = 1.60$, $p > 0.10$). Hence, when current preferences were available to serve as a basis for inferring past preferences, confidence in recall accuracy was high. However, when no anchors were available to guide preference reconstruction (as in the recall only condition), confidence was low. Recall confidence was also low when incentives for accuracy were present, because incentives that heighten concerns about accuracy also attenuate confidence (Kruglanski 1989; Mayseless and Kruglanski 1987).

6.6. Discussion

Robust within-subject preference reversals were observed when decision frames varied over time. These reversals were eliminated when the same decision frames were presented repeatedly over time. Although preference consistency varies dramatically as a function of intertemporal framing, decision makers are insensitive to the presence or absence of framing-induced shifts in preference. Instead, current preferences are constructed on the basis of available cues, and past preferences are reconstructed on the basis of current preferences. Moreover, decision makers assume that past and present preferences are similar. This illusion of preference stability persists regardless of whether preference reversals occur or not, even though preference reversals represent the most extreme form of preference instability.

It is interesting to note that robust within-subject preference reversals were observed even though the expected values favored the risky supplier in loss frame conditions. Framing effects are so readily induced that they are observed even when one alternative dominates the other in terms of expected values and even when expected values cannot be computed due to a lack of specific information about the choice options (Reyna and Brainerd 1991). In fact, framing effects are even more pronounced when the choice options are described in terms of relational gist (e.g., some, more, less) rather than in terms of specific outcome probabilities.

Consistent with the constructive perspective, preferences vary when frames vary, and preferences remain the same when frames remain the same. Moreover, current preferences influence recall for past preferences, and this reconstructive memory process leads to low recall accuracy when frames vary and high recall accuracy when frames remain the same. Indeed, recall performance did not differ from chance performance in the different frame condition, whereas recall accuracy was significantly greater than chance in the same frame condition. High levels of confidence in recall accuracy was also observed in different frame and same frame conditions, relative to the recall only control condition. This pattern suggests that subjects believed they were not just guessing, but, ironically, they also believed that having a basis for guessing (i.e., current preferences in different frame and same frame conditions) is better than having no basis for guessing (i.e., no current preferences in the recall only condition).

The results also suggest that incentives for accuracy reduce reconstructive processing, consistent with Hirt's (1990) findings. Incentives for accuracy also decrease confidence, consistent with Mayseless and Kruglanski's (1987) findings. Hence, inferential reconstruction of the past based on the present is not inevitable. Reconstructive memory processes are moderated by incentives and by other cognitive and motivational variables (Hirt 1990; Hirt et al. 1993).

320

Experimental Business Research

7.   STUDY 3

A key assumption of the Hirt/Ross reconstructive memory framework that was used to interpret the results of Study 2 is that people frequently expect their preferences to remain stable over time. Study 3 tested this assumption by measuring decision makers' expectations concerning preference stability or instability. The Hirt/Ross model suggests that preference stability should be expected even when preference-related knowledge and experience is expected to increase. This is an interesting contradiction because preferences frequently change as people become more knowledgeable about a topic (West, Brown, and Hoch 1996). For example, novice wine drinkers frequently prefer simple, sweet wines, whereas experts tend to prefer much more complex and subtle wines. Tastes and preferences frequently change as people gain knowledge and experience. Nevertheless, we expected the illusion of preference stability to persist.

7.1. Procedure

The subjects were 86 undergraduate business students at a large midwestern university. Subjects received a questionnaire containing twelve six-point scales ranging from 1 (strongly disagree) to 6 (strongly agree). Four of these scales assessed expectations about preference stability: Once I decide that I like something, I generally don't change my mind about it later; My personal preferences (for people, things, activities) tend to remain stable over time; When faced with a choice decision, if I determine a certain option is best today, it will probably still be my preferred option later; The choices I make are usually consistent from day to day, week to week, month to month. These items were averaged to form a single index (Cronbach's alpha = .79).

Expectations about knowledge stability were assessed on four scales: I know more now than I did when the quarter began; My general knowledge has increased steadily over time; As I gain more experiences in life, I expect knowledge of the world to grow; For me, learning is a process that never stops (Cronbach's alpha = .77).

Expectations about the stability of abilities and skills were assessed on four scales: My ability to make good decisions has improved greatly over time; My problem-solving skills are getting better and better; My decision-making skills continue to improve over time; In general, my proficiencies have grown dramatically over time (Cronbach's alpha = .89).

7.2. Results and Discussion

As predicted, the results revealed that subjects expected their preferences to remain more stable ($M = 4.32$) than the knowledge base on which their preferences were built ($M = 1.54$), $t(85) = 25.20$, $p < .001$, and than the problem-solving and decision-making skills that provide the foundation for preference formation ($M = 1.98$), $t(85) = 18.69$, $p < .001$. Consistent with the implications of the Hirt/Ross model, people expect their preferences to remain stable over time, and they expect their knowledge levels and decision-making skills and abilities to increase over time. Hence, the illusion of preference stability persists even in the face of expected change in knowledge and abilities.

8. GENERAL DISCUSSION

The results of the present experiments indicate that, consistent with the constructive perspective (Coupey et al. 1998; Payne et al. 1992, 1993; Slovic 1995), the manner in which decision options were represented or described produced robust between-subjects and within-subject framing effects. These effects were observed across many different decision scenarios, including the class scheduling, account management, and organizational buying scenarios. Both between-subjects and within-subject framing effects indicate that preferences are unstable, inconsistent, and malleable. However, because within-subject preference reversals reflect the most extreme type of phenomenon attributable to preference instability, the existence of within-subject framing-induced preference reversals provides compelling support for the constructive perspective.

The results of Experiments 1 and 2 extend the work of Coupey et al. (1998) by demonstrating that familiarity moderates the likelihood of violations of the principle of description invariance as well as the principle of procedural invariance. Together, these studies provide strong support for the constructive perspective, and provide useful information concerning the conditions under which construction processes are likely versus unlikely to occur. Familiarity is an important moderating variable because prior knowledge and experience increases the likelihood that an individual will have a previously-formed preference to retrieve from memory. When a previously-formed preference is not available in memory, preference elicitation forces the individual to construct a preference, on-line, at the time of measurement. Constructed preferences are often unstable because many different task and contextual cues influence rule selection and use, and different rules are likely to be selected and used as tasks or contexts vary (Payne et al. 1992, 1993). Inconsistent rule selection and use often results in unstable preferences.

The present results are consistent with the results of recent research showing that simple exposure to preference measures can lead people to construct preferences that would not have been formed otherwise (Morwitz, Johnson, and Schmittlein 1993). The rules and cues used following exposure to preference measures can be quite different from the rules and cues used in the absence of testing and measurement. Consequently, preferences formed during the measurement process may differ from preferences formed spontaneously while examing choice options without exposure to measurement.

Of course, construction processes are moderated by many cognitive and motivational factors (Payne et al. 1992, 1993). In some instances, decision makers may have relatively stable, consistent, and well-articulated preferences. Consistent with this hypothesis, the results of Study 1 indicate that preference consistency varies systematically as a function of task familiarity. Repetitive, familiar decision tasks are likely to lead to the development of schemata containing consistently-ordered, well-articulated preferences. Subsequently, decision makers can refer to these schemata when they encounter similar decision problems. In these situations, preference consistency is likely to be increased and the magnitude of between-subjects and within-subject framing effects is reduced.

The results of Study 2 suggest that constructed preferences can often serve as a basis for inferential reconstruction of past preferences. Memory for past preferences appears to be a function of three important factors: (a) the memory trace for the past preference, (b) the present preference, and (c) intuitive theories or expectations about the relationship between past and present preferences (Ross 1989). Consistent with this three-factor model, the results of Study 2 show that the memory trace for the past preference had a weak (marginally significant) but positive effect on recall, the present preference had a strong positive effect on recall, and the degree of perceived consistency between recalled and present preferences was greater than the degree of observed consistency between past and present preferences. Even when strong within-subject preference reversals were induced, recalled preferences were remarkably consistent with present preferences.

The illusion of preference stability that was observed in Experiments 2 and 3 is consistent with prior work by Ross (1989) on intuitive theories about stability or change between past and present events. People often expect change or improvement in their skills and abilities. Prior experience suggests that "practice makes perfect," and people are often motivated to believe that their abilities have improved with time (Kruglanski 1989; Kunda 1990). Conversely, people often expect lack of change or stability when it comes to personal dispositions (Ross 1989). Most people believe that personal traits, characteristics, attitudes, opinions, and beliefs change very little over time. The results of the present study suggest that personal preferences should be added to this list. Because preferences are expected to remain stable over time, past preferences are inferred to be similar to present preferences. This result was obtained even when past and present preferences were not at all similar.

It is important to emphasize that the illusion of preference stability can have either beneficial or deleterious effects on memory performance, depending on the actual relationship between past and present events. When past and present preferences happen to be the same, inferential reconstruction of past preferences on the basis of present preferences leads to highly accurate recall performance. Conversely, when past and present preferences differ, inferential reconstruction of the past from the present leads to poor memory performance. Past and present preferences frequently diverge due to variations in framing (Studies 1 and 2), the addition of new choice options (Huber, Payne, and Puto 1982; Huber and Puto 1983; Simonson 1989), the deletion of old choice options (Pratkanis and Farquhar 1992), tradeoff contrast and extremeness aversion (Simonson and Tversky 1992), short-run versus long-run perspectives (Wedell and Bockenholt 1990), and differences in processing mode (Slovic et al. 1990; Tversky et al. 1988). In each of these cases, recall for past preferences is likely to be highly inaccurate.

The illusion of preference stability has important implications for preference measurement and analysis. Market researchers routinely measure consumer preferences because they recognize the value of incorporating this information into product management decisions. Preference data is important in design-driven product development, in assessing the effectiveness of various positioning strategies, and in forecasting long-term demand and market growth. The diagnostic value of preference data, however, can be compromised if preferences are constructed on the basis of different cues and rules at different points in time. Consideration-set dynamics motivated by the addition of new choice options or the deletion of old choice options can often lead to highly unstable preferences. The illusion of preference stability persists, however, and leads consumers (and managers) to believe that current preferences will continue to influence subsequent decisions.

REFERENCES

Alba, Joseph W., and J. Wesley Hutchinson (1987). "Dimensions of Consumer Expertise." *Journal of Consumer Research* 13, 411–54.

Bettman, James R., and Mita Sujan (1987). "Effect of Framing on Evaluation of Comparable and Noncomparable Alternatives by Experts and Novice Consumers." *Journal of Consumer Research* 14, 141–54.

Butler, J. S., and Robert Moffitt (1982). "A Computationally Efficient Quadrature Procedure for the One-Factor Multinomial Probit Model." *Econometrica* 3, 761–4.

Coupey, Eloise, Julie R. Irwin, and John W. Payne (1998). "Product Category Familiarity and Preference Construction." *Journal of Consumer Research* 24, 459–68.

Feldman, Jack M., and John G. Lynch (1988). "Self-Generated Validity and Other Effects of Measurement on Belief, Attitude, Intention, and Behavior." *Journal of Applied Psychology* 73, 421–35.

Fischhoff, Baruch (1983). "Predicting Frames." *Journal of Experimental Psychology: Learning, Memory, and Cognition* 9, 103–16.

Fischhoff, Baruch (1991). "Value Elicitation: Is There Anything in There?" *American Psychologist* 46, 835–47.

Green, Paul E., and V. Srinivasan (1990). "Conjoint Analysis in Marketing Research: New Developments and Directions." *Journal of Marketing* 54, 3–19.

Greene, William H. (1990). *Econometric Analysis*. NY: Macmillan.

Greene, William H. (1991). *LIMDEP: User's Manual and Reference Guide, Version 6.* Bellport, NY: Econometric Software, Inc.

Hastie, Reid, and Bernadette Park (1986). "The Relationship between Memory and Judgment Depends on Whether the Judgment Task is Memory-Based or On-Line." *Psychological Review* 93, 258–68.

Hershey, J. C., and P. J. H. Shoemaker (1980). "Prospect Theory's Reflection Hypothesis: A Critical Examination." *Organizational Behavior and Human Performance* 25, 395–418.

Hirt, Edward R. (1990). "Do I See Only What I Expect? Evidence for an Expectancy-Guided Retrieval Model." *Journal of Personality and Social Psychology* 58, 937–51.

Hirt, Edward R., Grant A. Erickson, and Hugh E. McDonald (1993). "Role of Expectancy Timing and Outcome Consistency in Expectancy-Guided Retrieval." *Journal of Personality and Social Psychology* 65, 640–56.

Hirt, Edward R., and N. John Castellan (1988). "Probability and Category Redefinition in the Fault Tree Paradigm." *Journal of Experimental Psychology: Human Perception and Performance* 14, 122–31.

Huber, Joel, John W. Payne, and Christopher Puto (1982). "Adding Asymmetrically Dominated Althernatives: Violations of Regularity and the Similarity Hypothesis." *Journal of Consumer Research* 9, 90–8.

Huber, Joel, John W. Payne, and Christopher Puto (1983). "Market Boundaries and Product Choice: Illustrating Attraction and Substitution Effects." *Journal of Consumer Research* 10, 31–43.

Kahneman, Daniel, and Amos Tversky (1979). "Prospect Theory: An Analysis of Decision under Risk." *Econometrica* 47, 263–91.

Kahneman, Daniel, and Dan Lovallo (1993). "Timid Choices and Bold Forecasts: A Cognitive Perspective on Risk Taking." *Management Science* 39, 17–31.

Kahneman, Daniel, and Amos Tversky (1984). "Choices, Values, and Frames." *American Psychologist* 39, 341–50.

Kruglanski, Arie W. (1989). *Lay Epistemics and Human Knowledge: Cognitive and Motivational Bases*. NY: Plenum Press.

Kunda, Ziva (1990). "The Case for Motivated Reasoning." *Psychological Bulletin* 108, 480–98.

Levin, Irwin P., and Gary Gaeth (1988). "How Consumers are Affected by the Framing of Attribute Information before and after Consuming the Product." *Journal of Consumer Research* 15, 374–8.

Loftus, Elizabeth F., James A. Coan, and Jacqueline E. Pickrell (1996). "Manufacturing False Memories Using Bits of Reality." In *Implicit Memory and Metacognition*, edited by Lynne M. Reder, 195–220. Mahwah, NJ: Lawrence Erlbaum Associates.

Lynch, John G. (1985). "Uniqueness Issues in the Decompositional Modeling of Multiattribute Overall Evaluations: An Information Integration Perspective." *Journal of Marketing Research* 22, 1–19.

Lynch, John G., and Thomas K. Srull (1982). "Memory and Attentional Factors in Consumer Choice: Concepts and Research Methods." *Journal of Consumer Research* 9, 18–37.

Maheswaran, Durairaj, and Joan Meyers-Levy (1990). "The Influence of Message Framing and Issue Involvement." *Journal of Marketing Research* 27, 361–7.

Mayseless, Ofra, and Arie W. Kruglanski (1987). "What Makes You So Sure? Effects of Epistemic Motivations on Judgmental Confidence." *Organizational Behavior and Human Decision Processes* 39, 162–83.

Nisbett, R. E. (1993). *Rules for Reasoning*. Hillsdale, NJ: Lawrence Erlbaum Associates.

Payne, John W., James R. Bettman, and Eric J. Johnson (1992). "Behavioral Decision Research: A Constructive Processing Perspective." *Annual Review of Psychology* 43, 87–131.

Pratkanis, Anthony R., and Peter H. Farquhar (1992). "A Brief History of Research on Phantom Alternatives: Evidence for Seven Empirical Generalizations about Phantoms." *Basic and Applied Social Psychology* 13, 103–22.

Puto, Christopher P. (1987). "The Framing of Buying Decisions." *Journal of Consumer Research* 14, 301–15.

Qualls, William J., and Christopher P. Puto (1989). "Organizational Climate and Decision Framing: An Integrated Approach to Analyzing Industrial Buying Decisions." *Journal of Marketing Research* 26, 179–92.

Reyna, Valerie F., and Charles J. Brainerd (1991). "Fuzzy-Trace Theory and Framing Effects in Choice: Gist Extraction, Truncation, and Conversion." *Journal of Behavioral Decision Making* 4, 249–62.

Ross, Michael (1989). "Relation of Implicit Theories to the Construction of Personal Histories." *Psychological Review* 96, 341–57.

Schneider, Sandra L. (1992). "Framing and Conflict: Aspiration Level Contingency, the Status Quo, and Current Theories of Risky Choice." *Journal of Experimental Psychology: Learning, Memory, and Cognition* 18, 1040–57.

Simonson, Itamar (1989). "Choice Based on Reasons: The Case of Attraction and Compromise Effects." *Journal of Consumer Research* 16, 158–74.

Simonson, Itamar, and Amos Tversky (1992). "Choices in Context: Tradeoff Contrast and Extremeness Aversion." *Journal of Marketing Research* 29, 281–95.

Slovic, Paul (1995). "The Construction of Preference." *American Psychologist* 50, 364–71.

Slovic, Paul, Dale Griffin, and Amos Tversky (1990). "Compatibility Effects in Judgment and Choice." In *Insights in Decision Making: A Tribute to Hillel J. Einhorn*, edited by Robin M. Hogarth, 5–27. Chicago: University of Chicago Press.

Tversky, Amos, and Daniel Kahneman (1981). "The Framing of Decisions and the Psychology of Choice." *Science* 211, 453–8.

Tversky, Amos, and Daniel Kahneman (1986). "Rational Choice and the Framing of Decisions." *Journal of Business* 59, S251–78.

Tversky, Amos, Shmuel Sattath, and Paul Slovic (1988). "Contingent Weighting in Judgment and Choice." *Psychological Review* 95, 371–84.

Weber, Elke U., William M. Goldstein, and Sema Barlas (1995). "And Let Us Not Forget Memory: The Role of Memory Processes and Techniques in the Study of Judgment and Choice." In *The Psychology of Learning and Motivation*. Vol. 32, edited by Jerome Busemeyer, Reid Hastie, and Douglas L. Medin, 33–81. San Diego, CA: Academic Press.

Wedell, Douglas H., and Ulf Bockenholt (1990). "Moderation of Preference Reversals in the Long Run." *Journal of Experimental Psychology: Human Perception and Performance* 16, 429–38.

West, Patricia M., Christina L. Brown, and Stephen J. Hoch (1996). "Consumption Vocabulary and Preference Formation." *Journal of Consumer Research* 23, 120–35.

APPENDIX

In this section, we provide a discussion and derivation of the likelihood function for the estimation of the repeated-measure probit model.

To derive the likelihood function, we need to specify the probabilities of observing the sequence, Y_i of the distance dependent variable given the independent variables, $X_i = [X_{i1}, X_{i2}, \ldots, X_{iT}]$. Then, the likelihood function will be given by

$$L = \Pi_i \Pr[Y_i \mid X_i] \tag{A1}$$

where Π_i denotes the continuous product over all observations.

For the tth choice we can write

$$
\begin{aligned}
\Pr[Y_{it} = 1 \mid X_{it}, \tau_i] &= \Pr[Y_{it}^* \geq 0] \\
&= \Pr[\delta_{it} \geq -\beta_0 - X_{it}\beta - \tau_i] \\
&= \Pr[\delta_{it}/\sigma_\delta \geq (-\beta_0 - X_{it}\beta - \tau_i)/\sigma_\delta] \\
&= \Pr[\delta_{it}/\sigma_\delta \geq -(\beta_0 + X_{it}\beta)/\sigma_\delta - \sigma_\tau \tilde{\tau}_i/\sigma_\delta] \\
&= \phi[(\beta_0 + X_{it}\beta)/\sigma_\delta + \sigma_\tau \tilde{\tau}_i/\sigma_\delta],
\end{aligned}
\tag{A2}
$$

where $\phi[.]$ is the c.d.f. of the standard normal and $\tilde{\tau}_i \sim N(0,1)$. Noting that $\pi = \sigma_\tau/(\sigma_\tau^2 + \sigma_\delta^2)^{1/2}$ and $\sigma_\tau/\sigma_\delta = \rho(1 - \rho^2)^{-1/2}$, equation (A2) can now be written as:

$$\Pr[Y_{it} = 1 \mid X_{it}, \tau_i] = \phi\left[(\beta_0 + X_{it}\beta)/\sigma_\delta + \tilde{\tau}_i\rho(1 - \rho^2)^{-1/2}\right]. \tag{A3}$$

To obtain $\Pr[Y_{it} = 1 \mid X_{it}]$, we follow Butler and Moffitt (1982) and remove the conditioning on $\tilde{\tau}_i$ by integrating it out giving us:

$$\Pr[Y_{it} = 1 \mid X_{it}] = \int_{-\infty}^{\infty} \Phi[H_{it}]\Phi(\tilde{\tau}_i)d\tilde{\tau}_i, \tag{A4}$$

where $\Phi(.)$ is the p.d.f. of the standard normal, and

$$H_{it} = (\beta_0 + X_{it}\beta)/\sigma_\delta + \tilde{\tau}_i\rho(1 - \rho^2)^{-1/2}. \tag{A5}$$

Noting that $\Pr[Y_{it} = 0 \mid X_{it}] = 1 - \Pr[Y_{it} = 1 \mid X_{it}]$ and $1 - \Phi[a] = \Phi[-a]$ we can now write,

$$\Pr[Y_{it} = 0 \mid X_{it}] = \int_{-\infty}^{\infty} \Phi[-H_{it}]\Phi(\tilde{\tau}_i)d\tilde{\tau}_i. \tag{A6}$$

Combining equations (A4) and (A6), we can now express $\Pr[Y_{it} \mid X_{it}]$ as

$$-\Pr[Y_{it} \mid X_{it}] = \int_{-\infty}^{\infty} \Phi\{(H_{it})(2Y_{it} - 1)\} \times \Phi(\tilde{\tau}_i)d\tilde{\tau}_i. \tag{A7}$$

Note that substituting $Y_{it} = 1$ and $Y_{it} = 0$ in equation (A7) yields equation (A4) and (A6), respectively.

From equation (A7) we can now write the following expression for the probability of the sequence Y_i given X_i as follows:

$$\Pr[Y_i \mid X_i] = \int_{-\infty}^{\infty} \Pi_t \Phi\{(H_{it})(2Y_{it} - 1)\} \times \Phi(\tilde{\tau}_i)d\tilde{\tau}_i, \tag{A8}$$

where Π_t denotes the continuous product over all time periods. Substituting for $\Pr[Y_i|X_i]$ from equation (A8) in equation (A1) we can now write the likelihood function for the repeated measures probit model as

$$L = \Pi_i \int_{-\infty}^{\infty} \Pi_t \Phi\{(H_{it})(2Y_{it} - 1)\} \times \Phi(\tilde{\tau}_i) d\tilde{\tau}_i. \tag{A9}$$

Note from equation (A5) that similar to the standard bivariate probit model (Maddala 1983), we can estimate only scaled values of β_0 and β. Without loss of generality by making the standard probit model normalization of $\sigma_\delta = 1$ in equation (A5), we can now write the final expression for the likelihood function as

$$L = \Pi_i \int_{-\infty}^{\infty} \Pi_t \Phi\{(J_{it})(2Y_{it} - 1)\} \times \Phi(\tilde{\tau}_i) d\tilde{\tau}_i \tag{A10}$$

where $J_{it} = \beta_0 + X_{it}\beta + \tilde{\tau}_i \rho(1 - \rho^2)^{-1/2}$.

Part IV

BARGAINING AND CONTRACTS

Chapter 14

TRUST, RECIPROCITY, AND OTHER-REGARDING PREFERENCES: GROUPS VS. INDIVIDUALS AND MALES VS. FEMALES

James C. Cox
University of Arizona

1.   INTRODUCTION

Trust and reciprocity have attracted increasing attention as topics of research. Arrow (1974) explained that, because of asymmetric information, incomplete contracts, and the prohibitive transaction costs of perfect monitoring, much economic activity may require trust and reciprocity in order for mutual gains from exchange to be realized. And reciprocity may be essential to development of a modern economy in which much effort of highly-skilled labor cannot be effectively monitored.

Several recent studies, including Coleman (1990), Fukuyama (1995), Gambetta (1988), La Porta et al. (1997), and Putnam (1993), have argued that the level of trusting behavior in a society determines the performance of a society's institutions. This does not mean that these authors believe that social institutions are unimportant in themselves. It does mean that they have concluded that the same or similar institutions will perform differently depending on the level of trust in a society. Other studies, such as Knack and Keefer (1996) and La Porta et al. (1997), have reported positive estimated relationships between economic performance and trust.

EXPERIMENTAL BUSINESS RESEARCH. Copyright © 2002. Kluwer Academic Publishers. Boston. All rights reserved.

A question of interest concerns the identities of the players whose trust and reciprocity or other-regarding preferences are important to an economy? Are we only interested in the properties of decisions made by individuals or are the properties of decisions by small groups also central to the behavior we seek to understand? When studying decisions made by individuals, are we only interested in decisions made by both genders aggregated or are we interested in learning whether there may be systematic differences between females and males?

Experimental economics has focused primarily on the behavior of individual subjects. Little systematic work has been done to study the behavior of groups in the economic situations of interest. This may limit the external validity of the experiment results because many important economic decisions are made by small groups such families, boards of directors, and committees rather than individuals. As argued by Davis (1992), exporting results directly from individual-level experiments to group-level phenomena can be misleading.

There is an extensive literature in social psychology on small group decision-making. Principal topics in this literature include the social dynamics of group decision-making and group polarization in risky decisions. An overview of the literature is contained in Davis (1992). Experimental tests of expected utility theory using group decision-makers are reported in Bone, Hey, and Suckling (1997) and Kuon, Mathauschek, and Sadrieh (1999). Group and individual behavior patterns have also been compared in experiments with ultimatum games (Bornstein and Yaniv, 1998). The present paper extends the study of group decision-making to comparisons of individual and group decisions in the context of the investment game that involves decisions motivated by trust, reciprocity, and other-regarding preferences.

The recent economic history of highly-developed western economies is characterized by a steady movement of women into the labor force. This movement has included a gradual rise in the percentage of many types of managerial and professional jobs that are held by women. With women thus obtaining more decision-making power in the economy, it becomes increasingly relevant to predicting economic performance to know whether there are systematic differences in the economic behavior of men and women. Possible differences between the genders in tendencies to cooperate or defect have been studied in several contexts, including experiments with ultimatum games (Solnick, 1997; Eckel and Grossman, 1997), dictator games (Bolton and Katok, 1995; Eckel and Grossman, 1998), prisoner's dilemma games (Rapoport and Chammah, 1965; Frank et al., 1993; Ortmann and Tichy, 1999), public goods games (Brown-Kruse and Hummels, 1993; Norwell and Tinckler, 1994; Cadsby and Maynes, 1998), and the investment game (Croson and Buchan, 1999). This paper extends the study of gender differences to decisions involving trust, reciprocity, and other-regarding preferences with an experimental design that discriminates among the observable implications of these three motivations.

There is a large experimental literature that has produced replicable patterns of behavior that have been interpreted as trust and reciprocity. Some of the experimental designs use single one-shot matrix games.[1] Some others involve multiple-round experiments with single games interpreted as stylized labor markets.[2] The patterns of behavior in such experiments are inconsistent with the special-case interpretation of game theory in which payoffs (or utilities) depend only on the subjects' own monetary rewards in the experiments. But they cannot be definitively interpreted as exhibiting trust or reciprocity rather than other-regarding preferences because the experimental designs do not discriminate between the alternative motivations. Therefore, the experiment reported here uses the triadic game structure modeled in Cox (2000) to discriminate between decisions by males and females that are motivated by other-regarding preferences and decisions motivated by trust or reciprocity.

2. EXPERIMENTAL DESIGN AND PROCEDURES

The experiment sessions are run manually (i.e., not with computers). Each session contains an individual decision task ("Task 1") and a group decision task ("Task 2"). Decisions in Task 2 are made by groups with three members. The individual task precedes the group task in every session. At the end of a session, a coin is flipped in the presence of the subjects to determine which task has monetary payoff. The payoff procedure is double blind: (a) subject responses are identified only by letters that are private information of the individual subjects (in Task 1) or the committees (in Task 2); and (b) monetary payoffs are collected in private from sealed envelopes contained in lettered mailboxes. Decisions in the individual task are made in the single large room of the Economic Science Laboratory. Decisions in the group task are made in the breakout rooms of the Decision Behavior Laboratory. The two laboratories are located close to each other in McClelland Hall at the University of Arizona.

2.1. The Group Task

The experiment involves three treatments. Each treatment uses the same group task. The individual task differs across the three treatments. The group task is a group version of the investment game introduced by Berg, Dickhaut, and McCabe (1995). Individuals are randomly assigned to be members of three person groups, which are referred to in the subject instructions as "committees." Each second-mover ("Type Y") committee is given 30 one-dollar certificates as a show-up fee. Each first-mover ("Type X") committee is also given 30 one-dollar certificates as a show-up fee.[3] Each Type X committee is given the task of deciding whether it wants to transfer some, none, or all of its show-up fee to a paired Type Y committee. Any amount transferred is tripled by the experimenter. After the Type X committees have completed their decisions, each Type Y committee is given the task of deciding whether it wants to return some, none, or all of the tripled number of certificates it received to the paired committee in Type X that sent them. The Type X (resp., Type Y) committees are comprised of subjects who were Type X (resp. Type Y) in the preceding individual decision task.

The procedures used in the experiment are intended to ensure that the groups are unitary players. Thus, each group is given a $30 show-up fee as group property rather than each member of a three-person group being given a $10 show-up fee as individual property. Groups send and receive numbers of one-dollar certificates when interacting with other groups in the experiment. A group's money payoff is determined by the total number of one-dollar certificates assigned to it after both Type X and Type Y committees have made their decisions. The experimenters divide the group's payoff equally among the group members by placing one-third of it in each of three envelopes that are deposited in the group's mailbox.

2.2. The Three Individual Tasks

The different individual decision tasks used in the three treatments are as follows. Treatment A implements Game A, the investment game of Berg, Dickhaut, and McCabe (1995). Each individual of Type Y is given 10 one-dollar certificates as a show-up fee. Each individual of Type X is given 10 one-dollar certificates as a show-up fee and given the task of deciding whether he/she wants to transfer to a paired individual of Type Y none, some, or all of his/her show-up fee. Any amounts transferred are tripled by the experimenter. Then each individual of Type Y is given the task of deciding whether she/he wants to return some, all, or none of the tripled number of certificates received to the paired individual of Type X who sent them. Treatment B implements Game B, which involves an individual decision task that differs from Treatment A only in that the Type Y individuals do not have a decision to make; thus they do not have an opportunity to return any tokens that they receive.

In Game A, a first mover may send some of his/her $10 to the paired second mover because of altruistic preferences: it only costs $1 in own money payoff to increase the other person's money payoff by $3. Alternatively, a first mover in Game A may send some of her/his $10 to the paired second mover because of a trust that the second mover will share the profit on the investment obtained from the tripling of amounts sent. In contrast, in Game B the only reason for a first mover to send money is altruistic preferences because the second mover cannot return anything. Thus, the across-individuals measure of transfers due to trust is the difference between the numbers of tokens transferred in Treatments A and B.[4]

Treatment C implements Game C(n), which involves an individual decision task that differs from Treatment A as follows. First, Type X individuals do not have a decision to make. Type Y individuals are given 10 one-dollar certificates as a show-up fee. Type X individuals are given show-up fees in amounts equal to the amounts kept (i.e. *not* transferred) by the individual subjects in the experiments with Treatment A. Type Y subjects are given "additional certificates" in the amounts received from transfers by the Type X subjects in experiments with Treatment A. The subjects are informed with a table of the exact inverse relation between the number of additional certificates received by a Type Y subject and the show-up fee of the paired individual of Type X.

In Game A, a second mover may return some of the tripled amount of money sent by the paired first mover because of altruistic preferences. Alternatively, a second mover may return a positive amount of money to the paired first mover in Game A because of reciprocity: the second mover will know that if he/she receives a positive amount of money from the first mover it is because the first mover intended to make the transfer. In contrast, in Game C the only reason for a second mover to "return" anything is altruistic preferences because the first mover cannot send anything. Thus, the across-individuals measure of transfers due to reciprocity is the difference between the number of tokens returned in Treatments A and C.[5]

2.3. Other Design Features

The double blind payoffs are implemented by giving each individual and each committee an unmarked sealed envelope with a lettered key inside. Depending on the coin flip, one key or the other will be used by an individual or a committee to open a lettered mailbox to collect the appropriate money payoffs.

All of the above design features are common information given to the subjects except for one item. The subjects in Treatment C are *not* informed that the amounts of the Type X show-up fees and the Type Y additional certificates are determined by subject decisions in experiments with Treatment A.

All of the experimental sessions end with each subject being paid an additional $5 for filling out a questionnaire. Type X subjects and Type Y subjects have distinct questionnaires. The questions asked have three functions: (a) to provide additional data; (b) to provide a check for possible subject confusion about the decision tasks; and (c) to provide checks for possible recording errors by the experimenters and counting errors by the subjects.

Subjects did *not* write their names on the questionnaires. The additional data provided by the questionnaires include the subjects' reports of their payoff key letters in the individual and group tasks. This makes it possible to track individuals into groups without infringing upon the double blind feature of the protocol. Individuals are asked to state whether they are male or female. They are asked to explain the reasons for their decisions in both the individual and group tasks. During the first session involving Treatment B, three subjects asked questions (in the privacy of their breakout rooms) during the group task that seemed to reveal they had not understood the preceding individual task. This was confirmed by their answers on the questionnaires. This caused the author not to use the data for these three subjects in the data analysis reported in Table 1 and section 3. The three confused subjects caused the author to revise the Treatment B subject information form before running subsequent sessions with this treatment. In the last session with Treatment B, there was one repeat subject. Data for this subject are excluded from the data analysis reported in section 3 and data for the group including this subject are excluded from the data analysis reported in section 4.[6] The appendix reports results from analyses of two alternative data samples: (a) all of the individual subject data; and (b) data excluding decisions by the repeat subject and *all* subjects in the first session with Treatment B. Analyses of these alternative data samples imply the same conclusions as reported in section 3.

Data error checks provided by the questionnaires come from asking the subjects to report the numbers of tokens transferred, received, and returned in both tasks. These reports, together with two distinct records kept by the experimenters, provide accuracy checks that were used as follows. In one instance, the two experimenter data records contained different amounts for the number of tokens transferred by a Type X committee. It was possible to ascertain which amount was correct because all three of the individuals that were in that committee independently reported one of the two experimenters' numbers as the amount their committee transferred. In three other instances, the two experimenters' records contained the same odd number of certificates but all three members of the committees reported the same even numbers that were one certificate different than the experimenters' numbers. The differences appeared to have resulted from certificate counting errors by the subjects. In these instances, the data record reflects the numbers reported by the subjects as reflecting their *intended* decisions.

2.4. Experimental Procedures

The subjects first assembled in the sign-in room of the Economic Science Laboratory and recorded their names, student identification numbers, and signatures on a form. Then a monitor was chosen randomly from the subject sample (by drawing a ball from a bingo cage) and given the responsibility of ensuring that the experimenters followed the procedures contained in the subject instructions for calculating money payoffs. The monitor was paid $20 for this job. The other subjects were not informed of the amount of this payment in order to avoid the possible creation of a focal earnings figure. Next, the subjects were randomly divided into two equal-size groups, Group X and Group Y, and escorted into the large room of the Economic Science Laboratory. The procedures differed somewhat across the three treatments because of the properties of the experimental design. I will first explain in detail the procedures used in Treatment A and, subsequently, explain how procedures differed in Treatments B and C.

In a Treatment A session, the Group X subjects were seated at widely-separated computer terminals with privacy side and front partitions. (The computers were not used.) The Group Y subjects were standing at the back of the room at the beginning of the session with Treatment A. Each Group Y subject was given an envelope labeled "my show-up fee" that contained ten Task 1 $1 certificates. Each subject and the monitor were given copies of the instructions for Task 1 (the individual decision task). Then an experimenter (the author) read aloud the instructions. The instructions for all treatments and other forms and questionnaires are contained in an appendix available from the author. After the reading of the instructions was completed, the Group Y subjects were escorted back to the sign-in room by one of the experimenters. (The Group X subjects had no further contact with the Group Y subjects until all decisions in both decision tasks had been completed.) Then the Group X subjects were given the opportunity to raise their hands if they had questions. If a subject raised his/her hand, he/she was approached by an experimenter (the author) and given an opportunity to ask questions and receive answers in a low voice that could not be overheard by other subjects. When there were no more questions, the experimenter left the room and the monitor took over to conduct the first-mover individual decision task with the Group X subjects.

The monitor carried a large box that contained smaller boxes equal in number to the number of subjects. Each subject was given the opportunity to point to any remaining small box to indicate she wanted that one. (The boxes all looked the same to the author.) A subject opened her box to find an envelope labeled "my show-up fee" that contained ten Task One $1 dollar certificates. The box also contained an empty envelope labeled "certificates sent to a paired person in Group Y" and an envelope containing a lettered Task One mailbox key. Finally, the box contained a one-page form that summarized the nature of the first-mover individual decision task. All envelopes in the box were labeled with the letter on the mailbox key.

Subjects were given 10 minutes to complete this task. When a subject was finished, he put all of the envelopes except the key envelope back in the

box and summoned the monitor to collect the box. The monitor then carried
the large box full of small boxes into another room for data recording and
the preparation of boxes for the Group Y, second-mover subjects. The monitor
witnessed all data recording and Group Y box preparations.

While the boxes were being processed, one experimenter escorted the
Group X subjects out a side door of the Economic Science Laboratory and
down the hall to the committee breakout rooms of the Decision Behavior
Laboratory. Next, another experimenter escorted the Group Y subjects
through a different door from the sign-in room into the Economic Science
Laboratory to get ready for their second-mover decisions in the individual
decision task.

The Group Y subjects were given boxes by the monitor. Each box
contained an envelope with a lettered Task 1 mailbox key. The box contained two empty envelopes, one labeled "my certificates" and the other
labeled "certificates returned to the paired person in Group X." The box
contained the tripled number of certificates sent by the paired person in
Group X and a form summarizing the decision task. The Group Y subjects
had to decide how many of the certificates to put in the envelopes labeled
"my certificates" and "certificates returned to the paired person in Group
X." The Group Y subjects were given 10 minutes to complete the task.
When a subject was finished, she put all envelopes except the key envelope
back in the box and summoned the monitor to collect it. The monitor then
carried the large box of little boxes to another room and watched the data
recording.

The second-mover decisions in Task 1 were conducted simultaneously with the first-mover decisions in Task 2. The first-mover decisions in
Task 2 were made by three-person committees that were formed by the experimenter by the order in which the subjects entered the laboratory from
the hallway. Thus, the first three subjects were assigned to be in the first committee, the next three in the second committee, and so on. Each committee
was seated in its own small breakout room. Each member of each committee
was given the written subject instructions for Task 2. Then an experimenter
(the author) read aloud the instructions while all breakout room doors
remained open. Subjects were then given the opportunity to indicate whether
they had any questions. If there was a question, the experimenter entered the
appropriate breakout room and closed the door before the question was asked
and answered. When there were no more questions, the experimenter left and
the monitor took over. The monitor permitted the members of each committee to point to a small box contained in a large box to indicate which remaining box the committee wanted. A committee's box contained an envelope
labeled "our show-up fee" that contained 30 Task 2 $1 certificates. The box
also contained an envelope labeled "certificates sent to a paired committee in
Group Y" and an envelope containing a lettered Task 2 mailbox key. Finally,

the box contained a one-page summary of the group decision task. The committees were given 20 minutes to complete their tasks. When a committee was finished, it put all envelopes except the key envelope back in the box and summoned the monitor by opening the door to its breakout room. The monitor carried the large box full of little boxes to the processing room and watched the data recording and preparation of boxes for the Group Y committees. Next, an experimenter escorted the Group X subjects back to the sign-in room. After all of the Group X subjects were in the sign-in room and the door was closed, an experimenter escorted the Group Y subjects out a side door of the Economic Science Laboratory and down the hallway to the breakout rooms of the Decision Behavior Laboratory.

The Group Y subjects then made their Task 2, second-mover decisions. Each Group Y committee was given an envelope labeled "our show-up fee" that contained 30 Task 2 $1 certificates. The procedures for reading instructions, answering questions, and the role of the monitor were like those for the first-mover, Group X subjects. Each Group Y committee's box contained the tripled number of certificates sent to it by the paired committee in Group X. The box also contained an envelope with a Task 2 key, a summary instruction form, and two empty envelopes. The empty envelopes were labeled "our certificates" and "certificates returned to the paired committee in Group X."

After the Group Y committees finished their Task 2 decisions, they were escorted back down the hall to rejoin the Group X subjects in the Economic Science Laboratory. Next, an experimenter flipped a coin in the presence of all of the subjects and the monitor. The monitor announced whether the coin came up heads or tails. If heads (respectively, tails) then each Task 1 (respectively, Task 2) $1 certificate was exchanged for one United States dollar. While the subjects' money payoffs were calculated, they filled out the questionnaires. In addition to the salient money payoff, each subject was paid $5 upon depositing her completed questionnaire in a box. After the questionnaires were completed, the Group X subjects went together to obtain sealed envelopes containing their money payoffs from lettered mailboxes. They had been asked to exit the building after obtaining their envelopes and not to open their envelopes until out of the building. After the Group X subjects had left, the Group Y subjects obtained their payoff envelopes from the lettered mailboxes.

The procedures for Treatment B differed as follows from the Treatment A procedures explained above. The Group Y subjects did not make a decision in Task 1. The procedures for Treatment C differed as follows from those for Treatment A. At the beginning of Task 1, the Group Y subjects were seated in the Economic Science Laboratory and the Group X subjects were standing at the back. The Group X subjects did not make a decision in Task 1.

3.   MALE VS. FEMALE TRUST, RECIPROCITY, AND OTHER-REGARDING PREFERENCES

3.1. Trust and Other-Regarding Preferences

Data from Treatments A and B can be used to discriminate between amounts sent by first movers due to trust and amounts sent because of other-regarding preferences. The first and second columns of Table 1 report the mean amounts sent in Treatments A and B by males and females. There were 18 male and 12 female Type X subjects in Treatment A. Treatment B had 22 male and 16 female Type X subjects. The male subjects sent more than the female subjects in both Treatment A and Treatment B. For both males and females, the excess of the amounts sent in Treatment A over the amounts sent in Treatment B is not significantly greater than 0 by either the one tailed t-test for differences in means or the one-tailed Smirnov test. Therefore, neither males nor females exhibit significant trust in this experiment. Both females and males exhibit significant altruistic other-regarding preferences because the mean amount sent in Treatment B is more than two standard deviations away from zero for each gender. The males appear to be slightly more altruistic than the females because of the larger amount transferred by males than females in Treatment B. The larger amounts sent in Treatment B than in standard dictator games reveal the price-elasticity of demand for altruism: the own-price of increasing the other's payoff by $1.00 is only $0.33 in Treatment B whereas it is $1.00 in standard dictator games.

Table 1. Money Sent Due to Trust and Other-Regarding Preferences

Subjects	Treatment A Mean	Treatment B Mean	Means Test	Smirnov Test	$\hat{\alpha}$	$\hat{\beta}$	$\hat{\gamma}$	LR Test
Males	6.44 [2.66] {18}	6.27 [2.91] {22}	.172 (.423)[I]	.110 (>.10)[I]	...	...	...	...
Females	5.33 [2.42] {12}	5.19 [2.53] {16}	.146 (.438)[I]	.250 (>.10)[I]	...	...	...	...
Males vs. Females	...	...	...	...	6.62 (.000)	.067 (.464)[I]	−1.20 (.105)	2.62 (>.500)

p-values in parentheses.
[I] denotes a one-tailed test.
Standard deviations in brackets.
Number of subjects in braces.

The third row of Table 1 reports tobit estimates of the parameters of the model

$$S_t = \alpha + \beta D_t^A + \gamma D_t^F + \varepsilon_t \tag{1}$$

where S_t is the amount sent by the first mover in subject pair t and

$$D_t^A = 1, \text{ for Treatment A data} \tag{2}$$
$$ = 0, \text{ for Treatment B data}$$

and

$$D_t^F = 1, \text{ for female subject data} \tag{3}$$
$$ = 0, \text{ for male subject data.}$$

The bounds for the tobit estimation are the bounds imposed in the experimental design:

$$S_t \in [0,10]. \tag{4}$$

The estimate of β is not significantly greater than 0. This provides additional support for the conclusion that there is no evidence in these data of trust by first-mover subjects. Finally, note that the estimate of the coefficient, γ on the female dummy variable is negative but insignificant ($p = .105$). Thus the apparent difference between male and female altruism is not quite significant at 10% confidence.

3.2.   Reciprocity and Other-Regarding Preferences

Data from implementations of Treatments A and C can be used to discriminate between amounts returned by male and female second movers due to other-regarding preferences and amounts returned because of positive reciprocity. There were 17 male and 13 female Type Y subjects in each treatment.

The first row of Table 2 reports that, on average, the amounts returned by male second-mover subjects in Treatment A exceeded the amounts they were sent by first-mover subjects by $1.29. The comparison figure for females was $1.00. Thus, on average, the male second-mover subjects shared more of the profit created by the first movers than did the female subjects in Treatment A. In contrast, the average amount returned by the male subjects in Treatment C was $1.88 less than the additional amounts they were given by the experimenter. For females, the average amount returned in Treatment C was only $0.385 less than the average additional amount given to them. Two sample *t*-tests for differences in means detect a significant difference between the return

Table 2. Money Returned Due to Reciprocity and Other-Regarding Preferences

Subjects	Treatment A Ret. – Sent Mean	Treatment C Ret. – Given Mean	Means Test	Smirnov Test	$\hat{\alpha}$	$\hat{\beta}$	$\hat{\gamma}$	$\hat{\theta}$	LI Te
Males	1.29 [3.62] {17}	-1.88 [4.47] {17}	2.76 (.015)^I	.236 (>.10).	-.467 (.597)	.624 (.010)^I	.616 (.008)	.187 (.020)	28.9 (<.0
Females	1.00 [3.96] {13}	-.385 [5.19] {13}	1.38 (.226)^I	.154 (>.10)	6.56 (.009)	.402 (.179)^I	-.139 (.778)	.157 (.035)	10.4 (<.0.

p-values in parentheses.
^{I} denotes a one-tailed test.
Standard deviations in brackets.
Number of subjects in braces.

minus sent (or given) means for males ($p = .015$) but not for female subjects ($p = .226$). The contrast between these male and female means tests is consistent with a gender difference in reciprocity, but the Smirnov test does not detect significant reciprocity for either females or males.

The sixth through tenth columns of Table 2 report tobit estimates of the parameters of the following relation between amounts sent and amounts returned in Treatments A and C:

$$R_t = \alpha + \beta D_t S_t + \gamma S_t + \varepsilon_t \qquad (5)$$

where R_t is the amount returned by the second mover in subject pair t and

$$D_t = 1 \text{ for Treatment A data} \qquad (6)$$
$$= 0 \text{ for Treatment C data.}$$

The bounds for the tobit estimation are the bounds imposed by the experimental design:

$$R_t \in [0, 3S_t]. \qquad (7)$$

One would expect that the cone created by these bounds might produce heteroskedastic errors. In order to allow for the possibility of heteroskedastic errors, the tobit estimation procedure incorporates estimation of the θ parameter in the following model of multiplicative heteroskedasticity:

$$\sigma_t = \sigma e^{\theta S_t}. \qquad (8)$$

For the males, the estimate of β is significantly greater than 0 ($p = .010$). Hence the data for males provide support for behavior involving positive reciprocity. In contrast, the estimate of β for the female subjects is not significantly greater than 0 ($p = .179$). For males, the estimate of γ is significantly greater than 0; thus, the larger the amount a male received (the more unequal the payoffs before his decision), the larger the amount he returned. In that way, the males exhibited altruistic other-regarding preferences. For females, the estimate of γ is not significantly different from 0 but the estimate of α is significantly greater than 0; thus, on average the females also exhibited significant altruistic other-regarding preferences in Treatment C.

The differences between the estimated parameters of the tobit model for the male and female subjects are quite striking. In the male equation, the estimate of α is not significantly different from 0; the estimate of β is significantly greater than 0; and the estimate of γ is significantly different from 0. Thus the pattern of behavior for the males can be understood as not being significantly different from the following regularities: (a) if they get more then they return more ($\hat{\gamma} > 0$); and (b) if they know that they got more because of someone's intentional choice then they return even more than otherwise ($\hat{\beta} > 0$). The pattern of the estimates for the female data is very different, with the amount returned being approximately a constant amount ($\hat{\alpha} > 0$) that is independent of the amount sent ($\hat{\gamma} \cong 0$) and of whether the amount sent was the result of someone's intentional choice ($\hat{\beta} \cong 0$).

4.   SMALL GROUP VS. INDIVIDUAL BEHAVIOR IN THE INVESTMENT GAME

Data from the individual decision task of Treatment A together with data from the group decision task make possible both within-subjects and across-subjects comparisons of amounts sent and returned in the investment game by small groups and individuals.

4.1.   Within-Subjects Comparisons

The first three rows of Table 3 report the within-subjects comparisons of the 30 individual subjects' responses in the individual decision task of Treatment A with the 10 group responses by these same subjects in the group decision task of that treatment. One way to make the comparison between three-person groups and individuals is to compare group data with individual data multiplied by three. A two sample t-test for difference in means detects no significant difference ($p = .617$) between the mean number of tokens sent by the 10 committees in Treatment A and the mean of three times the number

Table 3. Group Effects on Money Sent and Returned

Decision	Comm. Mean	Ind. Mean	Means Test	Smirnov Test	$\hat{\alpha}$	$\hat{\beta}$	$\hat{\gamma}$	$\hat{\theta}$	LR Test
			WITHIN-SUBJECTS COMPARISONS						
Sent	16.5	6.00	−.504	.133	−8.81	1.31	.437	...	7.29
	[9.28]	[2.59]	(.617)	(.999)	(.580)	(.009)	(.508)		(<.10)
	{10}	{30}							
Returned	18.2	7.17	−.596	.233					
	[17.3]	[4.82]	(.555)	(.809)	.....	.....	.....	.....	.....
	{10}	{30}							
Returned	1.70	1.17	−.437	.267					
– Sent	[11.8]	[3.71]	(.664)	(.660)	.....	.....	.....	.....	.....
	{10}	{30}							
			ACROSS- AND WITHIN-SUBJECTS COMPARISONS						
Sent	18.2	6.00	.082	.133					
	[9.57]	[2.59]	(.935)	(.943)	.....	.....	.....	.....	.....
	{33}	{30}							
Returned	15.4	7.17	−1.48	.315					
	[17.7]	[4.82]	(.143)	(.088)	.....	.....	.....	.....	.....
	{33}	{30}							
Returned	−2.76	1.17	−1.98	.324	.415	−.651	1.12	.098	80.4
– Sent	[13.7]	[3.71]	(.053)	(.073)	(.736)	(.001)	(.000)	(.000)	(<.005)
	{33}	{30}							

p-values in parentheses.
Standard deviations in brackets.
Number of individual subjects or committees in braces.

of tokens sent by the 30 individuals in Treatment A. The means test for amounts returned is also insignificant ($p = .555$). The means test detects no significant difference ($p = .664$) between the mean excess of amounts returned over amounts sent by the 10 committees in Treatment A and three times the mean excess of amounts returned over amounts sent by the 30 individual subjects in Treatment A. None of the three Smirnov tests reveal significant differences between the tripled individual amounts and committee data in Treatment A.

The first row of Table 3 reports the results from tobit estimation of the parameters of the equation,

$$S_t = \alpha + \beta 3S_t^L + \gamma 3S_t^H + \varepsilon_t \tag{9}$$

where S_t^L is the lowest of the three group members' amounts sent in the individual task and S_t^H is the highest. This estimation uses committee and individual data from Treatment A. The estimation uses the bounds for groups imposed in the experiment design:

$$S_t \in [0,30]. \tag{10}$$

The question posed here is whether committees appear to send a weighted average of three times their low and high individual members' amounts sent. As reported in the first row of Table 3, the only significant coefficient is $\hat{\beta}$, the coefficient for three times the low amount sent ($p = .009$). Thus it appears that committees do not send a weighted average of triple their low and high members' amounts but, instead, mark-up three times the low amount.

4.2. Across- and Within-Subjects Comparisons

The bottom three rows of Table 3 use data from the 30 individual decision responses in Treatment A and the 33 group responses in all treatments to make mixed within- and across-subjects comparisons of individual and group decisions. The means test detects no significant difference ($p = .935$) between the mean number of tokens sent by the 33 groups and the mean of three times the number of tokens sent by the 30 individuals. The Smirnov test does not detect a significant difference between the distributions of amounts sent by the committees and individuals. The means test on amounts returned does not detect a significant difference ($p = .143$) but the Smirnov test is significant at 10% confidence ($p = .088$). The means test detects a significant difference ($p = .053$) between the mean excess of amounts returned over amounts sent by the 33 committees in all treatments and three times the mean excess of amounts returned over amounts sent by the 30 individual subjects in Treatment A. The Smirnov test on the distribution of differences between amounts returned and amounts sent is significant at 10% ($p = .073$) for comparison of the data of the 33 committees in all treatments and the 30 individuals in Treatment A.

The last row of Table 3 reports the results from tobit estimation of the parameters of the equation

$$R_t = \alpha + \beta D_t S_t + \gamma S_t + \varepsilon_t \tag{11}$$

where R_t is the amount returned by a committee or individual, S_t is the amount sent to that committee or individual, and

$$D_t = 1 \text{ for committee data} \tag{12}$$
$$= 0 \text{ for individual subject data from Treatment A.}$$

This estimation uses all of the committee data and the individual subject data from Treatment A. It also uses the bounds and heteroskedasticticity model given by equations (7) and (8). Note that $\hat{\beta}$, the estimate of the group effect on the generosity of second-mover return decisions, is significantly negative ($p = .001$). Thus small group second movers are less generous than individual second movers in returning money to the first movers. The experimental design does not permit us to ascertain whether the small groups are less generous because they are less altruistic or less positively reciprocal than the individuals.

5. CONCLUDING REMARKS

Results from the experiment with the triadic game structure make it possible to discriminate among male and female subjects' decisions motivated by other-regarding preferences and trust or reciprocity. Results are reported separately for male and female subjects in order to extend the study of gender differences to include possible differences in trusting and reciprocating behavior in one-shot games. Comparison of responses in the investment game and the first-mover dictator control treatment indicates that neither males nor females exhibited significant trust. Both females and males exhibited significant altruistic other-regarding preferences. The total amount of money sent by male first movers appears larger than the total amount sent by female first movers but is not significantly larger at 10% confidence. Turning our attention to second movers, we observe that males exhibited significant positive reciprocity but females did not.

The experimental design also makes it possible to compare the amounts sent and returned in the investment game by committees and individuals. Within-subjects comparison of the data for the 10 committees and 30 individuals in Treatment A yields the conclusion that there are no significant differences between committees and individuals in amounts sent or returned or in the differences between amounts returned and sent. There is a specific group composition effect on the determination of amounts sent by first-mover groups to second-mover groups: in determining the amount to send, groups appear to mark up three times the lowest amount sent by any of their three members rather than sending a weighted average of three times the low and high amounts sent by group members.

Across- and within-subjects comparisons of the 33 committees in all treatments with the 30 individuals in Treatment A yields the following conclusions. There is no significant difference between amounts sent by three-member groups and tripled amounts sent by individuals. The amounts returned by groups are significantly less than the tripled amounts returned by individuals by the Smirnov test but not by the means test. The difference between amounts returned and sent is significantly smaller for groups than for individuals by both the *t*-test and the Smirnov test. The conclusion that groups are significantly less generous than individuals in choosing how much to return to first movers is also supported by tobit estimation of the relation between amounts returned and amounts sent.

ACKNOWLEDGEMENT

Financial support was provided by the Decision Risk and Management Science Program, National Science Foundation (grant number SES-9818561). I am grateful for helpful comments and suggestions to the students in my Ph.D. seminar on experimental economics, most especially Cary A. Deck and Mary L. Rigdon, and to my colleagues, Ronald L. Oaxaca and John Wooders. Valuable research assistance was provided by Mary L. Rigdon, Marisa D. Bernal, Matthew E. Cox, Cary A. Deck, and Supriya Sarnikar.

NOTES

1. One prominent research program of this type includes the following papers: Berg, Dickhaut, and McCabe (1995); Hoffman, McCabe, Shachat, and Smith (1994); Hoffman, McCabe, and Smith (1996, 1998); McCabe, Rassenti, and Smith (1996, 1998); and Smith (1998).
2. A distinguished research program of this type includes the following papers: Fehr and Falk (1999), Fehr and Gächter (2000a,b), Fehr, Gächter, and Kirchsteiger (1996, 1997), and Fehr, Kirchsteiger, and Riedl (1993).
3. In the instructions given to the subjects (which are available on request), the names "Group X" and "Group Y" were used rather than Type X and Type Y.
4. This way of measuring trust is formally derived in Cox (2000).
5. This way of measuring reciprocity is formally derived in Cox (2000).
6. An experimenter recognized the subject as a repeat subject shortly after the experiment began. The double blind experimental protocol was discreetly compromised in order to learn this subject's identification letter (but not her name). This was done by silently counting the number of questionnaires that were sequentially deposited by the subjects in a stack in a collection box. It was determined that this subject's questionnaire was in position n in the stack. The subjects were not aware this was being done and all of their decisions had already been completed at the time the counting was done. This was the last session in the experiment.

REFERENCES

Arrow, K. (1974). *The Limits of Organization*. NY: Norton.
Berg, J., J. Dickhaut, and Kevin McCabe (1995). "Trust, Reciprocity, and Social History." *Games and Economic Behavior* 10, 122–42.

Bolton, G. E., and E. Katoc (1995). "An Experimental Test for Gender Differences in Beneficient Behavior." *Economics Letters* 48, 287–92.

Bone, J., J. Hey, and J. Suckling (1997). "Are Groups More Consistent than Individuals?" Discussion Paper, University of York.

Bornstein G., and I. Yaniv (1998). "Individual and Group Behavior in the Ultimatum Game: Are Groups More 'Rational' Players?" *Experimental Economics* 1, 109–18.

Brown-Kruse, J. L., and D. Hummels (1993). "Gender Effects in Laboratory Public Goods Contribution." *Journal of Economic Behavior and Organization* 22, 255–67.

Cadsby, C. B., and E. Maynes (1998). "Gender and Free-Riding in a Threshold Public Goods Game: Experimental Evidence." *Journal of Economic Behavior and Organization* 34, 603–40.

Coleman, J. (1990). *Foundations of Social Theory*. Cambridge, MA: Harvard University Press.

Cosmides, L., and J. Tooby (1992). "Cognitive Adaptations for Social Exchange." In *The Adapted Mind*, edited by J. Barkow, L. Cosmides, and J. Tooby. NY: Oxford University Press.

Cox, J. C. (2000). "Trust and Reciprocity: Implications of Game Triads and Social Contexts." Discussion Paper, University of Arizona.

Croson, R., and N. Buchan (1999). "Gender and Culture: International Experimental Evidence from Trust Games." *American Economic Review, Papers and Proceedings* 89, 386–91.

Davis, J. H. (1992). "Some Compelling Intuitions about Group Consensus Decisions: Theoretical and Empirical Research, and Interpersonal Aggregation Phenomena: Selected Examples, 1950–1990." *Organizational Behavior and Human Decision Processes* 52, 3–38.

Eckel, C. C., and P. J. Grossman (1997). "Chivalry and Solidarity in Ultimatum Games." Discussion Paper, Virginia Polytechnic and State University.

Eckel, C. C., and P. J. Grossman (1998). "Are Women Less Selfish than Men? Evidence from Dictator Experiments." *Economic Journal* 108, 726–35.

Fehr, E., and A. Falk (1999). "Wage Rigidity in a Competitive Incomplete Contract Market." *Journal of Political Economy* 107, 106–34.

Fehr, E., and S. Gächter (2000a). "Fairness and Retaliation: The Economics of Reciprocity." *Journal of Economic Perspectives* 14, 159–81.

Fehr, E., and S. Gächter (2000b). "Do Incentive Contracts Crowd out Voluntary Cooperation?" University of Zurich.

Fehr, E., S. Gächter, and G. Kirchsteiger (1996). "Reciprocal Fairness and Noncompensating Wage Differentials." *Journal of Institutional and Theoretical Economics* 152, 608–40.

Fehr, E., S. Gächter, and G. Kirchsteiger (1997). "Reciprocity as a Contract Enforcement Device: Experimental Evidence." *Econometrica* 65, 833–60.

Fehr, E., G. Kirchsteiger, and A. Riedl (1993). "Does Fairness Prevent Market Clearing? An Experimental Investigation." *Quarterly Journal of Economics* 108, 437–60.

Frank, R. H., T. Gilovich, and T. Regan (1993). "Does Studying Economics Inhibit Cooperation?" *Journal of Economic Perspectives* 7, 159–71.

Fukuyama, F. (1995). *Trust*. NY: Free Press.

Gambetta, D., ed. (1988) *Trust: Making and Breaking Cooperative Relations*. Cambridge: Blackwell.

Hoffman, E., K. A. McCabe, K. Shachat, and V. L. Smith (1994). "Preferences, Property Rights, and Anonymity in Bargaining Games." *Games and Economic Behavior* 7, 346–80.

Hoffman, E., K. A. McCabe, and V. L. Smith (1998). "Behavioral Foundations of Reciprocity: Experimental Economics and Evolutionary Psychology." *Economic Inquiry* 36, 335–52.

Knack, S., and P. Keefer (1996). "Does Social Capital Have an Economic Payoff? A Cross-Country Investigation." Discussion Paper, College Park, University of Maryland, ML.

Kuon, B., B. Mathauschek, and A. Sadrieh (1998). "Teams Take the Better Risks." Discussion Paper, University of Bonn.

La Porta, R., F. Lopez-de-Salanes, A. Shleifer, and R. W. Vishny (1997). "Trust in Large Organizations." *American Economic Review, Papers and Proceedings* 87, 333–8.

McCabe, K. A., S. J. Rassenti, and V. L. Smith (1996). "Game Theory and Reciprocity in Some Extensive Form Bargaining Games." *Proceedings of the National Academy of Sciences* 93, 13421–8.

McCabe, K. A., S. J. Rassenti, and V. L. Smith (1998). "Reciprocity, Trust, and Payoff Privacy in Extensive Form Bargaining Games." *Games and Economic Behavior* 24, 10–24.

Norwell, C., and S. Tinckler (1994). "The Influence of Gender on the Provision of a Public Good." *Journal of Economic Behavior and Organization* 25, 25–36.

Ortmann, A., and L. K. Tichy (1999). "Gender Differences in the Laboratory." *Journal of Economic Behavior and Organization* 39, 327–39.

Putnam, R. (1993). *Making Democracy Work: Civic Traditions in Modern Italy.* Princeton: Princeton University Press.

Rapoport, A., and A. M. Chammah (1965). "The Differences in Factors Contributing to the Level of Cooperation in the Prisoner's Dilemma Game." *Journal of Personality and Social Psychology* 2, 831–8.

Smith, V. L. (1998). "Distinguished Guest Lecture: The Two Faces of Adam Smith." *Southern Economic Journal* 65, 1–19.

Solnick, S. J. (1997). "Gender Differences in the Ultimatum Game." Discussion Paper, University of Miami.

APPENDIX: ALTERNATIVE TREATMENT B SUBJECT SAMPLES

Table 1A. Money Sent Due to Trust and Other-Regarding Preferences (using all of the data)

Subjects	Treatment A Mean	Treatment B Mean	Means Test	Smirnov Test	$\hat{\alpha}$	$\hat{\beta}$	$\hat{\gamma}$	LR Test
Males	6.44 [2.66] {18}	6.58 [2.98] {24}	−.139 (.563)	.111 (>.10)[I]	...	...	...	...
Females	5.33 [2.42] {12}	5.56 [2.55] {18}	−.222 (.594)	.250 (>.10)[I]	...	...	...	...
Males vs. Females	...	...	...	...	7.04 (.000)	−.271 (.364)[I]	−1.37 (.077)	3.17 (>.25)

p-values in parentheses.
[I] denotes a one-tailed test.
Standard deviations in brackets.
Number of subjects in braces.

Table 1B. Money Sent Due to Trust and Other-Regarding Preferences (deleting data from the first Treatment B session and the one repeat subject)

Subjects	Treatment A Mean	Treatment B Mean	Means Test	Smirnov Test	$\hat{\alpha}$	$\hat{\beta}$	$\hat{\gamma}$	LR Test
Males	6.44 [2.66] {18}	7.38 [2.47] {13}	−.940 (.840)[I]	.056 (>.10)[I]	...	...	...	...
Females	5.33 [2.42] {12}	5.08 [2.53] {13}	.256 (.399)[I]	.333 (>.10)[I]	...	...	...	...
Males vs. Females	...	...	...	...	7.53 (.000)	−.603 (.224)[I]	−1.83 (.020)	5.44 (>.10)

p-values in parentheses.
[I] denotes a one-tailed test.
Standard deviations in brackets.
Number of subjects in braces.

Chapter 15

WORK MOTIVATION, INSTITUTIONS, AND PERFORMANCE

D82
J41

Simon Gächter
University of St. Gallen, FEW-HSG

Armin Falk
University of Zürich

1.   INCOMPLETE CONTRACTS AND THE PROBLEM OF WORK MOTIVATION

> "... *motivation problems arise only because some plans cannot be described in a complete, enforceable contract.*"
> Milgrom and Roberts (1992, p. 127)

> "*A thorough understanding of internal incentive structures is critical [. . .], since these incentives determine to a large extent how individuals inside an organization behave.*"
> Baker, Jensen and Murphy (1988, p. 593)

Many economically important contracts are incomplete. This holds in particular for the employment relationship. Very often the labor contract just stipulates a wage payment and leaves out many details that actually determine performance (see, e.g., Baker, Jensen, and Murphy (1988)). Under conditions of incompletely specified obligations and only weak or absent explicit performance incentives the issue of motivation arises.

Let us start with a simple model, which describes the motivational problem that arises with incomplete contracts. In the main part of the present paper we will study experimental versions of this model. Suppose that a principal stipulates a contract that specifies a wage w and a *desired* effort level $\hat{e}$. Assume further that the principal's profit increases with the effort level. The principal can assure *at most* an effort level of e_0 from selfish and rational agents, i.e., only e_0 is "enforceable" via third parties like courts. The employment contract in this situation is incomplete since the principal cannot condition the wage payment on effort. The desired performance level $\hat{e}$ is just "cheap talk". Since effort is costly for the agent due to some disutility $c(e) > 0$ (with $c'(e) > 0$), it follows that, in case of $\hat{e} > e_0$, an agent who reduces effort below $\hat{e}$ will increase her net utility. Therefore, a rational profit-maximizing principal facing a selfish and rational agent cannot enforce $e > e_0$. How can principals in such a situation motivate their employees to work harder? Of course, this is an important question for the economics of organizations and for firms' employment policies.

This paper tries to shed light on ways to influence performance decisions under incomplete contracts. Actual human behavior within organizations is most likely influenced by conventions and social norms, intrinsic motivation, the striving for social approval, but also by the material incentives that are provided by payment schemes and the duration of the relationship. Many scholars have pointed out aspects of these arguments (see, e.g., Leibenstein (1979), Baker, Jensen, and Murphy (1988), Simon (1991), Lazear (1991), Frey (1997), Schlicht (1998), Malcomson and MacLeod (1998), Bewley (1999)).

In the main part of our paper we compare *four potential remedies* of contractual incompleteness: *reciprocity-based voluntary cooperation* (Section 2), *repeated interaction* (Section 3), *social embeddedness* (Section 4), and *incentive contracts* (Section 5). To achieve the comparison, we enrich the basic situation described above by varying the institutional environment. In our synopsis we draw on data collected by Fehr, Gächter, and Kirchsteiger (1997), Falk, Gächter and Kovács (1999) and Fehr and Gächter (2000), who analyzed different aspects of the contract enforcement problem *in isolation*. Our *comparison* of the institutional variations allows us to assess the behavioral impact of various incentive structures.

The main results of our comparative analysis are as follows: First, reciprocity-based voluntary cooperation clearly is a crucial motivation in all the experiments we investigate here. Second, the *effectiveness* of voluntary cooperation to improve performance depends on institutional and contractual arrangements: Enhanced possibilities for reciprocity, as they are, for instance, provided by a repeated interaction, considerably improve performance. Social exchange does not contribute to higher effort levels than those achieved with anonymous repeated interactions. Financial incentives in the form of a contractually determined wage cut in case of detected shirking, "crowd out reciprocity" and induce opportunism. In our concluding section we discuss some interesting links between our investigation of interaction effects of material incentives on people's propensity for voluntary cooperation, and the literature on "crowding out of intrinsic motivation", which has received considerable attention among practitioners as well as among academics interested in the effectiveness of incentive systems.

2. REMEDY I: VOLUNTARY COOPERATION

> *"A norm of reciprocity is, I suspect, no less universal and*
> *important an element of culture than the incest taboo (. . .)."*
> Alvin Gouldner (1960, p. 171)

Organizational theorists as well as personnel managers often stress the importance of an agent's general job attitude. For example, Williamson (1985) argues that under incomplete employment contracts "consummate cooperation" becomes important. He defines "consummate cooperation" as opposed to merely "perfunctory cooperation" as "an affirmative job attitude whereby gaps are filled, initiative is taken, and judgment is exercised in an instrumental way" (Williamson (1985), p. 262). Hence, in a work context that is incompletely specified, to behave "cooperatively", by showing "initiative" and "good judgment", may well be the particular expression of a reciprocal motivation that applies in the situation at hand.

How can the existence of reciprocity help the principal to elicit effort levels above e_0? Roughly speaking, reciprocity means that people reward kind acts and punish unkind ones. Let us assume that the kindness of a certain contract offer $(w, \hat{e})$ is determined by the *rent* the agent receives from the principal. This rent arises from the offer $(w, \hat{e})$ minus the opportunity costs of accepting $(w, \hat{e})$. If an agent is motivated by reciprocity considerations she will choose higher levels of e the higher the offered rent is. Thus, by offering sufficiently high rents principals may be capable of eliciting effort levels above e_0.[1]

2.1. The Experimental Design

In the following section we present an experiment that was designed to test the potential role of reciprocity as a contract enforcement device.[2] We describe this design in some detail because all other experiments reported in this paper are modifications of this design.

At the beginning of the experiment subjects were randomly allocated to their roles as "principals" and "agents". They played a version of the so-called "gift-exchange game" introduced by Fehr, Kirchsteiger and Riedl (1993). The **first stage** is a posted-bid-market. Subjects in the role of a principal post an employment contract that consists of a *wage* and a *desired effort level* $\hat{e}$. Wages

Table 1. Effort Levels and Costs of Effort

e	0.1	0.2	0.3	0.4	0.5	0.6	0.7	0.8	0.9	1
c(e)	0	1	2	4	6	8	10	12	15	18

have to be integers between 0 and 100 and the available effort levels are between 0.1 and 1 with increments of 0.1 (see Table 1).

In a given period, each principal can offer only one employment contract. After principals submit their contract offers, subjects in the role of agents, who accepted a contract, have to make an *actual* effort decision at the **second stage** of the game. An agent's choice of an effort level is associated with costs for the agent as indicated in Table 1. Principals also know Table 1.[3] After principals are informed about the effort decision of "their" agent, the second stage is completed and payoffs can be calculated. An agent's payoff at the end of the second stage is given by

$$u = w - c(e) \quad \text{upon acceptance}$$

$$u = 0 \qquad\qquad \text{otherwise}$$

where w denotes the accepted wage and $c(e)$ the costs of the agent's actual effort. In case an agent does not trade, she earns nothing. A principal's payoff is given by

$$\pi = ve - w \quad \text{upon acceptance}$$

$$\pi = 0 \qquad\quad \text{otherwise}$$

where v denotes a principal's redemption value, i.e., the maximal gross profitability of an agent for the principal (provided $e = 1$). The redemption value v was set at 100.

Our experimental design incorporates the motivational problem outlined in Section 1. Under the assumption of rationality and selfishness, no agent has an incentive to choose an effort level above 0.1 *regardless* of the wage payment. Principals, therefore, also have no reason to pay more than $w^* = 1$, which is just enough to induce a selfish agent to accept the contract.

Above we have argued that reciprocal voluntary cooperation may be an important contract enforcement device under conditions of incomplete contracts. Notice that in the two-stage-design described above it is basically the agents who have the opportunity to respond reciprocally to a principal's offer. However, most actual labor relations are long-term relationships and principals have opportunities to react to an agent's effort decision. For example, principals usually have many possibilities to influence an agent's utility of a given job, e.g., via promotion policies, access to fringe benefits, bonuses, and social sanctioning. To allow for the possibility that principals can respond to the agents' choices, Fehr, Gächter, and Kirchsteiger (1997) introduced a **third stage** into their design, in which principals have the opportunity to either punish or reward their agent at some cost. After having learned an agent's effort decision, a principal can choose a punishment/reward variable $p \in \{-1, -0.9, \dots, 1\}$. To punish ($p < 0$) or to reward ($p > 0$) is costly for a principal. The costs of punishment amount to $10|p|$. Notice that only in case of $p = 0$, i.e., if the principal neither rewards nor punishes, no costs arise. A punishment reduces the agent's gain at the end of the second stage by $25p$ whereas a reward gives the agent an additional payment of $25p$. To get some insight into agents' expectation formation when determining their actual effort at the second stage, agents in the three-stage treatment have to indicate the punishment/reward level p^e they *expect* from their principal, given their effort decision. Principals are not informed about the expected punishment/reward level. Notice that, since to punish or to reward is costly, the addition of a third stage does not alter the predictions derived under the assumption of rationality and selfishness.

In both the two- and three-stage treatment, agents and principals conclude contracts on a market. Principals post the contracts and agents choose among the available ones in a randomly determined order. Moreover, to induce competition among agents, there are more agents than principals (6 principals and 8 agents). After a two- or three-stage sequence is concluded, a new "trading day" starts where new principal-agent pairs are matched (in total there were twelve trading days). A total of 56 subjects participated in these experiments.

2.2. Procedures (of All Experiments Reported in This Paper)

After subjects' roles (which they kept throughout the whole experiment) were randomly determined, principals and agents were located in two different, yet adjacent, large rooms in which they sat remote from each other. They were given their written instructions, which included a set of control questions. The experiments did not start until all subjects answered all questions correctly. We can, therefore, safely assume that subjects fully understood the calculation of payoffs. Procedures and payoff functions were common knowledge, i.e., they were explained in the instructions and it was emphasized that they were the same for all principals and agents, respectively. Moreover, to ensure common knowledge, an experimenter orally summarized procedures and payoff functions.

All experiments reported in this paper were conducted manually. In two experiments (remedies I and IV), the "matching" of principals and agents was done in a market; in remedies II and III, the matching occurred in a bilateral

Table 2. Contractual Behavior – Summary Statistics

	wage	effort demanded $\hat{e}$	actual effort e
2-stage treatment	30.1	0.65	0.37
	(17.7)	(0.27)	(0.26)
3-stage treatment	27.3	0.72	0.63
	(7.2)	(0.13)	(0.28)

Note: Entries are averages over all twelve periods. Numbers in parentheses are standard deviations. Source: Fehr et al. (1997) and own calculations.

trading institution. In the market experiments principals orally submitted wage offers, which were transferred to the agents' room and there written on a chalkboard. Agents saw all wages and could then decide whether they wanted to accept them. In the bilateral trading institutions, principals made their wage offers by inserting them privately into their decision sheets. Then an experimenter collected the wage offers and transmitted them to the agents' room. Here, only the agent matched with a particular principal was informed about "her" principal's wage offer (a second experimenter in the agents' room wrote the wage offer into the agents' documentation sheets). After wages were settled, the agents made their effort choices in privacy. In all experiments, only the particular principal an agent was matched with was informed about it. Finally, principals and agents had to calculate profits. This ended a period. In all experiments (except those reported in the context of remedy III), identities of trading partners were never revealed and subjects were informed that they would never learn a trading partner's identity.

The experiments were conducted with students from different fields (except economics). They lasted between 1.5 and 2.5 hours. All subjects were paid according to their decisions and earned on average more than the opportunity cost of a typical students' job.

2.3. Hypotheses and Results

A first impression of the results is given by the summary statistics in Table 2, which reveals that the predictions of wages close to zero and effort levels of 0.1 are clearly refuted. Average wages and demanded effort levels are similar in both treatments. Moreover, principals' contractual offers are more homogeneous in the three-stage treatment (compare the standard deviations).

Table 2 also shows that the contract enforcement problem is lowest in the three-stage-treatment. Thus, behaviorally, principals' punishment and reward possibilities at the third stage were obviously credible. But even in the absence of punishment and rewards, on average, agents provided above-minimum effort levels.

In order to make the concept of agents' reciprocity measurable, it is necessary to define the kindness of an action. In our context, the rent $r = w - c(\hat{e})$ that is offered to the agents can be taken as an indicator of "generosity" (because it measures the excess payment over the necessary compensation of the disutility of the demanded effort). By the same token, the actual effort level indicates the kindness of an agent. Reciprocity, therefore, means that agents choose higher effort levels if principals offer them higher rents. Of course, actual effort behavior may also be correlated with expected punishments or rewards, respectively. We summarize these arguments in the following

RECIPROCITY HYPOTHESES:
1. *The **offered rent** is positively related to the demanded effort level.*
2. *Agents' **actual effort** choice will increase in the offered rent. In the three-stage treatment, agents' actual effort will also depend positively on the expected punishment/reward p^e.*
3. *Principals (i) **punish** less, the less agents deviate negatively from $\hat{e}$, and (ii) they **reward** more, the more agents deviate positively from $\hat{e}$.[4]*

Table 3 documents the formal regression models that we have used to test our behavioral hypotheses. The table reports three basic models. They relate directly to our behavioral hypotheses (1) to (3). Except for punishment and reward, the same models have been separately estimated for the two- and the three-stage treatments.

The results on Hypothesis (1) show that principals behaved differently in the two treatments. In the two-stage treatment principals appealed to agents' reciprocity since their offered rent increased in the demanded effort level. This was not the case in the three-stage treatment. In the latter, principals paid rents but their rent offers did not increase in the desired effort level. To the contrary, rents even declined in the effort level. However, the χ^2-statistic for the 3-stage model reveals that this model has no explanatory power. Hence, we conclude that principals' rent offers were more or less constant. Principals' strategic position is improved in the three-stage treatment since here principals have the "last word to say".

In the two-stage treatment, point 2 of our Reciprocity Hypothesis is confirmed by our data. Agents reciprocated higher offered rents with higher actual effort levels since the coefficient on the offered rent is positive and highly significant. In the three-stage treatment, agents' actual effort choice did not significantly depend on the offered rent (although the coefficient is positive), but

Table 3. Evidence on the Reciprocity Hypotheses

Dependent variables	offered rent		actual effort		punish/ reward
	r		e		p
Hypotheses	(1)		(2)		(3)
Explanatory variables:	2-stage	3-stage	2-stage	3-stage	3-stage
Constant	−0.671	21.496***	−0.066*	0.423***	0.277***
	(1.54)	(3.122)	(0.037)	(0.056)	(0.031)
e	37.948***	−6.521	–	–	–
	(2.228)	(4.416)			
r	–	–	0.021***	0.004	–
			(0.001)	(0.003)	
p^e	–	–	–	0.578***	–
				(0.057)	
$e - \hat{e}$	–	–	–	–	1.554***
					(0.151)
N	141	141	141	141	141
Log-L	−481.9	−473.8	−37.2	−31.7	$R^2 = 0.54$
χ^2	275.0***	2.18	138.0***	110.0***	$F = 105.2***$

Note: Since our dependent variables are censored below and above, the estimation procedure is censored regression. Since data are not independent within a session, we calculate robust standard errors with session as the independent unit. Model (3) is estimated with 2SLS (with *rent* and p^e as instruments), since $(e - \hat{e})$ is endogenously determined. The robust standard errors are in parentheses. * denotes significance at the 10-percent level, ** at the 5-percent level and *** at the 1-percent level. $\hat{e}$ denotes demanded effort, $c(\hat{e})$ are the implied effort costs (see Table 1), r denotes the offered rent (i.e., $w - c(\hat{e})$), and p^e is the agents' expected punishment/reward level. N denotes the number of observations. Data source: Fehr et al. (1997).

agents reacted highly positively to the expected punishment or reward. The lower the expected punishment or the higher the expected reward, the higher was the actual effort level.

Point 3 of our Reciprocity Hypothesis concerns principals' punishment and reward behavior at the third stage. An inspection of the right-hand column of Table 3 reveals that the effort deviation $e - \hat{e}$ was of overwhelming importance. The higher this deviation was, i.e., the less severe the contract enforcement problem, the higher was the reward or the lower was the punishment. This result shows that principals behaved reciprocally just as the agents. This fact had interesting and unexpected implications at the previous two stages. At the second stage, agents did not respond reciprocally but chose their effort level, quite rationally, given their correct expectations about principals' reciprocal propensity to reward or to punish. Consistent with this behavior, at the first stage, principals did not increase their offered rents in the desired effort level. Quite the contrary, the higher their demanded effort level was, the less generous was their job offer.

It is important to note that the observed reciprocity is not just the result of aggregating over all decisions. A detailed analysis at the individual level shows that, for instance in the two-stage treatment, roughly 60 percent of the agents exhibit a significantly positive rent-effort pattern (according to Spearman rank correlations). In the remainder of this paper, we take the observed amount of reciprocity-driven voluntary cooperation as a benchmark and focus on the question of *how* agents' voluntary cooperation is affected by extrinsic incentives.

3. REMEDY II: LONG-TERM CONTRACTS

> *". . . the two key requisites for co-operation to thrive are that the co-operation be based on reciprocity, and that the shadow of the future is important enough to make this reciprocity stable."*
> Robert Axelrod (1984, p. 173)

Labor relations can rarely be viewed as spot market transactions where anonymous trading partners interact only once. Rather, employers and employees often play a repeated game that opens up the possibility for implicit contracts and repeated game incentives (see, e.g. MacLeod and Malcomson (1998)). As Remedy I has shown, reciprocity-driven voluntary cooperation can mitigate the contract enforcement problem. Since a repeated interaction provides – in principle – material incentives for cooperation, the question arises whether these repeated game incentives are, indeed, compatible with reciprocal motivations. In the following, we describe an experiment that extends the design discussed above to allow for repeated interactions.

3.1. Experimental Design

The main treatment change compared to the 2-stage design described above is the following: Instead of interacting in a one-shot market, *randomly matched principals and agents remain paired for ten periods*. To control for the mere impact of repeated interaction, we compare the outcome of this treatment with a treatment where subjects were re-matched with ten *different* opponents. Thus, there were two treatments, a so-called "Stranger"-treatment, where subjects interacted only once, and a "Partner"-treatment, where subjects played a finitely repeated gift-exchange game.[5] The matching protocol was explained in the instructions and verbally emphasized in front of all subjects. A post-experimental debriefing confirmed the credibility of both matching protocols. In total, 90 subjects participated in this study.

3.2. Hypotheses and Results

In this finitely repeated gift exchange game agents who are not motivated by reciprocity may have an incentive to imitate reciprocity in order to build a reputation for being a reciprocator. However, the repeated interaction may also foster intrinsic reciprocity because a repeated interaction may create a chain of reciprocal obligations. Hence, in the Partner-treatment, we should observe at least as much reciprocity as in the Stranger-treatment, because reciprocal behavior for reputational reasons may add to (foster) intrinsic reciprocity (for a further discussion see Falk et al. (1999)).

THE REPEATED INTERACTION HYPOTHESIS:
1. *Wages and effort levels are positively correlated. In the **Stranger-treatment**, this measures the true amount of intrinsic reciprocity that may be present in all treatments. In the **Partner-treatment**, intrinsic reciprocal behavior may be confounded with extrinsic incentives. In particular, we hypothesize that the aggregate wage-effort relationship in the Partner-treatment is at least as steep as in the Stranger-treatment.*
2. *As a result, efforts in the Partner-treatment are – for a given wage – at least as high as in the Stranger-treatment.*

In the regression model presented in Table 4 the wage coefficient in the Stranger-treatment measures the slope of the wage-effort relationship. Agents in the Stranger-treatment clearly exhibit reciprocal behavior since the wage coefficient is positive and highly significant. This replicates the results of the two-stage treatment reported above. As further analyses have shown, there have been no significant spillovers between periods in the Stranger-treatment. Therefore, we take this coefficient to be the benchmark of genuine reciprocity, which is achieved in the absence of any extrinsic incentives.

The Repeated Interaction Hypothesis predicts a wage-effort relationship in the **Partner-treatment** that is at least as steep as in the benchmark of the Stranger-treatment. Column (2) shows that the wage-effort relation is steeper in the Partner- than in the Stranger-treatment. A χ^2-test confirms that the coefficient in the Partner-treatment is, indeed, significantly higher than in the Stranger-treatment.

The results show that the repeated interaction has fostered reciprocal behavior. Consequently, average effort levels should – for a given wage – be higher in the Partner-treatment than in the Stranger-treatment. Table 5 shows that this is, indeed, the case. Whereas wages are almost identical across

Table 4. Voluntary Cooperation in Repeated Interactions with Social Incentives (for Remedy III – See Next Section)

	Dependent variable: *effort*			
	Remedy II (Repeated Interaction)		Remedy III (Social embeddedness)	
Treatment: Independent variables:	(1) "Stranger"	(2) "Partner"	(3) "Approval face to face"	(4) "Approval social pressure"
constant		−0.421*** (0.1400)		
Wage × *Treatment*	0.016** (0.0021)	0.0202*** (0.0024) N = 613 log-L = −306.9 χ^2 = 71.2***	0.019*** (0.0027)	0.017*** (0.0027)

Note: Since our dependent variables are censored below and above, the estimation procedure is censored regression. Since data are not independent within a session (or bargaining pair, resp.), we calculate robust standard errors with session (in (1)) and bargaining pairs (in (2)–(4)) as the independent units. Forty subjects participated in the Stranger-treatment; in the Partner-treatment we had 25 independent pairs, and in the Approval treatments a total of 18 independent pairs participated in the experiments. We pool the data of all treatments and construct the independent variable as an interaction variable of wage and the respective treatment dummy. The treatments that relate to (3) and (4) are discussed in the next section. Data source: Falk et al. (1999), and own calculations.

Table 5. Contract Performance With and Without Repeated Interaction and With Social Incentives (for Remedy III – See Next Section)

	Remedy II (Repeated Interaction)				Remedy III (Social embeddedness)			
	"Stranger"		"Partner"		"Approval face to face"		"Approval social pressure"	
	Wage	effort	wage	effort	wage	effort	wage	effort
Mean	60.6	0.53	66.0	0.76	63.9	0.71	62.4	0.75
(std.dev.)	(11.6)	(0.31)	(11.7)	(0.23)	(18.4)	(0.25)	(11.4)	(0.26)

treatments, effort levels and thus efficiency are clearly higher in the Partner-treatment.

In summary, we conclude that a long-term interaction is quite an effective tool to induce better contractual performance. An analysis of *individual* behavior sheds light on the reasons for this observation. In both the Partner-

and the Stranger-treatment, there is a majority of subjects who is genuinely motivated by reciprocity. Sixty percent of the agents in the Stranger-treatment and even 72 percent of the agents in the Partner-treatment exhibit a significantly positive wage-effort relationship (according to Spearman rank correlations). Thus, the repeated interaction "crowds in" reciprocity. In a certain sense, both standard economic theory and reciprocity theory have a point in case. It is the *interaction* of both forces – the incentives provided by mere repeated interaction, and the social norm of reciprocity – that jointly mitigate the contract enforcement problem quite effectively.[6]

4.   REMEDY III: SOCIAL EMBEDDEDNESS

> *"When we seek economic goals in our interactions with others,*
> *these are usually combined with striving for sociability,*
> *approval, status, and power as well."*
> Mark Granovetter (1992, p. 234)

A natural feature of most real life employment relations is that they are characterized by *social interactions*. In most instances, work does not take place in a social vacuum, i.e., under completely anonymous conditions. Instead, employers and employees personally interact with each other. This social interaction may create yet another form of extrinsic incentives beyond those of the repeated interaction, namely, the expectation of emotionally prompted social approval or disapproval. The sociologist Peter Blau (1964) argues that social approval is a basic reward that people seek, a fact that is also highlighted by social psychologists. Moreover, a substantial amount of economic production takes place in personalized settings where communication and "identification" (Bohnet (1997)) allow social control to become effective.

4.1. Experimental Design

To test for the impact of social interaction, Falk et al. (1999) implemented two additional treatments. The two treatments varied in the degree of social embeddedness. As in the Partner-treatment, subjects interacted repeatedly. However, anonymity was lifted. In the "Face-to-Face" treatment the two subjects of a principal-agent pair were introduced to each other before they knew the rules of the game. Matched pairs were seated face-to-face. Subjects were not allowed to communicate verbally or with written comments. In the second treatment ("Social pressure"), subjects were again introduced and seated face-to-face. In addition, subjects were told that after the last round of the session they would have a chance for communication and discussion about what had happened during the experiment. Hence, subjects anticipated that after the final period they could exchange social approval and disapproval. Both treatments are thus parsimonious ways of lifting anonymity and inducing social approval and disapproval.[7]

4.2. Hypotheses and Results

A natural conjecture is that the approval incentives that are present in this experiment foster reciprocity. The reason is that people may not only feel obliged for intrinsic reasons to react reciprocally. These feelings may be reinforced by the presence of immediate expressions of approval or disapproval or by the expected exertion of social pressure (or approval) at the end of the experiment. Since in the approval treatment approval incentives are *added* to repeated game incentives, one may conjecture that the reciprocal relationship is strengthened compared to the anonymous Partner-treatment. For the Approval Hypothesis, therefore, the Partner-treatment serves as a baseline.

THE APPROVAL HYPOTHESIS:
Wages and effort levels are positively correlated. In all treatments intrinsic reciprocal behavior may be confounded with extrinsic incentives. In particular, we hypothesize
1. *The aggregate wage-effort relationship in the **Face-to-Face-treatment** is at least as steep as in the Partner-treatment.*
2. *In the **Social-Pressure treatment**, the wage-effort relation is at least as steep as in the Face-to-face-treatment.*
3. *As a result of 1 and 2, effort levels should – for a given wage – tend to increase compared to the Partner-treatment.*

In columns (3) and (4), of Table 4 we report the results of our regression analysis that tested Points 1 and 2 of the Approval Hypothesis. The data do not support them. In the **Face-to-Face treatment** we do not find any significant change of the slope of the wage-effort relationship relative to the Partner-treatment. The slope of the wage-effort relation in the **Social-Pressure treatment** is somewhat (but insignificantly) lower than in the Face-to-Face treatment.

Given the results of Table 4, it is no surprise that the role of the approval forces turns out to be limited. Although wages were rather similar in all three repeated game treatments, effort levels are not statistically higher than those achieved in the anonymous interaction of the Partner-treatment (compare Table 5). Hence, in these data approval incentives did not add to what had already been achieved by repeated interaction alone.

A comparison with the results reported in the previous section (compare Remedy II and III in Table 5) suggests that the mere fact that subjects interact repeatedly is capable of mitigating the contract enforcement problem. The approval incentives investigated in this section did not change very much this finding. This also holds at the individual level.

5.   REMEDY IV: INCENTIVE CONTRACTS

> *"Incentives are the essence of economics."*
> Canice Prendergast (1999, p.7)

So far we have neglected the possibility of *incentive devices*, which in reality are frequently used to mitigate the incentive problem. Principal-agent theory, information economics and contract theory, have all developed arguments about how the conflict of interest between agents and principals can be resolved (see Prendergast (1999) for a comprehensive survey).

For simplicity, we discuss the problem of incentive contracting in the framework introduced in Section 1. Suppose a principal has invested in some verification technology which allows with some probability $s > 0$ to prove in court that the desired effort level $\hat{e}$ has not been put forward. Of course, if this verification technology works perfectly (i.e., $s = 1$), the problem of incompleteness ceases to exist. Here, we do not analyze the optimal investment into a verification technology. For our purposes, it suffices to assume that the principal's (optimal) investment in its verification technology leads to $0 < s < 1$. Assume further that the principal offers the following contract: $(w, f, \hat{e})$, where f is a fine the agent has to pay if it can be verified that she has shirked, i.e., $e < \hat{e}$. Under the assumption of risk neutrality, an agent will not shirk (i.e., $e = \hat{e}$) if the "no-shirking condition" holds, i.e., if the expected fine exceeds the opportunity cost of not shirking:[8]

$$sf \geq c(\hat{e}).$$

Obviously, if f were unbounded *every* effort level $\hat{e}$ could be enforced as long as s is positive. Assume that f is bounded such that less than a maximum feasible effort choice can be enforced.[9] Then, there exists an optimal effort $\hat{e}^* \geq e_0$ that can be enforced by an optimal fine f^* such that the agent will just choose not to shirk.

5.1. Experimental Design

To test for the impact of incentive contracts on actual effort choices, Fehr and Gächter (2000) implemented a treatment that was similar to the stylized model introduced in the preceding paragraph.[10] This treatment is called "Incentive-treatment". In addition to a wage payment and a desired effort level, principals could also stipulate a *fine* an agent had to pay in case she was caught shirking (i.e., in case $e < \hat{e}$). The detection probability in this experiment was 1/3. The fine had to be chosen from an interval [0, 13]. Since introducing a fine at any level was costless for the principal, the optimal fine was $f^* = 13$. Hence, given that the principal actually chose $f^* = 13$, the expected wage reduction in case of verified shirking was 4.33. This implies that, according to the no-shirking condition (and the costs of effort as given in Table 1), principals could elicit *at most* an effort level of 0.4 (because $c(\hat{e} = 0.4) = 4$). To control for the impact of the incentive contract, Fehr and Gächter (2000) also replicated the two-stage design described in Section 2. They called this treatment the "Trust-treatment". The parameters in the Trust-treatment were the same as in the two-stage treatment of Section 2. One hundred and twenty six subjects participated in these experiments.

5.2. Hypotheses and Results

In contrast to the previous institutions and contracts, principals are now in a position to elicit at least $e^* > 0.1$, where e^* denotes the effort that is chosen by selfish and rational individuals, given the fine f and $c(\hat{e})$. For example, in case $f = 13$ and $\hat{e} = 0.4$, then $e^* = 0.4$; if $f = 10$ and $\hat{e} = 0.3$, then $e^* = 0.3$.[11] In the previous three sections we have seen that reciprocity is a major behavioral motivation that actually allowed the principals to elicit $e > e^* = 0.1$. Therefore, the question arises how performance incentives like those just outlined affect agents' willingness to cooperate or to reciprocate. In other words, are principals able to elicit $e > e^*$?

One possibility is that reciprocity actually gives rise to extra effort on top of what is enforced by financial incentives alone, i.e., $e - e^* > 0$, provided principals offer generous rents. Alternatively, it may well be that explicit performance incentives that threaten with a punishment in case of inferior performance, actually *reduce* the willingness to co-operate voluntarily and lead to effort choices that are *at most e^**. The financial incentives signal distrust and may, hence, "crowd out" voluntary cooperation.

THE CROWDING HYPOTHESES:
1. *In the Trust-treatment the same hypotheses hold as in the two-stage treatment of Section 2.*
2. *"Crowding In": The reciprocal relationship in the Incentive-treatment is **at least as steep** as in the Trust-treatment.*
3. *"Crowding Out": The reciprocal relationship in the Incentive-treatment is **less steep** as in the Trust-treatment.*

Since our dependent variables are censored below and above the estimation procedure

Table 7. Contractual Behavior in Trust and Incentive Contracts
– Summary Statistics

	wage	effort demanded $\hat{e}$	actual effort e
Trust treatment	28.1	0.63	0.35
	(17.4)	(0.26)	(0.25)
Incentive treatment	19.8	0.48	0.27
	(12.8)	(0.16)	(0.17)

Note: Entries are averages over all twelve periods. Numbers in
parentheses are standard deviations. Source: Fehr and Gächter
(2000) and own calculations.

trast to the Trust-treatment, where roughly 60 percent of the subjects exhibit
a significantly positive rent-effort relationship (according to Spearman rank
correlations). Indeed, a further data analysis shows that in the Incentive-
treatment high effort levels (i.e., those above 0.4) are chosen only in about 14
percent of all cases. In contrast, in the Trust-treatment about 35 percent of
effort choices are at least 0.5. Taken together, these results show that
reciprocity has been "crowded out" to a considerable degree by the incentive
contracts.

The overall efficiency effects of incentive contracting – as measured by
the average performance – are negative as well. Table 7 shows that the effort
levels, both the demanded and the actual one, are higher in the Trust-
treatment than in the Incentive-treatment. In the Incentive-treatment actual
effort levels are even lower than predicted by standard economic theory. This
implies that in our setup relying on trust and reciprocity induces at least as
high a performance as using incentive contracts.

This experiment has demonstrated that financial incentives can have
detrimental effects on voluntary cooperation. The question arises whether this
finding is a *general* property of incentive systems or just the result of the particular one studied here. This is a topic for future research. However, the findings in Anderhub, Gächter, and Königstein (1999), who study return sharing
as an incentive device in a simple principal-agent game, suggest that there are
incentive systems, which leave voluntary cooperation intact.

6.   SUMMARY AND DISCUSSION

In this paper we have provided a synoptic investigation of the empirical
importance and comparative merits of four remedies of contractual incompleteness discussed in the literature, namely, (1) reciprocity-based voluntary

cooperation, (2) long-term contracts, i.e., repeated interactions, (3) social embeddedness, and (4) incentive contracts. We summarize our findings as follows:

1.   In line with previous research and arguments about the importance of fair wages and gift exchanges advanced in the literature (e.g., by Akerlof (1982)), we find that both at the aggregate as well as at the individual level a **reciprocal motivation** can be a suitable contract enforcement device even in the absence of any extrinsic incentives. Its effectiveness, however, depends on the details of the interaction.

2.   A **repeated interaction** strongly mitigates the contract enforcement problem. In a certain sense, the possibility of a repeated interaction "crowds in" reciprocity (by generating a steeper reciprocal relationship than in one-shot encounters). At the individual level we find that many individuals who would act selfishly in the absence of repeated game incentives, imitate reciprocity in a repeated game. Hence, a long-term relationship is a very suitable contract enforcement device because it combines in a natural way standard economic incentives with the power of reciprocity that is even strengthened by them.

3.   **Social approval incentives** turned out to be rather weak in our experiments. They were, independently, not able to contribute significantly to a higher performance.

4.   Whereas the previous institutional arrangements provide rather favorable conditions for improved efficiency, **incentive contracts** have "crowded out" reciprocity and led to a high degree of opportunistic behavior. We see this as evidence that the introduction of pecuniary incentives into a reciprocal relationship bears "hidden costs" in the sense that it may weaken *total* incentives for effort provision.

Our results show an interesting parallel to recent findings on the subtleties of "intrinsic motivation", which can be defined as pursuing a particular activity for its own sake, without an apparent reward (see, e.g., Deci, Koestner and Ryan (1999) and Frey (1997)). Therefore, intrinsic motivation for the task may also help to mitigate the contract enforcement problem.

The issue of financial incentives in employment relations has recently received a lot of attention both among practitioners (see, e.g., Cairncross (1999) or Kohn (1993)) as well as among academics (see, e.g., Frey (1997)). In psychology, there is a debate over possible detrimental effects of incentives on "intrinsic work motivation", where some contend that incentives can lead to a "crowding out" of intrinsic motivation (see, e.g., Deci, Koestner and Ryan

(1999), whereas others cast doubt on such findings (e.g., Eisenberger and Cameron (1996)).

In our context, we refer to *reciprocity as an intrinsic motivation* because we see it as an innate psychic willingness to respond in kind. In the described experiments, the experimental task of an effort choice may be motivated by the intrinsic motivation of reciprocity although it is an artificial task which *as such* is most likely not done for any intrinsically satisfying reason.

We have just seen that the effectiveness of the intrinsic motivation of reciprocity depends crucially on the compatibility with extrinsic incentives. As, e.g., Frey (1997) shows, something similar holds for "intrinsic *work* motivation". Extrinsic incentives, like monetary rewards or the type of command an employer uses to enforce compliance, may interact adversely with the intrinsic work motivation. For example, a "crowding out effect" may occur if monetary incentives are used to motivate a task that once has been done without pecuniary incentives. Once monetary incentives are used, the task is only exerted for money and not for its own sake anymore. Similar crowding out effects can be observed by using "hard regulations" (Frey (1997), chap. 4)), like a punishment for non-compliance. The hard regulation is an external intervention that may be perceived as being *controlling* and undermining *self-determination*. With the intrinsic motivation of reciprocity, signalling distrust by threatening with a "stick" may have similar psychological effects and lead to the observed "crowding out of reciprocity" through incentive contracts discussed in the previous section.

"Crowding in" in the sense of improved performance is also possible. Enhanced possibilities for reciprocal exchanges "crowd in" reciprocal behavior and improve contractual performance. In intrinsic work motivation, a "crowding in" may occur if the external intervention is perceived as being supportive. This, for example, is the case if in a work relationship an agent is not given an honor or a prize for a particular task (which would tend to crowd out intrinsic motivation) but for his general dedication or performance (see Frey (1997, Chap. 10). In this case, it is more like a "gift" and it may increase intrinsic work motivation and performance, not least because of triggered reciprocity.

The important point with both intrinsic work motivation and reciprocity-based voluntary cooperation is how agents *perceive* the contractually incompletely regulated situation (see, e.g., Rousseau (1995) and the discussion in Gneezy and Rustichini (2000)). If agents perceive an extrinsic incentive as *supportive* there are no detrimental effects of extrinsic incentives. In our context, this seems to be the case with repeated game incentives, where the strategic incentives are perceived as complementary to motivational reciprocity. Introducing a financial incentive for a particular performance may change the perceived situation from one that is based on "good will" and the voluntary exchange of favors (or on intrinsic motivation for the task) to a relationship that is by and large "monetized": You get what you pay for – at the expense of intrinsic motivation or "good will".

In summary, reciprocity and the intrinsic motivation for a particular task (i.e., intrinsic *work* motivation) share similar features in their interplay with extrinsic incentives. The "trick" is to combine intrinsic and extrinsic incentives in contractual and institutional designs such that the extrinsic incentives respect the psychology that underlies reciprocity.

ACKNOWLEDGEMENT

This paper is part of the EU-TMR Research Network ENDEAR (FMRX-CT98-0238). We gratefully acknowledge financial support from the Swiss National Science Foundation (No. 1214-051000.97) and from the MacArthur Foundation, Network on Economic Environments and the Evolution of Individual Preferences and Social Norms. For helpful comments we are grateful to Werner Güth, Amnon Rapoport and the participants of the First Asian Conference on Experimental Business Research at the Hong Kong University of Science and Technology.

NOTES

1. From a psychological perspective there may be several reasons for agents' willingness to respond reciprocally, like equity considerations (Güth (1994)); inequity aversion (Fehr and Schmidt (1999), Bolton and Ockenfels (2000); intentions (Rabin (1993), Dufwenberg and Kirchsteiger (2000)); or a combination of inequity aversion and intentions (Falk and Fischbacher (1999)).
2. For further details, see Fehr, Gächter and Kirchsteiger (1997), in particular Section 6.
3. For simplicity the cost of the minimal effort was normalised to "zero". "Effort" can be interpreted as the monetary equivalent of the standard assumption of disutility of work, which increases in the effort level. The important point of both design features, the "normalisation" and the monetary costs, is that they set incentives that can be thought of being "isomorphic" to real world effort choices that are perceived as being onerous. See van Dijk, Sonnemans and van Winden (2001) for a "real effort" experiment on incentives systems. Moreover, to state the incentive problem as sharply as possible, we deliberately abstract from measurement problems of performance.
4. Formally this means that $(e - \hat{e})$ and p^e are expected to be positively correlated.
5. For further procedural details and experimental instructions see Falk et al. (1999).
6. See Gächter and Falk (1999) for a detailed analysis of individual behavior in repeated and one-shot gift-exchange games.
7. Communication during these experiments was not permitted. The reason is that communication is confounded with social pressure, internalised norms of keeping one's promises, coordination on particular wage and effort levels, etc. (see also Bohnet (1997)). For further discussion and detailed description of procedures see Falk et al. (1999).
8. Since, for simplicity, f does not depend on the amount of shirking, an agent who decides to shirk will always shirk fully, i.e., $e = e_0$, which implies with our parameters that $c(e_0) = 0$.

9. The real world is frequently characterized by constraints on principals' sanction opportunities. Such constraints may be imposed by law or by collective bargaining agreements. They may even arise endogenously because monitoring technologies may not allow the measurement of effort without error or because of problems of principals' moral hazard.
10. See Fehr and Gächter (2000) for detailed experimental instructions. This paper including instructions is available at *http://www.unizh.ch/iew/wp/iewwp034.pdf*.
11. Note that if the no-shirking condition $sf \geq c(\hat{e})$ does not hold (e.g., in case $f = 13$ and $\hat{e} > 0.4$), the optimal effort choice is $e^* = 0.1$.
12. To classify an effort choice as "reciprocal", one has to fix what is in the immediate self-interest of the reciprocator. In all previous two-stage experiments the agent always had – at least in the stage game – an incentive to choose the lowest effort $e = e^* = 0.1$. The use of fines leads to $e^* \geq 0.1$, which is now the correct benchmark for evaluating (reciprocal) effort choices. Notice further that our measure of generosity, the offered rent, is *not* affected by the use of a fine, which only determines what is in the employee's best material interest (i.e., e^*). Therefore, the fine is not included as a separate regressor.
13. Notice that the dependent variable is now $e - e^*$ (which is $e - 0.1$ in the Trust-treatment). If we estimate (3) with e as the dependent variable, the estimated coefficient of the variable r is 0.018, which is slightly lower than – but within keeping to – the estimated coefficient in model (2) of Table 3.

REFERENCES

Akerlof, George (1982). "Labor Contracts as a Partial Gift Exchange." *Quarterly Journal of Economics* 97, 543–69.
Anderhub, Vital, Simon Gächter, and Manfred Königstein (1999). "Efficient Contracting and Fair Play in a Simple Principal-Agent Experiment." Working Paper No. 18, Institute for Empirical Research in Economics, University of Zurich.
Axelrod, Robert (1984). *The Evolution of Cooperation.* NY: Basic Books.
Baker, George, Michael Jensen, and Kevin Murphy (1988). "Compensation and Incentives: Practice vs. Theory." *Journal of Finance* 43, 593–616.
Bewley, Truman (1999). *Why Wages Don't Fall during a Recession?* Cambridge, MA: Harvard University Press.
Blau, Peter (1964). *Exchange and Power in Social Life.* New Brunswick: Transaction Publishers.
Bohnet, Iris (1997). *Kooperation und Kommunikation. Eine ökonomische Analyse individueller Entscheidungen.* Tübingen: J.C.B. Mohr (Paul Siebeck).
Bolton, Gary, and Axel Ockenfels (2000). "ERC – A Theory of Equity, Reciprocity, and Competition." *American Economic Review* 90, 166–93.
Cairncross, Frances (1999). "A Survey of Pay." *The Economist* 351, 3–21.
Deci, Edward, Richard Koestner, and Richard Ryan (1999). "A Meta-Analytic Review of Experiments Examining the Effects of Extrinsic Rewards on Intrinsic Motivation." *Psychological Bulletin* 125, 627–68.
Dufwenberg, Martin, and Georg Kirchsteiger (2000). "Reciprocity and Wage Undercutting." *European Economic Review* 44, 1069–78.
Eisenberger, Robert, and Judy Cameron (1996). "Detrimental Effects of Reward. Reality or Myth?" *American Psychologist* 51, 1153–66.
Falk, Armin, and Urs Fischbacher (1999). "A Theory of Reciprocity." Working Paper No. 6, Institute for Empirical Research in Economics, University of Zurich.
Falk, Armin, Simon Gächter, and Judith Kovács (1999). "Intrinsic Motivations and Extrinsic

Incentives in a Repeated Game with Incomplete Contracts." *Journal of Economic Psychology* 20, 251–84.

Fehr, Ernst, Simon Gächter, and Georg Kirchsteiger (1997). "Reciprocity as a Contract Enforcement Device – Experimental Evidence." *Econometrica* 65, 833–60.

Fehr, Ernst, and Simon Gächter (2000). "Do Financial Incentives Crowd out Voluntary Cooperation?" Working Paper No. 34, Institute for Empirical Research in Economics, University of Zurich.

Fehr, Ernst, Georg Kirchsteiger, and Arno Riedl (1993). "Does Fairness Prevent Market Clearing? An Experimental Investigation." *Quarterly Journal of Economics* 108, 437–60.

Fehr, Ernst, and Klaus Schmidt (1999). "A Theory of Fairness, Competition and Cooperation." *Quarterly Journal of Economics* 114, 817–68.

Frey, Bruno (1997). *Not Just for the Money. An Economic Theory of Personal Motivation.* Cheltenham: Edward Elgar Publishing.

Gächter, Simon, and Armin Falk (1999). "Reputation or Reciprocity?" Working Paper No. 19, Institute for Empirical Research in Economics, University of Zurich.

Gneezy, Uri, and Aldo Rustichini (2000). "A Fine is a Price." *Journal of Legal Studies* 29, 1–17.

Gouldner, Alvin (1960). "The Norm of Reciprocity." *American Sociological Review* 25, 161–78.

Granovetter, Mark (1992). "The Sociological and Economic Approaches to Labour Market Analysis: A Social Structural View." In *The Sociology of Economic Life*, edited by Mark Granovetter and Richard Swedberg, 233–63. Boulder: Westview Press.

Güth, Werner (1994). "Distributive Justice. A Behavioural Theory and Empirical Evidence." In *Essays on Economic Psychology*, edited by Hermann Brandstätter and Werner Güth, 153–6. Berlin: Springer-Verlag.

Kohn, Alfie (1993). "Why Incentive Plans Cannot Work." *Harvard Business Review* 71, 54–63.

Lazear, Edward (1991). "Labour Economics and the Psychology of Organizations." *Journal of Economic Perspectives* 5, 89–110.

Leibenstein, Harvey (1979). "A Branch of Economics is Missing: Micro-Micro Theory." *Journal of Economic Literature* 17, 477–502.

MacLeod, Bentley, and James Malcomson (1998). "Markets and Motivation." *American Economic Review* 88, 388–411.

Milgrom, Paul, and John Roberts (1992). *Economics, Organization and Management.* NJ: Prentice Hall International.

Prendergast, Canice (1999). "The Provision of Incentives in Firms." *Journal of Economic Literature* 37, 7–63.

Rabin, Matthew (1993). "Incorporating Fairness into Game Theory and Economics." *American Economic Review* 83, 1281–302.

Rousseau, Denise (1995). *Psychological Contracts in Organizations. Understanding Written and Unwritten Agreements.* Thousand Oaks: SAGE Publications.

Schlicht, Ekkehart (1998). *On Custom in the Economy.* NY: Oxford University Press.

Simon, Herbert (1991). "Organizations and Markets." *Journal of Economic Perspectives* 5, 25–44.

van Dijk, Frans, Joep Sonnemans, and Frans van Winden (2001). "Incentive Systems in a Real Effort Experiment." *European Economic Review* 45(2), 187–214.

Williamson, Oliver (1985). *The Economic Institutions of Capitalism.* NY: Free Press.

Chapter 16

Using Experimental Data to Model Bargaining Behavior in Ultimatum Games

Haijin Lin
Carnegie Mellon University

C72

Shyam Sunder
Yale University

1.   INTRODUCTION

In ultimatum games two players bargain anonymously to divide a fixed amount between them, using a computer or human intermediary for communication. One player (proposer) proposes a division of the "pie" and the other player (responder) decides whether to accept the proposal. If accepted, the proposal is implemented so both players receive their agreed upon shares; if rejected, players receive nothing.

Harsanyi and Selten (1972) generalized the Nash equilibrium solution to provide a unique axiomatic equilibrium solution to this two-person bargaining game with incomplete information. Rubinstein (1985) showed that when the players try to maximize their own profits, there exists a unique subgame perfect equilibrium solution to this ultimatum bargaining problem: the proposer demands all but the smallest possible portion of the pie for himself, and the responder accepts any positive offer. However, the data gathered from most laboratory experiments on ultimatum or other noncooperative bargaining games exhibit significant discrepancies from these theoretical equilibrium solutions. The stylized facts are: proposers offer more than the minimal amount; responders reject not only the minimal but often even larger amounts.[1]

Literature on attempts to close this gap between the theory and data is large, and expanding fast. We do not attempt a review here.[2] These attempts can be approximately classified into four broad groups.[3] One approach is to consider the boundaries of the game the laboratory subjects are thought to be playing beyond its formal specification, and even beyond the walls of the laboratory (e.g., Hoffman et al. 1994, and Bolton and Zwick 1995). In a second approach subjects' beliefs and expectations about their environment, and possible dynamic modifications of these beliefs as the agents act and observe the results, are considered (e.g., Binmore et al. 1985, Binmore et al. 1995, Harrison and McCabe 1992, Slonim and Roth 1998, and Ochs and Roth 1989). A third approach is to add social (other regarding) arguments to agent preferences. These include fairness, envy, reciprocity, trust, intent, etc., e.g., Kahneman, Knetsch, and Thaler 1986, Bolton 1991, Bolton and Ockenfels 2000, Rabin 1993, Fehr and Schmidt 1999, Falk and Fischbacher 1998, and Berg et al. 1995. A fourth approach focuses on understanding and modeling the individual decision processes (e.g., Camerer et al. 1993, and Samuelson 2001). All these efforts are directed at developing theories to economically and simultaneously explain the agent behavior in ultimatum, and possibly other games.

We model the expectations of proposers on the basis of data gathered by others in several previous experiments.[4] In this framework, both the equal split (fairness) solution and the usual subgame perfect solution arise as special cases from different beliefs that might be held by the proposer. We ask: how well can a simple and controllable specification of preferences organize the data and theory in relation to each other by selecting the proposer's belief which are consistent with responder's rejections?

In Section 2, we examine the data from prior experiments, and use it in Sections 3 and 4 to develop and estimate two static models of the responder's behavior, and assess their effectiveness in organizing the responder data from previously published experiments. In Section 5, we develop a static model of optimal response of the proposer to the responder's behavior, and examine the ability of this model to organize the data from previously published experiments. Section 6 presents some concluding remarks.

2.   MODELING BEHAVIOR OF THE RESPONDER

The proposer of the division of the "pie" must assess the decision rule of the responder. It seems reasonable, *a priori*, for the proposer to assume that whether the responder accepts or rejects the proposal depends on what that proposal is. What do we know about the proposer's beliefs about this relationship? Subgame perfect predictions are often derived by assuming that the responder will accept any positive amount and reject only those proposals that offer her nothing. The rationale for this assumption is that in a single play game, if payoff from the game is the only argument of the responder's preference function, and preference is increasing in this argument, the responder is better off accepting any non-zero offer from the proposer. It is possible that the responder's preferences include arguments in addition to the absolute amount offered by the proposer. It is also possible that the responders may reject such offers to "educate" the population of proposers at large about the toughness of the responders in general. The issue can be resolved only by reference to data. We return to this issue in the concluding section after analyzing data from previously reported laboratory studies.

Slembeck (1999) reports the most extensive data relevant to our inquiry. In his experiment, Slembeck had 19 pairs of players play 20 consecutive rounds of a single-play ultimatum game anonymously. Identity and role of each member of the pairs remained fixed and anonymous through the twenty rounds.[5] Figure 1 shows the relative frequencies of responders' acceptance as a function of the fraction of the total pie demanded by the proposers for the entire pooled data set of 380 observations. The range of the proposer's demand between 0 and 1 is divided into ten equal intervals, and each interval is labeled by its mean value. The number of observations in each interval (from which relative frequencies are calculated) is shown above each bar. The relative frequency of acceptance is close to 100 percent when the proposer demands 30 percent or less of the total. Beyond this level, the relative frequency of acceptance progressively declines to about 10 percent when the proposer demands more than 90 percent of the pie. We repeated our analysis by partitioning the data into the early and late (first and last ten) rounds of the experiment to detect any effects of learning. The general result, that the chances of acceptance of the offer by the responder decline as the proposer demands more, remains unaltered through the early and later rounds.

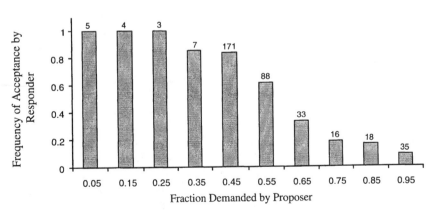

Figure 1. Frequency of Acceptance in Slembeck (1999) Data (No. of Observations at the Top of Each Bar)

The data reported in the published versions of other studies are not as detailed as in Slembeck. However, we analyzed the data from several other studies (Guth et al. (1982), Guth/Tietz (1988), Neelin et al. (1988), Ochs/Roth (1989)) of ultimatum games (either single play experiments, or from the last round of the multiple-play experiments). Results of this analysis are shown in Figure 2 in a format similar to the format of Figure 1. Panels A-E show the analysis of data from individual studies; Panel F shows the same analysis for data pooled from all five panels. Again, similar to Slembeck's data, we see a general pattern of declining relative frequency of acceptance by the responder as the proportion of the pie demanded by the proposer increases. Statistically, it is improbable for such a pattern to appear in data by random chance if the actual probability function matched the standard assumption that the probability of acceptance by the responder is constant at 1 over $0 \leq d_1 < 1$ and 0 at $d_1 = 1$.

The experimental data from the laboratory suggest that the probability of the responder accepting a proposal declines with the increase in the fraction of the pie demanded by the proposer. Is it reasonable to generalize this characteristic from laboratory to the field, and conclude that agents in economically significant work situations also have such a declining probability of acceptance? Whether fraction of the pie or the absolute magnitude of the offer is the relevant argument is not clear. Croson (1996) reports significant differences in the behavior of both players when proposals are presented in absolute versus fraction-of-the-pie amounts; and when the responders are or are not informed. However, as the size of the pie increases, so does the absolute dollar cost of rejection. Telser (1995) uses data for contracts of professional baseball players to show that their salaries and net marginal revenue products are consistent with the Law of Demand.

A second key question is: what should we assume the proposer believes about the responder's acceptance probability function.[6] There are many candidate assumptions to choose from. For example, predictions of the subgame perfect equilibrium are usually derived from the assumption that the proposer believes the responder will accept any offer greater than zero. This assumption is illustrated by the solid thick rectangular line marked a = 0 in Figure 3. Under this specific assessment of the responder's behavior, the proposer will demand almost the whole pie $(1 - \varepsilon)$, and the responder will accept the offer ε, where ε represents the smallest possible positive amount.[7]

Alternatively, we could assume that the proposer's assessment of the probability of acceptance by the responder declines, as the proposer demands a larger share. The class of functions that satisfy this condition is large and we need further restrictions to define a narrower class. One reasonable restriction would be that the function be non-increasing. An example of such a function, valued 1 at $d = 0$, and decreasing linearly to 0 as the demand of the proposer increases from 0 to 1, is shown by the thick dashed diagonal line in Figure 3 marked a = 100.[8]

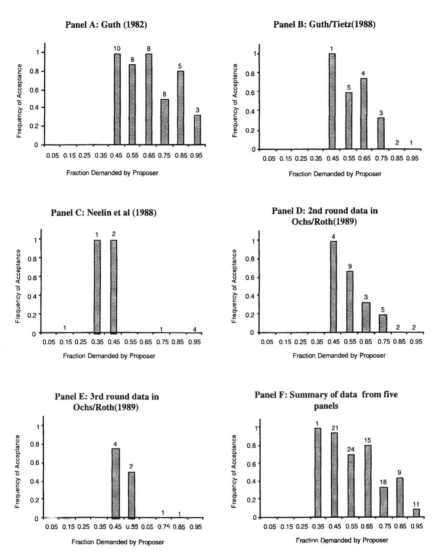

Figure 2. Frequency of Acceptance in Data from Other Prior Studies (No. of the Observations at the Top of Each Bar)

Given the problem of observability, how do we choose a candidate for the proposer's beliefs about the responder's probability of acceptance from a countless set of candidate beliefs? We start with Muth's (1961) rational expectation assumption: if economic agents have the ability to learn from experience, their beliefs about the probability distribution of their environment

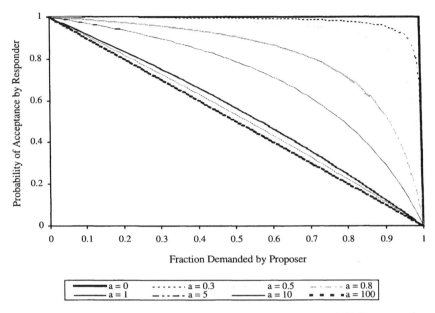

Figure 3. Hyperbolic Family of Probability of Acceptance Functions (with Parameter *a*)

should come arbitrarily close to the probability distribution of their environment itself.[9]

Applying the rational expectations assumption to the proposer's beliefs about the probability of acceptance of a proposal by the responder takes us back to the data presented in Figures 1 and 2. If these data are representative of the environment in which the ultimatum game is played, it is reasonable for us to assume that the proposer's beliefs about the responder's probability of acceptance should correspond to these data. In the following section, we identify a plausible class of non-increasing functions, and then estimate the parameters of the function from Slembeck's data.

3.   A CLASS OF HYPERBOLIC FUNCTIONS FOR RESPONDER'S PROBABILITY OF ACCEPTANCE

We would like to identify a class of concave downward sloping functions which are plausible candidates to have generated the data in Figures 1 and 2, and include the rectangular ($a = 0$ in Figure 3) and linear ($a \Rightarrow \infty$ in Figure 3) functions as special cases. In this section we consider the hyperbolic functions followed by piecewise linear functions in the following section.

We picked equilateral hyperbola as a function that might have these desired characteristics. Let $(f-b)(d-c) = \dfrac{a^2}{2}$, define the functional form where f is the probability of acceptance by the responder, d is the proposer's demand, and b and c should be functions of parameter a.

Since all those functions should pass through two points: $(0,1)$ and $(1,0)$, we can get two equations with two unknowns:

$$(1-b)(-c) = \frac{a^2}{2},\tag{1}$$

$$(-b)(1-c) = \frac{a^2}{2},\tag{2}$$

We solve these equations for b and c in terms of a, and derive two solutions for equilateral hyperbola f:

$$f = \frac{a^2}{2\left(d - \dfrac{1+\sqrt{1+2a^2}}{2}\right)} + \frac{1+\sqrt{1+2a^2}}{2},\tag{3}$$

and

$$f = \frac{a^2}{2\left(d - \dfrac{1-\sqrt{1+2a^2}}{2}\right)} + \frac{1-\sqrt{1+2a^2}}{2}.\tag{4}$$

Equations (3) and (4) define a single parameter family of hyperbolas. Equation (3) shows a class of concave functions and equation (4) a class of convex functions.

Figures 1 and 2 suggest that there is little drop in the probability of acceptance until the demand of the proposer exceeds 0.40 of the pie. The responder reacts to further increases in the proposer's demand by reducing the probability of acceptance. In Figure 3 as parameter a approaches zero, we get the rectangular function; when it increases without limit, the hyperbola becomes linear in the limit. We therefore choose the class of concave function (3) to represent the probability of acceptance as a function of the proposer's demand. Figure 3 also shows the hyperbolic functions as parameter a takes value 0, 0.3, 0.5, 0.8, 1, 5, 10, and 100. In the next section, we estimate (3) from Slembeck's experimental data.

(1) Estimating the Probability of Acceptance Function from Experimental Data

For statistical estimation of parameter a, we classify randomly chosen one half of Slembeck's raw data of 380 observations (19 fixed pairs of players played 20 rounds). We selected 190 observations from the odd-numbered rounds for odd-numbered pairs and the even-numbered rounds for even-numbered pairs (henceforth, called the first sub-sample) to estimate model (3). We then use the other half of the sample (henceforth called the second sub-sample) to cross validate the ability of the model to predict the behavior of responders.[10]

The observations are indexed $i = 1, 2, \ldots n$. Each observation consists of a pair (d_i, D_i), where d_i is the fraction of the pie demanded by the proposer, and D_i is the observed decision of the responder to accept ($D_i = 1$) or reject ($D_i = 0$) the proposer's proposal. We can rewrite equation (3) as $f_i = \phi(d_i, a)$, where f_i is the model value of the acceptance probability calculated from equation (3). We can write the sum of squared deviations between this model value of probability of acceptance and observed decisions of the responder as

$$S = \sum_{i=1}^{n} (D_i - \phi(d_i, a))^2. \tag{5}$$

We can solve this equation for the value of a that minimizes the sum of squared deviations S. Solver function in computer worksheet Excel is a convenient tool for doing this. This will give us the least squared error (LSE) estimate of a, denoted by $\hat{a}_{LSE}$.

An alternative way to estimate the value of parameter a is using the maximum likelihood method. Since (3) defines the probability of acceptance $\phi(d_i, a)$ for each demand, d_i, submitted by the proposer, the likelihood function is given by

$$L = \prod_{i=1}^{n} \phi(d_i, a)^{D_i} (1 - \phi(d_i, a))^{1-D_i} \tag{6}$$

Again, we can solve this equation for the value of a that maximizes the likelihood L. By using Solver function in computer worksheet Excel, we could get the Maximum Likelihood Estimate (MLE) of parameter a, denoted by $\hat{a}_{MLE}$.

Figure 4-Panel A shows the relative frequency chart prepared from the first sub-sample.[11] Acceptance probability functions, corresponding to LSE and MLE estimates of a ($\hat{a}_{LSE} = 1.57$ and $\hat{a}_{MLE} = 1.46$ respectively) given by equation (3) have been superimposed on the relative frequency chart. Panel B shows the estimation results for the second sub-sample which yields $\hat{a}_{LSE} = 1.42$ and $\hat{a}_{MLE} = 1.34$.[12]

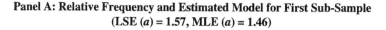

Panel A: Relative Frequency and Estimated Model for First Sub-Sample
(LSE (*a*) = 1.57, MLE (*a*) = 1.46)

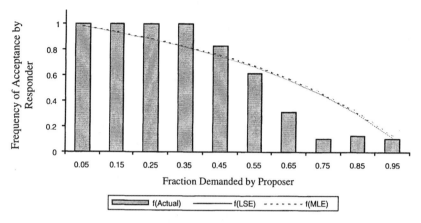

Panel B: Relative Frequency and Estimated Model for Second Sub-Sample
(LSE (*a*) = 1.42, MLE (*a*) = 1.34)

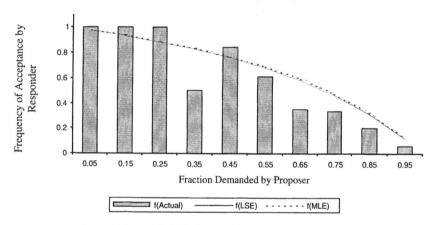

Figure 4. Static Model Estimated from Slembeck Data (1999)

(2) Statistical Test of the Model

The LSE and MLE are close to each other. We have arbitrarily chosen MLE to test whether we can reject the null hypothesis that the two sub-samples of the Slembeck data are drawn from the same distribution. Substituting MLE estimate 1.46 from the first sub-sample into (3), the estimated model from the first half of Slembeck's experimental data is:

Panel C: Relative Frequency and Estimated Linear Model for First Sub-Sample
(LSE $(a^P) = 0.335$, MLE $(a^P) = 0.40$)

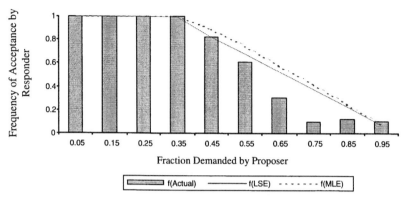

Panel D: Relative Frequency and Estimated Linear Model for Second Sub-Sample
(LSE $(a^P) = 0.347$, MLE $(a^P) = 0.45$)

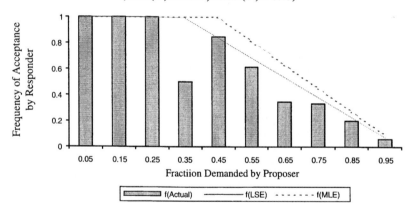

Figure 4.   Continued

$$\phi(d_i, \widehat{a}) = \frac{1.46^2}{2\left(d_i - \dfrac{1 + \sqrt{1 + 2*1.46^2}}{2}\right)} + \frac{1 + \sqrt{1 + 2 \times 1.46^2}}{2}$$

$$= \frac{1.0658}{d_i - 1.647} + 1.647 \tag{7}$$

We can assess the explanatory power of this model by applying it to the
second sub-sample. In other words, if our model could correctly describe

Slembeck's experimental result, the model should explain the variation in D_i of the second sub-sample. The null hypothesis is that the estimated model should apply to both outside and within the sample from which the estimates are derived. For this purpose, we use Chow's forecast test.[13] We know $1.26 < F_{0.01} < 1.29$. Since $1.01 < F_{0.01}$, we could not reject the null hypothesis at 1 percent level of significance, which means the estimated model is applicable to both the first and the second sub-sample. We also calculate the p-value relating to F-statistic of 1.01 in Appendix 1. The approximate p-value 0.5 provides no support for rejecting the null hypothesis, giving us some confidence in the predictive power of the estimated model.[14]

4. A PIECEWISE LINEAR CLASS OF FUNCTIONS FOR THE PROBABILITY OF ACCEPTANCE BY RESPONDERS

A second plausible candidate to describe the observed data can be identified as a piecewise linear model. Define parameter a^P as the critical value of the relative demand by the proposer. We hypothesize that when the proposer demands less than a^P, the responder accepts the offer with probability 1. On the other hand, when the proposer demands more than a^P, the responder's probability of acceptance is a linear decreasing function of the demand. See the following chart.[15]

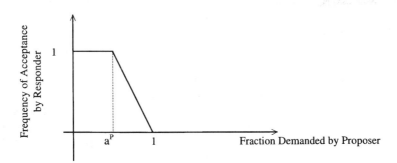

This functional form can be written as follows:

$$\left\{ \begin{array}{ll} f = 1, & if\, d \in [0, a^P) \\ f = \dfrac{1}{1-a^P} - \dfrac{d}{1-a^P}, & if\, d \in [a^P, 1] \end{array} \right\} \tag{8}$$

Now in order to combine these two linear models into one regression model, we define two dummy variable b_1 and b_2 as follows:

$$\left\{ b_1 = \begin{array}{l} 1,\ if\ d \in [0,a^P) \\ 0,\ otherwise \end{array} \right. and\ b_2 = \left. \begin{array}{l} 1,\ if\ d \in [a^P,1] \\ 0,\ otherwise \end{array} \right\}.$$

(9)

The final piecewise linear model will be: $f = b_1 + b_2 \left(\dfrac{1}{1-a^P} - \dfrac{d}{1-a^P} \right)$.

This linear model has only one parameter a^P since both b_1 and b_2 are determined by d and a^P. By using the first sub-sample, we could get the least squared error and maximum likelihood estimates for a^P. Define $f_i = \phi(d_i, a^P)$ as the estimated probability of acceptance by the responder conditional on each value of d_i. The sum of squared deviation between the model value $\phi(d_i, a^P)$ and the observed value D_i of the probability of acceptance is written as:

$$S = \sum_{i=1}^{n} (D_i - \phi(d_i, a^P))^2$$

(5A)

The likelihood function is written as:

$$L = \prod_{i=1}^{n} \phi(d_i, a^P)^{D_i} ((1 - \phi(d_i, a^P)))^{1-D}$$

(6A)

The Solver function in Excel helps us find the 0.335 as the LSE estimate and 0.40 as the MLE estimate. The explanation of the estimates is that if the proposer demands less than 0.335 (or 0.40 for MLE), the responder would accept the demand with probability 1; if the proposer demands 0.335 (or 0.40 for MLE) or more, the responder's probability of acceptance decreases proportionally with increase in the proposer's demand according to (8).

Figure 4-Panel C shows the relative frequency chart prepared from the first sub-sample. The probabilities of acceptance corresponding to the LSE and MLE estimates of parameter a^P in the piecewise linear model are superimposed to the bar chart. Panel D shows the relative frequency chart prepared from the second sub-sample which yields 0.347 and 0.45 as the LSE and MLE estimates of a^P respectively.[16]

Similar to the hyperbolic model testing, we randomly chose MLE estimate to test whether we could reject the null hypothesis that both two sub-samples are drawn from the following distribution:

$$\phi(d_i, 0.40) = b_1 + b_2 \left(\frac{1}{1-0.40} - \frac{d_i}{1-0.40} \right)$$

(10)

The Chow's forecast test can be applied here. F-statistics can be calculated as follows:

$$|F| = \left| \frac{(RSS_R - RSS_1)/(380 - n_1)}{RSS_1/(n_1 - k)} \right|$$

$$= \left| \frac{(246.0332 - 123.91)/(380 - 190)}{123.91/(190 - 1)} \right| \approx 0.9804$$

Since $0.9804 < F_{0.01}$, we could not reject the null hypothesis at 1 percent level of significance. The p-value for F-statistics of 0.9804 is 0.5542 (see Appendix 1),[17] which reinforces our confidence in the predictive power of the model.

5. OPTIMAL DEMAND DECISION OF THE PROPOSER

If the proposer knows that the probability of acceptance of the proposal by the responder is given by $\phi(d, a)$, and therefore depends on parameter a and their own decision d_i, they can choose their decision to maximize their own expected reward. Assuming that the proposer has a static estimate of parameter a from hyperbolic model (3), what is the optimal decision of the proposer?

Let $\pi(d, \phi)$ be the expected profit of the proposer from demanding d based on his expectation of the responder's decision rule:

$$\pi(d,\phi) = d\phi(d,a). \tag{11}$$

The proposer will choose the optimal demand d^* which meets the first and second order conditions (12) to maximize the expected profit $\pi(d,\phi)$:

$$\frac{\partial \pi(d,\phi)}{\partial d} = 0, \text{ and } \frac{\partial^2 \pi(d,\phi)}{\partial d^2} \leq 0 \tag{12}$$

Using (3), (11), and (12), we get the proposer's optimal decision rule in (12A)[18]:

$$d^* = \frac{1 + a^2 + \sqrt{1 + 2a^2} - \sqrt{a^2 + a^4 + a^2\sqrt{1 + 2a^2}}}{1 + \sqrt{1 + 2a^2}}. \tag{12A}$$

Figure 5 shows the relationship between parameter *a* and optimal demand *d**; the upper curve is for (3) and (12A), and the lower dotted curve for (4) and (12B). Under (3), the optimal demand of the proposer, *d**, is a decreasing function of *a*. Intuitively, parameter *a* can be explained as a "toughness" parameter about the proposer's assessment of the responder's bargaining posture. Greater the value of *a*, "tougher" the proposer assesses the responder to be. If the proposer believes that he is playing against a "softer" responder, he expects the latter to accept a smaller share of the pie, and therefore demands more for himself. The optimal demand increases as *a* decreases.[19]

We consider two extreme cases to fix ideas. If *a* is close to zero, the responder accepts just about any positive offer from the proposer, leading to the subgame perfect equilibrium as the solution. The other extreme case is when *a* increases without bound, and the optimal demand of the proposer converges to the equal-split solution.[20]

We compare the optimal decisions of the proposer predicted by the estimated model against the actual decisions of the proposer. Figure 6 makes this comparison based on Slembeck's data (1999). The proposer's relative demand is plotted on horizontal axis divided into ten equal segments from 0 to 1. The frequency of the proposer's demands falling into each decile is shown by the height of the vertical bars (left hand vertical scale). The dotted line in the chart shows the expected profit (see equation 11) of the proposer from submitting a demand equal to the midpoint of the interval (0.05, 0.15, 0.25, etc.) using the MLE estimate (a = 1.40) of *a* for the entire Slembeck (1999) sample. (The continuous line is for LSE estimate, a = 1.49). Optimal fractional demand

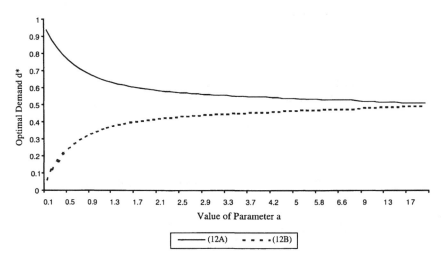

Figure 5. Relationship Between Hyperbolic Parameter *a* and Optimal Demand *d**

(LSE (*a*) = 1.49, MLE (*a*) = 1.40)

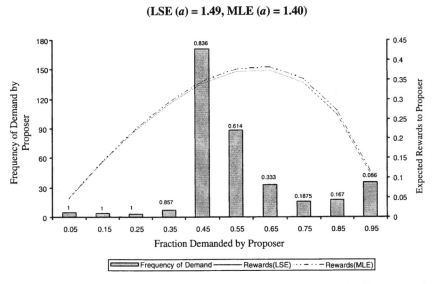

Figure 6. Frequency of Acceptance for the Full Slembeck (1999) Sample (Frequency of Acceptance at the Top of Each Bar) (LSE (*a*) = 1.49, MLE (*a*) = 1.40)

for the proposer based on MLE (LSE) estimate of *a* is 0.62 (0.61). Figure 6A shows the same data in the form of a cumulative frequency chart (thin line) of demands submitted by the proposer. Two thick lines (continuous line for the static model with a_{MLE} = 1.4, and broken line for *a* = 0 which corresponds to the assumption that the responder will accept any positive amount) in this figure are theoretical cumulative frequency charts to serve as benchmarks for comparison.

Both Figure 6 and Figure 6A suggest that the optimal demand model (12) captures the central tendency of the demand data. Perhaps we should not expect more from a static, cross-sectional single parameter model. It is also clear from these figures that the modal relative demand of the proposer at 50 percent of the pie lies well to the left of this theoretical optimum of the estimated model. About 36 percent of proposer demand lies at 50 percent and another about 24 percent lies between 50 percent and 62 percent. If the proposer stayed with the optimal demand of 0.62, he would have had an expected reward of 0.383 after considering the probability of rejection by the responder. Since the proposer deviated from this optimal, they had expected rewards of only 0.323, which is about 84 percent of the optimal expected reward. The actual ex post payoff of the proposer was 0.315 on average.

Since model (12) has no error term, there is no meaningful way of comparing the empirical relative frequencies in Figure 6 to the optimal prediction

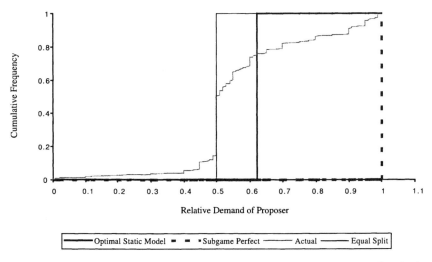

Figure 6A. Cumulative Frequency of the Proposer Relative Demand: Subgame Perfect, Static Model, Equal Split and Actual

of 0.62 (0.61). It is possible to add an error process and make comparisons using, for example, McKelvey and Palfrey's (1995) quantal response equilibrium. However, psychological and economic basis of such decision errors will require further specification and we do not include this exercise here.

6.   CONCLUDING REMARKS

This paper complements theoretical derivation of outcomes from *a priori* specification of beliefs and strategies by using experimental data to model and estimate human behavior in ultimatum bargaining games. The data show that the responder's probability of acceptance of an offer from the proposer declines progressively as the proposer demands a larger share of the pie. There is only about 10 percent chance that the responder will accept an offer of less than 10 percent of the pie. The overall acceptance rate by the responder is much higher. Does the proposer, anticipating rejection of small offers, choose to offer more? Or does the proposer value a more even split of the pie against higher personal consumption? We explore the extent to which we might be able to understand the proposer behavior without adding social arguments to his preferences.

We specify and estimate two global static models of proposer behavior.[21] The estimates suggest that while the responder rejects smaller offers with greater frequency, and the proposer behaves as if he knows this, and offers a fraction of the pie to the responder which approximates the amount that will maximize the proposer's expected reward. The data organizing power of the global static model dominates the predictions of the equal split (fairness) doctrine, as well as subgame perfect equilibrium derived from an extreme assumption about the responder behavior (this extreme assumption could have been, but is not chosen, by the estimation process). However, the model is far from organizing the data perfectly. We are currently developing and evaluating models that drop the global assumption in favor of person-specific parameters and drop the static assumption in favor of a dynamic adjustment process for the responder's rejection threshold and for the proposer's expectation of the rejection threshold.

If both the proposers and responders are driven purely by consideration of fairness in bargaining, 100 percent of the offers made by the proposer will be 50/50 splits, and all of them would be accepted, leading to 100 percent efficiency (total money made by the two bargaining agents as a percent of the maximum possible sum of money the two agents could have made).[22] In subgame perfect equilibrium based on the expectation that the responder will accept any positive amount, efficiency will again be 100 percent. The actual efficiency in Slembeck's (1999) data is 61.9 percent, which also matches the efficiency of the static model because it is fitted to the data. See Figure 7.

Models have different distributive consequences. In the subgame perfect equilibrium based on expectation of acceptance of minimal rewards by the responder, virtually 100 percent of the wealth will end up in the hands of the proposer and nothing with the responder. In a world driven by consideration of fairness alone, each player will receive 50 percent of total. If the world were described perfectly by our static model, only 38.3 percent of the maximum possible wealth will be in the hands of proposers and 23.6 percent in the hands of the responders (the two percentages add up to the efficiency of 61.9 percent). The actual distribution of wealth observed in Slembeck's data is more even, 31.5 percent to the proposer and 30.4 percent to the responder. See Figure 8.

If we return to Figure 6A that compares the cumulative frequencies of the actual proposer decision with the three models, it is clear that the equal split captures the modal behavior, and the static model covers the central tendency of the data. The subgame perfect equilibrium based on extreme assumption about the behavior of the responder lies at the right extreme, and does not seem to be a serious contender to organize the data.

One can defend selfishness as the motive for the proposer's "generosity;" if the proposer believes, for whatever reason, that the responder will reject an offer smaller than, say, fifty percent, selfishness is a better explanation of why he offers that much to the responder. It is not so much that the proposer wants

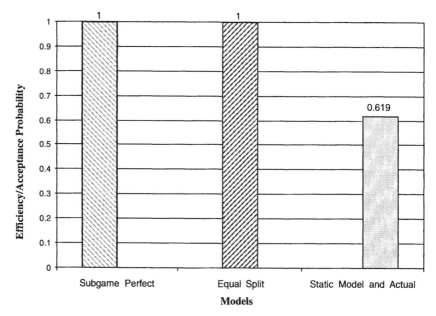

Figure 7. Efficiency and Probability of Acceptance by Responder

to be fair to the responder, but the proposer may expect that the responder may not want to be at the short end of the stick, and is willing to impose discipline on the proposer by denying herself the amount offered.

The argument for the responder is more complicated and less clear. First, there is some evidence in the part of the Slembeck (1999) data we did not analyze here that the responder has a "tougher" posture (higher probability of rejection) when she plays repeatedly against the same proposer than in playing against randomly drawn opponents in each round. Second, establishment of social norms may be driven by the "big-picture" self-interest of individuals. The responder may find that making a personal sacrifice by punishing the greedy proposer now in order to gain longer-term benefits of desirable social norms is well worth the investment. As Harkavay and Benson (1992) put it, "altruism pays." Even if the laboratory game is played only once, it is not unreasonable to recognize the externalities that may exist between even carefully designed laboratory games and the life outside the lab. Indeed experimental economics depends on such externalities between lab and the outside world for its value and validity of results. The responder's rejection of small offers can be seen as an investment in the establishment of social norms, a public good. Third, the responder may have competitive preferences along the lines suggested by Bolton where a large payoff to the proposer hurts her more

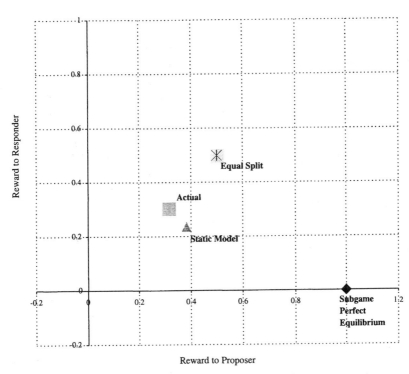

Figure 8. Model Comparison: Distribution of Rewards Between the Two Players

than zero payoff to herself. Fourth, the responder may act emotionally, not calculatively to maximize personal goals. Perhaps direct observations of brain or heart physiology may help enlighten us in this regard. In any case, in spite of repeated observations that the responder rejects nontrivial sums of money, it is not obvious that fairness is valued for itself, instead of being a means to more private goals.

One possibility is to develop models in which it is costly to formulate a set of strategies and to choose one from the set. This cost may arise not only from cognitive effort, but also from the time and observations necessary to accumulate data to evaluate the consequences of using a given strategy.[23] Given a positive cost, agents would be inclined to reuse a strategy from their tried and true arsenal in situations that may yield behavior close to Simon's (1955) satisficing under bounded rationality. Samuelson (2001) explicitly defines complexity cost as the limitation on reasoning resources. Without spelling out where this cost function comes from, he assumes complexity costs, as a function of the number of states and a shift parameter, directly and additively enter into individual payoff.

For the data at issue, our simple model works well, though its generalizability remains to be explored. Costa-Gomes and Zauner (2001) estimate a simple model of preferences, which is a linear combination of the monetary payoff of both the proposer and the responder and an error term, with Roth et al. (1991) data gathered in Israel, Japan, Slovenia and U.S. Unlike our study that takes the behavior of the responders as given, their model is more general in yielding a nested set of hypotheses about both the proposer as well as the responder behavior. They fail to reject the hypotheses that (1) the regard for the other player's payoff is independent of the role, proposer or responder, assigned to individuals; and (2) the proposers in Israel and Japan have no regard for responder payoff. They reject the hypotheses that (3) proposers are altruistic in any country; (4) the proposers in Slovenia and U.S. have no regard for responder payoff; and (5) responders have no regard for payoffs of proposers. Their result (2) is consistent with our approach, and result (4) contradicts it. They seem to have estimated and validated their model on the same data and we cannot tell if validating it separately would have made a difference. Our own results would not have changed much by being validated on the same sample.

In summary, for organizing laboratory data on proposer behavior in single-round ultimatum games, it may not be necessary to abandon or weaken the basic assumptions of individual preferences, and subgame perfect equilibrium. Using more realistic proposer beliefs about responder behavior seems to help. It has often been suggested that we must use social and cultural factors to understand bargaining behavior. People's beliefs and expectations of what others will do in a given situation are, perhaps, a good definition of culture and social norms in social sciences including economics.

ACKNOWLEDGEMENT

We are grateful to Professors Tilman Slembeck, Reinhard Tietz and Werner Guth for the use of their experimental data. We thank Jonathan Glover and the participants at the First Asian Conference on Experimental Business Research at Hong Kong University of Science and Technology for their comments on an earlier draft of the paper. We are especially grateful for Colin Camerer's detailed comments. We alone are responsible for any errors.

Notes

1. See, for example, Guth et al. (1982), Binmore et al. (1985), Guth and Tietz (1988), Neelin et al. (1988), and Ochs and Roth (1989).

2. See Thaler (1988), Guth and Tietz (1990), Roth (1995), and Bolton (1998) for some reviews.
3. The four broad approaches are not exclusive. They are defined in terms of the research focus on ultimatum games.
4. In the concluding section, we compare and discuss Costa-Gomes and Zauner (2001), which also used data for modeling behavior in ultimatum games.
5. While twenty rounds of repeated play against fixed opponents imparts certain features to this data not shared with single round games (e.g., Figure 1 versus Figure 2F), these data do allow us to conduct some preliminary investigations. These investigations will have to be followed by analysis of single play data.
6. Note that the probability density of responders' cutoff points being the first derivative of acceptance probability, is an equivalent specification. See Henrich and McElreath (2000), and Henrich and Smith (2000) for analysis based on a two-parameter truncated gausssian distribution of cutoff points.
7. This assumption implies that the cutoff points of responders are all concentrated in the narrow demand interval $(1-\varepsilon, 1)$.
8. This assumption implies that the cutoff points of responders are distributed uniformly in interval $(0,1)$. Also see Rapoport et al. (1996) for modeling of behavior in ultimatum games with uncertainty.
9. A simpler, deterministic version of this assumption is that the proposer's belief about the cutoff demand beyond which the responder will reject the proposal equals the cutoff point the proposer would use if he were a responder instead.
10. Note that the two sub-samples from this scheme of dividing the sample are not independent of each other. We repeated the analysis using mutually independent sub-samples consisting of 10 odd-numbered pairs (henceforth called the first independent sub-sample) for estimation and 9 even-numbered pairs (henceforth called the second independent sub-sample) for Chow's test. Results were essentially the same.
11. While the figure shows relative frequencies for 10 intervals only, estimation of a was carried out using 190 individual observations as specified above.
12. Estimates of a from the first independent sub-sample (see footnote 11 above) are $\hat{a}_{\text{LSE}} = 1.62$ and $\hat{a}_{\text{MLE}} = 1.53$; and $\hat{a}_{\text{LSE}} = 1.38$ and $\hat{a}_{\text{MLE}} = 1.28$ for the second independent sub-sample.
13. In the estimating sub-sample, first part of the data set, $n_1 = 190$. After regressing ϕ on d_i, we obtain residual sum of squares $RSS_1 = 32.73$. We apply the estimate from the first sub-sample to the entire data set of 380 observations to obtain $RSS_R = 66.12$. Calculate the F-statistics as follows:

$$|F| = \left| \frac{(RSS_R - RSS_1)/(380 - n_1)}{RSS_1/(n_1 - k)} \right| = \left| \frac{(66.12 - 32.73)/(380 - 190)}{32.73/(190 - 1)} \right| = 1.01$$

14. From analysis of the second independent sub-sample, we get $|F| = 1.019$ which yields the same statistical inference.
15. This specification is equivalent to assuming that the responders' cutoff points are distributed uniformly over interval $(a^P, 1)$.
16. Estimates of a^P from the first independent sub-sample (see footnote 11 above) are $\hat{a}^P_{\text{LSE}} = 0.321$ and $\hat{a}^P_{\text{MLE}} = 0.4499$, and $\hat{a}^P_{\text{LSE}} = 0.3629$ and $\hat{a}^P_{\text{MLE}} = 0.4999$ for the second independent sub-sample.
17. Alternative split of the sub-samples (see footnote 11) yields similar results, $|F| = 0.9739$.
18. If, we used (4) instead of (3), the optimal decision rule would be given by:

$$d^* = \frac{-1-a^2+\sqrt{1+2a^2}+\sqrt{a^2+a^4-a^2\sqrt{1+2a^2}}}{-1+\sqrt{1+2a^2}}. \tag{12B}$$

19. On the other hand, if we use (4), the proposer assesses the responder to be softer by assigning bigger value of a. Therefore, with small value of a, the proposer could only get smaller demand accepted by the responder. The optimal demand is decreasing as a decreases.

20. On the other hand, when we use (4), the optimal demand of the proposer is zero at $a = 0$ and converges to equal split as a increases without bound. See Figure 5.

21. Qualifier global indicates that the models assume that parameter is identical across players; static indicates that the parameter is assumed not to change with experience.

22. If the responders demanded fairness to the extent that they were willing to reject all offers of less than 50/50, the proposers who know this about responders would be forced to make 50/50 offers by their self-interest alone. If proposers valued fairness but the responders do not, we will see 50/50 splits even when responders accept smaller sums. Thus the extreme attachment to fairness on part of either or both players implies equal-split offers.

23. See Johnson et al. (2001) for evidence of insufficient data gathering and errors by untutored subjects in playing games in which they could do better by doing backward induction. Instruction in backward induction has significant impact on their behavior.

Bibliography

Berg, J. J. Dickhaut, and K. McCabe (1995). "Trust, Reciprocity and Social History." *Games and Economic Behavior* 10, 122–42.

Binmore, K., A. Shaked, and J. Sutton (1985). "Testing Noncooperative Bargaining Theory: A Preliminary Study." *American Economic Review* 75, 1178–80.

Binmore, K., J. Gale, and L. Samuelson (1995). "Learning to be Imperfect: The Ultimatum Game." *Games and Economic Behavior* 8, 56–90.

Bolton, G. E. (1991). "A Comparative Model of Bargaining: Theory and Evidence." *American Economic Review* 81, 1096–136.

Bolton, G. E. (1998). "Bargaining and Dilemma Games: From Laboratory Data Towards Theoretical Synthesis." *Experimental Economics* 1, 257–81.

Bolton, G. E., and A. Ockenfels (2000). "ERC: A Theory of Equity, Reciprocity, and Competition." *American Economic Review* 90, 166–93.

Bolton, G. E., and R. Zwick (1995). "Anonymity Verse Punishment in Ultimatum Bargaining." *Games and Economic Behavior* 10, 95–121.

Camerer, C., E. Johnson, T. Rymon, and S. Sen (1993). "Cognition and Framing in Sequential Bargaining for Gains and Losses." Ch. 1 in *Frontiers of Game Theory*, Edited by K. Binmore, A. Kirman, and P. Tani, 27–47. MIT.

Costa-Gomes, M., and K. G. Zauner (2001). "Ultimatum Bargaining Behavior in Israel, Japan, Slovenia, and the United States: A Social Utility Analysis." *Games and Economics Behavior* 34, 238–69.

Croson, R. T. A. (1996). "Information in Ultimatum Games: An Experimental Study." *Journal of Economic Behavior and Organization* 30, 197–212.

Falk, A., and U. Fischbacher (1998). "A Theory of Reciprocity." Working Paper, University of Zurich.

Fehr, E., and K. M. Schmidt (1999). "A Theory of Fairness, Competition and Cooperation." *Quarterly Journal of Economics* 114, 817–68.

Guth, W., and R. Tietz (1988). "Ultimatum Bargaining for a Shrinking Pie: An Experimental Analysis." In *Bounded Rational Behavior in Experimental Games and Markets, Proceedings of the Fourth Conference on Experimental Economics*, Edited by R. Tietz, W. Albers, and R. Selten, 111–28 NY: Springer Berlag.

Guth, W., and R. Tietz (1990). "Ultimatum Bargaining Behavior: A Survey and Comparison of Experimental Results." *Journal of Economic Psychology* 11, 417–49.

Guth, W., R. Schmittberger, and B. Schwarze (1982). "An Experimental Analysis of Ultimatum Bargaining," *Journal of Economic Behavior and Organization* 3, 367–88.

Harkavay, I., and L. Benson (1992). "Universities, Schools and the Welfare State." *Education Week on the Web*.

Harrison, G. W., and K. McCabe (1992). "Testing Noncooperative Bargaining Theory In Experiments." *Research in Experimental Economics* 5, 137–69.

Harsanyi, J. C., and R. Selten (1972). "A Generalized Nash Solution for Two-Person Bargaining Games with Incomplete Information." *Management Science* 18, 80–106.

Henrich, J., and N. Smith (2000). "Comparative Experimental Evidence from Peru, Chile & the U.S. Shows Substantial Variation among Social Groups." Working Paper, University of Michigan.

Henrich, J., and R. McElreath (2000). "Are Peasants Risk-Averse Decision Makers?" Working Paper, University of Michigan.

Hoffman, E., K. McCabe, K. Shachat, and V. L. Smith (1994). "Preferences, Property Rights, and Anonymity in Bargaining Games." *Games and Economic Behavior* 7, 346–80.

Johnson, E. J., C. Camerer, S. Sen, and T. Rymon (forthcoming 2001). "Detecting Failures of Backward Induction: Monitoring Information Search in Sequential Bargaining." *Journal of Economic Theory*.

Kahneman, D., J. L. Knetch, and R. H. Thaler (1986). "Fairness and Assumptions of Economics" *Journal of Business* 59, 285–300.

Mckelvey, R., and T. Palfrey (1995). "Quantal Response Equilibrium for Normal Form Games." *Games and Economic Behavior* 10, 6–38.

Muth, J. F. (1961). "Rational Expectations and the Theory of Price Movements," *Econometrica* 29, 315–35.

Neelin, J., H. Sonnenschein, and M. Spiegel (1988). "A Further Test of Noncooperative Bargaining Theory: Comment." *American Economic Review* 78, 824–36.

Ochs, J., and A. E. Roth (1989). "An Experimental Study of Sequential Bargaining." *American Economic Review* 79, 355–84.

Rabin, M. (1993). "Incorporating Fairness into Game Theory and Economics." *American Economic Review* 83, 1281–302.

Rapoport, A., J. A. Sundali, and D. A. Seale (1996). "Ultimatums in Two-Person Bargaining with One-Sided Uncertainty: Demand Games." *Journal of Economic Behavior and Organization* 30, 173–96.

Roth, A. E., V. Prasnikar, M. Fujiwara, and S. Zamil (1991). "Bargaining and Market Behavior in Jerusalem, Ljubljana, Pittsburgh and Tokyo: An Experimental Study." *American Economic Review* 81, 1068–95.

Rubinstein, A. (1985). "A Bargaining Model with Incomplete Information about Time Preference." *Econometrica* 53, 1151–72.

Samuelson, L. (2001). "Analogies, Adaptation, and Anomalies." *Journal of Economic Theory* 97, 320–66.

Simon, H. A. (1955). "A Behavioral Model of Rational Choice." *Quarterly Journal of Economics*, 69, 99–118.

Slembeck, T. (1999). "Reputations and Fairness in Bargaining – Experimental Evidence from a Repeated Ultimatum Game with Fixed Opponents." Working Paper, Department of Economics, University of St. Gallen.

Slonim, R., and A. E. Roth (1998). "Learning in High Stakes Ultimatum Games: An Experiment in the Slovak Republic." *Econometrica* 66, 569–96.

Telser, L. G. (1995). "The Ultimatum Game and the Law of Demand." *The Economic Journal* 105, 1519–23.

Thaler, R. H. (1988). "The Ultimatum Game." *Journal of Economic Perspectives* 2, 195–206.

APPENDIX 1

By the definition of p-value, we have

P-value $(1.01) = \Pr(x > 1.01)$

Notice here $x \sim F(190, 189)$

P-value $(1.01) = 1 - \Pr(x \leq 1.01)$

$$\Pr(x \leq 1.01) = \int_{-\infty}^{1.01} \frac{\Gamma\left(\dfrac{m+n}{2}\right) m^{\frac{m}{2}} n^{\frac{n}{2}}}{\Gamma\left(\dfrac{m}{2}\right)\Gamma\left(\dfrac{n}{2}\right)} \frac{x^{\frac{m}{2}-1}}{(mx+n)^{\frac{m+n}{2}}} dx$$

$$= \frac{\Gamma\left(\dfrac{190+189}{2}\right) * 190^{\frac{190}{2}} * 189^{\frac{189}{2}}}{\Gamma\left(\dfrac{190}{2}\right)\Gamma\left(\dfrac{189}{2}\right)} \int_{-\infty}^{1.01} \frac{x^{\frac{190}{2}-1}}{(190x+189)^{\frac{190+89}{21}}} dx$$

$$= \frac{\Gamma\left(\dfrac{379}{2}\right) * 190^{\frac{190}{2}} * 189^{\frac{189}{2}}}{\Gamma\left(\dfrac{190}{2}\right)\Gamma\left(\dfrac{189}{2}\right)} * 4.282985089554 * 10^{-490}$$

$$= 0.527$$

P-value $(1.01) = 1 - 0.527 = 0.473$

Similarly,

$$\Pr(x \leq 0.9804) = \frac{\Gamma\left(\dfrac{379}{2}\right) * 190^{\frac{190}{2}} * 189^{\frac{189}{2}}}{\Gamma\left(\dfrac{190}{2}\right)\Gamma\left(\dfrac{189}{2}\right)} \int_{-\infty}^{0.9804} \frac{x^{\frac{190}{2}-1}}{(190x+189)^{\frac{190+89}{21}}} dx$$

$$= 0.4458$$

P-value $(0.1093) = 1 - 0.4458 = 0.5542$

Author Index

Subject Index

The Authors

The Editors

Rami Zwick
Department of Marketing
Hong Kong University of Science
and Technology
Clear Water Bay, Kowloon
Hong Kong
mkzwick@ust.hk

Amnon Rapoport
Department of Management and
Policy
University of Arizona
McClelland Hall 405
Tucson, AZ 85721, USA
amnon@u.arizona.edu

Chapter Contributors

Vital Anderhub
Humboldt-University of Berlin
Department of Economics
Institute for Economic Theory III
Spandauer Str. 1
10178 Berlin, Germany
anderhub@wiwi.hu-berlin.de

Anirvan Banerji
Director of Research.
Economic Cycle Research Institute
(ECRI)
420 Lexington Avenue – Suite 1645
New York, NY 10170
anirvan@businesscycle.com

Paul J. Brewer
Department of Economics
Hong Kong University of Science
and Technology
Clear Water Bay, Kowloon
Hong Kong
pjb@smartmarkets.ust.hk

Colin F. Camerer
Div HSS 228-77
Caltech
Pasadena, CA 91125
camerer@hss.caltech.edu

Murali Chandrashekaran
College of Business Administration
University of Cincinnati
PO Box 210145
Cincinnati, OH 45221-0145
chandrm@email.uc.edu

James C. Cox
Department of Economics
401 McClelland Hall
University of Arizona
Tucson, AZ 85721-0108
jcox@bpa.arizona.edu

Ido Erev
Faculty of Industrial Engineering
and Management
Technion
Haifa, 32000, Israel
erev@techunix.technion.ac.il

Simon Gächter
University of St. Gallen
FEW-HSG
Varnbüelstrasse 14
Ch-9000 St. Gallen, Switzerland
simon.gaechter@unisg.ch

Werner Güth
Humboldt-University of Berlin
Department of Economics
Institute for Economic Theory III
Spandauer Str. 1
10178 Berlin, Germany
gueth@wiwi.hu-berlin.de

Yoichi Hizen
Department of Economics
University of Pennsylvania
3718 Locust Walk
Philadelphia, PA 19104-6297
hizen@ssc.upenn.edu

Soo Hong Chew
Department of Economics
Hong Kong University of Science
and Technology
Clear Water Bay, Kowloon
Hong Kong
shchew@ust.hk

John Dickhaut
University of Minnesota
Carlson School of Management
3-122 CSOM
321 19th Avenue South
Minneapolis, MN 55455
jdickhaut@csom.umn.edu

Armin Falk
University of Zürich
Institute for Empirical Research in
Economics
Blümlisalpstrasse 10, CH-8006
Zürich
falk@iew.unizh.ch

Sunil Gupta
Principal, Thinktodo, LLC and
Senior Consultant, David Shepard
Associates
305 Judd Road
Easton, CT 06612
sunil@thinktodo.com

Ernan Haruvy
School of Management, JO 51
University of Texas at Dallas
Richardson, Texas 75083-0688
eharuvy@utdallas.edu

Teck-Hua Ho
Marketing Department
University of Pennsylvania
1458 Steinberg Hall-Dietrich Hall
Philadelphia, PA 19104-6371
hoteck@wharton.upenn.edu

David Hsia
Citicorp
6400 Las Colinas Blvd, 3rd
Floor
Irving, TX 75039-2900
David_Hsia@AFCC.com

James J. Kellaris
College of Business
Administration
University of Cincinnati
PO Box 210145
Cincinnati, OH 45221-0145
James.Kellaris@UC.edu

Haijin Lin
Graduate School of Industrial
Administration
Carnegie Mellon University
Schenley Park
Pittsburgh, PA 15213
haijin@andrew.cmu.edu

Kevin McCabe
Departments of Economics and Law
George Mason University
4400 University Dr.
MSN 1B2
Fairfax, VA 22030
kmccabe@gmu.edu

James E. Parco
Department of Management and
Policy
University of Arizona
McClelland Hall 405
Tucson, AZ 85721
parco@u.arizona.edu

Vijay Rajan
University of Minnesota
Carlson School of Management
Minneapolis, MN 55455

Frank R. Kardes
College of Business Administration
University of Cincinnati
PO Box 210145
Cincinnati, OH 45221-0145
Frank.Kardes@uc.edu

Florian Knust
Humboldt-University of Berlin
Department of Economics
Institute for Economic Theory III
Spandauer Str. 1
10178 Berlin, Germany
knust@gmx.de

Alison King Chung Lo
Department of Marketing
Fuqua School of Business
Duke University, Box 90120
Durham, NC 27708
kcl5@mail.duke.edu

Naoko Nishimura
Faculty of Economics
Shinshu University
Matsumoto, Nagano 390-8621,
Japan
nnaoko@econ.shinshu-u.ac.jp

Nicole R. Peck
Kansas State University
Department of Psychology
492 Bluemont Hall
1100 Mid-Campus Drive
Manhattan, KS 66506-5302
npeck@ksu.edu

Mary Rigdon
George Mason University
Interdisciplinary Center for
Economic Science
3300 Washington Blvd, Room 400K
Arlington, VA, 22201
rigdon@econlab.arizona.edu

Tatsuyoshi Saijo
Institute of Social and Economic
Research
Osaka University
Ibaraki, Osaka 567-0047,
Japan
saijo@iser.osaka-u.ac.jp

Kip C. S. Smith
Kansas State University
Department of Psychology
492 Bluemont Hall
1100 Mid-Campus Drive
Manhattan, KS 66506-5302
kip@ksu.edu

Joel H. Steckel
Suite 8-87 Kaufman Management
Center
New York University
44 W. 4th Street
New York, NY 10012
jsteckel@stern.nyu.edu

William Waller
Department of Accounting
University of Arizona
1130 E. Helen Street, Room 301
Tucson, AZ 85721
wwaller@bpa.arizona.edu

Darryl A. Seale
Department of Management
University of Nevada Las Vegas
4505 Maryland Parkway
Las Vegas, NV 89154-6009
dseale@ccmail.nevada.edu

Vernon Smith
Professor of Economics and Law
George Mason University
Interdisciplinary Center for
Economic Science
3300 Washington Blvd, Room 400K
Arlington, VA, 22201
vsmith2@gmu.edu

Shyam Sunder
Yale School of Management
135 Prospect St.
P.O. Box 208200
New Haven, CT 06520-8200
shyam.sunder@yale.edu